B+T 2-65 (Kenley)

*The Age
of the Despots*

JOHN ADDINGTON SYMONDS

The Age
of the Despots

'Di questi adunque oziosi principi,
e di queste vilissime armi, sarà
piena la mia istoria'
—MACH. *Ist. Fior.* lib. i.

CAPRICORN BOOKS
G. P. PUTNAM'S SONS   New York

CAPRICORN EDITION, 1960

The Age of The Despots is Volume I of
Symonds' RENAISSANCE IN ITALY

TO

MY FRIEND

JOHN BEDDOE, M.D., F.R.S.

I DEDICATE MY WORK
ON
THE ITALIAN RENAISSANCE

PREFACE

TO

THE SECOND EDITION*

———◆———

THIS volume is the First Part of a work upon the
'Renaissance in Italy.' The Second Part treats of the
Revival of Learning. The Third, of the Fine Arts.
These have been already published. The Fourth Part
will be devoted to Italian Literature.

Owing to the extent of the ground I have attempted
to traverse, I feel conscious that the students of special
departments will find much to be desired in my handling of each part. In some respects I hope that the
several portions of the work may complete and illustrate each other. Many topics, for example, have been
omitted from Chapter VIII. in this volume because they
seemed better adapted to treatment in the future.

One of the chief difficulties which the critic has
to meet in dealing with the Italian Renaissance is the

* PUBLISHER'S NOTE.—This Preface was prefixed to the second
edition of this volume when it was issued independently.

determination of the limits of the epoch. Two dates, 1453 and 1527, marking respectively the fall of Constantinople and the sack of Rome, are convenient for fixing in the mind that narrow space of time during which the Renaissance culminated. But in order to trace its progress up to this point, it is necessary to go back to a far more remote period; nor, again, is it possible to maintain strict chronological consistency in treating of the several branches of the whole theme.

The books of which the most frequent use has been made in this first portion of the work are Sismondi's 'Républiques Italiennes;' Muratori's 'Rerum Italicarum Scriptores;' the 'Archivio Storico Italiano;' the seventh volume of Michelet's 'Histoire de France;' the seventh and eighth volumes of Gregorovius' 'Geschichte der Stadt Rom;' Ferrari's 'Rivoluzioni d' Italia;' Alberi's series of Despatches; Gino Capponi's 'Storia della Repubblica di Firenze;' and Burckhardt's 'Cultur der Renaissance in Italien.' To the last-named essay I must acknowledge especial obligations. It fell under my notice when I had planned, and in a great measure finished, my own work. But it would be difficult for me to exaggerate the profit I have derived from the comparison of my opinions with those of a writer so thorough in his learning and so delicate in his perceptions as Jacob Burckhardt, or the amount I owe to his acute and philosophical handling of the whole subject. I must also express a special debt to Ferrari, many of whose views I have adopted in the Chapter on 'Italian History,' written for the second edition of this volume. With regard to the alterations introduced into the substance of the book in this edition, it will be enough to say that I have endeavoured to bring each chapter up to the level of present knowledge.

In conclusion, I once more ask indulgence for a volume which, though it aims at a completeness of its own, is professedly but one part of a long inquiry.

CONTENTS

CHAPTER I

THE SPIRIT OF THE RENAISSANCE

CHAPTER II

ITALIAN HISTORY

CHAPTER III

THE AGE OF THE DESPOTS

CHAPTER IV

THE REPUBLICS

CHAPTER V

THE FLORENTINE HISTORIANS

CHAPTER VI

'THE PRINCE' OF MACHIAVELLI

CHAPTER VII

THE POPES OF THE RENAISSANCE

CHAPTER VIII

THE CHURCH AND MORALITY

CHAPTER IX

SAVONAROLA

CHAPTER X

CHARLES VIII

APPENDICES.

RENAISSANCE IN ITALY

CHAPTER I

THE SPIRIT OF THE RENAISSANCE

Difficulty of fixing Date—Meaning of word Renaissance—The Emanci-
pation of the Reason—Relation of Feudalism to the Renaissance—
Mediæval Warnings of the Renaissance—Abelard, Bacon, Joachim of
Flora, the Provençals, the Heretics, Frederick II.—Dante, Petrarch,
Boccaccio—Physical Energy of the Italians—The Revival of Learn-
ing—The Double Discovery of the World and of Man—Exploration
of the Universe and of the Globe—Science—The Fine Arts and
Scholarship—Art Humanises the Conceptions of the Church—Three
Stages in the History of Scholarship—The Age of Desire—The Age
of Acquisition—The Legend of Julia's Corpse—The Age of the
Printers and Critics—The Emancipation of the Conscience—The
Reformation and the Modern Critical Spirit—Mechanical Inven-
tions—The Place of Italy in the Renaissance.

THE word Renaissance has of late years received a more
extended significance than that which is implied in our English
equivalent—the Revival of Learning. We use it to denote
the whole transition from the Middle Ages to the Modern
World; and though it is possible to assign certain limits to
the period during which this transition took place, we cannot
fix on any dates so positively as to say—between this year
and that the movement was accomplished. To do so would
be like trying to name the days on which spring in any particular season began and ended. Yet we speak of spring as
different from winter and from summer. The truth is, that

in many senses we are still in mid-Renaissance. The evolution has not been completed. The new life is our own and is progressive. As in the transformation scene of some great Masque, so here the waning and the waxing shapes are mingled; the new forms, at first shadowy and filmy, gain upon the old; and now both blend; and now the old scene fades into the background; still, who shall say whether the new scene be finally set up?

In like manner we cannot refer the whole phenomena of the Renaissance to any one cause or circumstance, or limit them within the field of any one department of human knowledge. If we ask the students of art what they mean by the Renaissance, they will reply that it was the revolution effected in architecture, painting, and sculpture by the recovery of antique monuments. Students of literature, philosophy, and theology see in the Renaissance that discovery of manuscripts, that passion for antiquity, that progress in philology and criticism, which led to a correct knowledge of the classics, to a fresh taste in poetry, to new systems of thought, to more accurate analysis, and finally to the Lutheran schism and the emancipation of the conscience. Men of science will discourse about the discovery of the solar system by Copernicus and Galileo, the anatomy of Vesalius, and Harvey's theory of the circulation of the blood. The origination of a truly scientific method is the point which interests them most in the Renaissance. The political historian, again, has his own answer to the question. The extinction of feudalism, the development of the great nationalities of Europe, the growth of monarchy, the limitation of the ecclesiastical authority and the erection of the Papacy into an Italian kingdom, and in the last place the gradual emergence of that sense of popular freedom which exploded in the Revolution; these are the aspects of the movement which engross his attention. Jurists will describe the dissolution of legal fictions based upon the

False Decretals, the acquisition of a true text of the Roman Code, and the attempt to introduce a rational method into the theory of modern jurisprudence, as well as to commence the study of international law. Men whose attention has been turned to the history of discoveries and inventions will relate the exploration of America and the East, or will point to the benefits conferred upon the world by the arts of printing and engraving, by the compass and the telescope, by paper and by gunpowder; and will insist that at the moment of the Renaissance all these instruments of mechanical utility started into existence, to aid the dissolution of what was rotten and must perish, to strengthen and perpetuate the new and useful and life-giving. Yet neither any one of these answers taken separately, nor indeed all of them together, will offer a solution of the problem. By the term Renaissance, or new birth, is indicated a natural movement, not to be explained by this or that characteristic, but to be accepted as an effort of humanity for which at length the time had come, and in the onward progress of which we still participate. The history of the Renaissance is not the history of arts, or of sciences, or of literature, or even of nations. It is the history of the attainment of self-conscious freedom by the human spirit manifested in the European races. It is no mere political mutation, no new fashion of art, no restoration of classical standards of taste. The arts and the inventions, the knowledge and the books, which suddenly became vital at the time of the Renaissance, had long lain neglected on the shores of the Dead Sea which we call the Middle Ages. It was not their discovery which caused the Renaissance. But it was the intellectual energy, the spontaneous outburst of intelligence, which enabled mankind at that moment to make use of them. The force then generated still continues, vital and expansive, in the spirit of the modern world.

How was it, then, that at a certain period, about fourteen

centuries after Christ, to speak roughly, the intellect of the Western races awoke as it were from slumber and began once more to be active? That is a question which we can but imperfectly answer. The mystery of organic life defeats analysis; whether the subject of our inquiry be a germ-cell, or a phenomenon so complex as the commencement of a new religion, or the origination of a new disease, or a new phase in civilisation, it is alike impossible to do more than to state the conditions under which the fresh growth begins, and to point out what are its manifestations. In doing so, moreover, we must be careful not to be carried away by words of our own making. Renaissance, Reformation, and Revolution are not separate things, capable of being isolated; they are moments in the history of the human race which we find it convenient to name; while history itself is one and continuous, so that our utmost endeavours to regard some portion of it independently of the rest will be defeated.

A glance at the history of the preceding centuries shows that, after the dissolution of the fabric of the Roman Empire, there was no immediate possibility of any intellectual revival. The barbarous races which had deluged Europe had to absorb their barbarism: the fragments of Roman civilisation had either to be destroyed or assimilated: the Germanic nations had to receive culture and religion from the people they had superseded; the Church had to be created, and a new form given to the old idea of the Empire. It was further necessary that the modern nationalities should be defined, that the modern languages should be formed, that peace should be secured to some extent, and wealth accumulated, before the indispensable conditions for a resurrection of the free spirit of humanity could exist. The first nation which fulfilled these conditions was the first to inaugurate the new era. The reason why Italy took the lead in the Renaissance was, that Italy possessed a language, a favourable climate, political freedom, and commercial prosperity, at a time when other nations were still semi-barbarous. Where the human spirit had been buried in the decay of the Roman Empire, there it arose upon the ruins of that Empire; and the Papacy, called by Hobbes the ghost of the dead Roman Empire, seated, throned and crowned, upon the ashes thereof, to some extent bridged over the gulf between the two periods.

Keeping steadily in sight the truth that the real quality of the Renaissance was intellectual, that it was the emancipation of the reason for the modern world, we may inquire how feudalism was related to it. The mental condition of the Middle Ages was one of ignorant prostration before the idols of the Church—dogma and authority and scholasticism. Again, the nations of Europe during these centuries were bound down by the brute weight of material necessities. Without the power over the outer world which the physical sciences and useful arts communicate, without the ease of life which wealth and plenty secure, without the traditions of a civilised past, emerging slowly from a state of utter rawness, each nation could barely do more than gain and keep a difficult hold upon existence. To depreciate the work achieved during the Middle Ages would be ridiculous. Yet we may point out that it was done unconsciously—that it was a gradual and instinctive process of becoming. The reason, in one word, was not awake; the mind of man was ignorant of its own treasures and its own capacities. It is pathetic to think of the mediæval students poring over a single ill-translated sentence of Porphyry, endeavouring to extract from its clauses whole systems of logical science, and torturing their brains about puzzles hardly less idle than the dilemma of Buridan's donkey, while all the time, at Constantinople and at Seville, in Greek and Arabic, Plato and Aristotle were alive but sleeping, awaiting only the call of the Renaissance to bid them speak with voice intelligible to the modern mind.

It is no less pathetic to watch tide after tide of the ocean of humanity sweeping from all parts of Europe, to break in passionate but unavailing foam upon the shores of Palestine, whole nations laying life down for the chance of seeing the walls of Jerusalem, worshipping the sepulchre whence Christ had risen, loading their fleet with relics and with cargoes of the sacred earth, while all the time within their breasts and brains the spirit of the Lord was with them, living but unrecognised, the spirit of freedom which ere long was destined to restore its birthright to the world. Meanwhile the middle age accomplished its own work. Slowly and obscurely, amid stupidity and ignorance, were being forged the nations and the languages of Europe. Italy, France, Spain, England, Germany took shape. The actors of the future drama acquired their several characters, and formed the tongues whereby their personalities should be expressed. The qualities which render modern society different from that of the ancient world were being impressed upon these nations by Christianity, by the Church, by chivalry, by feudal customs. Then came a further phase. After the nations had been moulded, their monarchies and dynasties were established. Feudalism passed by slow degrees into various forms of more or less defined autocracy. In Italy and Germany numerous principalities sprang into pre-eminence; and though the nation was not united under one head, the monarchical principle was acknowledged. France and Spain submitted to a despotism, by right of which the king could say, 'L'Etat c'est moi.' England developed her complicated constitution of popular right and royal prerogative. At the same time the Latin Church underwent a similar process of transformation. The Papacy became more autocratic. Like the king, the Pope began to say, 'L'Eglise c'est moi.' This merging of the mediæval State and mediæval Church in the personal supremacy of King and Pope may be termed the special feature of the last age of feudalism which preceded the Renaissance. It was thus that the necessary conditions and external circumstances were prepared. The organisation of the five great nations, and the levelling of political and spiritual interests under political and spiritual despots, formed the prelude to that drama of liberty of which the Renaissance was the first act, the Reformation the second, the Revolution the third, and which we nations of the present are still evolving in the establishment of the democratic idea.

Meanwhile, it must not be imagined that the Renaissance burst suddenly upon the world in the fifteenth century without premonitory symptoms. Far from that: within the middle age itself, over and over again, the reason strove to break loose from its fetters. Abelard, in the twelfth century, tried to prove that the interminable dispute about entities and words was founded on a misapprehension. Roger Bacon, at the beginning of the thirteenth century, anticipated modern science, and proclaimed that man, by use of nature, can do all things. Joachim of Flora, intermediate between the two, drank one drop of the cup of prophecy offered to his lips, and cried that 'the Gospel of the Father was past, the Gospel of the Son was passing, the Gospel of the Spirit was to be.' These three men, each in his own way, the Frenchman as a logician, the Englishman as an analyst, the Italian as a mystic, divined the future but inevitable emancipation of the reason of mankind. Nor were there wanting signs, especially in Provence, that Aphrodite and Phœbus and the Graces were ready to resume their sway. The premature civilisation of that favoured region, so cruelly extinguished by the Church, was itself a reaction of nature against the restrictions imposed by ecclesiastical discipline ; while the songs of the wandering students, known under the title of *Carmina Burana*, indicate a revival of Pagan or pre-Christian feeling in the very stronghold of mediæval learning. We have, moreover, to remember the Cathari, the Paterini, the Fraticelli, the Albigenses, the Hussites—heretics in whom the new light dimly shone, but who were instantly exterminated by the Church. We have to commemorate the vast conception of the Emperor Frederick II., who strove to found a new society of humane culture in the South of Europe, and to anticipate the advent of the spirit of modern tolerance. He, too, and all his race were exterminated by the Papal jealousy. Truly we may say with Michelet that the Sibyl of the Renaissance kept offering her books in vain to feudal Europe. In vain because the time was not yet. The ideas projected thus early on the modern world were immature and abortive, like those headless trunks and zoophitic members of half-moulded humanity which, in the vision of Empedocles, preceded the birth of full-formed man. The nations were not ready. Franciscans imprisoning Roger Bacon for venturing to examine what God had meant to keep secret; Dominicans preaching crusades against the cultivated nobles of Toulouse; Popes stamping out the seed of enlightened Frederick; Benedictines erasing the masterpieces of classical literature to make way for their own litanies and lurries, or selling pieces of the parchment for charms; a laity devoted by superstition to saints and by sorcery to the devil; a clergy sunk in sensual sloth or fevered with demoniac zeal: these still ruled the intellectual destinies of Europe. Therefore the first anticipations of the Renaissance were fragmentary and sterile.

Then came a second period. Dante's poem, a work of conscious art, conceived in a modern spirit and written in a modern tongue, was the first true sign that Italy, the leader of the nations of the West, had shaken off her sleep. Petrarch followed. His ideal of antique culture as the everlasting solace and the universal education of the human race, his lifelong effort to recover the classical harmony of thought and speech, gave a direct impulse to one of the chief movements of the Renaissance—its passionate outgoing toward the ancient world. After Petrarch, Boccaccio opened yet another channel for the stream of freedom. His conception of human existence as joy to be accepted with thanksgiving, not as a gloomy error to be rectified by suffering, familiarised the fourteenth century with that form of semi-pagan gladness which marked the real Renaissance.

In Dante, Petrarch, and Boccaccio Italy recovered the consciousness of intellectual liberty. What we call the Renaissance had not yet arrived; but their achievement rendered its appearance in due season certain. With Dante the genius of the modern world dared to stand alone and to create confidently after its own fashion. With Petrarch the same genius reached forth across the gulf of darkness, resuming the tradition of a splendid past. With Boccaccio the same genius proclaimed the beauty of the world, the goodliness of youth and strength and love and life, unterrified by hell, unappalled by the shadow of impending death.

It was now, at the beginning of the fourteenth century, when Italy had lost indeed the heroic spirit which we admire in her Communes of the thirteenth, but had gained instead ease, wealth, magnificence, and that repose which springs from long prosperity, that the new age at last began. Europe was, as it were, a fallow field, beneath which lay buried the civilisation of the old world. Behind stretched the centuries of mediævalism, intellectually barren and inert. Of the future there were as yet but faint foreshadowings. Meanwhile, the force of the nations who were destined to achieve the coming transformation was unexhausted; their physical and mental faculties were unimpaired. No ages of enervating luxury, of intellectual endeavour, of life artificially preserved or ingeniously prolonged, had sapped the fibre of the men who were about to inaugurate the modern world. Severely

nurtured, unused to delicate living, these giants of the
Renaissance were like boys in their capacity for endurance,
their inordinate appetite for enjoyment. No generations,
hungry, sickly, effete, critical, disillusioned, trod them down.
Ennui and the fatigue that springs from scepticism, the
despair of thwarted effort, were unknown. Their fresh and
unperverted senses rendered them keenly alive to what was
beautiful and natural. They yearned for magnificence, and
instinctively comprehended splendour. At the same time the
period of satiety was still far off. Everything seemed possible
to their young energy ; nor had a single pleasure palled upon
their appetite. Born, as it were, at the moment when desires
and faculties are evenly balanced, when the perceptions are
not blunted nor the senses cloyed, opening their eyes for the
first time on a world of wonder, these men of the Renaissance
enjoyed what we may term the first transcendent springtide
of the modern world. Nothing is more remarkable than the
fulness of the life that throbbed in them. Natures rich in all
capacities and endowed with every kind of sensibility were
frequent. Nor was there any limit to the play of personality
in action. We may apply to them what Mr. Browning has
written of Sordello's temperament :

> A footfall there
> Suffices to upturn to the warm air
> Half germinating spices, mere decay
> Produces richer life, and day by day
> New pollen on the lily-petal grows,
> And still more labyrinthine buds the rose.

During the Middle Ages man had lived enveloped in a
cowl. He had not seen the beauty of the world, or had seen
it only to cross himself, and turn aside and tell his beads and
pray. Like S. Bernard travelling along the shores of the
Lake Leman, and noticing neither the azure of the waters,
nor the luxuriance of the vines, nor the radiance of the moun-

tains with their robe of sun and snow, but bending a thought-burdened forehead over the neck of his mule; even like this monk, humanity had passed, a careful pilgrim, intent on the terrors of sin, death, and judgment, along the highways of the world, and had scarcely known that they were sightworthy or that life is a blessing. Beauty is a snare, pleasure a sin, the world a fleeting show, man fallen and lost, death the only certainty, judgment inevitable, hell everlasting, heaven hard to win; ignorance is acceptable to God as a proof of faith and submission; abstinence and mortification are the only safe rules of life: these were the fixed ideas of the ascetic mediæval Church. The Renaissance shattered and destroyed them, rending the thick veil which they had drawn between the mind of man and the outer world, and flashing the light of reality upon the darkened places of his own nature. For the mystic teaching of the Church was substituted culture in the classical humanities; a new ideal was established, whereby man strove to make himself the monarch of the globe on which it is his privilege as well as destiny to live. The Renaissance was the liberation of the reason from a dungeon, the double discovery of the outer and the inner world.

An external event determined the direction which this outburst of the spirit of freedom should take. This was the contact of the modern with the ancient mind which followed upon what is called the Revival of Learning. The fall of the Greek Empire in 1453, while it signalised the extinction of the old order, gave an impulse to the now accumulated forces of the new. A belief in the identity of the human spirit under all previous manifestations and in its uninterrupted continuity was generated. Men found that in classical as well as Biblical antiquity existed an ideal of human life, both moral and intellectual, by which they might profit in the present. The modern genius felt confidence in its own energies when it learned what the ancients had achieved.

The guesses of the ancients stimulated the exertions of the moderns. The whole world's history seemed once more to be one.

The great achievements of the Renaissance were the discovery of the world and the discovery of man.[1] Under these two formulæ may be classified all the phenomena which properly belong to this period. The discovery of the world divides itself into two branches—the exploration of the globe, and that systematic exploration of the universe which is in fact what we call Science. Columbus made known America in 1492; the Portuguese rounded the Cape in 1497; Copernicus explained the solar system in 1507. It is not necessary to add anything to this plain statement; for, in contact with facts of such momentous import, to avoid what seems like commonplace reflection would be difficult. Yet it is only when we contrast the ten centuries which preceded these dates with the four centuries which have ensued, that we can estimate the magnitude of that Renaissance movement by means of which a new hemisphere has been added to civilisation. In like manner, it is worth while to pause a moment and consider what is implied in the substitution of the Copernican for the Ptolemaic system. The world, regarded in old times as the centre of all things, the apple of God's eye, for the sake of which were created sun and moon and stars, suddenly was found to be one of the many balls that roll round a giant sphere of light and heat, which is itself but one among innumerable suns attended each by a cortège of planets, and scattered, how we know not, through infinity. What has become of that brazen seat of the old gods, that Paradise to which an ascending Deity might be caught up through clouds, and hidden for a moment from the eyes of His disciples? The demonstration of the simplest truths of astronomy

[1] It is to Michelet that we owe these formulæ, which have passed into the language of history.

destroyed at a blow the legends that were most significant to the early Christians by annihilating their symbolism. Well might the Church persecute Galileo for his proof of the world's mobility. Instinctively she perceived that in this one proposition was involved the principle of hostility to her most cherished conceptions, to the very core of her mythology. Science was born, and the warfare between scientific positivism and religious metaphysic was declared. Henceforth God could not be worshipped under the forms and idols of a sacerdotal fancy; a new meaning had been given to the words: 'God is a Spirit, and they that worship Him must worship Him in spirit and in truth.' The reason of man was at last able to study the scheme of the universe, of which he is a part, and to ascertain the actual laws by which it is governed. Three centuries and a half have elapsed since Copernicus revolutionised astronomy. It is only by reflecting on the mass of knowledge we have since acquired, knowledge not only infinitely curious but also incalculably useful in its application to the arts of life, and then considering how much ground of this kind was acquired in the ten centuries which preceded the Renaissance, that we are at all able to estimate the expansive force which was then generated. Science, rescued from the hand of astrology, geomancy, alchemy, began her real life with the Renaissance. Since then, as far as to the present moment, she has never ceased to grow. Progressive and durable, Science may be called the first-born of the spirit of the modern world.

Thus by the discovery of the world is meant on the one hand the appropriation by civilised humanity of all corners of the habitable globe, and on the other the conquest by Science of all that we now know about the nature of the universe. In the discovery of man, again, it is possible to trace a twofold process. Man in his temporal relations, illustrated by Pagan antiquity, and man in his spiritual relations, illustrated by Biblical antiquity; these are the two regions, at first apparently distinct, afterwards found to be interpenetrative, which the critical and inquisitive genius of the Renaissance opened for investigation. In the former of these regions we find two agencies at work, art and scholarship. During the Middle Ages the plastic arts, like philosophy, had degenerated into barren and meaningless scholasticism—a frigid reproduction of lifeless forms copied technically and without inspiration from debased patterns. Pictures became symbolically connected with the religious feelings of the people, formulæ from which to deviate would be impious in the artist and confusing to the worshipper. Superstitious reverence bound the painter to copy the almond eyes and stiff joints of the saints whom he had adored from infancy; and, even had it been otherwise, he lacked the skill to imitate the natural forms he saw around him. But with the dawning of the Renaissance a new spirit in the arts arose. Men began to conceive that the human body is noble in itself and worthy of patient study. The object of the artist then became to unite devotional feeling and respect for the sacred legend with the utmost beauty and the utmost fidelity of delineation. He studied from the nude; he drew the body in every posture; he composed drapery, invented attitudes, and adapted the action of his figures and the expression of his faces to the subject he had chosen. In a word, he humanised the altar-pieces and the cloister-frescoes upon which he worked. In this way the painters rose above the ancient symbols, and brought heaven down to earth. By drawing Madonna and her Son like living human beings, by dramatising the Christian history, they silently substituted the love of beauty and the interests of actual life for the principles of the Church. The saint or angel became an occasion for the display of physical perfection, and to introduce 'un bel corpo ignudo' into the composition was of more moment to them than to represent the macerations of the Magdalen. Men thus learned to look beyond the relique and the host, and to forget the dogma in the lovely forms which gave it expression. Finally, when the classics came to aid this work of progress, a new world of thought and fancy, divinely charming, wholly human, was revealed to their astonished eyes. Thus art, which had begun by humanising the legends of the Church, diverted the attention of its students from the legend to the work of beauty, and lastly, severing itself from the religious tradition, became the exponent of the majesty and splendour of the human body. This final emancipation of art from ecclesiastical trammels culminated in the great age of Italian painting. Gazing at Michael Angelo's prophets in the Sistine Chapel, we are indeed in contact with ideas originally religious. But the treatment of these ideas is purely, broadly human, on a level with that of the sculpture of Pheidias. Titian's Virgin received into Heaven, soaring midway between the archangel who descends to crown her and the apostles who yearn to follow her, is far less a Madonna Assunta than the apotheosis of humanity conceived as a radiant mother. Throughout the picture there is nothing ascetic, nothing mystic, nothing devotional. Nor did the art of the Renaissance stop here. It went further, and plunged into Paganism. Sculptors and painters combined with architects to cut the arts loose from their connection with the Church by introducing a spirit and a sentiment alien to Christianity.

Through the instrumentality of art, and of all the ideas which art introduced into daily life, the Renaissance wrought for the modern world a real resurrection of the body, which, since the destruction of antique civilisation, had lain swathed up in hair-shirts and cerements within the tomb of the mediæval cloister. It was scholarship which revealed to men the wealth of their own minds, the dignity of human thought, the value of human speculation, the importance of human life regarded as a thing apart from religious rules and dogmas. During the Middle Ages a few students had possessed the poems of Virgil and the prose of Boethius—and Virgil at Mantua, Boethius at Pavia, had actually been honoured as saints—together with fragments of Lucan, Ovid, Statius, Juvenal, Cicero, and Horace. The Renaissance opened to the whole reading public the treasure-houses of Greek and Latin literature. At the same time the Bible in its original tongues was rediscovered. Mines of Oriental learning were laid bare for the students of the Jewish and Arabic traditions. The Aryan and Semitic revelations were for the first time subjected to something like a critical comparison. With unerring instinct the men of the Renaissance named the voluminous subject-matter of scholarship 'Litteræ Humaniores'—the more human literature, or the literature that humanises.

There are three stages in the history of scholarship during the Renaissance. The first is the age of passionate desire; Petrarch poring over a Homer he could not understand, and Boccaccio in his maturity learning Greek, in order that he might drink from the well-head of poetic inspiration, are the heroes of this period. They inspired the Italians with a thirst for antique culture. Next comes the age of acquisition and of libraries. Nicholas V., who founded the Vatican Library in 1453, Cosmo de' Medici, who began the Medicean Collection a little earlier, and Poggio Bracciolini, who ransacked all the cities and convents of Europe for manuscripts, together with the teachers of Greek, who in the first half of the fifteenth century escaped from Constantinople with precious freights of classic literature, are the heroes of this second period. It was an age of accumulation, of uncritical and indiscriminate enthusiasm. Manuscripts were worshipped by these men, just as the reliques of Holy Land had been adored by their great-grandfathers. The eagerness of the Crusades was re-vived in this quest of the Holy Grail of ancient knowledge.

Waifs and strays of Pagan authors were valued like precious gems, revelled in like odoriferous and gorgeous flowers, consulted like oracles of God, gazed on like the eyes of a beloved mistress. The good, the bad, and the indifferent received an almost equal homage. Criticism had not yet begun. The world was bent on gathering up its treasures, frantically bewailing the lost books of Livy, the lost songs of Sappho— absorbing to intoxication the strong wine of multitudinous thoughts and passions that kept pouring from those long-buried amphoræ of inspiration. What is most remarkable about this age of scholarship is the enthusiasm which pervaded all classes in Italy for antique culture. Popes and princes, captains of adventure and peasants, noble ladies and the leaders of the demi-monde, alike became scholars. There is a story told by Infessura which illustrates the temper of the times with singular felicity. On the 18th of April, 1485, a report circulated in Rome that some Lombard workmen had discovered a Roman sarcophagus while digging on the Appian Way. It was a marble tomb, engraved with the inscription, 'Julia, daughter of Claudius,' and inside the coffer lay the body of a most beautiful girl of fifteen years, preserved by precious unguents from corruption and the injury of time. The bloom of youth was still upon her cheeks and lips; her eyes and mouth were half open; her long hair floated round her shoulders. She was instantly removed, so goes the legend, to the Capitol; and then began a procession of pilgrims from all the quarters of Rome to gaze upon this saint of the old Pagan world. In the eyes of those enthusiastic worshippers, her beauty was beyond imagination or description: she was far fairer than any woman of the modern age could hope to be. At last Innocent VIII. feared lest the orthodox faith should suffer by this new cult of a heathen corpse. Julia was buried secretly and at night by his direction, and naught remained in the Capitol but her empty marble coffin. The tale, as told by Infessura, is repeated in Matarazzo and in Nantiporto with slight variations. One says that the girl's hair was yellow, another that it was of the glossiest black. What foundation for the legend may really have existed need not here be questioned. Let us rather use the mythus as a parable of the ecstatic devotion which prompted the men of that age to discover a form of unimaginable beauty in the tomb of the classic world.[1]

Then came the third age of scholarship—the age of the critics, philologers, and printers. What had been collected by Poggio and Aurispa had now to be explained by Ficino, Poliziano, and Erasmus. They began their task by digesting and arranging the contents of the libraries. There were then no short cuts to learning, no comprehensive lexicons, no dictionaries of antiquities, no carefully prepared thesauri of mythology and history. Each student had to hold in his brain the whole mass of classical erudition. The text and the canon of Homer, Plato, Aristotle, and the tragedians had to be decided. Greek type had to be struck. Florence, Venice, Basle, Lyons, and Paris groaned with printing-presses. The Aldi, the Stephani, and Froben toiled by night and day, employing scores of scholars, men of supreme devotion and of mighty brain, whose work it was to ascertain the right reading of sentences, to accentuate, to punctuate, to commit to the press, and to place beyond the reach of monkish hatred or of envious time that everlasting solace of humanity which exists in the classics. All subsequent achievements in the field of scholarship sink into insignificance beside the labours of these men, who needed genius, enthusiasm, and the sympathy

[1] The most remarkable document regarding the body of Julia which has yet been published is a Latin letter, written by Bartholomæus Fontius to his friend Franciscus Saxethus, minutely describing her, with details which appear to prove that he had not only seen but handled the corpse. It is printed in Janitschek, *Die Gesellschaft der R. in It.*: Stuttgart, 1879, p. 120.

cf Europe for the accomplishment of their titanic task. Virgil was printed in 1470, Homer in 1488, Aristotle in 1498, Plato in 1513. They then became the inalienable heritage of mankind. But what vigils, what anxious expenditure of thought, what agonies of doubt and expectation, were endured by those heroes of humanising scholarship, whom we are apt to think of merely as pedants! Which of us now warms and thrills with emotion at hearing the name of Aldus Manutius, or of Henricus Stephanus, or of Johannes Froben? Yet this we surely ought to do; for to them we owe in a great measure the freedom of our spirit, our stores of intellectual enjoyment, our command of the past, our certainty of the future of human culture.

This third age in the history of the Renaissance Scholarship may be said to have reached its climax in Erasmus; for by this time Italy had handed on the torch of learning to the northern nations. The publication of his 'Adagia' in 1500 marks the advent of a more critical and selective spirit, which from that date onward has been gradually gaining strength in the modern mind. Criticism, in the true sense of accurate testing and sifting, is one of the points which distinguish the moderns from the ancients; and criticism was developed by the process of assimilation, comparison, and appropriation, which was necessary in the growth of scholarship. The ultimate effect of this recovery of classic literature was, once and for all, to liberate the intellect. The modern world was brought into close contact with the free virility of the ancient world, and emancipated from the thraldom of unproved traditions. The force to judge and the desire to create were generated. The immediate result in the sixteenth century was an abrupt secession of the learned, not merely from monasticism, but also from the true spirit of Christianity. The minds of the Italians assimilated Paganism. In their hatred of mediæval ignorance, in their loathing of cowled and cloistered

fools, they flew to an extreme, and affected the manner of
an irrevocable past.   This extravagance led of necessity to a
reaction—in the north to Puritanism, in the south to what
has been termed the Counter-Reformation effected under
Spanish influences in the Latin Church.   But Christianity,
that most precious possession of the modern world, was never
seriously imperilled by the classical enthusiasm of the Renaissance ; nor, on the other hand, was the progressive emancipation of the reason materially retarded by the reaction it
produced.

The transition at this point to the third branch in the
discovery of man, the revelation to the consciousness of its
own spiritual freedom, is natural.   Not only did scholarship
restore the classics and encourage literary criticism ; it also
restored the text of the Bible, and encouraged theological
criticism.   In the wake of theological freedom followed a free
philosophy, no longer subject to the dogmas of the Church.
To purge the Christian faith from false conceptions, to liberate
the conscience from the tyranny of priests, and to interpret
religion to the reason, has been the work of the last centuries ;
nor is this work as yet by any means accomplished.   On the
one side Descartes and Bacon, Spinoza and Locke, are sons
of the Renaissance, champions of new-found philosophical
freedom ; on the other side, Luther is a son of the Renaissance, the herald of new found religious freedom.   The whole
movement of the Reformation is a phase in that accelerated
action of the modern mind which at its commencement we
call the Renaissance.   It is a mistake to regard the Reformation as an isolated phenomenon or as a mere effort to restore
the Church to purity.   The Reformation exhibits in the
region of religious thought and national politics what the
Renaissance displays in the sphere of culture, art, and science
—the recovered energy and freedom of the reason.   We are
too apt to treat of history in parcels, and to attempt to draw

lessons from detached chapters in the biography of the human race. To observe the connection between the several stages of a progressive movement of the human spirit, and to recognise that the forces at work are still active, is the true philosophy of history.

The Reformation, like the revival of science and of culture, had its mediæval anticipations and foreshadowings. The heretics whom the Church successfully combated in North Italy, France, and Bohemia were the precursors of Luther. The scholars prepared the way in the fifteenth century. Teachers of Hebrew, founders of Hebrew type—Reuchlin in Germany, Aleander in Paris, Von Hutten as a pamphleteer, and Erasmus as a humanist—contribute each a definite momentum. Luther, for his part, incarnates the spirit of revolt against tyrannical authority, urges the necessity of a return to the essential truth of Christianity, as distinguished from the idols of the Church, and asserts the right of the individual to judge, interpret, criticise, and construct opinion for himself. The veil which the Church had interposed between the human soul and God was broken down. The freedom of the conscience was established. Thus the principles involved in what we call the Reformation were momentous. Connected on the one side with scholarship and the study of texts, it opened the path for modern Biblical criticism. Connected on the other side with the intolerance of mere authority, it led to what has since been named rationalism— the attempt to reconcile the religious tradition with the reason, and to define the logical ideas that underlie the conceptions of the popular religious consciousness. Again, by promulgating the doctrine of personal freedom, and by connecting itself with national politics, the Reformation was linked historically to the Revolution. It was the Puritan Church in England, stimulated by the patriotism of the Dutch Protestants, which established our constitutional liberty, and introduced in America the general principle of the equality of men. This high political abstraction, latent in Christianity, evolved by criticism, and promulgated as a gospel in the second half of the last century, was externalised in the French Revolution. The work that yet remains to be accomplished for the modern world is the organisation of society in harmony with democratic principles.

Thus what the word Renaissance really means is new birth to liberty—the spirit of mankind recovering consciousness and the power of self-determination, recognising the beauty of the outer world, and of the body through art, liberating the reason in science and the conscience in religion, restoring culture to the intelligence, and establishing the principle of political freedom. The Church was the schoolmaster of the Middle Ages. Culture was the humanising and refining influence of the Renaissance. The problem for the present and the future is how through education to render knowledge accessible to all—to break down that barrier which in the Middle Ages was set between clerk and layman, and which in the intermediate period has arisen between the intelligent and ignorant classes. Whether the Utopia of a modern world, in which all men shall enjoy the same social, political, and intellectual advantages, be realised or not, we cannot doubt that the whole movement of humanity from the Renaissance onward has tended in this direction. To destroy the distinctions, mental and physical, which nature raises between individuals, and which constitute an actual hierarchy, will always be impossible. Yet it may happen that in the future no civilised man will lack the opportunity of being physically and mentally the best that God has made him.

It remains to speak of the instruments and mechanical inventions which aided the emancipation of the spirit in the modern age. Discovered over and over again, and offered at intervals to the human race at various times and on divers soils, no effective use was made of these material resources until the fifteenth century. The compass, discovered according to tradition by Gioja of Naples in 1302, was employed by Columbus for the voyage to America in 1492. The telescope, known to the Arabians in the Middle Ages, and described by Roger Bacon in 1250, helped Copernicus to prove the revolution of the earth in 1530, and Galileo to substantiate his theory of the planetary system. Printing, after numerous useless revelations to the world of its resources, became an art in 1438; and paper, which had long been known to the Chinese, was first made of cotton in Europe about 1000, and of rags in 1319. Gunpowder entered into use about 1320. As employed by the Genius of the Renaissance, each one of these inventions became a lever by means of which to move the world. Gunpowder revolutionised the art of war. The feudal castle, the armour of the knight and his battle-horse. the prowess of one man against a hundred, and the pride of aristocratic cavalry trampling upon ill-armed militia, were annihilated by the flashes of the cannon. Courage became more a moral than a physical quality. The victory was delivered to the brain of the general. Printing has established, as indestructible, all knowledge, and disseminated, as the common property of everyone, all thought; while paper has made the work of printing cheap. Such reflections as these, however, are trite, and must occur to every mind. It is far more to the purpose to repeat that not the inventions, but the intelligence that used them, the conscious calculating spirit of the modern world, should rivet our attention when we direct it to the phenomena of the Renaissance.

In the work of the Renaissance all the great nations of Europe shared. But it must never be forgotten that as a matter of history the true Renaissance began in Italy. It was there that the essential qualities which distinguish the modern from the ancient and the mediæval world were deve-

loped.   Italy created that new spiritual atmosphere of culture
and of intellectual freedom which has been the life-breath of
the European races.   As the Jews are called the chosen and
peculiar people of divine revelation, so may the Italians be
called the chosen and peculiar vessels of the prophecy of
the Renaissance.   In art, in scholarship, in science, in the
mediation between antique culture and the modern intellect,
they took the lead, handing to Germany and France and
England the restored humanities complete.   Spain and
England have since done more for the exploration and
colonisation of the world.   Germany achieved the labour of
the Reformation almost single-handed.   France has collected,
centralised, and diffused intelligence with irresistible energy.
But if we return to the first origins of the Renaissance, we
find that, at a time when the rest of Europe was inert, Italy
had already begun to organise the various elements of the
modern spirit, and to set the fashion whereby the other great
nations should learn and live.

CHAPTER II

ITALIAN HISTORY

AFTER a first glance into Italian history the student recoils as from a chaos of inscrutable confusion. To fix the moment of transition from ancient to modern civilisation seems impossible. There is no formation of a new people, as in the case of Germany or France or England, to serve as starting-point. Differ as the Italian races do in their original type; Gauls, Ligurians, Etruscans, Umbrians, Latins, Iapygians, Greeks have been fused together beneath the stress of Roman rule into a nation that survives political mutations and the disasters of barbarian invasions. Goths, Lombards, and Franks blend successively with the masses of this complex population, and lose the outlines of their several personalities. The Western Empire melts imperceptibly away. The Roman Church grows no less imperceptibly, and forms the Holy Roman Empire as the equivalent of its own spiritual greatness in the sphere of secular authority. These two institutions, the crowning monuments of Italian creative genius, dominate the Middle Ages, powerful as facts, but still more powerful as ideas. Yet neither of them controls the evolution of Italy in the same sense as France was controlled by the monarchical, and Germany by the federative, principle. The forces of the nation, divided and swayed from side to side by this commanding dualism, escaped both influences in so far as either Pope or Emperor strove to mould them into unity. Meanwhile the domination of Byzantine Greeks in the southern provinces, the kingdom of the Goths at Ravenna, the kingdom of the Lombards and Franks at Pavia, the incursions of Huns and Saracens, the kingdom of the Normans at Palermo, formed but accidents and moments in a national development which owed important modifications to each successive episode, but was not finally determined by any of them. When the Communes emerge into prominence, shaking off the supremacy of the Greeks in the South, vindicating their liberties against the Empire in the North, jealously guarding their independence from Papal encroachment in the centre, they have already assumed shapes of marked distinctness and bewildering diversity. Venice, Milan, Genoa, Florence, Bologna, Siena, Perugia, Amalfi, Lucca, Pisa, to mention only a few of the more notable, are indiscriminately called Republics. Yet they differ in their internal type no less than in external conditions. Each wears from the first and preserves a physiognomy that justifies our thinking and speaking of the town as an incarnate entity. The cities of Italy, down to the very smallest, bear the attributes of individuals. The mutual attractions and repulsions that presided over their growth have given them specific qualities which they will never lose, which will be reflected in their architecture, in their customs, in their language, in their policy, as well as in the institutions of their government. We think of them involuntarily as persons, and reserve for them epithets that mark the permanence of their distinctive characters. To treat of them collectively is almost impossible. Each has its own biography, and plays a part of consequence in the great drama of the nation. Accordingly the study of Italian politics, Italian literature, Italian art, is really not the study of one national genius, but of a whole family of cognate geniuses, grouped together, conscious of affinity, obeying the same general conditions, but issuing in markedly divergent characteristics. Democracies, oligarchies, aristocracies spring into being by laws of natural selection within the limits of a single province. Every municipality has a separate nomenclature for its magistracies, a somewhat different method of distributing administrative functions. In one place there is a Doge appointed for life ; in another the government is put into commission among officers elected for a period of months. Here we find a Patrician, a Senator, a Tribune ; there Consuls, Rectors, Priors, Ancients, Buonuomini, Conservatori. At one period and in one city the Podestà seems paramount; across the border a Captain of the People or a Gonfaloniere di Giustizia is supreme. Vicars of the Empire, Exarchs, Catapans, Rectors for the Church, Legates, Commissaries, succeed each other with dazzling rapidity. Councils are multiplied and called by names that have their origin and meaning buried in the dust of archæology. Consigli del Popolo, Credenza, Consiglio del Comune, Senato, Gran Consiglio, Pratiche, Parlamenti, Monti, Consiglio de' Savi, Arti, Parte Guelfa, Consigli di Dieci, di Tre, I Nove, Gli Otto, I Cento—such are a few of the titles chosen at random from the constitutional records of different localities.

Not one is insignificant. Not one but indicates some moment of importance in the social evolution of the state. Not one but speaks of civil strife, whereby the burgh in question struggled into individuality and defined itself against its neighbour. Like fossils in geological strata, these names survive long after their old uses have been forgotten, to guide the explorer in his reconstruction of a buried past. While one town appears to respect the feudal lordship of great families, another pronounces nobility to be a crime, and forces on its citizens the reality or the pretence of labour. Some recognise the supremacy of ecclesiastics. Others, like Venice, resist the least encroachment of the Church, and stand aloof from Roman Christianity in jealous isolation. The interests of one class are maritime, of another military, of a third industrial, of a fourth financial, of a fifth educational. Amalfi, Pisa, Genoa, and Venice depend for power upon their fleets and colonies; the little cities of Romagna and the March supply the Captains of adventure with recruits; Florence and Lucca live by manufacture; Milan by banking; Bologna, Padua, Vicenza, owe their wealth to students attracted by their universities. Foreign alliances or geographical affinities connect one centre with the Empire of the East, a second with France, a third with Spain. The North is overshadowed by Germany; the South is disquieted by Islam. The types thus formed and thus discriminated are vital, and persist for centuries with the tenacity of physical growths. Each differentiation owes its origin to causes deeply rooted in the locality. The freedom and apparent waywardness of nature, when she sets about to form crystals of varying shapes and colours, that shall last and bear her stamp for ever, have governed their uprising and their progress to maturity. At the same time they exhibit the keen jealousies and mutual hatreds of rival families in the animal kingdom. Pisa destroys Amalfi; Genoa, Pisa; Venice, Genoa; with ruthless and remorseless egotism in the conflict of commercial interests. Florence enslaves Pisa because she needs a way to the sea. Siena and Perugia, upon their inland altitudes, consume themselves in brilliant but unavailing efforts to expand. Milan engulfs the lesser towns of Lombardy. Verona absorbs Padua and Treviso. Venice extends dominion over the Friuli and the Veronese conquests. Strife and covetousness reign from the Alps to the Ionian Sea. But it is a strife of living energies, the covetousness of impassioned and puissant units. Italy as a whole is almost invisible to the student by reason of the many-sided, combative, self-centred crowd of numberless Italian communities. Proximity foments hatred and stimulates hostility. Fiesole looks down and threatens Florence. Florence returns frown for frown, and does not rest till she has made her neighbour of the hills a slave. Perugia and Assisi turn the Umbrian plain into a wilderness of wolves by their recurrent warfare. Scowling at one another across the Valdichiana, Perugia rears a tower against Chiusi, and Chiusi builds her Becca Questa in responsive menace. The tiniest burgh upon the Arno receives from Dante, the poet of this internecine strife and fierce town-rivalry, its stigma of immortalising satire and insulting epithet, for no apparent reason but that its dwellers dare to drink of the same water and to breathe the same air as Florence. It would seem as though the most ancient furies of antagonistic races, enchained and suspended for centuries by the magic of Rome, had been unloosed; as though the indigenous populations of Italy, tamed by antique culture, were reverting to their primal instincts, with all the discords and divisions introduced by the military system of the Lombards, the feudalism of the Franks, the alien institutions of the Germans, superadded to exasperate the passions of a nation blindly struggling against obstacles that block the channel of continuous progress. Nor is this the end of the perplexity. Not only are the cities at war with one another, but they are plunged in ceaseless strife within the circuit of their ramparts. The people with the nobles, the burghs with the castles, the plebeians with the burgher aristocracy, the men of commerce with the men of arms and ancient lineage, Guelfs and Ghibellines, clash together in persistent fury. One half the city expels the other

half.   The exiles roam abroad, cement alliances, and return
to extirpate their conquerors.   Fresh proscriptions and new
expulsions follow.   Again alliances are made and revolutions
accomplished, till the ancient feuds of the towns are crossed,
recrossed, and tangled in a web of madness that defies analysis.
Through the medley of quarrelling, divided, subdivided, and
intertwisted factions, ride Emperors followed by their bands
of knights, appearing for a season on vain quests, and with-
drawing after they have tenfold confounded the confusion.
Papal Legates drown the cities of the Church in blood, preach
crusades, fulminate interdictions, rouse insurrections in the
States that own allegiance to the Empire.   Monks stir republican revivals in old cities that have lost their liberties, or
assemble the populations of crime-maddened districts in aimless comedies of piety and false pacification, or lead them
barefooted and intoxicated with shrill cries of ' Mercy ' over
plain and mountain.   Princes of France, Kings of Bohemia
and Hungary, march and countermarch from north to south
and back again, form leagues, establish realms, head confede-
rations, which melt like shapes we form from clouds to nothing.
At one time the Pope and Emperor use Italy as the arena of
a deadly duel, drawing the congregated forces of the nation
into their dispute.   At another they join hands to divide the
spoil of ruined provinces.   Great generals with armies at their
backs start into being from apparent nothingness, dispute the
sovereignty of Italy in bloodless battles, found ephemeral
dynasties, and pass away like mists upon a mountain-side
beneath a puff of wind.   Conflict, ruin, desolation, anarchy
are ever yielding place to concord, restoration, peace, prosperity, and then recurring with a mighty flood of violence.
Construction, destruction, and reconstruction play their part
in crises that have to be counted by the thousands.

In the meantime, from this hurricane of disorder rises the
clear ideal of the national genius.   Italy becomes self-conscious

and attains the spiritual primacy of modern Europe. Art,
Learning, Literature, Statecraft, Philosophy, Science build a
sacred and inviolable city of the soul amid the tumult of seven
thousand revolutions, the dust and crash of falling cities, the
tramplings of recurrent invasions, the infamies and outrages
of tyrants and marauders who oppress the land. Unshaken
by the storms that rage around it, this refuge of the spirit,
raised by Italian poets, thinkers, artists, scholars, and discoverers, grows unceasingly in bulk and strength, until the
younger nations take their place beneath its ample dome.
Then, while yet the thing of wonder and of beauty stands in
fresh perfection, at that supreme moment when Italy is tranquil and sufficient to fulfil the noblest mission for the world,
we find her crushed and trampled under foot. Her tempestuous but splendid story closes in the calm of tyranny imposed
by Spain.

Over this vertiginous abyss of history, where the memories
of antique civilisation blend with the growing impulses of
modern life in an uninterrupted sequence of national consciousness ; through this many-chambered laboratory of conflicting principles, where the ideals of the Middle Age are
shaped, and laws are framed for Europe ; across this wonder-
land of waning and of waxing culture, where Goths, Greeks,
Lombards, Franks, and Normans come to form themselves by
contact with the ever-living soul of Rome ; where Frenchmen,
Spaniards, Swiss, and Germans at a later period battle for the
richest prize in Europe, and learn by conquest from the conquered to be men ; how shall we guide our course ? If we
follow the fortunes of the Church, and make the Papacy the
thread on which the history of Italy shall hang, we gain the
advantage of basing our narrative upon the most vital and
continuous member of the body politic. But we are soon
forced to lose sight of the Italians in the crowd of other
Christian races. The history of the Church is cosmopolitan.

The sphere of the Papacy extends in all directions around Italy taken as a local centre. ᶜ Its influence, moreover, was invariably one of discord rather than of harmony within the boundaries of the Peninsula. If we take the Empire as our standing-ground, we have to write the annals of a sustained struggle, in the course of which the Italian cities were successful, when they reduced the Emperor to the condition of an absentee, with merely nominal privileges. After Frederick II. the Empire played no important part in Italy until its rights were reasserted by Charles V. upon the platform of modern politics. A power so external to the true life of the nation, so successfully resisted, so impotent to control the development of the Italians, cannot be chosen as the central point of their history. If we elect the Republics, we are met with another class of difficulties. - The historian who makes the Commune his unit, who confines attention to the gradual development, reciprocal animosities, and final decadence of the Republics, can hardly do justice to the Kingdom of the Two Sicilies and the Papacy, which occupy no less than half the country. Again, the great age of the Renaissance, when all the free burghs accepted the rule of despots, and when the genius of the Italians culminated, is for him a period of downfall and degradation. Besides, he leaves the history of the Italian people before the starting-point of the Republics unexplained. ᵘ He has, at the close of their career, to account for the reason why these Communes, so powerful in self-development, so intelligent, so wealthy, and so capable of playing off the Pope against the Empire, failed to maintain their independence. In other words, he selects one phase of Italian evolution, and writes a narrative that cannot but be partial. If we make the Despots our main point, we repeat the same error in a worse form. The Despotisms imply the Communes as their predecessors. Each and all of them grew up and flourished on the soil of decadent or tired Republics.

Though they are all-important at one period of Italian history —the period of the present work—they do but form an episode in the great epic of the nation. He who attempts a general history of Italy from the point of view of the despotisms, is taking a single scene for the whole drama. Finally we might prefer the people—that people, instinctively and persistently faithful to Roman traditions, which absorbed into itself the successive hordes of barbarian invaders, civilised them, and adopted them as men of Italy ; that people which destroyed the kingdoms of the Goths and Lombards, humbled the Empire at Legnano, and evolved the Communes ; that people which resisted alien feudalism, and spent its prime upon eradicating every trace of the repugnant system from its midst ; that people which finally attained to the consciousness of national unity by the recovery of scholarship and culture under the dominion of despotic princes. This people is Italy. But the documents that should throw light upon the early annals of the people are deficient. It does not appear upon the scene before the reign of Otho I. Nor does it become supreme till after the Peace of Constance. Its biography is bound up with that of the republics and the despots. Before the date of their ascendency we have to deal with Bishops of Rome, Emperors of the East and West, Exarchs and Kings of Italy, the feudal Lords of the Marches, the Dukes and Counts of Lombard and Frankish rulers. Through that long period of incubation, when Italy freed herself from dependence upon Byzantium, created the Papacy and formed the second Roman Empire, the people exists only as a spirit resident in Roman towns and fostered by the Church, which effectually repelled all attempts at monarchical unity, playing the Lombards off against the Goths, the Franks against the Lombards, the Normans against the Greeks, merging the Italian Kingdom in the Empire when it became German, and resisting the Empire of its own creation when the towns at last were strong enough to stand alone. To speak about the people in this early period is, therefore, to invoke a myth ; to write its history is the same as writing an ideal history of mediæval Europe.

The truth is that none of these standpoints in isolation suffices for the student of Italy. Her inner history is the history of social and intellectual progress evolving itself under the conditions of attraction and repulsion generated by the double ideas of Papacy and Empire. Political unity is everywhere and at all times imperiously rejected. The most varied constitutional forms are needed for the self-effectuation of a race that has no analogue in Europe. The theocracy of Rome, the monarchy of Naples, the aristocracy of Venice, the democracy of Florence, the tyranny of Milan are equally instrumental in elaborating the national genius that gave art, literature, and mental liberty to modern society. The struggles of city with city for supremacy or bare existence, the internecine wars of party against party, the never-ending clash of principles within the States, educated the people to multifarious and vivid energy. In the course of those long complicated contests, the chief centres acquired separate personalities, assumed the physiognomy of conscious freedom, and stamped the mark of their own spirit on their citizens. At the end of all discords, at the close of all catastrophes, we find in each of the great towns a population released from mental bondage and fitted to perform the work of intellectual emancipation for the rest of Europe. Thus the essential characteristic of Italy is diversity, controlled and harmonised by an ideal rhythm of progressive movement.[1] We who are mainly

---

[1] See Guicciardini (*Op. Ined.* vol. i. p. 28) for an eloquent demonstration of the happiness, prosperity, and splendour conferred on the Italians by the independence of their several centres. He is arguing against Machiavelli's lamentation over their failure to achieve national unity.

occupied in this book with the Italian genius as it expressed itself in society, scholarship, fine art, and literature, at its most brilliant period of renascence, may accept this fact of political dismemberment with acquiescence. It was to the variety of conditions offered by the Italian communities that we owe the unexampled richness of the mental life of Italy. Yet it is impossible to overlook the weakness inflicted on the people by those same conditions when the time came for Italy to try her strength against the nations of Europe.[1] It was then shown that the diversities which stimulated spiritual energy were a fatal source of national instability. The pride of the Italians in their local independence, their intolerance of unification under a single head, the jealousies that prevented them from forming a permanent confederation, rendered them incapable of coping with races which had yielded to the centripetal force of monarchy. If it is true that the unity of the nation under a kingdom founded at Pavia would have deprived the world of much that Italy has yielded in the sphere of thought and art, it is certainly not less true that such centralisation alone could have averted the ruin of the sixteenth century, which gives the aspect of a tragedy to much of my work on the Renaissance.

Without seeking to attack the whole problem of Italian history, two main topics must be briefly discussed in the present chapter, before entering on the proper matter of this work. The first relates to the growth of the Communes, which preceded, necessitated, and determined the despotisms of the fifteenth century. The second raises the question why

[1] This was the point urged by Machiavelli, in the *Principe*, the *Discorsi*, and the *Art of War*. With keener political insight than Guicciardini, he perceived that the old felicity of Italy was about to fail her through the very independence of her local centres, which Guicciardini rightly recognised as the source of her unparalleled civilisation and wealth. The one thing needful in the shock with France and Spain was unity.

Italian differs from any other national history, why the people failed to achieve unity either under a sovereign or in a powerful confederation. These two subjects of inquiry are closely connected and interdependent. They bring into play the several points that have been indicated as partially and imperfectly explanatory of the problem of Italy. But, since I have undertaken to write neither a constitutional nor a political history, but a history of culture at a certain epoch, it will be enough to treat of these two questions briefly, with the special view of showing under what conditions the civilisation of the Renaissance came to maturity in numerous independent Communes, reduced at last by necessary laws of circumstance to tyranny ; and how it was checked at the point of transition to its second phase of modern existence, by political weakness inseparable from the want of national coherence in the shock with mightier military races.

Modern Italian history may be said to begin with the retirement of Honorius to Ravenna and the subsequent foundation of Odoacer's Kingdom in 476. The Western Empire ended, and Rome was recognised as a Republic. When Zeno sent the Goths into Italy, Theodoric established himself at Ravenna, continued the institutions and usages of the ancient Empire, and sought by blending with the people to naturalise his alien authority. Rome was respected as the sacred city of ancient culture and civility. Her Consuls, appointed by the Senate, were confirmed in due course by the Greek Emperor ; and Theodoric made himself the vicegerent of the Cæsars rather than an independent sovereign. When we criticise the Ostro-Gothic occupation by the light of subsequent history, it is clear that this exclusion of the capital from Theodoric's conquest and his veneration for the Eternal City were fatal to the unity of the Italian realm. From the moment that Rome was separated from the authority of the Italian Kings, there existed two powers in the peninsula—the one secular, monarchical, with the military strength of the barbarians imposed upon its ancient municipal organisation; the other ecclesiastical, pontifical, relying on the undefined ambitions of S. Peter's See and the unconquered instincts of the Roman people scattered through the still surviving cities.[1] Justinian, bent upon asserting his rights as the successor of the Cæsars, wrested Italy from the hands of the Goths; but scarcely was this revolution effected when Narses, the successor of Belisarius, called a new nation of barbarians to support his policy in Italy. Narses died before the advent of the Lombards; but they descended, in forces far more formidable than the Goths, and established a second kingdom at Pavia. Under the Lombard domination Rome was left untouched. Venice, with her population gathered from the ruins of the neighbouring Roman cities, remained in quasi-subjection to the Empire of the East. Ravenna became a Greek garrison, ruling the Exarchate and Pentapolis under the name of the Byzantine Emperors. The western coast escaped the Lombard domination; for Genoa grew slowly into power upon her narrow cornice between hills and sea, while Pisa defied the barbarians intrenched in military stations at Fiesole and Lucca. In like manner the islands. Sicily, Sardinia, and Corsica, were detached from the Lombard Kingdom; and the maritime cities of Southern Italy, Bari, Naples, Amalfi, and Gaeta, asserted independence under the shadow of the Greek ascendency. What the Lombards achieved in their conquest, and what they failed to accomplish, decided the future of Italy. They broke the country up into unequal blocks: for while the inland regions

[1] When I apply the term Roman here and elsewhere to the inhabitants of the Italian towns, I wish to indicate the indigenous Italic populations moulded by Roman rule into homogeneity. The resurgence of this population and its reattainment of intellectual consciousness by the recovery of past traditions and the rejection of foreign influence constitutes the history of Italy upon the close of the Dark Ages.

of the north obeyed Pavia, while the great duchies of Spoleto
in the centre and of Benevento in the south owned the
nominal sway of Alboin's successors,[1] Venice and the
Riviera, Pisa and the maritime republics of Apulia and
Calabria, Ravenna and the islands, repelled their sovereignty.
Rome remained inviolable beneath the ægis of her ancient
prestige, and the decadent Empire of the East was too inert
to check the freedom of the towns which recognised its titular
supremacy.

The kingdom of the Lombards endured two centuries,
and left ineffaceable marks upon Italy. A cordon of military
cities was drawn round the old Roman centres in Lombardy,
Tuscany, and the Duchy of Spoleto. Pavia rose against
Milan, which had been a second Rome, Cividale against
Aquileia, Fiesole against Florence, Lucca against Pisa. The
country was divided into Duchies and Marches; military
service was exacted from the population, and the laws of the
Lombards, *asininum jus, quoddam jus quod faciebant reges
per se*, as the jurists afterwards defined them, were imposed
upon the descendants of Roman civilisation. Yet the outlying cities of the sea-coasts, as we have already seen, were
independent; and Rome remained to be the centre of revolutionary ideas, the rallying-point of a policy inimical to
Lombard unity. Not long after their settlement, the princes
of the Lombard race took the fatal step of joining the
Catholic communion, whereby they strengthened the hands
of Rome and excluded themselves from tyrannising in the
last resort over the growing independence of the Papal
See. The causes of their conversion from Arianism to orthodox Latin Christianity are buried in obscurity. But it is

---

[1] It will be remembered by students of early Italian history that
Benevento and Spoleto joined the Church in her war upon the Lombard
kingdom. Spoleto was broken up. Benevento survived as a Lombard
duchy till the Norman Conquest.

probable that they were driven to this measure by the
rebelliousness of their great vassals and the necessity of
resting for support upon the indigenous populations they had
subjugated. Rome, profiting by the errors and the weakness
of her antagonists, extended her spiritual dominion by enforcing sacraments, ordeals, and appeals to ecclesiastical
tribunals, organised her hierarchy under Gregory the Great,
and lost no opportunity of enriching and aggrandising her
bishoprics. In 718 she shook off the yoke of Byzantium by
repelling the heresies of Leo the Isaurian ; and when this
insurrection menaced her with the domestic tyranny of the
Lombard Kings, who possessed themselves of Ravenna in
728, she called the Franks to her aid against the now powerful realm. Stephen II. journeyed in 753 to Gaul, named
Pippin Patrician of Rome, and invited him to the conquest of
Italy. In the war that followed, the Franks subdued the
Lombards, and Charles the Great was invested with their
kingdom and crowned Emperor in 800 by Leo III. at Rome.

The famous compact between Charles the Great and the
Pope was in effect a ratification of the existing state of
things. The new Emperor took for himself and converted
into a Frankish Kingdom all the provinces that had been
wrested from the Lombards. He relinquished to the
Papacy Rome with its patrimony, the portions of Spoleto and
Benevento that had already yielded to the See of S. Peter,
the southern provinces that owned the nominal ascendency of
Byzantium, the islands and the cities of the Exarchate and
Pentapolis which formed no part of the Lombard conquest.
By this stipulation no real temporal power was accorded to
the Papacy, nor did the new Empire surrender its paramount
rights over the peninsula at large. The Italian Kingdom,
transferred to the Franks in 800, was the kingdom founded
by the Lombards ; while the outlying and unconquered
districts were placed beneath the protectorate of the power

which had guided their emancipation. Thus the dualism introduced into Italy by Theodoric's veneration for Rome, and confirmed by the failure of the Lombard conquest, was ratified in the settlement whereby the Pope gave a new Empire to Western Christendom. Venice, Pisa, Genoa, and the maritime Republics of the south, excluded from the kingdom, were left to pursue their own course of independence ; and this is the chief among many reasons why they rose so early into prominence. Rome consolidated her ancient patrimonies and extended her rectorship in the centre, while the Frankish kings, who succeeded each other through eight reigns, developed the Regno upon feudal principles by parcelling the land among their Counts. New marches were formed, traversing the previous Lombard fabric and introducing divisions that decentralised the kingdom. Thus the great vassals of Ivrea, Verona, Tuscany, and Spoleto raised themselves against Pavia. The monarchs, placed between the Papacy and their ambitious nobles, were unable to consolidate the realm ; and when Berengar, the last independent sovereign, strove to enforce the declining authority of Pavia, he was met with the resistance and the hatred of the nation.

The kingdom Berengar attempted to maintain against his vassals and the Church was virtually abrogated by Otho I., whom the Lombard nobles summoned into Italy in 951. When he reappeared in 961, he was crowned Emperor at Rome, and assumed the title of the King of Italy. Thus the Regno was merged in the Empire, and Pavia ceased to be a capital. Henceforth the two great potentates in the peninsula were an unarmed Pontiff and an absent Emperor. The subsequent history of the Italians shows how they succeeded in reducing both these powers to the condition of principles, maintaining the pontifical and imperial ideas, but repelling the practical authority of either potentate. Otho created new marches and gave them to men of German origin. The houses of Savoy and Montferrat rose into importance in his reign. To Verona were entrusted the passes between Germany and Italy. The Princes of Este at Ferrara held the keys of Po, while the family of Canossa accumulated fiefs that stretched from Mantua across the plain of Lombardy, over the Apennines to Lucca, and southward to Spoleto. Thus the ancient Italy of Lombards and Franks was superseded by a new Italy of German feudalism, owing allegiance to a suzerain whose interests detained him in the provinces beyond the Alps. At the same time the organisation of the Church was fortified. The Bishops were placed on an equality with the Counts in the chief cities, and Viscounts were created to represent their civil jurisdiction. It is difficult to exaggerate the importance of Otho's concessions to the Bishops. During the preceding period of Frankish rule about one third of the soil of Italy had been yielded to the Church, which had the right of freeing its vassals from military service ; and since the ecclesiastical sees were founded upon ancient sites of Roman civilisation, without regard to the military centres of the barbarian kingdoms, the new privileges of the Bishops accrued to the benefit of the indigenous population. Milan, for example, down-trodden by Pavia, still remained the major See of Lombardy. Aquileia, though a desert, had her patriarch, while Cividale, established as a fortress to coerce the neighbouring Roman towns, was ecclesiastically but a village. At this epoch a third power emerged in Italy. Berengar had given the cities permission to inclose themselves with walls in order to repel the invasions of the Huns.[1] Otho respected their right of self-defence, and from the date of his coronation the history of the free burghs begins in Italy. It is at first closely connected with the changes

---

[1] It is worthy of notice that to this date belongs the war-chant of the Modenese sentinels, with its allusions to Troy and Hector, which is recognised as the earliest specimen of the Italian hendecasyllabic metre.

wrought by the extinction of the kingdom of Pavia, by the
exaltation of the clergy, and by the dislocation of the previous
system of feud-holding, which followed upon Otho's determination to remodel the country in the interest of the German
Empire. The Regno was abolished. The ancient landmarks
of nobility were altered and confused. The cities under their
Bishops assumed a novel character of independence. Those
of Roman origin, being ecclesiastical centres, had a distinct
advantage over the more recent foundations of the Lombard
and the Frankish monarchs. The Italic population everywhere emerged and displayed a vitality that had been crushed
and overlaid by centuries of invasion and military oppression.

The burghs at this epoch may be regarded as luminous
points in the dense darkness of feudal aristocracy.[1] Gathering
round their Cathedral as a centre, the towns inclose their
dwellings with bastions, from which they gaze upon a country
bristling with castles, occupied by serfs, and lorded over by
the hierarchical nobility. Within the city the Bishop and
the Count hold equal sway ; but the Bishop has upon his
side the sympathies and passions of the burghers. The first
effort of the towns is to expel the Count from their midst.

---

[1] It is not necessary to raise antiquarian questions here relating to
the origin of the Italian Commune. Whether regarded as a survival of
the ancient Roman *municipium* or as an offshoot from the Lombard *guild*,
it was a new birth of modern times, a new organism evolved to express the
functions of Italian as different from ancient Roman or mediæval Lombard life. The affection of the people for their past induced them to
use the nomenclature of Latin civility for the officers and councils of
the Commune. Thus a specious air of classical antiquity, rather literary
and sentimental than real, was given to the Commune at the outset.
Moreover, it must be remembered that Rome itself had suffered no substantial interruption of republican existence during the dark ages.
Therefore the free burghs, though their vitality was the outcome of
wholly new conditions, though they were built up of guilds and associa-
tions representing interests of modern origin, flattered themselves with
an uninterrupted municipal succession from the Roman era, and pointed
for proof to the Eternal City.

Some accident of misrule infuriates the citizens. They fly to arms and are supported by the Bishop. The Count has to retire to the open country, where he strengthens himself in his castle.[1] Then the Bishop remains victor in the town, and forms a government of rich and noble burghers, who control with him the fortunes of the new-born state. At this crisis we begin to hear for the first time a word that has been much misunderstood. The *Popolo* appears upon the scene. Interpreting the past by the present, and importing the connotation gained by the word *people* in the revolutions of the last two centuries, students are apt to assume that the Popolo of the Italian burghs included the whole population. In reality it was at first a close aristocracy of influential families, to whom the authority of the superseded Counts was transferred in commission, and who held it by hereditary right.[2] Unless we firmly grasp this fact, the subsequent vicissitudes of the Italian commonwealths are unintelligible, and the elaborate definitions of the Florentine doctrinaires lose half their meaning. The internal revolutions of the free cities were almost invariably caused by the necessity of enlarging the Popolo, and extending its franchise to the non-privileged inhabitants. Each effort after expansion provoked an obsti-

[1] The Italian word *contado* is a survival from this state of things. It represents a moment in the national development when the sphere of the Count outside the city was defined against the sphere of the municipality. The *Contadini* are the people of the Contado, the Count's men.

[2] Even Petrarch, in his letter to four Cardinals (Lett. Fam. xi. 16, ed. Fracassetti) on the reformation of the Roman Commonwealth, recommends the exclusion of the neighbouring burghs and all strangers, inclusive of the Colonna and Orsini families, from the franchise. None but pure Romans, how to be discovered from the *colluvies omnium gentium* deposited upon the Seven Hills by centuries of immigration he does not clearly say, should be chosen to revive the fallen majesty of the Republic. See in particular the peroration of his argument (op. cit. vol. iii. p. 95). In other words, he aims at a narrow Popolo, a *pura cittadinanza*, in the sense of Cacciaguida, Par. xvi.

nate resistance from those families who held the rights of burghership; and thus the technical terms *primo popolo*, *secondo popolo*, *popolo grasso*, *popolo minuto*, frequently occurring in the records of the Republics, indicate several stages in the progress from oligarchy to democracy. The constitution of the city at this early period was simple. At the head of its administration stood the Bishop, with the Popolo of enfranchised burghers. The *Commune* included the Popolo, together with the non-qualified inhabitants, and was represented by Consuls, varying in number according to the division of the town into quarters.[1] Thus the Commune and the Popolo were originally separate bodies; and this distinction has been perpetuated in the architecture of those towns which still can show a Palazzo del Popolo apart from the Palazzo del Commune. Since the affairs of the city had to be conducted by discussion, we find Councils corresponding to the constituent elements of the burgh. There is the *Parlamento*, in which the inhabitants meet together to hear the decisions of the Bishop and the Popolo, or to take measures in extreme cases that affect the city as a whole; the *Gran Consiglio*, which is only open to duly qualified members of the Popolo; and the *Credenza*, or privy council of specially delegated burghers, who debate on matters demanding secrecy and diplomacy. Such, generally speaking, and without regard to local differences, was the internal constitution of an Italian city during the supremacy of the Bishops.

In the North of Italy not a few of the greater vassals, among whom may be mentioned the houses of Canossa, Montferrat, Savoy, and Este, creations of the Salic Emperors, looked with favour upon the development of the towns, while

---

[1] In some places we find as many as twelve Consuls. It appears that both the constituent families of the Popolo and the numbers of the Consuls were determined by the Sections of the city, so many being told off for each quarter.

some nobles went so far as to constitute themselves feudatories of Bishops.[1]   The angry warfare carried on against Canossa by the Lombard barons has probably to be interpreted by the jealousy this popular policy excited.   At the same time, while Lombardy and Tuscany were establishing their municipal liberties, a sympathetic movement began in Southern Italy, which resulted in the conquest of Apulia, Calabria, and Sicily by the Normans.   Omitting all the details of this episode, than which nothing more dramatic is presented by the history of modern nations, it must be enough to point out here that the Normans finally severed Italy from the Greek Empire, gave a monarchical stamp to the south of the peninsula, and brought the Regno they consolidated into the sphere of national politics under the protection of the Pope.   Up to the date of their conquest Southern Italy had a separate and confused history.   It now entered the Italian community, and by the peculiar circumstances of its cession to the Holy See was destined in the future to become the chief instrument whereby the Popes disturbed the equilibrium of the peninsula in furtherance of their ambitious schemes.

The greatness of the Roman cities under the popular rule of their Bishops is illustrated by Milan, second only to Rome in the last days of the Empire.   Milan had been reduced to the condition of abject misery by the Kings, who spared no pains to exalt Pavia at the expense of her elder sister.   After the dissolution of the kingdom, she started into new life, and in 1037 her archbishop, Heribert, was singled out by Conrad II. as the protagonist of the episcopal revolution against feudalism.[2]   Heribert was in truth the hero of the burghs in their first strife for independence.   It was he who devised the

[1] The Pelavicini of S. Donnino, for example, gave themselves to Parma.

[2] He was summoned before the Diet of Pavia for having dispossessed a noble of his feud.

Carroccio, an immense car drawn by oxen, bearing the banner of the Commune, with an altar and priests ministrant, around which the pikemen of the city mustered when they went to war. This invention of Heribert's was soon adopted by the cities throughout Italy. It gave cohesion and confidence to the citizens, reminded them that the Church was on their side in the struggle for freedom, and served as symbol of their military strength in union. The first authentic records of a Parliament, embracing the nobles of the Popolo, the clergy, and the multitude, are transmitted to us by the Milanese Chronicles, in which Heribert figures as the president of a republic. From this date Milan takes the lead in the contests for municipal independence. Her institutions, like that of the Carroccio, together with her tameless spirit, are communicated to the neighbouring cities of Lombardy, cross the Apennines, and animate the ancient burghs of Tuscany.

Having founded their liberties upon the episcopal presidency, the cities now proceeded to claim the right of choosing their own Bishops. They refused the prelates sent them by the Emperor, and demanded an election by the Chapters of each town. This privilege was virtually won when the war of Investitures broke out in 1073. After the death of Gregory VI. in 1046, the Emperors resolved to enforce their right of nominating the Popes. The first two prelates imposed on Rome, Clement II. and Damasus II., died under suspicion of poison. Thus the Roman people refused a foreign Pope, as the Lombards had rejected the Bishops sent to rule them. The next Popes, Leo IX. and Victor II., were persuaded by Hildebrand, who now appears upon the stage, to undergo a second election at Rome by the clergy and the people. They escaped assassination. But the fifth German, Stephen X., again died suddenly; and now the formidable monk of Soana felt himself powerful enough to cause the election of his own candidate, Nicholas II. A Lateran council, inspired by Hildebrand, transferred the election of Popes to the Cardinals, approved by the clergy and people of Rome, and confirmed the privilege of the cities to choose their Bishops, subject to Papal ratification. In 1073 Hildebrand assumed the tiara as Gregory VII., and declared a war that lasted more than forty years against the Empire. At its close in 1122 the Church and the Empire were counterposed as mutually exclusive autocracies, the one claiming illimitable spiritual sway, the other recognised as no less illimitably paramount in civil society. From the principles raised by Hildebrand and contested in the struggles of this duel, we may date those new conceptions of the two chief powers of Christendom which found final expression in the theocratic philosophy of the *Summa* and the imperial absolutism of the *De Monarchiâ*. Meanwhile the Empire and the Papacy, while trying their force against each other, had proved to Italy their essential weakness. What they gained as ideas, controlling the speculations of the next two centuries, they lost as potentates in the peninsula. It was impossible for either Pope or Emperor to carry on the war without bidding for the support of the cities; and therefore, at the end of the struggle, the free burghs found themselves strengthened at the expense of both powers. Still it must not be forgotten that the wars of Investitures, while they developed the independent spirit and the military energies of the Republics, penetrated Italy with the vice of party conflict. The ineradicable divisions of Guelf and Ghibelline were a heavy price to pay for a step forward on the path of emancipation; nor was the ecclesiastical revolution, which tended to Italianise the Papacy, while it magnified its cosmopolitan ascendency, other than a source of evil to the nation.

The forces liberated in the cities by these wars brought the Consuls to the front. The Bishops had undermined the feudal fabric of the kingdom, depressed the Counts, and

restored the Roman towns to prosperity. During the war
both Popolo and Commune grew in vigour, and their Consuls
began to use the authority that had been conquered by the
prelates. At first the Consuls occupied a subordinate position
as men of affairs and notaries, needed to transact the business
of the mercantile inhabitants. They now took the lead as
political agents of the first magnitude, representing the city in
its public acts, and superseding the ecclesiastics. The Popolo
was enlarged by the admission of new burgher families, and
the ruling caste, though still oligarchical, became more fairly
representative of the inhabitants. This progress was inevitable, when we remember that the cities had been organised
for warfare, and that, except their Consuls, they had no
officials who combined civil and military functions. Under
the jurisdiction of the Consuls Roman law was everywhere
substituted for Lombard statutes, and another strong blow
was thus dealt against decaying feudalism. The school
of Bologna eclipsed the University of Pavia. Justinian's
Code was studied with passionate energy, and the Italic people
enthusiastically reverted to the institutions of their past. In
the fable of the Codex of the *Pandects* brought by Pisa from
Amalfi we can trace the fervour of this movement, whereby the
Romans of the cities struggled after resurrection.

One of the earliest manifestations of municipal vitality
was the war of city against city, which began to blaze with
fury in the first half of the twelfth century, and endured so
long as free towns lasted to perpetuate the conflict. No
sooner had the burghs established themselves beneath the
presidency of their Consuls than they turned the arms they
had acquired in the war of independence against their
neighbours. The phenomenon was not confined to any single
district. It revealed a new necessity in the very constitution
of the commonwealths. Penned up within the narrow limits
of their petty dependencies, throbbing with fresh life, over-

flowing with a populace inured to warfare, demanding channels for their energies in commerce, competing with each other on the paths of industry, they clashed in deadliest duels for breathing space and means of wealth. The occasions that provoked one Commune to declare war upon its rival were trivial. The animosity was internecine and persistent. Life or death hung in the balance. It was a conflict for ascendency that brought the sternest passions into play, and decided the survival of the fittest among hundreds of competing cities. The deeply rooted jealousies of Roman and feudal centres, the recent partisanship of Papal and Imperial principles, embittered this strife. But what lay beneath all superficial causes of dissension was the economic struggle of communities, for whom the soil of Italy already had begun to seem too narrow. So superabundant were the forces of her population, so vast were the energies emancipated by her attainment of municipal freedom, that this mighty mother of peoples could not afford equal sustenance to all her children. New-born, they had to strangle one another as they hung upon the breasts that gave them nourishment. It was impossible for the Emperor to overlook the apparent anarchy of his fairest province. Therefore, when Frederick Barbarossa was elected in 1152, his first thought was to reduce the Garden of the Empire to order. Soon after his election he descended into Lombardy and formed two leagues among the cities of the North, the one headed by Pavia, the centre of the abrogated kingdom, the other by Milan, who inherited the majesty of Rome and contained within her loins the future of Italian freedom. It is not necessary to follow in detail the conflict of the Lombard burghs with Frederick, so enthusiastically described by their historian, Sismondi. It is enough for our present purpose to remember that in the course of that contention both leagues made common cause against the Emperor, drew the Pope Alexander III. into their quarrel, and at last in

1183, after the victory of Legnano had convinced Frederick of
his weakness, extorted by the Peace of Constance privileges
whereby their autonomy was amply guaranteed and recognised.
The advantages won by Milan, who sustained the brunt of the
Imperial onslaughts, and by the splendour of her martyrdom
surmounted the petty jealousies of her municipal rivals, were
extended to the cities of Tuscany. After the date of that
compact signed by the Emperor and his insurgent subjects,
the burghs obtained an assured position as a third power
between the Empire and the Church. The most remarkable
point in the history of this contention is the unanimous submission of the Communes to what they regarded as the just
suzerainty of Cæsar's representative. Though they were
omnipotent in Lombardy, they took no measures for closing
the gates of the Alps against the Germans. The Emperor
was free to come and go as he listed; and when peace was
signed, he reckoned the burghers who had beaten him by arms
and policy among his loyal vassals. Still, the spirit of independence in Italy had been amply asserted. This is notably
displayed in the address presented to Frederick, before his
coronation, by the Senate of Rome. Regenerated by Arnold
of Brescia's revolutionary mission, the Roman people assumed
its antique majesty in these remarkable words : ' Thou wast a
stranger ; I have made thee citizen : thou camest from regions
beyond the Alps ; I have conferred on thee the principality.' [1]

[1] 'Hospes eras, civem feci. Advena fuisti ex transalpinis partibus,
principem constitui. Quod meum jure fuit, tibi dedi.' See *Ottonis
Episcopi Frisingensis Chronicon*, De Rebus Gestis Frid. i. Imp. Lib. ii.
cap. 21. Basileæ, 1569. The Legates appointed by the Senate met the
Emperor at Sutri, and delivered the oration of which the sentence just
quoted was part. It began : ' Urbis legati nos, rex optime, ad tuam a
Senatu, populoque Romano destinati sumus excellentiam,' and contained
this remarkable passage : ' Orbis imperium affectas, coronam præbitura
gratanter assurgo, jocanter occurro. . . . indebitum clericorum excus-
surus jugum.' If the words are faithfully reported, the Republic
separates itself abruptly from the Papacy, and claims a kind of preco-

Presumptuous boast as this sounded in the ears of Frederick, it proved that the Italic nation had now sharply defined itself against the Church and the barbarians. It still accepted the Empire, because the Empire was the glory of Italy, the crown that gave to her people the presidency of civilisation. It still recognised the authority of the Church, because the Church was the eldest daughter of Italy emergent from the wrecks of Roman society. But the nation had become conscious of its right to stand apart from either.

Strengthened by their contest with Frederick Barbarossa, recognised in their rights as belligerent powers, and left to their own guidance by the Empire, the cities were now free to prosecute their wars upon the remnants of feudalism. The town, as we have learned to know it, was surrounded by a serried rank of castles, where the nobles held still undisputed authority over serfs of the soil. Against this cordon of fortresses every city with singular unanimity directed the forces it had formed in the preceding conflicts. At the same time the municipal struggles of Commune against Commune lost none of their virulence. The Counts, pressed on all sides by the towns that had grown up around them, adopted the policy of pitting one burgh against another. When a noble was attacked by the township near his castle, he espoused the animosities of a more distant city, compromised his independence by accepting the captaincy or lieutenancy of communes hostile to his natural enemies, and thus became the servant or

dence in honour before the Empire. Frederick is said to have interrupted the Legates in a rage before they could finish their address, and to have replied with angry contempt. The speech put into his mouth is probably a rhetorical composition, but it may have expressed his sentiments. ' Multa de Romanorum sapientia seu fortitudine hactenus audivimus, magis tamen de sapientia. Quare satis mirari non possumus. quod verba vestra plus arrogantiæ tumore insipida quam sale sapientiæ condita sentimus. . . . . Fuit, fuit quondam in hac Republica virtus. Quondam dico, atque o utinam tam veraciter quam libenter nunc dicere possemus,' &c.

ally of a Republic. In his desperation he emancipated his serfs, and so the folk of the Contado profited by the dissensions of the cities and their feudal masters. This new phase of republican evolution lasted over a long and ill-defined period, assuming different characters in different centres; but the end of it was that the nobles were forced to submit to the cities. They were admitted to the burghership, and agreed to spend a certain portion of every year in the palaces they raised within the circuit of the walls. Thus the Counts placed themselves beneath the jurisdiction of the Consuls, and the Italic population absorbed into itself the relics of Lombard, Frank, and German aristocracy. Still the gain upon the side of the republics was not clear. Though the feudal lordship of the nobles had been destroyed, their wealth, their lands, and their prestige remained untouched. In the city they felt themselves but aliens. Their real home was still the castle on the neighbouring mountain. Nor, when they stooped to become burghers, had they relinquished the use of arms. Instead of building peaceable dwelling-houses in the city, they filled its quarters with fortresses and towers, whence they carried on feuds among themselves and imperilled the safety of the streets. It was speedily discovered that the war against the Castles had become a war against the Palaces, and that the arena had been transferred from the open Contado to the Piazza and the barricade. The authority of the Consuls proved insufficient to maintain an equilibrium between the people and the nobles. Accordingly a new magistrate started into being, combining the offices of supreme justiciary and military dictator. When Frederick Barbarossa attempted to govern the rebellious Lombard cities in the common interest of the Empire, he established in their midst a foreign judge, called Podestà, *quasi habens potestatem Imperatoris in hac parte*. This institution only served at the moment to inflame and embitter the resistance of the Communes; but the title of

Podestà was subsequently conferred upon the official summoned
to maintain an equal balance between the burghers and the
nobles.   He was invariably a foreigner, elected for one year,
entrusted with summary jurisdiction in all matters of dispute,
exercising the power of life and death, and disposing of the
municipal militia.   The old constitution of the Commune
remained to control this dictator and to guard the independence of the city.   All the Councils continued to act, and the
Consuls were fortified by the formation of a College of
Ancients or Priors.   The Podestà was created with the
express purpose of effecting a synthesis between two rival
sections of the burgh.   He was never regarded as other than
an alien to the city, adopted as a temporary mediator and
controller of incompatible elements.   The lordship of the
burgh still resided with the Consuls, who from this time
forward began to lose their individuality in the College of the
Signoria—called *Priori, Anziani,* or *Rettori,* as the case might
be in various districts.

The Italian republics had reached this stage when
Frederick II. united the Empire and the kingdom of the
Two Sicilies.   It was a crisis of the utmost moment for
Italian independence.   Master of the South, Frederick sought
to reconquer the lost prerogatives of the Empire in Lombardy
and Tuscany ; nor is it improbable that he might have succeeded in uniting Italy beneath his sway but for the violent
animosity of the Church.   The warfare of extermination
carried on by the Popes against the house of Hohenstauffen
was no proof of their partiality for the cause of freedom.
They dreaded the reality of a kingdom that should base itself
on Italy and be the rival of their own authority.   Therefore
they espoused the cause of the free burghs against Frederick,
and when the North was devastated by his Vicars, they
preached a crusade against Ezzelino da Romano.   In the
convulsions that shook Italy from North to South the parties

of Guelf and Ghibelline took shape, and acquired an ineradicable force. All the previous humours and discords of the nation were absorbed by them. The Guelf party meant the burghers of the consular Communes, the men of industry and commerce, the upholders of civil liberty, the friends of democratic expansion. The Ghibelline party included the naturalised nobles, the men of arms and idleness, the advocates of feudalism, the politicians who regarded constitutional progress with disfavour. That the banner of the Church floated over the one camp, while the standard of the Empire rallied to itself the hostile party, was a matter of comparatively superficial moment. The true strength of the war lay in the population, divided by irreconcilable ideals, each eager to possess the city for itself, each prepared to die for its adopted principles. The struggle is a social struggle, played out within the precincts of the Commune, for the supremacy of one or the other moiety of the whole people. A city does not pronounce itself either Guelf or Ghibelline till half the burghers have been exiled. The victorious party organises the government in its own interest, establishes itself in a Palazzo apart from the Commune, where it develops its machinery at home and abroad, and strengthens its finance by forced contributions and confiscations.[1] The exiles make common cause with members of their own faction in an adverse burgh ; and thus, by the diplomacy of Guelfs and Ghibellines, the most distant centres are drawn into the network of a common dualism. In this way we are justified in saying that Italy achieved her national consciousness through strife and conflict ; for the Communes ceased to be isolated, cemented by temporary leagues, or engaged in merely local conflicts. They were brought together and connected by the sympathies and antipathies of an antagonism which em-

[1] It is enough to refer to the importance of the *Parte Guelfa* in the history of Florence.

braced and dominated the municipalities, set Republics and Regno on equal footing, and merged the titular leaders of the struggle, Pope and Emperor, in the uncontrollable tumult. The issue was no vulgar one ; no merely egotistic interests were at stake. Guelfs and Ghibellines alike interrogated the oracle, with perfect will to obey its inspiration for the common good. But they read the utterances of the Pythia in adverse senses. The Ghibelline heard Italy calling upon him to build a citadel that should be guarded by the lance and shield of chivalry, where the hierarchies of feudalism, ranged beneath the daïs of the Empire, might dispense culture and civil order in due measure to the people. The Guelf believed that she was bidding him to multiply arts and guilds within the burgh, beneath the mantle of the Pope, who stood for Christ, the preacher of equality and peace for all mankind, in order that the beehive of industry should in course of time evolve a civil order and a culture representative of its own freely acting forces.

During the stress and storm of the fierce warfare carried on by Guelfs and Ghibellines, the Podestà fell into the second rank. He had been created to meet an emergency ; but now the discord was too vehement for arbitration. A new functionary appears, with the title of *Captain of the People.* Chosen when one or other of the factions gains supreme power in the burgh, he represents the victorious party, takes the lead in proscribing their opponents, and ratifies on his responsibility the changes introduced into the constitution. The old magistracies and councils, meanwhile, are not abrogated. The Consiglio del Popolo, with the Capitano at his head, takes the lead ; and a new member, called the Consiglio della Parte, is found beside them, watchful to maintain the policy of the victorious faction. But the Consiglio del Commune, with the Podestà, who has not ceased to exercise judicial functions, still subsists. The Priors form the Signory as of old. The Credenza goes on working, and the Gran Consiglio represents the body of privileged burghers. The party does but tyrannise over the city it has conquered, and manipulates the ancient constitution for its own advantage. In this clash of Guelf with Ghibelline the beneficiaries were the lower classes of the people. Excluded from the Popolo of episcopal and consular revolutions, the trades and industries of the great cities now assert their claims to be enfranchised. The advent of the *Arti* is the chief social phenomenon of the crisis.[1] Thus the final issue of the conflict was a new Italy, deeply divided by factions that were little understood, because they were so vital, because they represented two adverse currents of national energy, incompatible, irreconcilable, eternal in antagonism as the poles. But this discordant nation was more commercial and more democratic. Families of merchants rose upon the ruins of the old nobility. Roman cities of industry reduced their military rivals of earlier or later origin to insignificance. The plain, the river, and the port asserted themselves against the mountain fastness and the barrack-burgh. The several classes of society, triturated, shaken together, levelled by warfare and equalised by industry, presented but few obstacles to the emergence of commanding personalities, however humble, from their ranks. Not only had the hierarchy of feudalism disappeared; but the constitution of the city itself was confused, and the Popolo, whether 'primo' or 'secondo' or even 'terzo,' was diluted with recently enfranchised Contadini and all kinds of 'novi homines.'[2] The Divine Comedy, written after the culmi-

---

[1] The history of Florence illustrates more clearly than that of any other town the vast importance acquired by trades and guilds in politics at this epoch of the civil wars.

[2] This is the sting of Cacciaguida's scornful lamentation over Florence (*Par.* xvi).

> Ma la cittadinanza, ch' è or mista
> Di Campi e di Certaldo e di Figghine,
> Pura vedeasi nell' ultimo artista.
> *   *   *   *

nation of the Guelf and Ghibelline dissensions, yields the measure of their animosity. Dante finds no place in Hell, Heaven, or Purgatory for the souls who stood aloof from strife, the angels who were neither Guelf nor Ghibelline in Paradise. His Vigliacchi, 'wretches who never lived,' because they never felt the pangs or ecstasies of partisanship, wander homeless on the skirts of Limbo, among the abortions and offscourings of creation. Even so there was no standing-ground in Italy outside one or the other hostile camp. Society was riven down to its foundation. Rancours dating from the thirteenth century endured long after the great parties ceased to have a meaning. They were perpetuated in customs, and expressed themselves in the most trivial details. Banners, ensigns, and heraldic colours followed the divisions of the factions. Ghibellines wore the feathers in their caps upon one side, Guelfs upon the other. Ghibellines cut fruit at table crosswise, Guelfs straight down. In Bergamo some Calabrians were murdered by their host, who discovered from their way of slicing garlic that they sided with the hostile party. Ghibellines drank out of smooth, and Guelfs out of chased, goblets. Ghibellines wore white, and Guelfs red, roses. Yawning, passing in the street, throwing dice, gestures in speaking or swearing, were used as pretexts for distinguishing the one half of Italy from the other. So late as the middle of the fifteenth century, the Ghibellines of Milan tore Christ from the high-altar of the Cathedral at Crema and burned him because he turned his face to the Guelf shoulder. Every great city has a tale of love and death that carries the

Tal fatto è fiorentino, e cambia e merca,
Che si sarebbe volto a Simifonti,
Là dove andava l' avolo alla cerca.

*　　　*　　　*　　　*

Sempre la confusione delle persone
Principio fu del mal della cittade,
Come del corpo il cibo che s' appone.

contention of its adverse families into the region of romance and legend. Florence dated her calamities from the insult offered by Buondelmonte dei Buondelmonti to the Amidei in a broken marriage. Bologna never forgot the pathos of Imelda Lambertazzi stretched in death upon her lover Bonifazio Gieremei's corpse. The story of Romeo and Juliet at Verona is a myth which brings both factions into play, the well-meaning intervention of peace-making monks, and the ineffectual efforts of the Podestà to curb the violence of party warfare.

So deep and dreadful was the discord, so utter the exhaustion, that the distracted Communes were fain at last to find some peace in tyranny. At the close of their long quarrel with the house of Hohenstauffen, the Popes called Charles of Anjou into Italy. The final issue of that policy for the nation at large will be discussed in another portion of this work. It is enough to point out here that, as Ezzelino da Romano introduced despotism in its worst form as a party leader of the Ghibellines, so Charles of Anjou became a typical tyrant in the Guelf interest. He was recognised as chief of the Guelf party by the Florentines, and the kingdom of the Two Sicilies was conferred upon him as the price of his dictatorship. The republics almost simultaneously entered upon a new phase. Democratised by the extension of the franchise, corrupted, to use Machiavelli's phrase, in their old organisation of the Popolo and Commune, they fell into the hands of tyrants, who employed the prestige of their party, the indifference of the Vigliacchi, and the peace-loving instincts of the middle class for the consolidation of their selfish autocracy.[1]

[1] Not to mention the republics of Lombardy and Romagna, which took the final stamp of despotism at the beginning of the fourteenth century, it is noticeable that Pisa submitted to Uguccione da Faggiuola, Lucca to Castruccio Castracane, and Florence to the Duke of Athens. The revolution of Pisa in 1316 delivered it from Uguccione; the premature death of Castruccio in 1328 destroyed the Tuscan duchy he was

Placing himself above the law, manipulating the machinery of the State for his own ends, substituting the will of a single ruler for the clash of hostile passions in the factions, the tyrant imposed a forcible tranquillity upon the city he had grasped. The Captaincy of the people was conferred upon him.[1] The Councils were suffocated and reduced to silence. The aristocracy was persecuted for the profit of the plebs. Under his rule commerce flourished; the towns were adorned with splendid edifices; foreign wars were carried on for the aggrandisement of the State without regard to factious rancours. Thus the tyrant marked the first emergence of personality supreme within the State, resuming its old forces in an autocratic will, superseding and at the same time consciously controlling the mute, collective, blindly working impulses of previous revolutions. His advent was welcomed as a blessing by the recently developed people of the cities he reduced to peace. But the great families and leaders of the parties regarded him with loathing, as a reptile spawned by the corruption and disease of the decaying body politic. In their fury they addressed themselves to the two chiefs of Christendom. Boniface VIII., answering to this appeal, called in a second Frenchman, Charles of Valois, with the titles of Marquis of Ancona, Count of Romagna, Captain of Tuscany, who was bidden to reduce Italy to order on Guelf principles. Dante in his mountain solitudes invoked the Emperor, and Italy beheld the powerless march of Henry VII. Neither Pope nor Emperor was strong enough to control the currents of the factions which were surely whirling Italy into the abyss of despotism. Boniface died of grief after Sciarra Colonna,

building up upon the basement of Ghibellinism; while the rebellion of 1343 averted tyranny from Florence for another century.

[1] Machiavelli's *Vita di Castruccio Castracane*, though it is rather a historical romance than a trustworthy biography, illustrates the gradual advances made by a bold and ambitious leader from the Captaincy of the people, conferred upon him for one year, to the tyranny of his city.

the terrible Ghibelline's outrage at Anagni, and the Papal Court was transferred to Avignon in 1316. Henry VII. expired, of poison probably, at Buonconvento, in 1313. The parties tore each other to fragments. Tyrants were murdered. Whole families were extirpated. Yet these convulsions bore no fruit of liberty. The only exit from the situation was in despotism—the despotism of a jealous oligarchy as at Florence, or the despotism of new tyrants in Lombardy and the Romagna.[1]

Meanwhile the perils to which the tyrants were exposed taught them to employ cruelty and craft in combination. From the confused and spasmodic efforts of the thirteenth century, when Captains of the people and leaders of the party seized a momentary gust of power, there arose a second sort of despotism, more cautious in its policy, more methodic in its use of means to ends, which ended by metamorphosing the Italian cities and preparing the great age of the Renaissance. It would be sentimental to utter lamentations over this change, and unphilosophical to deplore the diminution of republican liberty as an unmixed evil. The divisions of Italy and the weakness of both Papacy and Empire left no other solution of the political problem. All branches of the municipal administration, strained to the cracking-point by the tension of party conflict, were now isolated from the organism, abnormally developed, requiring the combining effort of a single thinker to reunite their scattered forces in one system or

---

[1] The Divine Comedy is, under one of its aspects, the Epic of Italian tyranny, so many of its episodes are chosen from the history of the civil wars :

> Chè le terre d' Italia tutte piene
> Son di tiranni ; ed un Marcel diventa
> Ogni villan che parteggiando viene.

These lines occur in the apostrophe to Italy (*Purg.* vi.), where Dante refers to the Empire, idealised by him as the supreme authority in Europe.

absorb them in himself. The indirect restraints which a
calmer period of municipal vitality had placed upon tyrannic
ambition were removed by the levelling of classes and the
presentation of an equal surface to the builder of the palace-
dome of monarchy. Moreover, it must be remembered that
what the Italians then understood by freedom was municipal
autonomy controlled by ruling houses in the interest of the
few. These considerations need not check our sympathy with
Florence in the warfare she carried on against the Milanese
tyrants. But they should lead us to be cautious in adopting
the conclusions of Sismondi, who saw Italian greatness only
in her free cities. The obliteration of the parties beneath
despotism was needed, under actual conditions, for that development of arts and industry which raised Italy to a first
place among civilised nations. Of the manners of the Despots,
and of the demoralisation they encouraged in the cities of
their rule, enough will be said in the succeeding chapters,
which set forth the social conditions of the Renaissance in
Italy. But attention should here be called to the general
character of despotic authority, and to the influence the Despots
exercised for the pacification of the country. We are not
justified by facts in assuming that had the free burghs continued independent, arts and literature would have risen to a
greater height. Venice, in spite of an uninterrupted republican
career, produced no commanding men of letters, and owed
much of her splendour in the art of painting to aliens from
Cadore, Castelfranco, and Verona. Genoa remained silent
and irresponsive to the artistic movement of Italy until the
last days of the republic, when her independence was but
a shadow. Pisa, though a burgh of Tuscany, displayed no
literary talent, while her architecture dates from the first
period of the Commune. Siena, whose republican existence
lasted longer even than that of Florence, contributed nothing
of importance to Italian literature. The art of Perugia was

developed during the ascendency of despotic families. The
painting of the Milanese School owed its origin to Lodovico
Sforza, and survived the tragic catastrophes of his capital,
which suffered more than any other from the brutalities of
Spaniards and Frenchmen. Next to Florence, the most
brilliant centres of literary activity during the bright days of
the Renaissance were princely Ferrara and royal Naples.
Lastly, we might insist upon the fact that the Italian language
took its first flight in the court of imperial Palermo, while
republican Rome remained dumb throughout the earlier stage
of Italian literary evolution. Thus the facts of the case
seem to show that culture and republican independence were
not so closely united in Italy as some historians would seek
to make us believe. On the other hand it is impossible to
prove that the despotisms of the fifteenth century were necessary to the perfecting of art and literature. All that can be
safely advanced upon this subject, is that the pacification of
Italy was demanded as a preliminary condition, and that this
pacification came to pass through the action of the princes,
checked and equilibrated by the oligarchies of Venice and
Florence. It might further be urged that the Despots were
in close sympathy with the masses of the people, shared their
enthusiasms, and promoted their industry. When the classical
revival took place at the close of the fourteenth century, they
divined this movement of the Italic races to resume their past,
and gave it all encouragement. To be a prince and not to be
the patron of scholarship, the pupil of humanists, and the
founder of libraries, was an impossibility. In like manner
they employed their wealth upon the development of arts and
industries. The great age of Florentine painting is indis-
solubly connected with the memories of Casa Medici. Rome
owes her magnificence to the despotic Popes. Even the
pottery of Gubbio was a creation of the ducal house of
Urbino.

After the death of Henry VII. and the beginning of the Papal exile at Avignon, the Guelf party became the rallying-point of municipal independence, with its headquarters in Florence. Ghibellinism united the princes in an opposite camp. 'The Guelf party,' writes Giovanni Villani, 'forms the solid and unalterable basis of Italian liberty, and is so antagonistic to all tyranny that, if a Guelf become a tyrant, he must of necessity become at the same moment Ghibelline.' Milan, first to assert the rights of the free burghs, was now the chief centre of despotism; and the events of the next century resume themselves in the long struggle between Florence and the Visconti. The chronicle of the Villani and the Florentine history of Poggio contain the record of this strife, which seemed to them the all-important crisis of Italian affairs. In the Milanese annals of Galvano Fiamma and Mussi, on the other hand, the advantages of a despotic sovereignty in giving national coherence, the crimes of the Papacy, which promoted anarchy in its ill-governed States, and the prospect of a comprehensive Italian tyranny under the great house of the Visconti, are eloquently pleaded. The terms of the main issue being thus clearly defined, we may regard the warfare carried on by Bertrand du Poiet and Louis of Bavaria in the interests of Church and Empire, the splendid campaigns of Egidio d'Albornoz, and the delirious cruelty of Robert of Geneva, no less than the predatory excursions of Charles IV., as episodical. The main profits of those convulsions, which drowned Italy in blood during nearly all the fourteenth century, accrued to the Despots, who held their ground in spite of all attempts to dispossess them. The greater houses, notably the Visconti, acquired strength by revolutions in which the Church and Empire neutralised each other's action. The lesser families struck firm roots into cities, infuriated rather than intimidated by such acts of violence as the massacres of Faenza and Cesena in 1377. The relations of the imperial and pontifical parties were confused; while even in the centre of republican independence, at Florence, social changes, determined in great measure by the exhaustion of the city in its conflict, prepared the way for the Medicean tyranny. Neither the Church nor the Empire gained steady footing in Italy, while the prestige of both was ruined.[1] Municipal freedom, instead of being enlarged, was extinguished by the ambition of the Florentine oligarchs, who, while they spent the last florin of the Commune in opposing the Visconti, never missed an opportunity of enslaving the sister burghs of Tuscany. In a word, the destiny of the nation was irresistibly impelling it toward despotism.

In order to explain the continual prosperity of the princes amid the clash of forces brought to bear against them from so many sides, we must remember that they were the partisans of social order in distracted burghs, the heroes of the middle classes and the multitude, the quellers of faction, the administrators of impartial laws, and the aggrandisers of the city at the expense of its neighbours. Ser Gorello, singing the praises of the Bishop Guido dei Tarlati di Pietra Mala, who ruled Arezzo in the first half of the fourteenth century, makes the Commune say: [2] 'He was the lord so valiant and magnificent, so full of grace and daring, so agreeable to both Guelfs and Ghibellines. He, for his virtue, was chosen by common consent to be the master of my people. Peace and justice were the beginning, middle, and end of his lordship, which

---

[1] Machiavelli, in his *Istorie Fiorentine* (Firenze, 1818, vol. i. pp. 47, 48), points out how the competition of the Church and Empire, during the Papacies of Benedict XII. and Clement VI. and the reign of Louis, strengthened the tyrants of Lombardy, Romagna, and the March. Each of the two contending powers gave away what did not belong to them, bidding against each other for any support they might obtain from the masters of the towns.

[2] *Mur. Scr. R. It.* xv. 826. Compare what G. Merula wrote about Azzo Visconti: 'He conciliated the people to him by equal justice without distinction of Guelf or Ghibelline.'

removed all discord from the State. By the greatness of his valour I grew in territory round about. Every neighbour reverenced me, some through love and some through dread; for it was dear to them to rest beneath his mantle.' These verses set forth the qualities which united the mass of the populations to their new lords. The Despot delivered the industrial classes from the tyranny and anarchy of faction, substituting a reign of personal terrorism that weighed more heavily upon the nobles than upon the artisans or peasants. Ruling more by perfidy, corruption, and fraud than by the sword, he turned the leaders of parties into courtiers, brought proscribed exiles back into the city as officials, flattered local vanity by continuing the municipal machinery in its functions of parade, and stopped the mouths of unruly demagogues by making it their pecuniary interest to preach his benefits abroad. So long as the burghers remained peaceable beneath his sway and refrained from attacking him in person, he was mild. But at the same moment the gallows, the torture-chamber, the iron cage suspended from the giddy height of palace-roof or church-tower, and the dreadful dungeons, where a prisoner could neither stand nor lie at ease, were ever ready for the man who dared dispute his authority. That authority depended solely on his personal qualities of will, courage, physical endurance. He held it by intelligence, being as it were an artificial product of political necessities, an equilibrium of forces, substituted without legal title for the Church and Empire, and accumulating in his despotic individuality the privileges previously acquired by centuries of Consuls, Podestàs, and Captains of the people. The chief danger he had to fear was conspiracy; and in providing himself against this peril he expended all the resources suggested by refined ingenuity and heightened terror. Yet, when the Despot was attacked and murdered, it followed of necessity that the successful conspirator became in turn a tyrant. 'Cities,' wrote Machiavelli,[1] 'that are once corrupt and accustomed to the rule of princes, can never acquire freedom, even though the prince with all his kin be extirpated. One prince is needed to extinguish another; and the city has no rest except by the creation of a new lord, unless it chance that one burgher by his goodness and great qualities may during his lifetime preserve its temporary independence.' Palace intrigues, therefore, took the place of Piazza revolutions, and dynasties were swept away to make room for new tyrants without material change in the condition of the populace.

It was the universal policy of the Despots to disarm their subjects. Prompted by considerations of personal safety, and demanded by the necessity of extirpating the factions, this measure was highly popular. It relieved the burghers of that most burdensome of all public duties, military service. A tax on silver and salt was substituted in the Milanese province for the conscription, while the Florentine oligarchs, actuated probably by the same motives, laid a tax upon the country. The effect of this change was to make financial and economical questions all-important, and to introduce a new element into the balance of Italian powers. The principalities were transformed into great banks, where the lords of cities sat in their bureau, counted their money, and calculated the cost of wars or the value of towns they sought to acquire by bargain. At first they used their mercenary troops like pawns, buying up a certain number for some special project, and dismissing them when it had been accomplished. But in course of time the mercenaries awoke to the sense of their own power, and placed themselves beneath captains who secured them a certainty of pay with continuity of profitable service. Thus the Condottieri came into existence, and Italy beheld the spectacle of moving despotisms, armed and mounted, seeking to effect

[1] *Discorsi*, i. 17.

establishment upon the weakest, worst-defended points of the peninsula. They proved a grave cause of disquietude alike to the tyrants and the republics; and until the settlement of Francesco Sforza in the Duchy of Milan, when the employers of auxiliaries had come to understand the arts of dealing with them by perfidy, secret assassination, and a system of elaborate counter-checks, the equilibrium of power in Italy was seriously threatened. The country suffered at first from marauding excursions conducted by piratical leaders of adventurous troops, by Werner of Urslingen, the Conte Lando, and Fra Moriale; afterwards from the discords of Braccio da Montone and Sforza Attendolo, incessantly plotting to carve duchies for themselves from provinces they had been summoned by a master to subdue. At this period gold ruled the destinies of Italy. The Despots, relying solely on their exchequer for their power, were driven to extortion. Cities became bankrupt, pledged their revenues, or sold themselves to the highest bidder.[1] Indescribable misery oppressed the poorer classes and the peasants. A series of obscure revolutions in the smaller despotic centres pointed to a vehement plebeian reaction against a state of things that had become unbearable. The lower classes of the burghers rose against the 'popolani grassi,' and a new class of princes emerged at the close of the crisis. Thus the plebs forced the Bentivogli on Bologna and the Medici on Florence, the Baglioni on Perugia and the Petrucci on Siena.

The emergence of the Condottieri at the beginning of the fourteenth century, the anarchy they encouraged for their own aggrandisement, and the financial distress which ensued upon the substitution of mercenary for civic warfare, com-

---

[1] Perugia, for example, farmed out the tax upon her country population for 12,000 florins, upon her baking-houses for 7,266, upon her wine for 4,000, upon her lake for 5,200, upon contracts for 1,500. Two bankers accepted the Perugian loan at this price in 1388.

pleted the democratisation of the Italian cities, and marked a new period in the history of despotism. From the date of Francesco Sforza's entry into Milan as conqueror in 1450, the princes became milder in their exercise of power and less ambitious. Having begun by disarming their subjects, they now proceeded to lay down arms themselves, employing small forces for the protection of their person and the State, engaging more cautiously in foreign strife, and substituting diplomacy, wherever it was possible, for warfare. Gold still ruled in politics, but it was spent in bribery. To the ambitious military schemes of Gian Galeazzo Visconti succeeded the commercial cynicism of Cosimo de' Medici, who enslaved Florence by astute demoralisation.[1] The spirit of the age was materialistic and positive. The Despots held their state by treachery, craft, and corruption. The element of force being virtually eliminated, intelligence at last gained undivided sway; and the ideal statecraft of Machiavelli was realised with more or less completeness in all parts of the peninsula. At this moment and by these means Italy obtained a brief but golden period of peace beneath the confederation of her great powers. Nicholas V. had restored the Papal Court to Rome in 1447, where he assumed the manners of despotism and counted as one among the Italian Signori. Lombardy remained tranquil under the rule of Francesco Sforza, and Tuscany under that of the Casa Medici. The kingdom of Naples, conquered by Alfonso of Aragon in 1442, was equally ruled in the spirit of enlightened despotism, while Venice, who had so long formed a state apart, by her recent acquisition of a domain on terra firma, entered the community of Italian politics. Thus the country had finally resolved itself into five grand constituent elements —the Duchy of Milan, the Republic of S. Mark, Florence,

[1] I have attempted to analyse Cosimo's method in the article on 'Florence and the Medici,' *Studies and Sketches in Italy*.

Rome, and the kingdom of Naples—all of them, though widely differing in previous history and constitutional peculiarities, now animated by a common spirit.[1] Politically they tended to despotism ; for though Venice continued to be a republic, the government of the Venetian oligarchy was but despotism put into commission. Intellectually, the same enthusiasm for classical studies, the same artistic energy, and the same impulse to revive Italian literature brought the several centres of the nation into keener sympathy than they had felt before. A network of diplomacy embraced the cities ; and round the leaders of the confederation were grouped inferior burghs, republican or tyrannical as the case might be, like satellites around the luminaries of a solar system. When Constantinople was taken by the Turks in 1453, Italy felt the need of suppressing her old jealousies, and Nicholas V. induced the four great powers to sign with him a treaty of peace and amity. The political tact and sagacity of Lorenzo de' Medici enabled him to develop and substantiate the principle of balance then introduced into Italian politics ; nor was there any apparent reason why the equilibrium so hardly won, so skilfully maintained, should not have subsisted but for Lodovico Sforza's invitation to the French in 1494. Up to that date the more recent wars of Italy had been principally caused by the encroachments of Venice and the nepotism of successive Popes. They raised no new enthusiasm hostile to the interests of peace. The Empire was eliminated and forgotten as an obsolete antiquity. Italy seemed at last determined to manage her own affairs by mutual agreement between the five great powers.

Still the ground beneath this specious fabric of diplomacy

---

[1] This centralisation of Italy in five great powers was not obtained without the depression or total extinction of smaller cities. Ferrari counts seventeen towns, who died, to use his forcible expression, at the close of the civil wars. *Storia delle Rivoluzioni d' Italia*, iii. 239.

rung hollow. The tyrannies represented a transient political necessity. They were not the product of progressive social growth, satisfying and regulating organic functions of the nation. Far from being the final outcome of a slow, deliberate accretion in the states they had absorbed, we see in them the climax of conflicting humours, the splendid cancers and imposthumes of a desperate disease. That solid basis of national morality which grounds the monarch firm upon the sympathies and interests of the people whom he seems to lead, but whom he in reality expresses, failed them. There-fore each individual Despot trembled for his throne, while Italy, as in the ominous picture drawn by her historian, felt that all the elements were combining to devour her with a coming storm. The land of earthquakes divined a cataclysm, to cope with which she was unable. An apparently insignifi-cant event determined the catastrophe. The Sforza appealed to France, and after the disastrous descent of Charles VIII. the whole tide of events turned. Instead of internal self-government by any system of balance, Italy submitted to a succession of invasions terminating in foreign tyranny.

The problem why the Italians failed to achieve the unity of a coherent nation has been implicitly discussed in the foregoing pages upon the history of the Communes and the development of despotism. We have already seen that their conception of municipal independence made a narrow oli-garchy of enfranchised burghers lords of the city, which in its turn oppressed the country and the subject burghs of its domain. Every conquest by a republic reduced some village or centre of civil life to the condition of serfdom. The voices of the inhabitants were no longer heard debating questions that affected their interests. They submitted to dictation from their masters, the enfranchised few in the ascendent commonwealth. Thus, as Guicciardini pointed out in his 'Considerations on the Discourses of Machiavelli,' the subjection of Italy by a dominant republic would have meant the extinction of numberless political communities and the sway of a close oligarchy from the Alps to the Ionian Sea. The 3,200 burghers who constituted Florence in 1494, or the nobles of the Golden Book at Venice, would by such unification of the country under a victorious republic have become sovereigns, administering the resources of the nation for their profit. The dread of this catastrophe rendered Venice odious to her sister commonwealths at the close of the fifteenth century, and justified, according to Guicciardini's views of history, the action taken by Cosimo de' Medici in 1450, when he rendered Milan strong by supporting her despot, Francesco Sforza.[2] In a word, republican freedom, as the term is now understood, was unknown in Italy. Municipal autonomy, implying the right of the municipality to rule its conquests for its own particular profit, was the dominant idea. To have advanced from this stage of thought to the highly developed conception of a national republic, centralising the forces of Italy and at the same time giving free play to its local energies, would have been impossible. This kind of republican unity implies a previous unification of the people in some other form of government. It furthermore demands a system of representation extended to all sections of the nation. Their very nature, therefore, prevented the republican institutions won by the Italians in the early Middle Ages from sufficing for their independence in a national republic.

It may with more reason be asked in the next place why Italy did not become a monarchy, and again why she never produced a confederation, uniting the Communes as the Swiss Cantons were combined for mutual support and self-defence. When we attack the first of these two questions, our immediate answer must be that the Italians had a rooted

[1] *Op. Ined.* vol. i. p. 28. [2] *Ib.* vol. iii. p. 8.

disinclination for monarchical union.[1] Their most strenuous efforts were directed against it when it seemed to threaten them. It may be remembered that they were not a new people, needing concentration to secure their bare existence. Even during the great days of ancient Rome they had not been what we are wont to call a nation, but a confederacy of municipalities governed and directed by the mistress of the globe. When Rome passed away, the fragments of the body politic in Italy, though rudely shaken, retained some portion of the old vitality that joined them to the past. It was to the past rather than the future that the new Italians looked; and even as they lacked initiative forces in their literature, so in their political systems they ventured on no fresh beginning. Though Rome herself was ruined, the shadow of the name of Rome, the mighty memory of Roman greatness, still abode with them. Instead of a modern capital and a modern king, they had an idea for their rallying-point, a spiritual city for their metropolis. Nor was there any immediate reason why they should have sacrificed their local independence in order to obtain the security afforded by a sovereign. It was not till a later epoch that Italy learned by bitter experience that unity at any cost would be acceptable, face to face with the organised armies of modern Europe. But when the chance of securing that safeguard was offered in the Middle Ages, it must have been bought by subjection to foreigners, by toleration of feudalism, by the extinction of Roman culture in the laws and customs of barbarians. Thus

[1] Guicciardini (*Op. Ined.* i. 29) remarks: 'O sia per qualche fato d' Italia, o per la complessione degli uomini temperata in modo che hanno ingegno e forze, non è mai questa provincia stata facile a ridursi sotto uno imperio.' He speaks again of her disunion as 'quello modo di vivere che è più secondo la antiquissima consuetudine e inclinazione sua.' But Guicciardini, with that defect of vision which rendered him incapable of appreciating the whole situation while he analysed its details so profoundly, was reckoning without the great nations of Europe. See above, pp. 34, 35.

it is not too much to say that the Italians themselves rejected it. Moreover, the problem of unifying Italy in a monarchy was never so practically simple as that of forming nations out of the Teutonic tribes. Not only was the instinct of clanship absent, but before the year 800 all attempts to establish a monarchical state were thwarted by the still formidable proximity of the Greek Empire and by the growing power of ecclesiastical Rome. We have seen how the Goths erred by submitting to the Empire and merging their authority in a declining organisation. We have seen again how the Lombards erred by adopting Catholic Christianity and thus entangling themselves in the policy of Papal Rome. Both Goths and Lombards committed the mistake of sparing the Eternal City; or it may be more accurate to say that neither of them were strong enough to lay hands of violence upon the sacred and mysterious metropolis and hold it as their seat of monarchy against the world. So long as Rome remained independent, neither Ravenna nor Pavia could head a kingdom in the peninsula. Meanwhile Rome lent her prestige to the advancement of a spiritual power which, subject to no dynastic weakness, with the persistent force of an idea that cannot die, was bent on subjugating Europe. The Papacy needed Italy as the basis of its operations, and could not brook a rival that might reduce the See of S. Peter to the level of an ordinary bishopric. Rome, therefore, generation after generation, upheld the so-called liberties of Italy against all comers; and when she summoned the Franks, it was to break the growing power of the Lombard monarchs. The pact between the Popes and Charles the Great, however we may interpret its meaning, still further removed the possibility of a kingdom by dividing Italy into two sections with separate allegiances; and since the sway of neither Pope nor Emperor, the one unarmed the other absent, was stringent enough to check the growth of independent cities, a third and all-important factor was added to the previous checks upon national unity.

After 1200 the problem changes its aspect. We have now to ask ourselves why, when the struggle with the Empire was over, when Frederick Barbarossa had been defeated at Legnano, when the Lombard and the Tuscan Leagues were in full vigour, before the Guelf and Ghibelline factions had confused the mainsprings of political activity, and while the national militia was still energetic, the Communes did not advance from the conception of local and municipal independence to that of national freedom in a confederacy similar to the Swiss Bund. The Italians, it may be suggested, saw no immediate necessity for a confederation that would have limited the absolute autonomy of their several parcels. Only the light cast by subsequent events upon their early history makes us perceive that they missed an unique opportunity at this moment. What they then desired was freedom for expansion each after his own political type, freedom for the development of industry and commerce, freedom for the social organisation of the city beloved by its burghers above the nation as a whole. Special difficulties, moreover, lay in the way of confederation. The Communes were not districts, like the Swiss Cantons, but towns at war with the Contado round them and at war among themselves. Mutually jealous and mistrustful, with a country population that but partially obeyed their rule, these centres of Italian freedom were in a very different position from the peasant communities of Schwytz, Uri, Unterwalden. Italy, moreover, could not have been federally united without the consent of Naples and the Church. The kingdom of the Two Sicilies, rendered definitely monarchical by the Norman Conquest, offered a serious obstacle; and though the Regno might have been defied and absorbed by a vigorous concerted movement from the North and centre, there still remained the opposition of the Papacy. It had been the recent policy of the Popes to support the free burghs in their war with Frederick. But they did this only because they could not tolerate a rival near their base of spiritual power; and the very reasons which had made them side with the cities in the wars of liberation would have roused their hostility against a federative union. To have encouraged an Italian Bund, in the midst of which they would have found the Church unarmed and on a level with the puissant towns of Lombardy and Tuscany, must have seemed to them a suicidal error. Such a coalition, if attempted, could not but have been opposed with all their might; for the whole history of Italy proves that Machiavelli was right when he asserted that the Church had persistently maintained the nation in disunion for the furtherance of her own selfish ends. We have furthermore to add the prestige which the Empire preserved for the Italians, who failed to conceive of any civilised human society whereof the representative of Cæsar should not be the God-appointed head. Though the material power of the Emperors was on the wane, it still existed as a dominant idea. Italy was still the Garden of the Empire no less than the Throne of Christ on earth. After the burghs had wrung what they regarded as their reasonable rights and privileges from Frederick, they laid down their arms, and were content to flourish beneath the imperial shadow. To raise up a political association as a bulwark against the Holy Roman Empire, and by the formation of this defence to become an independent and united nation, instead of remaining an aggregate of scattered townships, would have seemed to their minds little short of sacrilege. Up to this point the Church and the Empire had been, theoretically at least, concordant. They were the sun and moon of a sacred social system which ruled Europe with light and might. But the Wars of Investiture placed them in antagonism, and the result of that quarrel was still further to divide the Italians, still further to remove the hope of national unity

into the region of things unattainable. The great parties
accentuated communal jealousies and gave external form and
substance to the struggles of town with town. So far distant
was the possibility of confederation on a grand scale that every
city strove within itself to establish one of two contradictory
principles, and the energies of the people were expended in a
struggle that set neighbour against neighbour on the field of
war and in the market-place. The confusion, exhaustion, and
demoralisation engendered by these conflicts determined the
advent of the Despots ; and after 1400 Italy could only have
been united under a tyrant's iron rule. At such an universal
despotism Gian Galeazzo Visconti was aiming when the
plague cut short his schemes. Cesare Borgia played his
highest stakes for it. Leo X. dreamed of it for his family.
Machiavelli, at the end of the ' Principe,' when the tragedy of
Italy was almost accomplished, invoked it. But even for this
last chance of unification it was now too late. The great
nations of Europe were in movement, and the destinies of
Italy depended upon France and Spain. When Charles V.
remained victor in the struggle of the sixteenth century, he
stereotyped and petrified the divisions of Italy in the interest
of his own dynastic policy. The only Italian power that remained unchangeable throughout all changes was the Papacy
—the first to emerge into prominence after the decay of the
old Western Empire, the last to suffer diminution in spite of
vicissitudes, humiliations, schisms, and internal transformation. As the Papacy had created and maintained a divided
Italy, as it had opposed itself to every successive prospect of
unification, so it survived the extinction of Italian independence, and lent its aid to that imperial tyranny whereby the
disunion of the nation was confirmed and prolonged till the
present century.

CHAPTER III

THE AGE OF THE DESPOTS

THE fourteenth and fifteenth centuries may be called the
Age of the Despots in Italian history, as the twelfth and
thirteenth are the Age of the Free Burghs, and as the
sixteenth and seventeenth are the Age of Foreign Enslavement. It was during the age of the Despots that the
conditions of the Renaissance were evolved, and that the
Renaissance itself assumed a definite character in Italy.
Under tyrannies, in the midst of intrigues, wars, and

revolutions, the peculiar individuality of the Italians obtained its ultimate development. This individuality, as remarkable for salient genius and diffused talent as for self-conscious and deliberate vice, determined the qualities of the Renaissance and affected by example the whole of Europe. Italy led the way in the education of the Western races, and was the first to realise the type of modern as distinguished from classical and mediæval life.

During this age of the Despots, Italy presents the spectacle of a nation devoid of central government and comparatively uninfluenced by feudalism. The right of the Emperor had become nominal, and served as a pretext for usurpers rather than as a source of order. The visits, for instance, of Charles IV. and Frederick III. were either begging expeditions or holiday excursions, in the course of which ambitious adventurers bought titles to the government of towns, and meaningless honours were showered upon vain courtiers. It was not till the reign of Maximilian that Germany adopted a more serious policy with regard to Italy, which by that time had become the central point of European intrigue. Charles V. afterwards used force to reassert imperial rights over the Italian cities, acting not so much in the interest of the Empire as for the aggrandisement of the Spanish monarchy. At the same time the Papacy, which had done so much to undermine the authority of the Empire, exercised a power at once anomalous and ill-recognised except in the immediate States of the Church. By the extinction of the House of Hohenstauffen and by the assumed right to grant the investiture of the kingdom of Naples to foreigners, the Popes not only struck a death-blow at imperial influence, but also prepared the way for their own exile to Avignon. This involved the loss of the second great authority to which Italy had been accustomed to look for the maintenance of some sort of national coherence. Moreover, the Church, though impotent to unite all Italy beneath her own sway, had power enough to prevent the formation either by Milan or Venice or Naples of a substantial kingdom. The result was a perpetually recurring process of composition, dismemberment, and recomposition, under different forms, of the scattered elements of Italian life. The Guelf and Ghibelline parties, inherited from the wars of the thirteenth century, survived the political interests which had given them birth, and proved an insurmountable obstacle, long after they had ceased to have any real significance, to the pacification of the country.[1] The only important state which maintained an unbroken dynastic succession of however disputed a nature at this period was the kingdom of the Two Sicilies. The only great republics were Venice, Genoa, and Florence. Of these, Genoa, after being reduced in power and prosperity by Venice, was overshadowed by the successive lords of Milan; while Florence was destined at the end of a long struggle to fall beneath a family of despots. All the rest of Italy, especially to the north of the Apennines, was the battlefield of tyrants, whose title was illegitimate—based, that is to say, on no feudal principle, derived in no regular manner from the Empire, but generally held as a gift or extorted as a prize from the predominant parties in the great towns.

If we examine the constitution of these tyrannies, we find abundant proofs of their despotic nature. The succession from father to son was always uncertain. Legitimacy of birth was hardly respected. The last La Scalas were bastards. The house of Aragon in Naples descended from a bastard. Gabriello Visconti shared with his half-brothers the heritage of Gian Galeazzo. The line of the Medici was continued by

[1] So late as 1526 we find the burlesque poet Folengo exclaiming (*Orlandino*, ii. 59)—

Chè se non fusser le gran parti in quella,
Dominerebbe il mondo Italia bella.

princes of more than doubtful origin. Suspicion rested on the birth of Frederick of Urbino. The houses of Este and Malatesta honoured their bastards in the same degree as their lawful progeny. The great family of the Bentivogli at Bologna owed their importance at the end of the fifteenth century to an obscure and probably spurious pretender, dragged from the wool-factories of Florence by the policy of Cosimo de' Medici. The sons of Popes ranked with the proudest of aristocratic families. Nobility was less regarded in the choice of a ruler than personal ability. Power once acquired was maintained by force, and the history of the ruling families is one long catalogue of crimes. Yet the cities thus governed were orderly and prosperous. Police regulations were carefully established and maintained by governors whose interest it was to rule a quiet state. Culture was widely diffused without regard to rank or wealth. Public edifices of colossal grandeur were multiplied. Meanwhile the people at large were being fashioned to that self-conscious and intelligent activity which is fostered by the modes of life peculiar to political and social centres in a condition of continued rivalry and change.

Under the Italian despotisms we observe nearly the opposite of all the influences brought to bear in the same period upon the nations of the North. There is no gradual absorption of the great vassals in monarchies, no fixed allegiance to a reigning dynasty, no feudal aid or military service attached to the tenure of the land, no tendency to centralise the whole intellectual activity of the race in any capital, no suppression of individual character by strongly biassed public feeling, by immutable law, or by the superincumbent weight of a social hierarchy. Everything, on the contrary, tends to the free emergence of personal passions and personal aims. Though the vassals of the Despot are neither his soldiers nor his loyal lieges, but his courtiers and taxpayers, the continual object of his cruelty and fear, yet each subject has the chance of becoming a prince like Sforza or a companion of princes like Petrarch. Equality of servitude goes far to democratise a nation, and common hatred of the tyrant leads to the combination of all classes against him. Thence follows the fermentation of arrogant and self-reliant passions in the breasts of the lowest as well as the highest.[1] The rapid mutations of government teach men to care for themselves and to depend upon themselves alone in the battle of the world; while the necessity of craft and policy in the conduct of complicated affairs sharpens intelligence. The sanction of all means that may secure an end under conditions of social violence encourages versatility unprejudiced by moral considerations. At the same time the freely indulged vices of the sovereign are an example of self-indulgence to the subject, and his need of lawless instruments is a practical sanction of force in all its forms. Thus to the play of personality, whether in combat with society and rivals, or in the gratification of individual caprice, every liberty is allowed. Might is substituted for right, and the sense of law is supplanted by a mere dread of coercion. What is the wonder if a Benvenuto Cellini should be the outcome of the same society as that which formed a Cesare Borgia? What is the miracle if Italy under these circumstances produced original characters and many-sided intellects in greater profusion than any other nation at any other period, with the single exception of Greece on her emergence from the age of her Despots? It was the misfortune of Italy that the age of the Despots was succeeded, not by an age of free political existence, but by one of foreign servitude.

Frederick II. was at the same time the last emperor who maintained imperial sway in Italy in person, and also the

[1] See Guicciardini, 'Dialogo del Reggimento di Firenze,' *Op. Ined.* vol. ii. p. 53, for a critique of the motives of tyrannicide in Italy.

beginner of a new system of government which the Despots afterwards pursued. His establishment of the Saracen colony at Nocera, as the nucleus of an army ready to fulfil his orders with scrupulous disregard for Italian sympathies and customs, taught all future rulers to reduce their subjects to a state of unarmed passivity, and to carry on their wars by the aid of German, English, Swiss, Gascon, Breton, or Hungarian mercenaries, as the case might be. Frederick, again, derived from his Mussulman predecessors in Sicily the arts of taxation to the utmost limits of the national capacity, and founded a precedent for the levying of tolls by a Catasto or schedule of the properties attributed to each individual in the state. He also destroyed the self-government of burghs and districts, by retaining for himself the right to nominate officers, and by establishing a system of judicial jurisdiction which derived authority from the throne. Again, he introduced the example of a prince making profit out of the industries of his subjects by monopolies and protective duties. In this path he was followed by illustrious successors—especially by Sixtus IV. and Alfonso II. of Aragon, who enriched themselves by trafficking in the corn and olive-oil of their famished provinces. Lastly, Frederick established the precedent of a court formed upon the model of that of Oriental Sultans, in which chamberlains and secretaries took the rank of hereditary nobles, and functions of state were confided to the body-servants of the monarch. This court gave currency to those habits of polite culture, magnificent living, and personal luxury which played so prominent a part in all subsequent Italian despotism. It is tempting to overstrain a point in estimating the direct influence of Frederick's example. In many respects doubtless he was merely somewhat in advance of his age; and what we may be inclined to ascribe to him personally, would have followed in the natural evolution of events. Yet it remains a fact that he first realised the type of cultivated despotism which prevailed throughout Italy in the fourteenth and fifteenth centuries. Italian literature began in his court, and many Saracenic customs of statecraft were transmitted through him from Palermo to Lombardy.

While Frederick foreshadowed the comparatively modern tyrants of the coming age, his Vicar in the North of Italy, Ezzelino da Romano, represented the atrocities towards which they always tended to degenerate. Regarding himself with a sort of awful veneration as the divinely appointed scourge of humanity, this monster in his lifetime was execrated as an aberration from the ' kindly race of men,' and after his death he became the hero of a fiendish mythus. But in the succeeding centuries of Italian history his kind was only too common ; the immorality with which he worked out his selfish aims was systematically adopted by princes like the Visconti, and reduced to rule by theorists like Machiavelli. Ezzelino, a small, pale, wiry man, with terror in his face and enthusiasm for evil in his heart, lived a foe to luxury, cold to the pathos of children, dead to the enchantment of women. His one passion was the greed of power, heightened by the lust for blood. Originally a noble of the Veronese Marches, he founded his illegal authority upon the captaincy of the Imperial party delegated to him by Frederick. Verona, Vicenza, Padua, Feltre, and Belluno made him their captain in the Ghibelline interest, conferring on him judicial as well as military supremacy. How he fearfully abused his power, how a crusade was preached against him,[1] and how he died in silence like a boar at bay, rending from his wounds the dressings that his foes had placed to keep him alive are notorious matters of history. At Padua alone he erected eight prisons, two of which contained as many as three hundred captives each ; and though the executioner never

[1] Alexander IV. issued letters for this crusade in 1255. It was preached next year by the Archbishop of Ravenna.

ceased to ply his trade there, they were always full. These dungeons were designed to torture by their noisomeness, their want of air, and light and space. Ezzelino made himself terrible not merely by executions and imprisonments but also by mutilations and torments. When he captured Friola he caused the population, of all ages, sexes, occupations, to be deprived of their eyes, noses, and legs, and to be cast forth to the mercy of the elements. On another occasion he walled up a family of princes in a castle and left them to die of famine. Wealth, eminence, and beauty attracted his displeasure no less than insubordination or disobedience. Nor was he less crafty than cruel. Sons betrayed their fathers, friends their comrades, under the fallacious safeguard of his promises. A gigantic instance of his scheming was the coup-de-main by which he succeeded in entrapping 11,000 Paduan soldiers, only 200 of whom escaped the miseries of his prisons. Thus by his absolute contempt of law, his inordinate cruelty, his prolonged massacres, and his infliction of plagues upon whole peoples, Ezzelino established the ideal in Italy of a tyrant marching to his end by any means whatever. In vain was the humanity of the race revolted by the hideous spectacle. Vainly did the monks assemble pity-stricken multitudes upon the plain of Paquara to atone with tears and penitence for the insults offered to the saints in heaven by Ezzelino's fury. It laid a deep hold upon the Italian imagination, and, by the glamour of loathing that has strength to fascinate, proved in the end contagious. We are apt to ask ourselves whether such men are mad—whether in the case of a Nero or a Maréchal de Retz or an Ezzelino the love of evil and the thirst for blood are not a monomaniacal perversion of barbarous passions which even in a cannibal are morbid.[1] Is there in fact such a thing as Hæmatomania, Blood-madness? But if we answer this question in the affirmative, we shall have to place how

[1] See Appendix, No. I.

many Visconti, Sforzeschi, Malatesti, Borgias, Farnesi, and princes of the houses of Anjou and Aragon in the list of these maniacs ? Ezzelino was indeed only the first of a long and horrible procession, the most terror-striking because the earliest, prefiguring all the rest.

Ezzelino's cruelty was no mere Berserkir fury or Lycan-thropia coming over him in gusts and leaving him exhausted. It was steady and continuous. In his madness, if such we may call this inhumanity, there was method ; he used it to the end of the consolidation of his tyranny. Yet, inasmuch as it passed all limits and prepared his downfall, it may be said to have obtained over his nature the mastery of an in-sane appetite. While applying the nomenclature of disease to these exceptional monsters, we need not allow that their atrocities were, at first at any rate, beyond their control. Moral insanity is often nothing more than the hypertrophy of some vulgar passion—lust, violence, cruelty, jealousy, and the like. The tyrant, placed above law and less influenced by public opinion than a private person, may easily allow a greed for pleasure or a love of bloodshed to acquire morbid pro-portions in his nature. He then is not unjustly termed a monomaniac. Within the circle of his vitiated appetite he proves himself irrational. He becomes the puppet of passions which the sane man cannot so much as picture to his fancy, the victim of desire, ever recurring and ever destined to remain unsatisfied ; nor is any hallucination more akin to lunacy than the mirage of a joy that leaves the soul thirstier than it was before, the paroxysm of unnatural pleasure which wearies the nerves that crave for it.

In Frederick, the modern autocrat, and Ezzelino, the legendary tyrant, we obtain the earliest specimens of two types of despotism in Italy. Their fame long after their death powerfully affected the fancy of the people, worked itself into the literature of the Italians, and created a consiousness of tyranny in the minds of irresponsible rulers.

During the fourteenth and fifteenth centuries we find, roughly speaking, six sorts of despots in Italian cities.[1] Of these the *first* class, which is a very small one, had a dynastic or hereditary right accruing from long seignorial possession of their several districts.   The most eminent are the houses of Montferrat and Savoy, the Marquises of Ferrara, the Princes of Urbino. At the same time it is difficult to know where to draw the line between such hereditary lordship as that of the Este family, and tyranny based on popular favour.   The Malatesti of Rimini, Polentani of Ravenna, Manfredi of Faenza, Ordelaffi of Forli, Chiavelli of Fabriano, Varani of Camerino, and others, might claim to rank among the former, since their cities submitted to them without a long period of republican independence like that which preceded despotism in the cases to be next mentioned.   Yet these families styled themselves Captains of the burghs they ruled ; and in many instances they obtained the additional title of Vicars of the Church.[2]   Even the Estensi were made hereditary captains of Ferrara at the end of the thirteenth century, while they also acknowledged the supremacy of the Papacy.   There was in fact no right outside the Empire in Italy ; and Despots of whatever origin or complexion gladly accepted the support which a title derived from the Empire, the Church, or the People might give.   Brought to the front amid the tumults of the civil wars, and accepted as pacificators of the factions by the multitude, they gained the confirmation of their anomalous authority by representing themselves to be lieutenants or vice-gerents of the three great powers.   The *second* class comprise

[1] This classification must of necessity be imperfect, since many of the tyrannies belong in part to two or more of the kinds which I have mentioned.

[2] See Guicc. *Ist.* end of Book 4.

those nobles who obtained the title of Vicars of the Empire, and built an illegal power upon the basis of imperial right in Lombardy. Of these, the Della Scala and Visconti families are illustrious instances. Finding in their official capacity a ready-made foundation, they extended it beyond its just limits, and in defiance of the Empire constituted dynasties. The *third* class is important. Nobles charged with military or judicial power, as Capitani or Podestàs, by the free burghs, used their authority to enslave the cities they were chosen to administer. It was thus that almost all the numerous tyrants of Lombardy, Carraresi at Padua, Gonzaghi at Mantua, Rossi and Correggi at Parma, Torrensi and Visconti at Milan, Scotti at Piacenza, and so forth, first erected their despotic dynasties. This fact in the history of Italian tyranny is noticeable. The fount of honour, so to speak, was in the citizens of these great burghs. Therefore, when the limits of authority delegated to their captains by the people were overstepped, the sway of the princes became confessedly illegal. Illegality carried with it all the consequences of an evil conscience, all the insecurities of usurped dominion, all the danger from without and from within to which an arbitrary governor is exposed. In the *fourth* class we find the principle of force still more openly at work. To it may be assigned those Condottieri who made a prey of cities at their pleasure. The illustrious Uguccione della Faggiuola, who neglected to follow up his victory over the Guelfs at Monte Catini, in order that he might cement his power in Lucca and Pisa, is an early instance of this kind of tyrant. His successor, Castruccio Castracane, the hero of Machiavelli's romance, is another. But it was not until the first half of the fifteenth century that professional Condottieri became powerful enough to found such kingdoms as that, for example, of Francesco Sforza at Milan.[1] The *fifth* class

[1] John Hawkwood (died 1393), the English adventurer, held Cotignola and Bagnacavallo from Gregory XI. In the second half of the fifteenth

includes the nephews or sons of Popes. The Riario principality of Forli, the Della Rovere of Urbino, the Borgia of Romagna, the Farnese of Parma, form a distinct species of despotisms; but all these are of a comparatively late origin. Until the Papacies of Sixtus IV. and Innocent VIII. the Popes had not bethought them of providing in this way for their relatives. Also, it may be remarked, there was an essential weakness in these tyrannies. Since they had to be carved out of the States of the Church, the Pope who had established his son, say in Romagna, died before he could see him well confirmed in a province which the next Pope sought to wrest from his hands, in order to bestow it on his own favourite. The fabric of the Church could not long have stood this disgraceful wrangling between Papal families for the dynastic possession of Church property. Luckily for the continuance of the Papacy, the tide of counter-reformation which set in after the sack of Rome and the great Northern Schism, put a stop to nepotism in its most barefaced form.

There remains the *sixth* and last class of despots to be mentioned. This again is large and of the first importance. Citizens of eminence, like the Medici at Florence, the Bentivogli at Bologna, the Baglioni of Perugia, the Vitelli of Città

century the efforts of the Condottieri to erect tyrannies were most frequent. Braccio da Montone established himself in Perugia in 1416, and aspired, not without good grounds for hope, to acquiring the kingdom of Italy. Francesco Sforza, before gaining Milan, had begun to form a despotism at Ancona. Sforza's rival, Giacomo Piccinino, would probably have succeeded in his own attempt, had not Ferdinand of Aragon treacherously murdered him at Naples in 1465. In the disorganisation caused by Charles VIII., Vidovero of Brescia in 1495 established himself at Cesena and Castelnuovo, and had to be assassinated by Pandolfo Malatesta at the instigation of Venice. After the death of Gian Galeazzo Visconti, in 1402, the generals whom he had employed in the consolidation of his vast dominions attempted to divide the spoil among themselves. Naples, Venice, Milan, Rome, and Florence were in course of time made keenly alive to the risk of suffering a captain of adventure to run his course unchecked.

di Castello, the Gambacorti of Pisa, like Pandolfo Petrucci in
Siena (1502), Roméo Pepoli, the usurer of Bologna (1323),
the plebeian Alticlinio and Agolanti of Padua (1313), Giovanni
Vignate, the millionaire of Lodi (1402), acquired more than
their due weight in the conduct of affairs, and gradually
tended to tyranny. In most of these cases great wealth was
the original source of despotic ascendency. It was not uncommon to buy cities together with their Signory. Thus the
Rossi bought Parma for 35,000 florins in 1333 ; the Appiani
sold Pisa ; Astorre Manfredi sold Faenza and Imola in 1377.
In 1444 Galeazzo Malatesta sold Pesaro to Alessandro Sforza,
and Fossombrone to Urbino ; in 1461 Cervia was sold to
Venice by the same family. Franceschetto Cibo purchased
the County of Anguillara. Towns at last came to have their
market value. It was known that Bologna was worth
200,000 florins, Parma 60,000, Arezzo 40,000, Lucca 30,000,
and so forth. But personal qualities and nobility of blood
might also produce Despots of the sixth class. Thus the
Bentivogli claimed descent from a bastard of King Enzo,
son of Frederick II., who was for a long time an honourable prisoner in Bologna. The Baglioni, after a protracted
struggle with the rival family of Oddi, owed their supremacy
to ability and vigour in the last years of the fifteenth century.
But the neighbourhood of the Papal power, and their own
internal dissensions, rendered the hold of this family upon
Perugia precarious. As in the case of the Medici and the
Bentivogli, many generations might elapse before such burgher
families assumed dynastic authority. But to this end they
were always advancing.

The history of the bourgeois Despots proves that Italy
in the fifteenth century was undergoing a natural process
of determination toward tyranny. Sismondi may attempt to
demonstrate that Italy was 'not answerable for the crimes
with which she was sullied by her tyrants.' But the facts

show that she was answerable for choosing Despots instead of remaining free, or rather that she instinctively obeyed a law of social evolution by which princes had to be substituted for municipalities at the end of those fierce internal conflicts and exhausting wars of jealousy which closed the Middle Ages. Machiavelli, with all his love of liberty, is forced to admit that in his day the most powerful provinces of Italy had become incapable of freedom. ' No accident, however weighty and violent, could ever restore Milan or Naples to liberty, owing to their utter corruption. This is clear from the fact that after the death of Filippo Visconti, when Milan tried to regain freedom, she was unable to preserve it.'[1] Whether Machiavelli is right in referring this incapacity for self-government to the corruption of morals and religion may be questioned. But it is certain that throughout the states of Italy, with the one exception of Venice, causes were at work inimical to republics and favourable to despotisms.

It will be observed in this classification of Italian tyrants that the tenure of their power was almost uniformly forcible. They generally acquired it through the people in the first instance, and maintained it by the exercise of violence. Rank had nothing to do with their claims. The bastards of Popes, who like Sixtus IV. had no pedigree, merchants like the Medici, the son of a peasant like Francesco Sforza, a rich usurer like Pepoli, had almost equal chances with nobles of the ancient houses of Este, Visconti, or Malatesta. The chief point in favour of the latter was the familiarity which through long years of authority had accustomed the people to their

[1] *Discorsi*, i. 17. The Florentine philosopher remarks in the same passage, ' Cities, once corrupt, and accustomed to the rule of a prince, can never acquire their freedom even though the prince with all his kith and kin be extirpated. One prince is needed to extinguish another; and the city has no rest except by the creation of a new lord, unless one burgher by his goodness and his great qualities may chance to preserve its independence during his lifetime.'

rule. When exiled, they had a better chance of return to power than parvenus, whose party-cry and ensigns were comparatively fresh and stirred no sentiment of loyalty—if indeed the word loyalty can be applied to that preference for the established and the customary which made the mob, distracted by the wrangling of doctrinaires and intriguers, welcome back a Bentivoglio or a Malatesta. Despotism in Italy as in ancient Greece was democratic. It recruited its ranks from all classes and erected its thrones upon the sovereignty of the peoples it oppressed. The impulse to the free play of ambitious individuality which this state of things communicated was enormous. Capacity might raise the meanest monk to the chair of S. Peter's, the meanest soldier to the duchy of Milan. Audacity, vigour, unscrupulous crime were the chief requisites for success. It was not till Cesare Borgia displayed his magnificence at the French Court, till the Italian adventurer matched himself with royalty in its legitimate splendour, that the lowness of his origin and the frivolity of his pretensions appeared in any glaring light.[1] In Italy itself, where there existed no time-honoured hierarchy of classes and no fountain of nobility in the person of a sovereign, one man was a match for another, provided he knew how to assert himself. To the conditions of a society based on these principles we may ascribe the unrivalled emergence of great personalities among the tyrants, as well as the extraordinary tenacity and vigour of such races as the Visconti. In the contest for power and in the maintenance of an illegal authority, the picked athletes came to the front. The struggle by which they established their tyranny, the efforts by which they defended

[1] Brantôme, *Capitaines Etrangers*, Discours 48, gives an account of the entrance of the Borgia into Chinon in 1498, and adds : 'The king being at the window saw him arrive, and there can be no doubt how he and his courtiers ridiculed all this state, as unbecoming the petty Duke of Valentinois.'

it against foreign foes and domestic adversaries, trained them to endurance and to daring. They lived habitually in an atmosphere of peril which taxed all their energies. Their activity was extreme, and their passions corresponded to their vehement vitality. About such men there could be nothing on a small or mediocre scale. When a weakling was born in a despotic family, his brothers murdered him, or he was deposed by a watchful rival. Thus only gladiators of tried capacity and iron nerve, superior to religious and moral scruples, dead to national affection, perfected in perfidy, scientific in the use of cruelty and terror, employing first-rate faculties of brain and will and bodily powers in the service of transcendent egotism, only the *virtuosi* of political craft as theorised by Machiavelli, could survive and hold their own upon this perilous arena.

The life of the Despot was usually one of prolonged terror. Immured in strong places on high rocks, or confined to gloomy fortresses like the Milanese Castello, he surrounded his person with foreign troops, protected his bedchamber with a picked guard, and watched his meat and drink lest they should be poisoned. His chief associates were artists, men of letters, astrologers, buffoons, and exiles. He had no real friends or equals, and against his own family he adopted an attitude of fierce suspicion, justified by the frequent intrigues to which he was exposed.[1] His timidity verged on monomania. Like Alfonso II. of Naples, he was tortured with the ghosts of starved or strangled victims ; like Ezzelino, he felt the mysterious fascination of astrology ; like Filippo Maria Visconti, he trembled at the sound of thunder, and set one

---

[1] See what Guicciardini in his *History of Florence* says about the suspicious temper of even such a tyrant as the cultivated and philosophical Lorenzo de' Medici. See too the incomparably eloquent and penetrating allegory of *Sospetto*, and its application to the tyrants of Italy in Ariosto's *Cinque Canti* (C. 2. St. 1–9).

band of body-guards to watch another next his person. He dared not hope for a quiet end. No one believed in the natural death of a prince : princes must be poisoned or poignarded.[1] Out of thirteen of the Carrara family, in little more than a century (1318–1435) three were deposed or murdered by near relatives, one was expelled by a rival from his state, four were executed by the Venetians. Out of five of the La Scala family three were killed by their brothers, and a fourth was poisoned in exile.

To enumerate all the catastrophes of reigning families occurring in the fifteenth century alone, would be quite impossible within the limits of this chapter. Yet it is only by dwelling on the more important that any adequate notion of the perils of Italian despotism can be formed. Thus Girolamo Riario was murdered by his subjects at Forlì (1488), and Francesco Vico dei Prefetti in the Church of S. Sisto at Viterbo[2] (1387). At Lodi in 1402 Antonio Fisiraga burned

[1] Our dramatist Webster, whose genius was fascinated by the crimes of Italian despotism, makes the Duke of Bracciano exclaim on his death-bed :—

'O thou soft natural Death, thou art joint-twin
To sweetest Slumber ! no rough-bearded comet
Stares on thy mild departure ; the dull owl
Beats not against thy casement ; the hoarse wolf
Scents not thy carrion : pity winds thy corse,
Whilst horror waits on princes.'

Instances of domestic crime might be multiplied by the hundred. Besides those which will follow in these pages, it is enough to notice the murder of Giovanni Francesco Pico, by his nephew, at Mirandola (1533) ; the murder of his uncle by Oliverotto da Fermo ; the assassination of Giovanni Varano by his brothers at Camerino (1434) ; Ostasio da Polenta's fratricide (1322) ; Obizzo da Polenta's fratricide in the next generation, and the murder of Ugolino Gonzaga by his brothers ; Gian Francesco Gonzaga's murder of his wife ; the poisoning of Francesco Sforza's first wife, Polissena, Countess of Montalto, with her little girl, by her aunt ; and the murder of Galeotto Manfredi, by his wife, at Faenza (1488).

[2] The family of the Prefetti fed up the murderer in their castle, and then gave him alive to be eaten by their hounds.

the chief members of the ruling house of Vistarini on the public square, and died himself of poison after a few months. His successor in the tyranny, Giovanni Vignate, was imprisoned by Filippo Maria Visconti in a wooden cage at Pavia, and beat his brains out in despair against its bars. At the same epoch Gabrino Fondulo slaughtered seventy of the Cavalcabò family together in his castle of Macastormo, with the purpose of acquiring their tyranny over Cremona. He was afterwards beheaded as a traitor at Milan (1425). Ottobon Terzi was assassinated at Parma (1408), Nicolà Borghese at Siena (1499), Altobello Dattiri at Todi (about 1500), Raimondo and Pandolfo Malatesta at Rimini, and Oddo Antonio di Montefeltro at Urbino (1444).[1] The Varani were massacred to a man in the church of S. Dominic at Camerino (1434), the Trinci at Foligno (1434), and the Chiavelli of Fabriano in church upon Ascension Day (1435). This wholesale extirpation of three reigning families introduces one of the most romantic episodes in the history of Italian despotism. From the slaughter of the Varani one only child, Giulio Cesare, a boy of two years old, was saved by his aunt Tora. She concealed him in a truss of hay and carried him to the Trinci at Foligno. Hardly had she gained this refuge, when the Trinci were destroyed, and she had to fly with her burden to the Chiavelli at Fabriano. There the same scenes of bloodshed awaited her. A third time she took to flight, and now concealed her precious charge in a nunnery. The boy was afterwards stolen from the town on horseback by a soldier of adventure. After surviving three massacres of kith and kin, he returned as despot at the age of twelve to

---

[1] Sforza Attendolo killed Terzi by a spear-thrust in the back. Pandolfo Petrucci murdered Borghese, who was his father-in-law. Raimondo Malatesta was stabbed by his two nephews disguised as hermits. Dattiri was bound naked to a plank and killed piecemeal by the people, who bit his flesh, cut slices out, and sold and ate it—distributing his living body as a sort of infernal sacrament among themselves.

Camerino, and became a general of distinction. But he was not destined to end his life in peace. Cesare Borgia finally murdered him, together with three of his sons, when he had reached the age of sixty. Less romantic but not less significant in the annals of tyranny is the story of the Trinci. A rival noble of Foligno, Pietro Rasiglia, had been injured in his honour by the chief of the ruling house. He contrived to assassinate two brothers, Nicolà and Bartolommeo, in his castle of Nocera; but the third, Corrado Trinci, escaped, and took a fearful vengeance on his enemy. By the help of Braccio da Montone he possessed himself of Nocera and all its inhabitants, with the exception of Pietro Rasiglia's wife, whom her husband flung from the battlements. Corrado then butchered the men, women, and children of the Rasiglia clan, to the number of three hundred persons, accomplishing his vengeance with details of atrocity too infernal to be dwelt on in these pages. It is recorded that thirty-six asses laden with their mangled limbs paraded the streets of Foligno as a terror-striking spectacle for the inhabitants. He then ruled the city by violence, until the warlike Cardinal dei Vitelleschi avenged society of so much mischief by destroying the tyrant and five of his sons, in the same year. Equally fantastic are the annals of the great house of the Baglioni at Perugia. Raised in 1389 upon the ruins of the bourgeois faction called Raspanti, they founded their tyranny in the person of Pandolfo Baglioni, who was murdered together with sixty of his clan and followers by the party they had dispossessed. The new Despot, Biordo Michelotti, was stabbed in the shoulders with a poisoned dagger by his relative, the abbot of S. Pietro. Then the city, in 1416, submitted to Braccio da Montone, who raised it to unprecedented power and glory. On his death it fell back into new discords, from which it was rescued again by the Baglioni in 1466, now finally successful in their prolonged

warfare with the rival family of Oddi.   But they did not hold
their despotism in tranquillity.   In 1500 one of the members
of the house, Grifonetto degli Baglioni, conspired against his
kinsmen and slew them in their palaces at night.   As told by
Matarazzo, this tragedy offers an epitome of all that is most
brilliant and terrible in the domestic feuds of the Italian
tyrants.[1]   The vicissitudes of the Bentivogli at Bologna present
another series of catastrophes, due less to their personal
crimes than to the fury of the civil strife that raged around
them.   Giovanni Bentivoglio began the dynasty in 1400.   The
next year he was stabbed to death and pounded in a wine-vat
by the infuriated populace, who thought he had betrayed
their interests in battle.   His son Antonio was beheaded by
a Papal Legate, and numerous members of the family on
their return from exile suffered the same fate.   In course of
time the Bentivogli made themselves adored by the people ;
and when Piccinino imprisoned the heir of their house,
Annibale, in the castle of Varano, four youths of the
Marescotti family undertook his rescue at the peril of their
lives, and raised him to the Signory of Bologna.   In 1445
the Canetoli, powerful nobles, who hated the popular dynasty,
invited Annibale and all his clan to a christening feast, where
they exterminated every member of the reigning house.   Not
one Bentivoglio was left alive.   In revenge for this massacre,
the Marescotti, aided by the populace, hunted down the
Canetoli for three whole days in Bologna, and nailed their
smoking hearts to the doors of the Bentivoglio palace.   They
then drew from his obscurity in Florence the bastard Santi
Bentivoglio, who found himself suddenly lifted from a wool-
factory to a throne.   Whether he was a genuine Bentivoglio
or not, mattered little.   The house had become necessary to
Bologna, and its popularity had been baptized in the blood.

[1] See the article ' Perugia ' in my *Sketches in Italy and Greece.*

shed of four massacres. What remains of its story can be briefly told. When Cesare Borgia besieged Bologna, the Marescotti intrigued with him, and eight of their number were sacrificed by the Bentivogli in spite of their old services to the dynasty. The survivors, by the help of Julius II., returned from exile in 1536, to witness the final banishment of the Bentivogli and to take part in the destruction of the palace, where their ancestors had nailed the hearts of the Canetoli upon the walls.

To multiply the records of crime revenged by crime, of force repelled by violence, of treason heaped on treachery, of insult repaid by fraud, would be easy enough. Indeed, a huge book might be compiled containing nothing but the episodes in this grim history of despotism, now tragic and pathetic, now terror-moving in sublimity of passion, now despicable by the baseness of the motives brought to light, at one time revolting through excess of physical horrors, at another fascinating by the spectacle of heroic courage, intelligence, and resolution. Enough, however, has been said to describe the atmosphere of danger in which the tyrants breathed and moved, and from which not one of them was ever capable of finding freedom. Even a princely house so well based in its dynasty and so splendid in its parade of culture as that of the Estensi offers a long list of terrific tragedies. One princess is executed for adultery with her stepson (1425); a bastard's bastard tries to seize the throne, and is put to death with all his kin (1493); a wife is poisoned by her husband to prevent her poisoning him (1493); two brothers cabal against the legitimate heads of the house, and are imprisoned for life (1506). Such was the labyrinth of plot and counterplot, of force repelled by violence, in which the princes praised by Ariosto and by Tasso lived.

Isolated, crime-haunted, and remorseless, at the same time fierce and timorous, the despot not unfrequently made of vice a fine art for his amusement, and openly defied humanity. His pleasures tended to extravagance. Inordinate lust and refined cruelty sated his irritable and jaded appetites. He destroyed pity in his soul, and fed his dogs with living men, or spent his brains upon the invention of new tortures. From the game of politics again he won a feverish pleasure, playing for states and cities as a man plays chess, and endeavouring to extract the utmost excitement from the varying turns of skill and chance. It would be an exaggeration to assert that all the princes of Italy were of this sort. The saner, better, and nobler among them—men of the stamp of Gian Galeazzo Visconti, Can Grande della Scala, Francesco and Lodovico Sforza, found a more humane enjoyment in the consolidation of their empire, the cementing of their alliances, the society of learned men, the friendship of great artists, the foundation of libraries, the building of palaces and churches, the execution of vast schemes of conquest. Others, like Galeazzo Visconti, indulged a comparatively innocent taste for magnificence. Some, like Sigismondo Pandolfo Malatesta, combined the vices of a barbarian with the enthusiasm of a scholar. Others again, like Lorenzo de' Medici and Frederick of Urbino, exhibited the model of moderation in statecraft and a noble width of culture. But the tendency to degenerate was fatal in all the despotic houses. The strain of tyranny proved too strong. Crime, illegality, and the sense of peril, descending from father to son, produced monsters in the shape of men. The last Visconti, the last La Scalas, the last Sforzas, the last Malatestas, the last Farnesi, the last Medici are among the worst specimens of human nature.

Macaulay's brilliant description of the Italian tyrant in his essay on Machiavelli deserves careful study. It may, however, be remarked that the picture is too favourable. Macaulay omits the darker crimes of the Despots, and draws his portrait almost exclusively from such men as Gian Galeazzo Visconti, Francesco and Lodovico Sforza, Frederick of Urbino, and Lorenzo de' Medici. The point he is seeking to establish—that political immorality in Italy was the national correlative to Northern brutality—leads him to idealise the polite refinement, the disciplined passions, the firm and astute policy, the power over men, and the excellent government which distinguished the noblest Italian princes. When he says, 'Wanton cruelty was not in his nature: on the contrary, where no political object was at stake, his disposition was soft and humane;' he seems to have forgotten Gian Maria Visconti, Corrado Trinci, Sigismondo Pandolfo Malatesta, and Cesare Borgia. When he writes, 'His passions, like well-trained troops, are impetuous by rule, and in their most headstrong fury never forget the discipline to which they have been accustomed,' he leaves Francesco Maria della Rovere, Galeazzo Maria Sforza, Pier Luigi Farnese, Alexander VI., out of the reckoning. If all the Despots had been what Macaulay describes, the revolutions and conspiracies of the fourteenth and fifteenth centuries would not have taken place. It is, however, to be remarked that in the sixteenth century the conduct of the tyrant toward his subjects assumed an external form of mildness. As Italy mixed with the European nations, and as tyranny came to be legalised in the Italian states, the Despots developed a policy not of terrorism but of enervation (Lorenzo de' Medici is the great example), and aspired to be paternal governors.

What I have said about Italian despotism is no mere fancy picture. The actual details of Milanese history, the innumerable tragedies of Lombardy, Romagna, and the Marches of Ancona, during the ascendency of despotic families, are far more terrible than any fiction; nor would it be easy for the imagination to invent so perplexing a mixture of savage

barbarism with modern refinement. Savonarola's denunciations [1] and Villani's descriptions of a Despot read like passages
from Plato's Republic, like the most pregnant of Aristotle's
criticisms upon tyranny. The prologue to the sixth book of
Matteo Villani's Chronicle may be cited as a fair specimen of
the judgment passed by contemporary Italian thinkers upon
their princes (Libro Sesto, cap. i.) : ' The crimes of Despots
always hinder and often neutralise the virtues of good men.
Their pleasures are at variance with morality. By them the
riches of their subjects are swallowed up. They are foes to
men who grow in wisdom and in greatness of soul in their
dominions. They diminish by their imposts the wealth of the
peoples ruled by them. Their unbridled lust is never satiated,
but their subjects have to suffer such outrages and insults as
their fancy may from time to time suggest. But inasmuch
as the violence of tyranny is manifested to all eyes by these
and many other atrocities, we need not enumerate them afresh.
It is enough to select one feature, strange in appearance but
familiar in fact ; for what can be more extraordinary than to
see princes of ancient and illustrious lineage bowing to the
service of Despots, men of high descent and time-honoured
nobility frequenting their tables and accepting their bounties ?
Yet if we consider the end of all this, the glory of tyrants often
turns to misery and ruin. Who can exaggerate their wretchedness ? They know not where to place their confidence;
and their courtiers are always on the look-out for the Despot's
fall, gladly lending their influence and best endeavours to
undo him in spite of previous servility. This does not happen
to hereditary kings, because their conduct toward their
subjects, as well as their good qualities and all their circum-

[1] See the passage condensed from his Sermons in Villari's Life of
Savonarola (Eng. Tr. vol. ii. p. 62). The most thoroughgoing analysis
of despotic criminality is contained in Savonarola's *Tractato circa el
Reggimento e Governo della Città di Firenze*, trattato ii. cap. 2. *Della
Malitia e pessime Conditioni del Tyranno.*

stances, are of a nature contrary to that of tyrants. Therefore the very causes which produce and fortify and augment tyrannies, conceal and nourish in themselves the sources of their overthrow and ruin. This indeed is the greatest wretchedness of tyrants.'

It may be objected that this sweeping criticism, from the pen of a Florentine citizen at war with Milan, partakes of the nature of an invective. Yet abundant proofs can be furnished from the chronicles of burghs which owed material splendour to their despots, confirming the censure of Villani. Matarazzo, for example, whose sympathy with the house of Baglioni is so striking, and who exults in the distinction they conferred upon Perugia, writes no less bitterly concerning the pernicious effects of their misgovernment.[1] It is to be noticed that Villani and Matarazzo agree about the special evils brought upon the populations by their tyrants. Lust and violence take the first place. Next comes extortion ; then the protection of the lawless and the criminal against the better sort of citizens. But the Florentine, with intellectual acumen, lays his finger on one of the chief vices of their rule. They retard the development of mental greatness in their states, and check the growth of men of genius. Ariosto, in the comparative calm of the sixteenth century, when tyrannies had yielded to the protectorate of Spain, sums up the records of the past in the following memorable passage :[2] 'Happy the kingdoms where an open-hearted and blameless man gives law ! Wretched indeed and pitiable are those where injustice and cruelty hold sway, where burdens ever greater and more grievous are laid upon the people by tyrants like those who now abound in Italy, whose infamy will be recorded through years to come as no less black than Caligula's or Nero's.' Guicciardini, with pregnant brevity, observes :[3] ' The mortar

[1] *Arch. Stor.* xvi. 102. See my *Sketches in Italy and Greece*, p. 84.
[2] Cinque Canti, ii. 5. [3] *Ricordi Politici*, ccxlii.

with which the states of tyrants are cemented is the blood of the citizens.'

In the history of Italian despotism two points of first-rate importance will demand attention. The first is the process by which the greater tyrannies absorbed the smaller during the fourteenth century. The second is the relation of the chief Condottieri to the tyrants of the fifteenth century. The evolution of these two phenomena cannot be traced more clearly than by a study of the history of Milan, which at the same time presents a detailed picture of the policy and character of the Italian Despot during this period. The dynasties of Visconti and Sforza from 1300 to 1500 bridged over the years that intervened between the Middle Age and the Renaissance, between the period of the free burghs and the period during which Italy was destined to become the theatre of the action of more powerful nations. Their alliances and diplomatic relations prepared the way for the interference of foreigners in Italian affairs. Their pedigree illustrates the power acquired by military adventurers in the peninsula. The magnitude of their political schemes displays the most soaring ambition which it was ever granted to Italian princes to indulge. The splendour of their court and the intelligence of their culture bear witness to the high state of civilisation which the Italians had reached.

The power of the Visconti in Milan was founded upon that of the Della Torre family, who preceded them as Captains-General of the people at the end of the thirteenth century. Otho, Archbishop of Milan, first laid a substantial basis for the dominion of his house by imprisoning Napoleone Della Torre and five of his relatives in three iron cages in 1277, and by causing his nephew Matteo Visconti to be nominated both by the Emperor and by the people of Milan as Imperial Vicar. Matteo, who headed the Ghibelline party in Lombardy, was the model of a prudent Italian Despot.

From the date 1311, when he finally succeeded in his attempts upon the sovereignty of Milan, to 1322, when he abdicated in favour of his son Galeazzo, he ruled his states by force of character, craft, and insight, more than by violence or cruelty. Excellent as a general, he was still better as a diplomatist, winning more cities by money than by the sword. All through his life, as became a Ghibelline chief at that time, he persisted in fierce enmity against the Church. But just before his death a change came over him. He showed signs of superstitious terror, and began to fear the ban of excommunication which lay upon him. This weakness alarmed the suspicions of his sons, terrible and wolf-like men, whom Matteo had hitherto controlled with bit and bridle. They therefore induced him to abdicate in 1322, and when in the same year he died, they buried his body in a secret place, lest it should be exhumed and scattered to the winds in accordance with the Papal edict against him.[1] Galeazzo, his son, was less fortunate than Matteo, surnamed Il Grande by the Lombards. The Emperor Louis of Bavaria threw him into prison on the occasion of his visit to Milan in 1327, and only released him at the intercession of his friend Castruccio Castracane. To such an extent was the growing tyranny of the Visconti still dependent upon their office delegated from the Empire. This Galeazzo married Beatrice d' Este, the widow of Nino di Gallura, of whom Dante speaks in the eighth canto of the 'Purgatory,' and had by her a son named

[1] We may compare what Dante puts into the mouth of Manfred in the 'Purgatory' (canto iii.). The great Ghibelline poet here protests against the use of excommunication as a political weapon. His sense of justice will not allow him to believe that God can regard the sentence of priests and pontiffs, actuated by the spite of partisans: yet the examples of Frederick II. and of this Matteo Visconti prove how terrifying, even to the boldest, those sentences continued to be. Few had the resolute will of Galeazzo Pico di Mirandola, who expired in 1499 under the ban of the Church, which he had borne for sixteen years.

Azzo. Azzo bought the city, together with the title of Imperial Vicar, from the same Louis who had imprisoned his father.[1] When he was thus seated in the tyranny of his grandfather, he proceeded to fortify it further by the addition of ten Lombard towns, which he reduced beneath the supremacy of Milan. At the same time he consolidated his own power by the murder of his uncle Marco in 1329, who had grown too mighty as a general. Giovio describes him as fair of complexion, blue-eyed, curly-haired, and subject to the hereditary disease of gout.[2] Azzo died in 1339, and was succeeded by his uncle Lucchino. In Lucchino the darker side of the Visconti character appears for the first time. Cruel, moody, and jealous, he passed his life in perpetual terror. His nephews, Galeazzo and Barnabas, conspired against him, and were exiled to Flanders. His wife, Isabella Fieschi, intrigued with Galeazzo and disgraced him by her amours with Ugolino Gonzaga and Dandolo the Doge of Venice. Finally suspicion rose to such a pitch between this ill-assorted couple, that, while Lucchino was plotting how to murder Isabella, she succeeded in poisoning him in 1349. In spite of these domestic calamities, Lucchino was potent as a general and governor. He bought Parma from Obizzo d' Este, and made the town of Pisa dependent upon Milan. Already in his policy we can trace the encroachment which characterised the schemes of the Milanese Despots, who were always plotting to advance their foot beyond the Apennines as a prelude to the complete subjugation of Italy. Lucchino

[1] This was in 1328. Azzo agreed to pay 25,000 florins. The vast wealth of the Visconti amassed during their years of peaceful occupation always stood them in good stead when bad times came, and when the Emperor was short of cash. Azzo deserves special commendation from the student of art for the exquisite octagonal tower of S. Gottardo, which he built of terra cotta with marble pilasters, in Milan. It is quite one of the loveliest monuments of mediæval Italian architecture.

[2] Lucchino and Galeazzo Visconti were both afflicted with gout, the latter to such an extent as to be almost crippled.

left sons, but none of proved legitimacy.[1] Consequently he was succeeded by his brother Giovanni, son of old Matteo il Grande, and Archbishop of Milan. This man, the friend of Petrarch, was one of the most notable characters of the four-teenth century. Finding himself at the head of sixteen cities, he added Bologna to the tyranny of the Visconti in 1350, and made himself strong enough to defy the Pope. Clement VI., resenting his encroachments on the Papal terri-tory, summoned him to Avignon. Giovanni Visconti replied that he would march thither at the head of 12,000 cavalry and 6,000 infantry. In the Duomo of Milan he ascended his throne with the crosier in his left hand and a drawn sword in his right; and thus he is always represented in pictures. The story of Giovanni's answer to the Papal Legate is well told by Corio:[2] 'After Mass in the Cathedral the great-hearted Archbishop unsheathed a flashing sword, which he had girded on his thigh, and with his left hand seized the cross, saying, "This is my spiritual sceptre, and I will wield the sword as my temporal, in defence of all my empire."' Afterwards he sent couriers to engage lodgings for his soldiers and his train for six months. Visitors to Avignon found no room in the city, and the Pope was fain to decline so terrible a guest. In 1353 Giovanni annexed Genoa to the Milanese principality, and died in 1354, having established the rule of the Visconti over the whole of the North of Italy, with the exception of Piedmont, Verona, Mantua, Ferrara, and Venice.

The reign of the Archbishop Giovanni marks a new epoch in the despotism of the Visconti. They are now no longer the successful rivals of the Della Torre family or dependants on imperial caprice, but self-made sovereigns, with a well-

[1] This would not have been by itself a bar to succession in an Italian tyranny. But Lucchino's bastards were not of the proper stuff to continue their father's government, while their fiery uncle was precisely the man to sustain the honour and extend the power of the Visconti.

[2] *Storia di Milano*, 1554, p. 223.

established power in Milan and a wide extent of subject
territory. Their dynasty, though based on force and maintained by violence, has come to be acknowledged; and we
shall soon see them allying themselves with the royal houses
of Europe. After the death of Giovanni, Matteo's sons were
extinct. But Stefano, the last of his family, had left three
children, who now succeeded to the lands and cities of the
house. They were named Matteo, Bernabo, and Galeazzo.
Between these three princes a partition of the heritage of
Giovanni Visconti was effected. Matteo took Bologna, Lodi,
Piacenza, Parma, Bobbio, and some other towns of less
importance. Bernabo received Cremona, Crema, Brescia, and
Bergamo. Galeazzo held Como, Novara, Vercelli, Asti, Tor-
tona, and Alessandria. Milan and Genoa were to be ruled by
the three in common. It may here be noticed that the dismemberment of Italian despotisms among joint-heirs was a
not unfrequent source of disturbance and a cause of weakness
to their dynasties. At the same time the practice followed
naturally upon the illegal nature of the tyrant's title. He
dealt with his cities as so many pieces of personal property,
which he could distribute as he chose, not as a coherent
whole to be bequeathed to one ruler for the common benefit
of all his subjects. In consequence of such partition, it became the interest of brother to murder brother, so as to effect
a reconsolidation of the family estates. Something of the
sort happened on this occasion. Matteo abandoned himself
to bestial sensuality; and his two brothers, finding him both
eeble and likely to bring discredit on their rule, caused him
to be assassinated in 1355.[1] They then jointly swayed the
Milanese, with unanimity remarkable in despots. Galeazzo
was distinguished as the handsomest man of his age. He
was tall and graceful, with golden hair, which he wore in long

[1] M. Villani, v. 81. Compare Corio, p. 230. Corio gives the date
1356

plaits, or tied up in a net, or else loose and crowned with flowers. Fond of display and magnificence, he spent much of his vast wealth in shows and festivals, and in the building of palaces and churches. The same taste for splendour led him to seek royal marriages for his children. His daughter Violante was wedded to the Duke of Clarence, son of Edward III. of England, who received with her for dowry the sum of 200,000 golden florins, as well as five cities bordering on Piedmont.[1] It must have been a strange experience for this brother of the Black Prince, leaving London, where the streets were still unpaved, the houses thatched, the beds laid on straw, and where wine was sold as medicine, to pass into the luxurious palaces of Lombardy, walled with marble, and raised high above smooth streets of stone. Of his marriage with Violante, Giovio gives some curious details. He says that Galeazzo on this occasion made splendid presents to more than 200 Englishmen, so that he was reckoned to have outdone the greatest kings in generosity. At the banquet Gian Galeazzo, the bride's brother, leading a choice company of well-born youths, brought to the table with each course fresh gifts.[2] 'At one time it was a matter of sixty most beautiful horses with trappings of silk and silver ; at another, plate, hawks, hounds, horse-gear, fine cuirasses, suits of armour fashioned of wrought steel, helmets adorned with crests, surcoats embroidered with pearls, belts, precious jewels set in gold, and great quantities of cloth of gold and crimson stuff for making raiment. Such was the profusion of this banquet that the remnants taken from the table were enough and to spare for 10,000 men.' Petrarch, we may remember, assisted at this festival and sat among the princes. It was

---

[1] Namely, Alba, Cuneo, Carastra, Mondovico, Braida. See Corio, p. 238, who adds sententiously, ' il che quasi fu l' ultima roina del suo stato.'

[2] Corio (pp. 239, 240) gives the bill of fare of the banquet.

thus that Galeazzo displayed his wealth before the feudal nobles of the North, and at the same time stretched the hand of friendly patronage to the greatest literary man of Europe. Meanwhile he also married his son Gian Galeazzo to Isabella, daughter of King John of France, spending on this occasion, it is said, a similar sum of money for the honour of a royal alliance.[1]

Galeazzo held his court at Pavia. His brother reigned at Milan. Bernabo displayed all the worst vices of the Visconti. His system of taxation was most oppressive, and at the same time so lucrative that he was able, according to Giovio's estimate, to settle nine of his daughters at the expense of something like two millions of gold pieces. A curious instance of his tyranny relates to his hunting establishment. Having saddled his subjects with the keep of 5,000 boarhounds, he appointed officers to go round and see whether these brutes were either too lean or too well-fed to be in good condition for the chase. If anything appeared defective in their management, the peasants on whom they were quartered had to suffer in their persons and their property.[2] This Bernabo was also

[1] Sismondi says he gave 600,000 florins to Charles, the brother of Isabella, but authorities differ about the actual amount.

[2] 'Per cagione di questa caccia continoamente teneva cinque mila cani, e la maggior parte di quelle distribuiva alla custodia de i cittadini, e anche a i contadini, i quali niun altro cane che quelli potevano tenere. Questi due volte il mese erano tenuti a far la mostra. Onde trovandoli macri in gran somma di danari erano condannati, e se grossi erano, incolpandoli del troppo, erano multati; se morivano, li pigliava il tutto.' —Corio, p. 247.

Read M. Villani, vii. 48, for the story of a peasant who was given to Bernabo's dogs to be devoured for having killed a hare. Corio (p. 247) describes the punishments which he inflicted on his subjects who were convicted of poaching—eyes put out, houses burned, &c. A young man who dreamed of killing a boar had an eye put out and a hand cut off because he imprudently recounted his vision of sport in sleep. On one occasion he burned two friars who ventured to remonstrate. We may compare Pontanus, *De Immanitate*, vol. i. pp. 318, 320, for similar cruelty in Ferdinand, King of Naples.

remarkable for his cold-blooded cruelty. Together with his brother, he devised and caused to be publicly announced by edict that State criminals would be subjected to a series of tortures extending over the space of forty days. In this infernal programme every variety of torment found a place, and days of respite were so calculated as to prolong the lives of the victims for further suffering, till at last there was little left of them that had not been hacked and hewed and flayed away.[1] To such extremities of terrorism were the Despots driven in the maintenance of their illegal power.

Galeazzo died in 1378, and was succeeded in his own portion of the Visconti domain by his son Gian Galeazzo. Now began one of those long, slow, internecine struggles which were so common between the members of the ruling families in Italy. Bernabo and his sons schemed to get possession of the young prince's estate. He, on the other hand, determined to supplant his uncle, and to reunite the whole Visconti principality beneath his own sway. Craft was the weapon which he chose in this encounter. Shutting himself up in Pavia, he made no disguise of his physical cowardice, which was real, while he simulated a timidity of spirit wholly alien to his temperament. He pretended to be absorbed in religious observances, and gradually induced his uncle and cousins to despise him as a poor creature whom they could make short work of when occasion served. In 1385, having thus prepared the way for treason, he avowed his intention of proceeding on a pilgrimage to Our Lady of Varese. Starting from Pavia with a body-guard of Germans, he passed near Milan, where his uncle and cousins came forth to meet him. Gian Galeazzo feigned a courteous greeting; but when he saw his relatives within his grasp, he gave a watchword in German to his troops, who surrounded Bernabo and took him prisoner with his sons. Gian Galeazzo marched

[1] This programme may be read in Sismondi, iv. 282.

immediately into Milan, poisoned his uncle in a dungeon, and proclaimed himself sole lord of the Visconti heirship.[1]

The reign of Gian Galeazzo, which began with this coup-de-main (1385–1402), forms a very important chapter in Italian history. We may first see what sort of man he was, and then proceed to trace his aims and achievements. Giovio describes him as having been a remarkably sedate and thoughtful boy, so wise beyond his years that his friends feared he would not grow to man's estate. No pleasures in after-life drew him away from business. Hunting, hawking, women, had alike no charms for him. He took moderate exercise for the preservation of his health, read and meditated much, and relaxed himself in conversation with men of letters. Pure intellect, in fact, had reached to perfect independence in this prince, who was far above the boisterous pleasures and violent activities of the age in which he lived. In the erection of public buildings he was magnificent. The Certosa of Pavia and the Duomo of Milan owed their foundation to his sense of splendour. At the same time he completed the palace of Pavia, which his father had begun, and which he made the noblest dwelling-house in Europe. The University of Pavia was raised by him from a state of decadence to one of great prosperity, partly by munificent endowments and partly by a wise choice of professors. In his military undertakings he displayed a kindred taste for vast engineering projects. He contemplated and partly carried out a scheme for turning the Mincio and the Brenta from their channels, and for drying up the lagoons of Venice. In this way he purposed to attack his last great enemy, the Republic of S. Mark, upon her strongest point. Yet in the midst of these huge designs he was able to attend to the most trifling details of economy. His love of order was so precise that he may be said to have

[1] The narrative of this coup-de-main may be read with advantage in Corio, p. 258.

applied the method of a banker's office to the conduct of a
state. It was he who invented Bureaucracy by creating a
special class of paid clerks and secretaries of departments.
Their duty consisted in committing to books and ledgers the
minutest items of his private expenditure and the outgoings
of his public purse ; in noting the details of the several taxes,
so as to be able to present a survey of the whole state
revenue ; and in recording the names and qualities and claims
of his generals, captains, and officials. A separate office was
devoted to his correspondence, of all of which he kept accurate copies.[1] By applying this mercantile machinery to the
management of his vast dominions, at a time when public
economy was but little understood in Europe, Gian Galeazzo
raised his wealth enormously above that of his neighbours.
His income in a single year is said to have amounted to
1,200,000 golden florins, with the addition of 800,000 golden
florins levied by extraordinary calls.[2] The personal timidity
of this formidable prince prevented him from leading his
armies in the field. He therefore found it necessary to employ
paid generals, and took into his service all the chief Condottieri of the day, thus giving an impulse to the custom
which was destined to corrupt the whole military system of
Italy. Of these men, whom he well knew how to choose,
he was himself the brain and moving principle. He

[1] Giovio is particular upon these points : ' Ho veduto io ne gli armari
de' suoi Archivi maravigliosi libri in carta pecora, i quali contenevano
d' anno in anno i nomi de' capitani, condottieri, e soldati vecchi, e le
paghe di ogn' uno, e 'l rotulo delle cavallerie, et delle fanterie : v' erano
anco registrate le copie delle lettere le quali negli importantissimi
maneggi di far guerra o pace, o egli haveva scritto ai principi o haveva
ricevuto da loro.'

[2] The description given by Corio (pp. 260, 266-68) of the dower in
money, plate, and jewels brought by Valentina Visconti to Louis
d'Orléans is a good proof of Gian Galeazzo's wealth. Besides the town
of Asti, she took with her in money 400,000 golden florins. Her gems
were estimated at 68,858 florins, and her plate at 1,667 marks of Paris.
The inventory is curious.

might have boasted that he never took a step without calculating the cost, carefully considering the object, and pro-
portioning the means to his end. How mad to such a man
must have seemed the Crusaders of previous centuries, or
the chivalrous Princes of Northern Germany and Burgundy,
who expended their force upon such unprofitable and
impossible undertakings as the subjugation, for instance, of
Switzerland! Not a single trait in his character reminds us
of the Middle Ages, unless it be that he was said to care for
reliques with a superstitious passion worthy of Louis XI.
Sismondi sums up the description of this extraordinary Despot
in the following sentences, which may be quoted for their
graphic brevity : 'False and pitiless, he joined to immeasurable
ambition a genius for enterprise, and to immovable constancy
a personal timidity which he did not endeavour to conceal.
The least unexpected motion near him threw him into a
paroxysm of nervous terror. No prince employed so many
soldiers to guard his palace, or took such multiplied precautions of distrust. He seemed to acknowledge himself the
enemy of the whole world. But the vices of tyranny had not
weakened his ability. He employed his immense wealth without prodigality; his finances were always flourishing; his cities
well garrisoned and victualled; his army well paid; all the
captains of adventure scattered throughout Italy received
pensions from him, and were ready to return to his service
whenever called upon. He encouraged the warriors of the
new Italian school ; he knew well how to distinguish, reward,
and win their attachment.'[1] Such was the tyrant who aimed
at nothing less than the reduction of the whole of Italy
beneath the sway of the Visconti, and who might have
achieved his purpose had not his career of conquest been
checked by the Republic of Florence, and afterwards cut short
by a premature death.

[1] *History of the Italian Republics* (1 vol. Longmans), p. 190.

At the time of his accession the Visconti had already rooted
out the Correggi and Rossi of Parma, the Scotti of Piacenza,
the Pelavicini of San Donnino, the Tornielli of Novara, the
Ponzoni and Cavalcabò of Cremona, the Beccaria and
Languschi of Pavia, the Fisiraghi of Lodi, the Brusati of
Brescia. Their viper had swallowed all these lesser snakes.[1]
But the Carrara family still ruled at Padua, the Gonzaga at
Mantua, the Este at Ferrara, while the great house of Scala
was in possession of Verona. Gian Galeazzo's schemes were
first directed against the Scala dynasty. Founded, like that
of the Visconti, upon the imperial authority, it rose to its
greatest height under the Ghibelline general Can Grande and
his nephew Mastino in the first half of the fourteenth century
(1312–51). Mastino had himself cherished the project of an
Italian Kingdom ; but he died before approaching its accomplishment. The degeneracy of his house began with his three
sons. The two younger killed the eldest ; of the survivors the
stronger slew the weaker and then died in 1374, leaving his
domains to two of his bastards. One of these, named Antonio,
killed the other in 1381,[2] and afterwards fell a prey to
the Visconti in 1387. In his subjugation of Verona Gian
Galeazzo contrived to make use of the Carrara family, although
these princes were allied by marriage to the Scaligers, and
had everything to lose by their downfall. He next proceeded
to attack Padua, and gained the co-operation of Venice. In
1388 Francesco da Carrara had to cede his territory to
Visconti's generals, who in the same year possessed themselves
for him of the Trevisan Marches. It was then that the
Venetians saw too late the error they had committed in

[1] Il Biscione, or the Great Serpent, was the name commonly given
to the tyranny of the Visconti (see M. Villani, vi. 8). in allusion to their
ensign of a naked child issuing from a snake's mouth.

[2] Corio, p. 255, tells how the murder was accomplished. Antonio
tried to make it appear that his brother Bartolommeo had met his death
in the prosecution of infamous amours.

suffering Verona and Padua to be annexed by the Visconti, when they ought to have been fortified as defences interposed between his growing power and themselves. Having now made himself master of the North of Italy,[1] with the exception of Mantua, Ferrara, and Bologna, Gian Galeazzo turned his attention to these cities. Alberto d' Este was ruling in Ferrara ; Francesco da Gonzaga in Mantua. It was the Visconti's policy to enfeeble these two princes by causing them to appear odious in the eyes of their subjects.[2] Accordingly he roused the jealousy of the Marquis of Ferrara against his nephew Obizzo to such a pitch that Alberto beheaded him together with his mother, burned his wife, and hung a third member of his family, besides torturing to death all the supposed accomplices of the unfortunate young man. Against the Marquis of Mantua Gian Galeazzo devised a still more diabolical plot. By forged letters and subtly contrived incidents he caused Francesco da Gonzaga to suspect his wife of infidelity with his secretary.[3] In a fit of jealous fury Francesco ordered the execution of his wife, the mother of several of his children, together with the secretary. Then he discovered the Visconti's treason. But it was too late for anything but impotent hatred. The infernal device had been successful ; the Marquis of Mantua was no less discredited than

[1] Savoy was not in his hands, however, and the Marquisate of Montferrat remained nominally independent, though he held its heir in a kind of honourable confinement. Venice, too, remained in formidable neutrality, the spectator of the Visconti's conquests.

[2] The policy adopted by the Visconti against the Estensi and the Gonzaghi was that recommended by Machiavelli (*Disc.* iii. 32): ' quando alcuno vuole o che un popolo o un principe levi al tutto l' animo ad uno accordo, non ci è altro modo più vero, nè più stabile, che fargli usare qualche grave sceleratezza contro a colui con il qual tu non vuoi che l' accordo si faccia.'

[3] This lady was a first cousin as well as sister-in-law of Gian Galeazzo Visconti, who in second marriage had taken Caterina, daughter of Bernabo Visconti, to wife. This fact makes his perfidy the more disgraceful.

the Marquis of Ferrara by his crime. It would seem that these men were not of the stamp and calibre to be successful villains, and that Gian Galeazzo had reckoned upon this defect in their character. Their violence caused them to be rather loathed than feared. The whole of Lombardy was now prostrate before the Milanese tyrant. His next move was to set foot in Tuscany. For this purpose Pisa had to be acquired; and here again he resorted to his devilish policy of inciting other men to crimes by which he alone would profit in the long run. Pisa was ruled at that time by the Gambacorta family, with an old merchant named Pietro at their head. This man had a friend and secretary called Jacopo Appiano, whom the Visconti persuaded to turn Judas, and to entrap and murder his benefactor and his children. The assassination took place in 1392. In 1399 Gherardo, son of Jacopo Appiano, who held Pisa at the disposal of Gian Galeazzo, sold him this city for 200,000 florins.[1] Perugia was next attacked. Here Pandolfo, chief of the Baglioni family, held a semi-constitutional authority, which the Visconti first helped him to transmute into a tyranny, and then, upon Pandolfo's assassination, seized as his own.[2] All Italy and even Germany had now begun to regard the usurpations of the Milanese Despot with alarm. But the sluggish Emperor Wenceslaus refused to take action against him; nay, in 1395 he granted to the Visconti the investiture of the

[1] The Appiani retired to Piombino, where they founded a petty despotism. Appiano's crime, which gave a tyranny to his children, is similar to that of Tremacoldo, who murdered his masters, the Vistarini of Lodi, and to that of Luigi Gonzaga, who founded the Ducal house of Mantua by the murder of his patron, Passerino Buonacolsi..

[2] Pandolfo was murdered in 1393. Gian Galeazzo possessed himself of Perugia in 1400, having paved his way for the usurpation by causing Biordo Michelotti, the successor of the Baglioni, to be assassinated by his friend Francesco Guidalotti. It will be noticed that he proceeded slowly and surely in the case of each annexation, licking over his prey after he had throttled it and before he swallowed it, like a boa-constrictor.

Duchy of Milan for 100,000 florins, reserving only Pavia for himself. In 1399 the Duke laid hands on Siena ; and in the next two years the plague came to his assistance by enfeebling the ruling families of Lucca and Bologna, the Guinizzi and the Bentivogli, so that he was now able to take possession of those cities.

There remained no power in Italy, except the Republic of Florence and the exiled but invincible Francesco da Carrara, to withstand his further progress. Florence delayed his conquests in Tuscany. Francesco managed to return to Padua. Still the peril which threatened the whole of Italy was imminent. The Duke of Milan was in the plenitude of manhood—rich, prosperous, and full of mental force. His acquisitions were well cemented ; his armies in good condition ; his treasury brim full ; his generals highly paid. All his lieutenants in city and in camp respected the iron will and the deep policy of the despot who swayed their action from his arm-chair in Milan. He alone knew how to use the brains and hands that did him service, to keep them mutually in check, and by their regulated action to make himself not one but a score of men. At last, when all other hope of independence for Italy had failed, the plague broke out with fury in Lombardy. Gian Galeazzo retired to his isolated fortress of Marignano in order to escape infection. Yet there in 1402 he sickened. A comet appeared in the sky, to which he pointed as a sign of his approaching death—'God could not but signalise the end of so supreme a ruler,' he told his attendants. He died aged 55. Italy drew a deep breath. The danger was passed.

The systematic plan conceived by Gian Galeazzo for the enslavement of Italy, the ability and force of intellect which sustained him in its execution, and the power with which he bent men to his will, are scarcely more extraordinary than the sudden dissolution of his dukedom at his death. Too timid to take the field himself, he had trained in his service a band of great commanders, among whom Alberico da Barbiano, Facino Cane, Pandolfo Malatesta, Jacopo dal Verme, Gabrino Fondulo, and Ottobon Terzo were the most distinguished. As long as he lived and held them in leading strings, all went well. But at his death his two sons were still mere boys. He had to entrust their persons, together with the conduct of his hardly won dominions, to these captains in conjunction with the Duchess Catherine and a certain Francesco Barbavara. This man had been the Duke's body-servant, and was now the paramour of the Duchess. The generals refused to act with them; and each seized upon such portions of the Visconti inheritance as he could most easily acquire. The vast tyranny of the first Duke of Milan fell to pieces in a day. The whole being based on no legal right, but held together artificially by force and skill, its constituent parts either reasserted their independence or became the prey of adventurers.[1] Many scions of the old ejected families recovered their authority in the subject towns. We hear again of the Scotti at Piacenza, the Rossi and Correggi at Parma, the Benzoni at Crema, the Rusconi at Como, the Soardi and Colleoni at Bergamo, the Landi at Bòbbio, the Cavalcabò at Cremona. Facino Cane appropriated Alessandria; Pandolfo Malatesta seized Brescia; Ottobon Terzo established himself in Parma. Meanwhile Giovanni Maria Visconti was proclaimed Duke of Milan, and his brother Filippo Maria occupied Pavia. Gabriello, a bastard son of the first Duke, fortified himself in Crema.

In the despotic families of Italy, as already hinted, there was a progressive tendency to degeneration. The strain of tyranny sustained by force and craft for generations, the

---

[1] The anarchy which prevailed in Lombardy after Gian Galeazzo's death makes it difficult to do more than signalise a few of these usurpations. Corio, pp. 292 et seq., contains the details.

abuse of power and pleasure, the isolation and the dread in which the despots lived habitually, bred a kind of hereditary madness.[1] In the case of Giovanni Maria and Filippo Maria Visconti these predisposing causes of insanity were probably intensified by the fact that their father and mother were first cousins, the grandchildren of Stefano, son of Matteo il Grande. Be this as it may, the constitutional ferocity of the race appeared as monomania in Giovanni, and its constitutional timidity as something akin to madness in his brother. Gian Maria, Duke of Milan in nothing but in name, distinguished himself by cruelty and lust. He used the hounds of his ancestors no longer in the chase of boars, but of living men. All the criminals of Milan, and all whom he could get denounced as criminals, even the participators in his own enormities, were given up to his infernal sport. His huntsman, Squarcia Giramo, trained the dogs to their duty by feeding them on human flesh, and the Duke watched them tear his victims in pieces with the avidity of a lunatic.[2] In 1412 some Milanese nobles succeeded in murdering him, and threw his mangled corpse into the street. A prostitute is said to have covered it with roses. Filippo Maria meanwhile had married the widow of Facino Cane,[3] who brought him nearly half a million of florins for dowry, together with her husband's

[1] I may refer to Dr. Maudesley (*Mind and Matter*) for a scientific statement of the theory of madness developed by accumulated and hereditary vices.

[2] Corio, p. 301, mentions by name Giovanni da Pusterla and Bertolino del Maino as 'lacerati da i cani del Duca.' Members of the families of these men afterwards helped to kill him.

[3] Beatrice di Tenda, the wife of Facino Cane, was twenty years older than the Duke of Milan. As soon as the Visconti felt himself assured in his duchy, he caused a false accusation to be brought against her of adultery with the youthful Michele Oranbelli, and, in spite of her innocence, beheaded her in 1418. Machiavelli relates this act of perfidy with Tacitean conciseness (*Ist. Fior.* lib. i. vol. i. p. 55): 'Dipoi per esser grato de' benefici grandi, come sono quasi sempre tutti i Principi, accusò Beatrice sua moglie di stupro e la fece morire.'

soldiers and the cities he had seized after Gian Galeazzo's death. By the help of this alliance Filippo was now gradually recovering the Lombard portion of his father's dukedom. The minor cities, purged by murder of their usurpers, once more fell into the grasp of the Milanese Despot, after a series of domestic and political tragedies that drenched their streets with blood. Piacenza was utterly depopulated. It is recorded that for the space of a year only three of its inhabitants remained within the walls.

Filippo, the last of the Visconti tyrants, was extremely ugly, and so sensitive about his ill-formed person that he scarcely dared to show himself abroad. He habitually lived in secret chambers, changed frequently from room to room, and when he issued from his palace refused salutations in the streets. As an instance of his nervousness, the chroniclers report that he could not endure to hear the noise of thunder.[1] At the same time he inherited much of his father's insight into character, and his power of controlling men more bold and active than himself. But he lacked the keen decision and broad views of Gian Galeazzo. He vacillated in policy and kept planning plots which seemed to have no object but his own disadvantage. Excess of caution made him surround the captains of his troops with spies, and check them at the moment when he feared they might become too powerful. This want of confidence neutralised the advantage which he might have gained by his choice of fitting instruments. Thus his selection of Francesco Sforza for his general against the Venetians in 1431 was a wise one. But he could not attach the great soldier of fortune to himself. Sforza took the pay

[1] The most complete account of Filippo Maria Visconti written by a contemporary is that of Piero Candilo Decembrio (Muratori, vol. xx.). The student must, however, read between the lines of this biography, for Decembrio, at the request of Leonello d'Este, suppressed the darker colours of the portrait of his master. See the correspondence in Rosmini's Life of Guarino da Verona.

of Florence against his old patron, and in 1441 forced him to a ruinous peace; one of the conditions of which was the marriage of the Duke of Milan's only daughter, Bianca, to the son of the peasant of Cotignola. Bianca was illegitimate, and Filippo Maria had no male heir. The great family of the Visconti had dwindled away. Consequently, after the Duke's death in 1447, Sforza found his way open to the Duchy of Milan, which he first secured by force and then claimed in right of his wife. An adverse claim was set up by the House of Orleans, Louis of Orleans having married Valentina, the legitimate daughter of Gian Galeazzo.[1] But both of these claims were invalid, since the investiture granted by Wenceslaus to the first duke excluded females. So Milan was once again thrown open to the competition of usurpers.

The inextinguishable desire for liberty in Milan blazed forth upon the death of the last duke. In spite of so many generations of Despots, the people still regarded themselves as sovereign, and established a republic. But a state which had served the Visconti for nearly two centuries, could not in a moment shake off its weakness and rely upon itself alone. The republic, feeling the necessity of mercenary aid, was short-sighted enough to engage Francesco Sforza as commander-in-chief against the Venetians, who had availed themselves of the anarchy in Lombardy to push their power west of the Adda.

Sforza, though the ablest general of the day, was

[1] This claim of the House of Orleans to Milan was one source of French interference in Italian affairs. Judged by Italian custom, Sforza's claim through Bianca was as good as that of the Orleans princes through Valentina, since bastardy was no real bar in the peninsula. It is said that Filippo Maria bequeathed his duchy to the Crown of Naples, by a will destroyed after his death. Could this bequest have taken effect, it might have united Italy beneath one sovereign. But the probabilities are that the jealousies of Florence, Venice, and Rome against Naples would have been so intensified as to lead to a bloody war of succession, and to hasten the French invasion.

precisely the man whom common prudence should have prompted the burghers to mistrust. In one brilliant campaign he drove the Venetians back beyond the Adda, burned their fleet at Casal Maggiore on the Po, and utterly defeated their army at Caravaggio. Then he returned as conqueror to Milan, reduced the surrounding cities, blockaded the Milanese in their capital, and forced them to receive him as their Duke in 1450. Italy had lost a noble opportunity. If Florence and Venice had but taken part with Milan, and had stimulated the flagging energies of Genoa, four powerful republics in federation might have maintained the freedom of the whole peninsula and have resisted foreign interference. But Cosimo de' Medici, who was silently founding the despotism of his own family in Florence, preferred to see a duke in Milan ; and Venice, guided by the Doge Francesco Foscari, thought only of territorial aggrandisement. The chance was lost. The liberties of Milan were extinguished. A new dynasty was established in the duchy, grounded on a false hereditary claim, which, as long as it continued, gave a sort of colour to the superior but still illegal pretensions of the house of Orleans. It is impossible at this point in the history of Italy to refrain from judging that the Italians had become incapable of local self-government, and that the prevailing tendency to despotism was not the result of accidents in any combination, but of internal and inevitable laws of evolution.

It was at this period that the old despotisms founded by Imperial Vicars and Captains of the People came to be supplanted or crossed by those of military adventurers, just as at a somewhat later time the Condottiere and the Pope's nominee were blent in Cesare Borgia. This is therefore the proper moment for glancing at the rise and influence of mercenary generals in Italy, before proceeding to sketch the history of the Sforza family.

After the wars in Sicily, carried on by the Angevine princes, had ceased (1302), a body of disbanded soldiers, chiefly foreigners, was formed under Fra Ruggieri, a Templar, and swept the South of Italy. Giovanni Villani marks this as the first sign of the scourge which was destined to prove so fatal to the peace of Italy.[1] But it was not any merely accidental outbreak of Banditti, such as this, which established the Condottiere system. The causes were far more deeply seated, in the nature of Italian despotism and in the peculiar requirements of the republics. We have already seen how Frederick II. found it convenient to employ Saracens in his warfare with the Holy See. The same desire to procure troops incapable of sympathising with the native population induced the Scala and Visconti tyrants to hire German, Breton, Swiss, English, and even Hungarian guards. These foreign troops remained at the disposal of the tyrants and superseded the national militia. The people of Italy were reserved for taxation; the foreigners carried on the wars of the princes. Nor was this policy otherwise than popular. It relieved all classes from the conscription, leaving the burgher free to ply his trade, the peasant to till his fields, and disarming the nobles who were still rebellious and turbulent within the city walls. The same custom gained ground among the Republics. Rich Florentine citizens preferred to stay at home at ease, or to travel abroad for commerce, while they entrusted their military operations to paid generals.[2] Venice, jealous of her own citizens, raised no levies in her immediate territory, and made a rule of never confiding her armies to Venetians. Her admirals,

[1] VIII. 51.
[2] We may remember how the Spanish general Cardona, in 1325, mis-used his captaincy of the Florentine forces to keep rich members of the republican militia in unhealthy stations, extorting money from them as the price of freedom from perilous or irksome service.

Indeed, were selected from the great families of the Lagoons. But her troops were placed beneath the discipline of foreigners. The warfare of the Church, again, had of necessity to be conducted on the same principles ; for it did not often happen that a Pope arose like Julius II., rejoicing in the sound of cannon and the life of camps. In this way principalities and republics gradually denationalised their armies, and came to carrying on campaigns by the aid of foreign mercenaries under paid commanders. The generals, wishing as far as possible to render their troops movable and compact, suppressed the infantry, and confined their attention to perfecting the cavalry. Heavy-armed cavaliers, officered by professional captains, fought the battles of Italy ; while despots and republics schemed in their castles, or debated in their council-chambers, concerning objects of warfare about which the soldiers of fortune were indifferent. The pay received by men-at-arms was more considerable than that of the most skilled labourers in any peaceful trade. The perils of military service in Italy, conducted on the most artificial principles, were but slight ; while the opportunities of self-indulgence— of pillage during war and of pleasure in the brief intervals of peace—attracted all the hot blood of the country to this service.[1] Therefore, in course of time, the profession of Condottieri fascinated the needier nobility of Italy, and the ranks of their men-at-arms were recruited by townsfolk and peasants, who deliberately chose a life of adventure.

At first the foreign troops of the despots were engaged as body-guards, and were controlled by the authority of their employers. But the captains soon rendered themselves

---

[1] Matarazzo, in his Chronicle of Perugia, gives a lively picture of an Italian city, in which the nobles for generations followed the trade of Condottieri, while the people enlisted in their bands—to the utter ruin of the morals and the peace of the community.

independent, and entered into military contracts on their own account. The first notable example of a roving troop existing for the sake of pillage, and selling its services to any bidder, was the so-called Great Company (1343), commanded by the German Guarnieri, or Duke Werner, who wrote upon his corslet : 'Enemy of God, of Pity, and of Mercy.' This band was employed in 1348 by the league of the Montferrat, La Scala, Carrara, Este, and Gonzaga houses, formed to check the Visconti.

'In the middle of the fourteenth century,' writes Sismondi,[1] 'all the soldiers who served in Italy were foreigners : at the end of the same century they were all, or nearly all, Italian.' This sentence indicates a most important change in the Condottiere system, which took place during the lifetime of Gian Galeazzo Visconti. Alberico da Barbiano, a noble of Romagna, and the ancestor of the Milanese house of Belgiojoso, adopted the career of Condottiere, and formed a Company, called the Company of S. George, into which he admitted none but Italians. The consequence of this rule was that he Italianised the profession of mercenary arms for the future. All the great captains of the period were formed in his ranks, during the course of those wars which he conducted for the Duke of Milan. Two rose to paramount importance —Braccio da Montone, who varied his master's system by substituting the tactics of detached bodies of cavalry for the solid phalanx in which Barbiano had moved his troops ; and Sforza Attendolo, who adhered to the old method. Sforza got his name from his great physical strength. He was a peasant of the village of Cotignola, who, being invited to quit the mattock for a sword, threw his pickaxe into an oak, and cried, 'If it stays there, it is a sign that I shall make my fortune.' The axe stuck in the tree and Sforza went forth to found a line of dukes.[1] After the death of Barbiano in 1409, Sforza and Braccio separated and formed two distinct companies, known as the Sforzeschi and Bracceschi, who carried on between them, sometimes in combination, but usually in opposition, all the wars of Italy for the next twenty years. These old comrades, who had parted in pursuit of their several advantage, found that they had more to lose than to gain by defeating each other in any bloody or inconveniently decisive engagement. Therefore they adopted systems of campaigning which should cost them as little as possible, but which enabled them to exhibit a chess-player's capacity for designing clever checkmates.[2] Both Braccio and Sforza died in 1424, and were succeeded respectively by Nicolo Piccinino and Francesco Sforza. These two men became in their turn the chief champions of Italy. At the same time other Condottieri rose into notice. The Malatesta family at Rimini, the ducal house of Urbino, the Orsini and the Vitelli of the Roman

[1] This is the commonly received legend. Corio, p. 255, does not draw attention to the lowness of Sforza's origin, but says that he was only twelve years of age when he enlisted in the corps of Boldrino di Panigale, condottiere of the Church. His robust physical qualities were hereditary for many generations in his family. His son Francesco was tall and well made, the best runner, jumper, and wrestler of his day. He marched, summer and winter, bareheaded ; needed but little sleep ; was spare in diet, and self-indulgent only in the matter of women. Galeazzo Maria, though stained by despicable vices, was a powerful prince, who ruled his duchy with a strong arm. Of his illegitimate daughter, Caterina, the wife of Girolamo Riario, a story is told, which illustrates the strong coarse vein that still distinguished this brood of princes. [See Dennistoun, *Dukes of Urbino*, vol. i. p. 292, for Boccalini's account of the Siege of Forli, sustained by Caterina in 1488. Compare Sismondi, vol. vii. p. 251.] Caterina Riario Sforza, as a woman, was no unworthy inheritor of her grandfather's personal heroism and genius for government.

[2] I shall have to notice the evils of this system in another place, while reviewing the *Principe* of Machiavelli. In that treatise the Florentine historian traces the whole ruin of Italy during the sixteenth century to the employment of mercenaries.

States, the Varani of Camerino, the Baglioni of Perugia, and the younger Gonzaghi furnished republics and princes with professional leaders of tried skill and independent resources The vassals of these noble houses were turned into men-at-arms, and the chiefs acquired more importance in their roving military life than they could have gained within the narrow circuit of their little states.

The biography of one of these Condottieri deserves special notice, since it illustrates the vicissitudes of fortune to which such men were exposed, as well as their relations to their patrons. Francesco Carmagnuola was a Piedmontese. He first rose into notice at the battle of Monza in 1412, when Filippo Maria Visconti observed his capacity and bravery, and afterwards advanced him to the captaincy of a troop. Having helped to reduce the Visconti duchy to order, Carmagnuola found himself disgraced and suspected without good reason by the Duke of Milan; and in 1426 he took the pay of the Venetians against his old master. During the next year he showed the eminence of his abilities as a general; for he defeated the combined forces of Piccinino, Sforza, and other captains of the Visconti, and took them prisoners at Macalo. Carmagnuola neither imprisoned nor murdered his foes.[1] He

[1] Such an act of violence, however consistent with the morality of a Cesare Borgia, a Venetian Republic, or a Duke of Milan, would have been directly opposed to the code of honour in use among Condottieri. Nothing, indeed, is more singular among the contradictions of this period than the humanity in the field displayed by hired captains. War was made less on adverse armies than on the population of provinces. The adventurers respected each other's lives, and treated each other with courtesy. They were a brotherhood who played at campaigning, rather than the representatives of forces seriously bent on crushing each other to extermination. Machiavelli says (*Princ.* cap. xii.) 'Aveano usato ogni industria per levar via a se e a' soldati la fatica e la paura, non s' ammazzando nelle zuffe, ma pigliandosi prigioni e senza taglia.' At the same time the license they allowed themselves against the cities and the districts they invaded is well illustrated by the pillage of Piacenza in 1447 by Francesco Sforza's troops. The anarchy of a sack lasted forty

gave them their liberty, and four years later had to sustain a defeat from Sforza at Soncino. Other reverses of fortune followed, which brought upon him the suspicion of bad faith or incapacity. When he returned to Venice, the state received their captain with all honours, and displayed unusual pomp in his admission to the audience of the Council. But no sooner had their velvet clutches closed upon him, than they threw him into prison, instituted a secret impeachment of his conduct, and on May 5, 1432, led him out with his mouth gagged to execution on the Piazza. No reason was assigned for this judicial murder. Had Carmagnuola been convicted of treason? Was he being punished for his ill success in the campaign of the preceding years? The Republic of Venice, by the secresy in which she enveloped this dark act of vengeance, sought to inspire the whole body of her officials with vague alarm.

But to return to the Duchy of Milan. Francesco Sforza entered the capital as conqueror in 1450, and was proclaimed Duke. He never obtained the sanction of the Empire to his title, though Frederick III. was proverbially lavish of such honours. But the great Condottiere, possessing the substance, did not care for the external show of monarchy. He ruled firmly, wisely, and for those times well, attending to the prosperity of his states, maintaining good discipline in his cities, and losing no ground by foolish or ambitious schemes. Louis XI. of France is said to have professed himself Sforza's pupil in statecraft, than which no greater tribute could be paid to his political sagacity. In 1466 he died, leaving three sons, Galeazzo, Duke of Milan, the Cardinal Ascanio, and Lodovico, surnamed Il Moro.

'Francesco's crown,' says Ripamonti, 'was destined to pass to more than six inheritors, and these five successions

days, during which the inhabitants were indiscriminately sold as slaves, or tortured for their hidden treasure. Sism. vi. 170.

were accomplished by a series of tragic events in his family. Galeazzo, his son, was murdered because of his abominable crimes, in the presence of his people, before the altar, in the middle of the sacred rites. Giovanni Galeazzo, who followed him, was poisoned by his uncle Lodovico. Lodovico was imprisoned by the French, and died of grief in a dungeon.[1] One of his sons perished in the same way; the other, after years of misery and exile, was restored in his childless old age to a throne which had been undermined, and when he died, his dynasty was extinct. This was the recompense for the treason of Francesco to the State of Milan. It was for such successes that he passed his life in perfidy, privation, and danger.' In these rapid successions we trace, besides the demoralisation of the Sforza family, the action of new forces from without. France, Germany, and Spain appeared upon the stage ; and against these great powers the policy of Italian despotism was helpless.

We have now reached the threshold of the true Renaissance, and a new period is being opened for Italian politics. The despots are about to measure their strength with the nations of the North. It was Lodovico Sforza who, by his invitation of Charles VIII. into Italy, inaugurated the age of Foreign Enslavement. His biography belongs, therefore, to another chapter. But the life of Galeazzo Maria, husband of Bona of Savoy, and uncle by marriage to Charles VIII. of France, forms an integral part of that history of the Milanese Despots which we have hitherto been tracing. In him the passions of Gian Maria Visconti were repeated with the addition of extravagant vanity. We may notice in particular his parade-expedition in 1471 to Florence, when he flaunted the wealth

---

[1] In the castle of Loches, there is said to be a roughly painted wall-picture of a man in a helmet over the chimney in the room known as his prison, with this legend, *Voilà un qui n'est pas content.* Tradition gives it to Il Moro.

extorted from his Milanese subjects before the sober-minded citizens of a still free city. Fifty palfreys for the Duchess, fifty chargers for the Duke, trapped in cloth of gold; a hundred men-at-arms and five hundred foot soldiers for a body-guard ; five hundred couples of hounds and a multitude of hawks; preceded him. His suite of courtiers numbered two thousand on horseback : 200,000 golden florins were expended on this pomp. Machiavelli ('Ist. Fior.' lib. 7) marks this visit of the Duke of Milan as a turning-point from austere simplicity to luxury and license in the manners of the Florentines, whom Lorenzo de' Medici was already bending to his yoke. The most extravagant lust, the meanest and the vilest cruelty, supplied Galeazzo Maria with daily recreation.[1] He it was who used to feed his victims on abominations or to bury them alive, and who found a pleasure in wounding or degrading those whom he had made his confidants and friends. The details of his assassination, in 1476, though well known, are so interesting that I may be excused for pausing to repeat them here ; especially as they illustrate a moral characteristic of this period which is intimately connected with despotism. Three young nobles of Milan, educated in the classic literature by Montano, a distinguished Bolognese scholar, had imbibed from their studies of Greek and Latin history an ardent thirst for liberty and a deadly hatred of tyrants.[2] Their names were Carlo Visconti, Girolamo Olgiati, and Giannandrea Lampugnani. Galeazzo Sforza had wounded the two latter in the points which men hold dearest—their honour and

[1] Allegretto Allegretti, Diari Sanesi, in Muratori, xxiii. p. 777, and Corio, p. 425, should be read for the details of his pleasures. See too his character by Machiavelli, Ist. Fior. lib. 7, vol. ii. p. 316. Yet Giovio calls him a just and firm ruler, stained only with the vice of unbridled sensuality.

[2] The study of the classics, especially of Plutarch, at this time, as also during the French Revolution, fired the imagination of patriots. Lorenzino de' Medici appealed to the example of Timoleon in 1537, and Pietro Paolo Boscoli to that of Brutus in 1513.

their property [1]—by outraging the sister of Olgiati and by depriving Lampugnani of the patronage of the Abbey of Miramondo. The spirit of Harmodius and Virginius was kindled in the friends, and they determined to rid Milan of her Despot. After some meetings in the garden of S. Ambrogio, where they matured their plans, they laid their project of tyrannicide as a holy offering before the patron saint of Milan.[2] Then having spent a few days in poignard exercise for the sake of training,[3] they took their place within the precincts of S. Stephen's Church. There they received the sacrament and addressed themselves in prayer to the Proto-martyr, whose fane was about to be hallowed by the murder of a monster odious to God and man. It was on the morning of December 26, 1476, that the duke entered San Stefano. At one and the same moment the daggers of the three conspirators struck him—Olgiati's in the breast, Visconti's in the back, Lampugnani's in the belly. He cried 'Ah Dio!' and fell dead upon the pavement. The friends were unable to make their escape; Visconti and Lampugnani were killed on the spot; Olgiati was seized, tortured, and torn to death.

In the interval which elapsed between the rack and the pincers, Olgiati had time to address this memorable speech to the priest who urged him to repent: 'As for the noble action for which I am about to die, it is this which gives my conscience peace; to this I trust for pardon from the Judge of all. Far from repenting, if I had to come ten times to

---

[1] 'Le ingiurie conviene che siano nella roba, nel sangue, o nell' onore . . . . La roba e l' onore sono quelle due cose che offendono più gli uomini che alcun' altra offesa, e dalle quali il principe si debbe guardare: perchè e' non può mai spogliare uno tanto che non gli resti un coltello da vendicarsi; non può tanto disonorare uno che non gli resti un animo ostinato alla vendetta.' Mach. *Disc.* iii. 6.

[2] See Olgiati's prayer to Saint Ambrose in Sismondi, vii. 87, and in Mach. *Ist. Fior.* lib. 7.

[3] Giovanni Santi's chronicle, quoted by Dennistoun, vol. i. p. 223, describes the conspirators rehearsing on a wooden puppet.

life in order ten times to die by these same torments, I should not hesitate to dedicate my blood and all my powers to an object so sublime.' When the hangman stood above him, ready to begin the work of mutilation, he is said to have exclaimed: ' Mors acerba, fama perpetua, stabit vetus memoria facti—my death is untimely, my fame eternal, the memory of the deed will last for aye.' He was only twenty-two years of age.[1] There is an antique grandeur about the outlines of this story, strangely mingled with mediæval Catholicism in the details, which makes it typical of the Renaissance. Conspiracies against rulers were common at the time in Italy; but none were so pure and honourable as this. Of the Pazzi Conjuration (1478), which Sixtus IV. directed to his everlasting infamy against the Medici, I shall have to speak in another place. It is enough to mention here in passing the patriotic attempt of Girolamo Gentile against Galeazzo Sforza at Genoa in 1476, and the more selfish plot of Nicolo d'Este, in the same year, against his uncle Ercole, who held the Marquisate of Ferrara to the prejudice of his own claim. The latter tragedy was rendered memorable by the vengeance taken by Ercole. He beheaded Nicolo and his cousin Azzo together with twenty-five of his comrades, effectually preventing by this bloodshed any future attempt to set aside his title. Falling as these four conspiracies do within the space of two years, and displaying varied features of antique heroism, simple patriotism, dynastic dissension, and ecclesiastical perfidy, they present examples of the different forms and causes of political tragedies with a noteworthy and significant conciseness.[2]

[1] The whole story may be read in Ripamonti, under the head of ' Confessio Olgiati ; ' in Corio, who was a page of the Duke's and an eye-witness of the murder ; and in the seventh book of Machiavelli's *History*. Sismondi's summary and references, vol. vii. pp. 86–90, are very full.

[2] It is worthy of notice that very many tyrannicides took place in

Such was the actual condition of Italy at the end of the fifteenth century. Neither public nor private morality in our sense of the word existed. The crimes of the tyrants against their subjects and the members of their own families had produced a correlative order of crime in the people over whom they tyrannised. Cruelty was met by conspiracy. Tyrannicide became honourable; and the proverb, ' He who gives his own life can take a tyrant's,' had worked itself into popular language. At this point it may be well to glance at the opinions concerning public murder which prevailed in Italy. Machiavelli, in the ' Discorsi,' iii. 6, discusses the whole subject with his usual frigid and exhaustive analysis. It is no part of his critical method to consider the morality of the matter. He deals with the facts of history scientifically. The esteem in which tyrannicide was held at Florence is proved by the erection of Donatello's Judith in 1495, at the gate of the Palazzo Pubblico, with this inscription, *exemplum salutis publicæ cives posuere.* All the political theorists agree that to rid a state of its despot is a virtuous act. They only differ about its motives and its utility. In Guicciardini's ' Reggimento di Firenze ' ('Op. Ined.' vol. ii. pp. 53, 54, 114) the various motives of tyrannicide are discussed, and it is concluded that *pochissimi sono stati quelli che si siano mossi meramente per amore della libertà della sua patria, a' quali si conviene suprema laude.*[1] Donato Giannotti (' Opere,' vol. i.

Church—for example, the murders of Francesco Vico dei Prefetti, of the Varani, the Chiavelli, Giuliano de' Medici, and Galeazzo Maria Sforza. The choice of public service, as the best occasion for the commission of these crimes, points to the guarded watchfulness maintained by tyrants in their palaces and on the streets. Banquets and festivities offered another kind of opportunity; and it was on such occasions that domestic tragedies, like Oliverotto's murder of his uncle and Grifonetto Baglioni's treason, were accomplished.

[1] ' Very few indeed have those been, whose motive for tyrannicide was a pure love of their country's liberty; and these deserve the highest praise.'

p. 341) bids the conspirator consider whether the mere destruction of the Despot will suffice to restore his city to true liberty and good government—a caution by which Lorenzino de' Medici in his assassination of Duke Alessandro might have profited; for he killed one tyrant in order only to make room for another.   Lorenzino's own Apology (Varchi, vol. iii. pp. 283–295) is an important document, as showing that the murderer of a Despot counted on the sympathy of honourable men.   So, too, is the verdict of Boscolo's confessor (' Arch. Stor. ' vol. i. p. 309), who pronounced that conspiracy against a tyrant was no crime.   Nor did the demoralisation of the age stop here.   Force, which had been substituted for Law in government, became, as it were, the mainspring of society.   Murders, poisoning, rapes, and treasons were common incidents of private as of public life.[1]   In cities like Naples bloodguilt could be atoned for at an inconceivably low rate.   A man's life was worth scarcely more than that of a horse.   The palaces of the nobles swarmed with professional cut-throats, and the great ecclesiastics claimed for their abodes the right of sanctuary. Popes sold absolution for the most horrible excesses, and granted indulgences beforehand for the commission of crimes of lust and violence.   Success was the standard by which acts were judged; and the man who could help his friends, intimidate his enemies, and carve a way to fortune for

---

[1] It is quite impossible to furnish a complete view of Italian society under this aspect.   Students must be referred to the stories of the novelists, who collected the more dramatic incidents and presented them in the form of entertaining legends.   It may suffice here to mention Bartolommeo Colleoni, Angelo Poliziano, and Pontano, all of whom owed their start in life to the murder of their respective fathers by assassins; to Varchi and Filelfo, whose lives were attempted by cut-throats; to Cellini, Perugino, Masaccio, Berni, in each of whose biographies poison and the knife play their parts.   If men of letters and artists were exposed to these perils, the dangers of the great and noble may be readily imagined.

himself by any means he chose, was regarded as a hero. Machiavelli's use of the word *virtù* is in this relation most instructive. It has altogether lost the Christian sense of *virtue*, and retains only so much of the Roman *virtus* as is applicable to the courage, intellectual ability, and personal prowess of one who has achieved his purpose, be that what it may. The upshot of this state of things was that individuality of character and genius obtained a freer scope at this time in Italy than during any other period of modern history.

At the same time it must not be forgotten that during this period the art and culture of the Renaissance were culminating. Filelfo was receiving the gold of Filippo Maria Visconti. Guarino of Verona was instructing the heir of Ferrara, and Vittorino da Feltre was educating the children of the Marquis of Mantua. Lionardo was delighting Milan with his music and his magic world of painting. Poliziano was pouring forth honeyed eloquence at Florence. Ficino was expounding Plato. Boiardo was singing the prelude to Ariosto's melodies at Ferrara. Pico della Mirandola was dreaming of a reconciliation of the Hebrew, Pagan, and Christian traditions. It is necessary to note these facts in passing ; just as when we are surveying the history of letters and the arts, it becomes us to remember the crimes and the madness of the despots who patronised them. This was an age in which even the wildest and most perfidious of tyrants felt the ennobling influences and the sacred thirst of knowledge. Sigismondo Pandolfo Malatesta, the Lord of Rimini, might be selected as a true type of the princes who united a romantic zeal for culture with the vices of barbarians.[1] The coins which bear the portraits of this man, together with the medallions carved in red Verona

[1] For a fuller account of him, see my *Sketches in Italy and Greece*, article 'Rimini.'

marble on his church at Rimini, show a narrow forehead, protuberant above bushy eyebrows, a long hooked nose, hollow cheeks, and petulant, passionate, compressed lips. The whole face seems ready to flash with sudden violence, to merge its self-control in a spasm of fury. Sigismondo Pandolfo Malatesta killed three wives in succession, violated his daughter, and attempted the chastity of his own son. So much of him belongs to the mere savage. He caused the magnificent church of S. Francesco at Rimini to be raised by Leo Alberti in a manner more worthy of a Pagan Pantheon than of a Christian temple. He encrusted it with exquisite bas-reliefs in marble, the triumphs of the earliest Renaissance style, carved his own name and ensigns upon every scroll and frieze and point of vantage in the building, and dedicated a shrine there to his concubine—*Divæ Isottæ Sacrum.* So much of him belongs to the Neo-Pagan of the fifteenth century. He brought back from Greece the mortal remains of the philosopher Gemistos Plethon, buried them in a sarcophagus outside his church, and wrote upon the tomb this epigraph : ' These remains of Gemistus of Byzantium, chief of the sages of his day, Sigismondo Pandolfo Malatesta, son of Pandolfo, commander in the war against the king of the Turks in the Morea, induced by the mighty love with which he burns for men of learning, brought hither and placed within this chest. 1466.' He, the most fretful and turbulent of men, read books with patient care, and bore the contradictions of pedants in the course of long discussions on philosophy and arts and letters. So much of him belonged to the new spirit of the coming age, in which the zeal for erudition was a passion, and the spell of science was stronger than the charms of love. At the same time, as Condottiere, he displayed all the treasons, duplicities, cruelties, sacrileges, and tortuous policies to which the most accomplished villain of the age could have aspired.

It would be easy, following in the steps of Tiraboschi, o describe the patronage awarded in the fifteenth century to men of letters by princes—the protection extended by Nicholas III. of Ferrara to Guarino and Aurispa—the brilliant promise of his son Leonello, who corresponded with Poggio, Filelfo, Guarino, Francesco Barbaro, and other scholars—the liberality of Duke Borso, whose purse was open to poor students. Or we might review the splendid culture of the Court of Naples, where Alfonso committed the education of his terrible son Ferdinand to the care of Lorenzo Valla and Antonio Beccadelli.[1] More insight, however, into the nature of Italian despotism in all its phases may be gained by turning from Milan to Urbino, and by sketching a portrait of the good Duke Frederick.[2] The life of Frederick, Count of Montefeltro, created Duke of Urbino in 1474 by Pope Sixtus IV., covers the better part of the fifteenth century (b. 1422, d. 1482). A little corner of old Umbria lying between the Apennines and the Adriatic, Rimini and Ancona, formed his patrimony. Speaking roughly, the whole duchy was but forty miles square, and the larger portion consisted of bare hillsides and ruinous ravines. Yet this poor territory became the centre of a splendid court. 'Federigo,' says his biographer, Muzio, 'maintained a suite so numerous and distinguished as to rival any royal household.' The chivalry of Italy flocked to Urbino in order to learn manners and the art of war from the most noble general of his day. 'His household,' we

[1] The Panormita; author, by the way, of the shameless *Hermaphroditus*. This fact is significant. The moral sense was extinct when such a pupil was entrusted to such a tutor.

[2] For the following details I am principally indebted to *The Memoirs of the Dukes of Urbino*, by James Dennistoun; 3 vols., Longmans, 1851. Vespasiano's Life of Duke Frederick (*Vite di uomini illustri*, pp. 72-112) is one of the most charming literary portaits extant. It has, moreover, all the value of a personal memoir. for Vespasiano had lived in close relation with the Duke as his librarian.

hear from Vespasiano, 'which consisted of 500 mouths entertained at his own cost, was governed less like a company of soldiers than a strict religious community. There was no gaming nor swearing, but the men conversed with the utmost sobriety.' In a list of the court officers we find forty-five counts of the duchy and of other states, seventeen gentlemen, five secretaries, four teachers of grammar, logic, and philosophy, fourteen clerks in public offices, five architects and engineers, five readers during meals, four transcribers of MSS. The library, collected by Vespasiano during fourteen years of assiduous labour, contained copies of all the Greek and Latin authors then discovered, the principal treatises on theology and church history, a complete series of Italian poets, historiographers, and commentators, various medical, mathematical, and legal works, essays on music, military tactics and the arts, together with such Hebrew books as were accessible to copyists. Every volume was bound in crimson and silver, and the whole collection cost upwards of 30,000 ducats. For the expenses of so large a household, and the maintenance of this fine library, not to mention a palace that was being built and churches that required adornment, the mere revenues of the duchy could not have sufficed. Federigo owed his wealth to his engagements as a general. Military service formed his trade. 'In 1453,' says Dennistoun, 'his war-pay from Alfonso of Naples exceeded 8,000 ducats a month, and for many years he had from him and his son an annual peace-pension of 6,000 in name of past services. At the close of his life, when captain-general of the Italian league, he drew in war 165,000 ducats of annual stipend, 45,000 being his own share; in peace, 65,000 in all.' As a Condottiere, Federigo was famous in this age of broken faith for his plain dealing and sincerity. Only one piece of questionable practice—the capture of Verucchio in 1462 by a forged letter pretending to come from Sigismondo Malatesta—stained his character for honesty. To his soldiers in the field he was considerate and generous ; to his enemies compassionate and merciful.[1] 'In military science,' says Vespasiano, 'he was excelled by no commander of his time; uniting energy with judgment, he conquered by prudence as much as by force. The like wariness was observed in all his affairs ; and in none of his many battles was he worsted. Nor may I omit the strict observance of good faith, wherein he never failed. All to whom he once gave his word might testify to his inviolate performance of it.' The same biographer adds that 'he was singularly religious, and most observant of the Divine commands. No morning passed without his hearing mass upon his knees.'

While a boy, Federigo had been educated in the school of Vittorino da Feltre at Mantua. Gian Francesco Gonzaga invited that eminent scholar to his court in 1425 for the education of his sons and daughter, assembling round him subordinate teachers in grammar, mathematics, music, painting, dancing, riding, and all noble exercises. The system supervised by Vittorino included not only the acquisition of scholarship, but also training in manly sports and the cultivation of the moral character. Many of the noblest Italians were his pupils. Ghiberto da Correggio, Battista Pallavicini, Taddeo Manfredi of Faenza, Gabbriello da Cremona, Francesco da Castiglione, Niccolo Perrotti, together with the Count of Montefeltro, lived in Vittorino's house, associating with the poorer students whom the benevolent philosopher instructed for the love of learning. Ambrogio Camaldolese in a letter to Niccolo Niccoli gives this animated picture of the Mantuan school : 'I went again to visit Vittorino and to see his Greek books. He came to meet me with the

[1] See the testimony of Francesco di Giorgio ; Dennistoun, vol. i. p. 259. The sack of Volterra was, however, a blot upon his humanity.

children of the prince, two sons and a daughter of seven years. The elder boy is eleven, the younger five. There are also other children of about ten, sons of nobles, as well as other pupils. He teaches them Greek, and they can write that language well. I saw a translation from Saint Chrysostom made by one of them which pleased me much.' And again a few years later : ' He brought me Giovanni Lucido, son of the Marquis, a boy of about fourteen, whom he has educated, and who then recited two hundred lines composed by him upon the shows with which the Emperor was received in Mantua. The verses were most beautiful, but the sweetness and elegance of his recitation made them still more graceful. He also showed me two propositions added by him to Euclid, which prove how eminent he promises to be in mathematical studies. There was also a little daughter of the Marquis of about ten, who writes Greek beautifully ; and many other pupils, some of noble birth, attended them.' The medal struck by Pisanello in honour of Vittorino da Feltre bears the ensign of a pelican feeding her young from a wound in her own breast—a symbol of the master's self-sacrifice.[1] I intend to return in the second volume of this work to Vittorino. It is enough here to remark that in this good school the Duke of Urbino acquired that solid culture which distinguished him through life. In after years, when the cares of his numerous engagements fell thick upon him, we hear from Vespasiano that he still prosecuted his studies, reading Aristotle's ' Ethics,' ' Politics,' and ' Physics,' listening to the works of S. Thomas Aquinas and Scotus read aloud, perusing at one time the Greek fathers and at another the Latin historians.[2] How profitably he spent his day at Urbino may be gathered from

[1] Prendilacqua, the biographer of Vittorino, says that he died so poor that his funeral expenses had to be defrayed.

[2] Pius II. in his Commentaries gives an interesting account of the conversations concerning the tactics of the ancients which he held with Frederick, in 1461, in the neighbourhood of Tivoli.

this account of his biographer : 'He was on horseback at
daybreak with four or six mounted attendants, and not more,
and with one or two foot servants unarmed. He would ride
out three or four miles, and be back again when the rest of
his court rose from bed. After dismounting, he heard mass.
Then he went into a garden open at all sides, and gave
audience to those who listed until dinner-time. At table, all
the doors were open ; any man could enter where his lordship
was, for he never ate except with a full hall. According to
the season he had books read out as follows—in Lent, spiritual
works ; at other times, the history of Livy—all in Latin.
His food was plain ; he took no comfits, and drank no wine,
except drinks of pomegranate, cherry, or apples.' After dinner
he heard causes, and gave sentence in the Latin tongue.
Then he would visit the nuns of Santa Chiara, or watch the
young men of Urbino at their games, using the courtesy of
perfect freedom with his subjects. His reputation as a patron
of the arts and of learning was widely spread. 'To hear him
converse with a sculptor,' says Vespasiano, 'you would have
thought he was a master of the craft. In painting, too, he
displayed the most acute judgment ; and as he could not find
among the Italians worthy masters of oil colours, he sent to
Flanders for one, who painted for him the philosophers and
poets and doctors of the Church. He also brought from
Flanders masters in the art of tapestry.' Pontano, Ficino,
and Poggio dedicated works of importance to his name ; and
Pirro Perrotti, in the preface to his uncle's 'Cornucopia,'
draws a quaint picture of the reception which so learned a
book was sure to meet with at Urbino.[1] But Frederick was

---

[1] The preface to the original edition of the *Cornucopia* is worth
reading for the lively impression which it conveys of Federigo's personality : 'Admirabitur in te divinam illam corporis proceritatem,
membrorum robur eximium, venerandam oris dignitatem, ætatis
maturam gravitatem, divinam quandam majestatem cum humanitate
conjunctam, totum præterea talem qualem esse oportebat eum

not merely an accomplished prince. Concurrent testimony proves that he remained a good husband and a constant friend throughout his life, that he controlled his natural quickness of temper, and subdued the sensual appetites which in that age of lax morality he might have indulged without reproach. In his relations to his subjects he showed what a paternal monarch should be, conversing familiarly with the citizens of Urbino, accosting them with head uncovered, inquiring into the necessities of the poorer artisans, relieving the destitute, dowering orphan girls, and helping distressed shopkeepers with loans. Numerous anecdotes are told which illustrate his consideration for his old servants, and his anxiety for the welfare and good order of his state. At a time when the Pope and the King of Naples were making money by monopolies of corn, the Duke of Urbino filled his granaries from Apulia, and sold bread during a year of scarcity at a cheap rate to his poor subjects. Nor would he allow his officers to prosecute the indigent for debts incurred by such purchases. He used to say : 'I am not a merchant ; it is enough to have saved my people from hunger.' We must remember that this excellent prince had a direct interest in maintaining the prosperity and goodwill of his duchy. His profession was warfare, and the district of Urbino supplied him with his best troops. Yet this should not diminish the respect due to the foresight and benevolence of a Condottiere who knew how to carry on his calling with humanity and generosity. Federigo wore the Order of the Garter, which Henry VII. conferred on him, the Neapolitan Order of the Ermine, and the Papal decorations of the Rose, the Hat, the Sword. He served three pontiffs, two kings of Naples, and two dukes of Milan. The Republic of Florence and more than one Italian League

principem quem nuper pontifex maximus et universus senatus omnium rerum suarum et totius ecclesiastici imperii ducem moderatoremque constituit.'

appointed him their general in the field. If his military career was less brilliant than that of the two Sforzas, Piccinino, or Carmagnuola, he avoided the crimes to which ambition led some of these men and the rocks on which they struck. At his death he transmitted a flourishing duchy, a cultivated court, a renowned name, and the leadership of the Italian League to his son, Guidobaldo.

The young Duke, whose court, described by Castiglione, may be said to have set the model of good breeding to all Europe, began life under the happiest auspices. From his tutor, Odasio of Padua, we hear that even in boyhood he cared only for study and for manly sports. His memory was so retentive that he could repeat whole treatises by heart after the lapse of ten or fifteen years, nor did he ever forget what he had resolved to retain. In the Latin and Greek languages he became an accomplished scholar,[1] and, while he appreciated the poets, he showed peculiar aptitude for philosophy and history. But his development was precocious. His zeal for learning and the excessive ardour with which he devoted himself to physical exercises undermined his constitution. He became an invalid and died childless, after exhibiting to his court for many years an example of patience in sickness, and of dignified cheerfulness under the restraints of enforced inaction. His wife, Elizabetta Gonzaga, one of the most famous women of her age, was no less a pattern of noble conduct and serene contentment.

Such were the two last princes of the Montefeltro dynasty.[2]

[1] It is not easy to say what a panegyrist of that period intended by 'a complete knowledge of Greek,' or 'fluent Greek writing,' in a prince. I suspect, however, that we ought not to understand by these phrases anything like a real familiarity with Greek literature, but rather such superficial knowledge as would enable a reader of Latin books to understand allusions and quotations. Poliziano, it may be remarked, thought it worth while to flatter Guidobaldo in a Greek epigram.

[2] After Guidobaldo's death the duchy was continued by the Della Rovere family, one of whom, Giovanni, Prefect of Rome and nephew of Sixtus IV., married the Duke's sister Giovanna in 1474.

breeding, the amenities of intercourse, the pleasures of the intellect, scarcely existed outside the sphere of courts; for one effect of the Revival of Learning had been to make the acquisition of polite knowledge difficult, and the proletariat was less cultivated then than in the age of Dante. Men of ambition who desired to acquire a reputation whether as soldiers or as poets, as politicians or as orators, came to court and served their chosen prince in war or at the council-table, or even in humbler offices of state. To be able, therefore, to conduct himself with dignity, to know how to win the favour of his master and to secure the goodwill of his peers, to retain his personal honour and to make himself respected without being hated, to inspire admiration and to avoid envy, to outshine all honourable rivals in physical exercises and the craft of arms, to maintain a creditable equipage and retinue, to be instructed in the arts of polite intercourse, to converse with ease and wit, to be at home alike in the tilting-yard, the banquet-hall, the boudoir, and the council-chamber, to understand diplomacy, to live before the world and yet to keep a fitting privacy and distance—these and a hundred other matters were the climax and perfection of the culture of a gentleman. Courts being now the only centres in which it was possible for a man of birth and talents to shine, it followed that the perfect courtier and the perfect gentleman were synonymous terms. Castiglione's treatise may therefore be called an essay on the character of the true gentleman as he appeared in Italy. Eliminating all qualities that are special to any art or calling, he defines those essential characteristics which were requisite for social excellence in the sixteenth century. It is curious to observe how unchangeable are the laws of real politeness and refinement. Castiglione's courtier is, with one or two points of immaterial difference, a modern gentleman, such as all men of education at the present day would wish to be.

The first requisite in the ideal courtier is that he must be noble. The Count of Canossa, who proposed the subject of debate, lays down this as an axiom. Gaspar Pallavicino denies the necessity.[1] But after a lively discussion, his opinion is overruled, on the ground that, although the gentle virtues may be found among people of obscure origin, yet a man who intends to be a courtier must start with the prestige of noble birth. Next he must be skilful in the use of weapons and

---

[1] Italy, earlier than any other European nation, developed theoretical democracy. Dante had defined true nobility to consist of personal excellence in a man or in his ancestors; he also called ' nobiltà ' sister of ' filosofia.' Poggio in his Dialogue *De Nobilitate*, into which he introduces Niccolo Niccoli and Lorenzo de' Medici (Cosimo's brother), decides that only merit constitutes true nobility. Hawking and hunting are far less noble occupations than agriculture; descent from a long line of historic criminals is no honour. French and English castle-life, and the robber-knighthood of Germany, he argues, are barbarous. Lorenzo pleads the authority of Aristotle in favour of noble blood; Poggio contests the passage quoted, and shows the superiority of the Latin word ' nobilitas ' (distinction) over the Greek term εὐγένεια (good birth). The several kinds of aristocracy in Italy are then discussed. In Naples the nobles despise business and idle their time away. In Rome they manage their estates. In Venice and Genoa they engage in commerce. In Florence they either take to mercantile pursuits or live upon the produce of their land in idleness. The whole way of looking at the subject betrays a liberal and scientific spirit, wholly free from prejudice. Machiavelli (*Discorsi*, i. 55) is very severe on the aristocracy, whom he defines as ' those who live in idleness on the produce of their estates, without applying themselves to agriculture or to any other useful occupation.' He points out that the Venetian nobles are not properly so called, since they are merchants. The different districts of Italy had widely different conceptions of nobility. Naples was always aristocratic, owing to its connection with France and Spain. Ferrara maintained the chivalry of courts. Those states, on the other hand, which had been democratised, like Florence, by republican customs, or like Milan, by despotism, set less value on birth than on talent and wealth. It was not until the age of the Spanish ascendency (latter half of sixteenth century) that Cosimo I. withdrew the young Florentines from their mercantile pursuits and enrolled them in his order of S. Stephen, and that the patricians of Genoa carried daggers inscribed ' for the chastisement of villeins.'

courageous in the battle-field. He is not, however, bound to have the special science of a general, nor must he in times of peace profess unique devotion to the art of war : that would argue a coarseness of nature or vainglory. Again, he must excel in all manly sports and exercises, so as, if possible, to beat the actual professors of each game or feat of skill on their own ground. Yet here also he should avoid mere habits of display, which are unworthy of a man who aspires to be a gentleman and not an athlete. Another indispensable quality is gracefulness in all he does and says. In order to secure this elegance, he must beware of every form of affectation : ' Let him shun affectation, as though it were a most perilous rock ; and let him seek in everything a certain carelessness, to hide his art, and show that what he says or does comes from him without effort or deliberation.' This vice of affectation in all its kinds, and the ways of avoiding it, are discussed with a delicacy of insight which would do credit to a Chesterfield of the present century, sending forth his son into society for the first time. Castiglione goes so far as to condemn the pedantry of far-fetched words and the coxcombry of elaborate costumes, as dangerous forms of affectation. His courtier must speak and write with force and freedom. He need not be a purist in his use of language, but may use such foreign phrases and modern idioms as are current in good society, aiming only at simplicity and clearness. He must add to excellence in arms polite culture in letters and sound scholarship, avoiding that barbarism of the French, who think it impossible to be a good soldier and an accomplished student at the same time. Yet his learning should be always held in reserve, to give brilliancy and flavour to his wit, and not brought forth for merely erudite parade. He must have a practical acquaintance with music and dancing ; it would be well for him to sing and touch various stringed and keyed instruments, so as to relax his own spirits and to make himself agreeable to ladies. If he can compose verses and sing them to his own accompaniment, so much the better. Finally, he ought to understand the arts of painting and sculpture; for criticism, even though a man be neither poet nor artist, is an elegant accomplishment. Such are the principal qualities of the Cortegiano.

The precepts which are laid down for the use of his acquirements and his general conduct resolve themselves into a strong recommendation of tact and caution. The courtier must study the nature of his prince, and show the greatest delicacy in approaching him, so as to secure his favour, and to avoid wearying him with importunities. In tendering his advice he must be modest; but he should make a point of never sacrificing his own liberty of judgment. To obey his master in dishonourable things would be a derogation from his dignity; and if he discovers any meanness in the character of the prince, it is better to quit his service.[1] A courtier must be careful to create beforehand a favourable opinion of himself in places he intends to visit. Much stress is laid upon his choice of clothes and the equipment of his servants. In these respects he should aim at combining individuality with simplicity, so as to produce an impression of novelty without extravagance or eccentricity. He must be very cautious in his friendships, selecting his associates with care, and admitting only one or two to intimacy.

In connection with the general subject of tact and taste, the Cardinal Bibbiena introduces an elaborate discussion of the different sorts of jokes, which proves the high value attached in Italy to all displays of wit. It appears that even

[1] From many passages in the *Cortegiano* it is clear that Castiglione is painting the character of an independent gentleman, to whom self-culture in all humane excellence is of far more importance than the acquisition of the art of pleasing. Circumstances made the life of courts the best obtainable; but there is no trace of French 'œil-de-bœuf' servility.

practical jokes were not considered in bad taste, but that irreverence and grossness were tabooed as boorish. Mere obscenity is especially condemned, though it must be admitted that many jests approved of at that time would now appear intolerable. But the essential point to be aimed at then, as now, was the promotion of mirth by cleverness, and not by mere tricks and clumsy inventions.

In bringing this chapter on Italian Despotism in the fourteenth and fifteenth centuries to a conclusion, it will be well to cast a backward glance over the ground which has been traversed. A great internal change took place and was accomplished during this period. The free burghs which flourished in the twelfth and thirteenth centuries gave place to tyrannies, illegal for the most part in their origin, and maintained by force. In the absence of dynastic right, violence and ˉcraft were instruments by means of which the Despots founded and preserved their power. Yet the sentiments of the Italians at large were not unfavourable to the growth of principalities. On the contrary, the forces which move society, the inner instinct of the nation, and the laws of progress and development, tended year by year more surely to the consolidation of despotisms. City after city lost its faculty for self-government, until at last Florence, so long the centre of political freedom, fell beneath the yoke of her merchant princes. It is difficult for the historian not to feel either a monarchical or a republican bias. Yet this internal and gradual revolution in the states of Italy may be regarded neither as a matter for exultation in the cause of sovereignty, nor for lamentation over the decay of liberty. It was but part of an inevitable process which the Italians shared, according to the peculiarities of their condition, in common with the rest of Europe.

In tracing the history of the Visconti and the Sforzas our attention has been naturally directed to the private and political vices of the Despot. As a contrast to so much violence and treachery, we have studied the character of one of the best princes produced in this period. Yet it must be borne in mind that the Duke of Urbino was far less representative of his class than Francesco Sforza, and that the aims and actions of Gian Galeazzo Visconti formed the ideal to which an Italian prince of spirit, if he had the opportunity, aspired. The history of art and literature in this period belongs to another branch of the inquiry ; and a separate chapter must be devoted to the consideration of political morality as theorised by the Italians at the end of these two centuries of intrigue. But having insisted on the violence and vices of the tyrants, it seemed necessary to close the review of their age by describing the Italian nobleman as court-life made him. Castiglione shows him at the very best : the darker shadows of the picture are omitted ; the requirements of the most finished culture and the tone of the purest society in Italy are depicted with the elegance of a scholar and the taste of a true gentleman. The fact remains that the various influences at work in Italy during the age of the Despots had rendered the conception of this ideal possible. Nowhere else in Europe could a portrait of so much dignity and sweetness, combining the courage of a soldier with the learning of a student and the accomplishments of an artist, the liberality of freedom with the courtesies of service, have been painted from the life and been recognised as the model which all members of polite society should imitate. Nobler characters and more heroic virtues might have been produced by the Italian commonwealths if they had continued to enjoy their ancient freedom of self-government. Meanwhile we must render this justice to Italian despotism, that beneath its shadow was developed the type of the modern gentleman.

CHAPTER IV

THE REPUBLICS

The different Physiognomies of the Italian Republics—The Similarity of
their Character as Municipalities—The Rights of Citizenship—
Causes of Disturbance in the Commonwealths—Belief in the
Plasticity of Constitutions—Example of Genoa—Savonarola's Con-
stitution—Machiavelli's Discourse to Leo X.—Complexity of In-
terests and Factions—Example of Siena—Small Size of Italian
Cities—Mutual Mistrust and Jealousy of the Commonwealths—The
notable Exception of Venice—Constitution of Venice—Her Wise
System of Government—Contrast of Florentine Vicissitudes—The
Magistracies of Florence—Balia and Parlamento—The Arts of the
Medici—Comparison of Venice and Florence in respect to Intel-
lectual Activity and Mobility—Parallels between Greece and Italy—
Essential Differences—The Mercantile Character of Italian Burghs—
The ' Trattato del Governo della Famiglia '—The Bourgeois Tone of
Florence, and the Ideal of a Burgher—Mercenary Arms.

THE despotisms of Italy present the spectacle of states
founded upon force, controlled and moulded by the will of
princes, whose object in each case has been to maintain
usurped power by means of mercenary arms and to deprive
the people of political activity. Thus the Italian principalities, however they may differ in their origin, the character
of their administration, or their relation to Church and
Empire, all tend to one type. The egotism of the Despot,
conscious of his selfish aims and deliberate in their execution,
formed the motive principle in all alike.

The republics on the contrary are distinguished by strongly
marked characteristics. The history of each is the history

of the development of certain specific qualities, which
modified the type of municipal organisation common to them
all. Their differences consist chiefly in the varying forms
which institutions of a radically similar design assumed, and
also in those peculiar local conditions which made the
Venetians Levant merchants, the Perugians captains of
adventure, the Genoese admirals and pirates, the Florentines
bankers, and so forth. Each commonwealth contracted a
certain physiognomy through the prolonged action of external
circumstances and by the maintenance of some political pre-
dilection. Thus Siena, excluded from maritime commerce
by its situation, remained, broadly speaking, faithful to the
Ghibelline party ; while Perugia at the distance of a few
miles, equally debarred from mercantile expansion, maintained
the Guelf cause with pertinacity. The annals of the one city
record a long succession of complicated party quarrels,
throughout the course of which the State continued free ; the
Guelf leanings of the other exposed it to the gradual encroachment of the Popes, while its civic independence was
emperilled and enfeebled by the contests of a few noble
families. Lucca and Pistoja in like manner are strongly contrasted, the latter persisting in a state of feud and faction
which delivered it bound hand and foot to Florence, the
former after many vicissitudes attaining internal quiet under
the dominion of a narrow oligarchy.

But while recognising these differences, which manifest
themselves partly in what may be described as national
characteristics, and partly in constitutional varieties, we may
trace one course of historical progression in all except Venice.
This is what natural philosophers might call the morphology
of Italian commonwealths. To begin with, the Italian
republics were all municipalities. That is, like the Greek
states, they consisted of a small body of burghers, who alone
had the privileges of government, together with a larger

population, who, though they paid taxes and shared the commercial and social advantages of the city, had no voice in its administration. Citizenship was hereditary in those families by whom it had been once acquired, each republic having its own criterion of the right, and guarding it jealously against the encroachments of non-qualified persons. In Florence, for example, the burgher must belong to one of the Arts.[1] In Venice his name must be inscribed upon the Golden Book. The rivalries to which this system of municipal government gave rise were a chief source of internal weakness to the commonwealths. Nor did the burghers see far enough or philosophically enough to recruit their numbers by a continuous admission of new members from the wealthy but unfranchised citizens.[2] This alone could have saved them from the death by dwindling and decay to which they were exposed. The Italian conception of citizenship may be set forth in the words of one of their acutest critics, Donato Giannotti, who writes concerning the electors in a state :[3] 'Non dico tutti gli abitanti della terra, ma tutti quelli che hanno grado ; cioè che hanno acquistato, o eglino o gli antichi loro, facultà d' ottenere i magistrati ; e in somma che sono *participes imperandi et parendi.*' No Italian had any notion of representative government in our sense of the term.

[1] Villari, *Life of Savonarola*, vol. i. p. 259, may be consulted concerning the further distinction of Benefiziati, Statuali, Aggravezzati, at Florence. See also Varchi, vol. i. pp. 165-70. Consult Appendix ii.

[2] It must be mentioned that a provision for admitting deserving individuals to citizenship formed part of the Florentine Constitution of 1495. The principle was not, however, recognised at large by the republics.

[3] On the Government of Siena (vol. i. p. 351 of his collected works): 'I say not all the inhabitants of the state, but all those who have rank ; that is, who have acquired, either in their own persons or through their ancestors, the right of taking magistracy, in short those who are participes imperandi et parendi.' What has already been said in Chapter II. about the origin of the Italian Republics will explain this definition of burghership.

The problem was always how to put the administration of the state most conveniently into the hands of the fittest among those who were qualified as burghers, and how to give each burgher his due share in the government; not how to select men delegated from the whole population. The wisest among their philosophical politicians sought to establish a mixed constitution, which should combine the advantages of principality, aristocracy, and democracy. Starting with the fact that the eligible burghers numbered some 5,000, and with the assumption that among these the larger portion would be content with freedom and a voice in the administration, while a certain body were ambitious of honourable distinctions, and a few aspired to the pomp of titular presidency, they thought that these several desires might be satisfied and reconciled in a republic composed of a general assembly of the citizens, a select Senate, and a Doge. In these theories the influence of Aristotelian studies [1] and the example of Venice are apparent. At the same time it is noticeable that no account whatever is taken of the remaining 95,000 who contributed

[1] It would be very interesting to trace in detail the influence of Aristotle's *Politics* upon the practical and theoretical statists of the Renaissance. The whole of Giannotti's works; the discourses of de' Pazzi, Vettori, Acciaiuoli, and the two Guicciardini on the State of Florence (*Arch. St. It.* vol. i.); and Machiavelli's *Discorso sul Reggimento di Firenze*, addressed to Leo X., illustrate in general the working of Aristotelian ideas. At Florence, in 1495, Savonarola urged his Constitution on the burghers by appeals to Aristotle's doctrine and to the example of Venice [see Segni, p. 15, and compare the speeches of Pagolo Antonio Soderini and Guido Antonio Vespucci, in Guicciardini's *Istoria d' Italia*, vol. ii. p. 155 of Rosini's edition, on the same occasion]. Segni, p. 86, mentions a speech of Pier Filippo Pandolfini, the arguments of which, he says, were drawn from Aristotle and illustrated by Florentine history. The Italian doctrinaires seem to have imagined that, by clever manipulation of existing institutions, they could construct a state similar to that called πολιτεία by Aristotle, in which all sections of the community should be fairly represented. Venice, meanwhile, was a practical instance of the possible prosperity of such a constitution with a strong oligarchical complexion.

their wealth and industry to the prosperity of the city.[1] The theory of the State rests upon no abstract principle like that of the divine right of the Empire, which determined Dante's speculation in the Middle Ages, or that of the divine right of kings, with which we Englishmen were made familiar in the seventeenth century, or that again of the rights of men, on which the democracies of France and America were founded. The right contemplated by the Italian politicians is that of the burghers to rule the commonwealth for their advantage. As a matter of fact, Venice was the only Italian republic which maintained this kind of oligarchy with success through centuries of internal tranquillity. The rest were exposed to a series of revolutions which ended at last in their enslavement.

Intolerant of foreign rule, and blinded by the theoretical supremacy of the Empire to the need of looking beyond its own municipal institutions, each city in the twelfth century sought to introduce such a system into the already existing machinery of the burgh as should secure its independence and place the government in the hands of its citizens. But the passing of bad laws, or the non-observance of wise regulations, or, again, the passions of individuals and parties, soon disturbed the equilibrium established in these little communities. Desire for more power than their due prompted one section of the burghers to violence. The love of independence, or simple insubordination, drove another portion to resistance. Matters were further complicated by resident or neighbouring nobles. Then followed the wars of factions, proscriptions, and exiles.

[1] These numbers, 100,000 for the population, and 5,000 for the burghers, are stated roundly. In Florence, when the Consiglio Maggiore was opened in 1495, it was found that the Florentines altogether numbered about 90,000, while the qualified burghers were not more than 3,200. In 1581 the population of Venice numbered 134,890, whereof 1,843 were adult patricians [see below, p. 164].

Having banished their rivals, the party in power for the time being remodelled the institutions of the republic to suit their own particular interest. Meanwhile the opposition in exile fomented every element of discontent within the city, which this short-sighted policy was sure to foster. Sudden revolutions were the result, attended in most cases by massacres consequent upon the victorious return of the outlaws. To the action of these peccant humours—*umori* is the word applied by the elder Florentine historians to the troubles attendant upon factions—must be added the jealousy of neighbouring cities, the cupidity of intriguing princes, the partisanship of the Guelfs and Ghibellines, the treason and the egotism of mercenary generals, and the false foreign policy which led the Italians to rely for aid on France or Germany or Spain. Little by little, under the prolonged action of these disturbing forces, each republic in turn became weaker, more confused in policy, more mistrustful of itself and its own citizens, more subdivided into petty but ineradicable factions, until at last it fell a prey either to some foreign potentate, or to the Church, or else to an ambitious family among its members. The small scale of the Italian commonwealths, taken singly, favoured rapid change, and gave an undue value to distinguished wealth or unscrupulous ability among the burghers. The oscillation between democracy and aristocracy and back again, the repetition of exhausting discords, and the demoralising influences of occasional despotism, so broke the spirit of each commonwealth that in the end the citizens forgot their ancient zeal for liberty, and were glad to accept tyranny for the sake of the protection it professed to extend to life and property.

To these vicissitudes all the republics of Italy, with the exception of Venice, were subject. In like manner, they shared in common the belief that constitutions could be made at will, that the commonwealth was something plastic, capable of taking the complexion and the form impressed upon it by speculative politicians. So firmly rooted was this conviction, and so highly self-conscious had the statesmen of Italy become, partly by the experience of their shifting history, and partly by their study of antiquity, that the idea of the State as something possessed of organic vitality can scarcely be said to have existed among them. The principle of gradual growth, which gives its value, for example, to the English Constitution, was not recognised by the Italians. Nor again had their past history taught them the necessity, so well divined and recognised by the Greek statesmen, of maintaining a fixed character at any cost in republics, which, in spite of their small scale, aspired to permanence.[1] The most violent and arbitrary changes which the speculative faculty of a theorist could contrive, or which the prejudices of a party could impose, seemed to them not only possible but natural.

A very notable instance of this tendency to treat the State as a plastic product of political ingenuity is afforded by the annals of Genoa. After suffering for centuries from the vicissitudes common to all Italian free cities—discords between the Guelf and Ghibelline factions, between the nobles and the people, between the enfranchised citizens and the proletariat—after submitting to the rule of foreign masters, especially of France and Milan, and after being torn in pieces by the rival houses of Adorni and Fregosi, the Genoese at last received liberty from the hands of Andrea Doria in 1528. They then proceeded to form a new Constitution for the protection of their freedom ; and in order to destroy the memory of the old parties which had caused their ruin, they obliterated all their family names with the exception of twenty, under one or other of which the whole body of citizens were bound to enrol them-

---

[1] The value of the ἦθος was not wholly unrecognised by political theorists. Giannotti (vol. i. p. 160, and vol. ii. p. 13), for example, translates it by the word 'temperamento.'

selves.[1] This was nothing less than an attempt to create new *gentes* by effacing the distinctions established by nature and tradition. To parallel a scheme so artificial in its method, we must go back to the history of Sicyon and the changes wrought in the Dorian tribes by Cleisthenes.

Short of such violent expedients as these, the whole history of towns like Florence reveals a succession of similar attempts. When, for example, the Medici had been expelled in 1494, the Florentines found themselves without a working constitution, and proceeded to frame one. The matter was at first referred to two eminent jurists, Guido Antonio Vespucci and Paolo Antonio Soderini, who argued for and against the establishment of a Grand Council on the Venetian model, before the Signory in the Palazzo. At this juncture Savonarola in his Sermon for the third Sunday in Advent [2] suggested that each of the sixteen Companies should form a plan, that these should be submitted to the Gonfaloniers, who should choose the four best, and that from these four the Signory should select the most perfect. At the same time he pronounced himself in favour of an imitation of the Venetian Consiglio Grande. His scheme, as is well known, was adopted.[3] Running through the whole political writings of the Florentine philosophers and historians, we find the same belief in artificial and arbitrary alterations of the state.

---

[1] See Varchi, *St. F.* lib. vii. cap. 8.

[2] December 12, 1494.

[3] Segni (pp. 15, 16) says that Savonarola deserved to be honoured for this Constitution by the Florentines no less than Numa by the Romans. Varchi (vol. i. p. 169) judges the Consiglio Grande to have been the only good institution ever adopted by the Florentines. We may compare Giannotti (*Sopra la Repubblica di Siena*, p. 346) for a similar opinion. Guicciardini, both in the *Storia d' Italia* and the *Storia di Firenze*, gives to Savonarola the whole credit of having passed this Constitution. Nardi and Pitti might be cited to the same effect. None of these critics doubt for a moment that what was theoretically best ought to have been found practically feasible.

Machiavelli pronounces his opinion that, in spite of the corruption of Florence, a wise legislator might effect her salvation.[1]
Skill alone was needed. There lay the wax; the scientific
artist had only to set to his hand and model it.

This is the dominant thought which pervades his treatise
on the right ordering of the State of Florence addressed to
Leo X.[2] A more consummate piece of political mechanism
than that devised by Machiavelli in this essay can hardly be
imagined. It is like a clock with separate actions for hours,
minutes, seconds, and the revolutions of the moon and planets.
All the complicated interests of parties and classes in the state,
the traditional pre-eminence of the Medicean family, the rights
of the Church, and the relation of Florence to foreign powers,
have been carefully considered and provided for. The defect
of this consummate work of art is that it remained a mere
machine, devised to meet the exigencies of the moment, and
powerless against such perturbations as the characters and
passions of living men must introduce into the working of a
Commonwealth. Had Florence been a colony established in
a new country with no neighbours but savages, or had it been
an institution protected from without against the cupidity of

---

[1] *St. Fior.* lib. iii. 1: 'Firenze a quel grado è pervenuta che facilmente da uno savio dator di leggi potrebbe essere in qualunque forma di
governo riordinata.'

[2] The language of this treatise is noteworthy. After discoursing on
the differences between republics and principalities, and showing that
Florence is more suited to the former, and Milan to the latter, form of
government, he says: 'Ma perchè *fare* principato dove starebbe bene
repubblica,' etc. . . . . 'sì perchè Firenze *è subietto attissimo di pigliare
questa forma,*' etc. The phrases in italics show how thoroughly Machiavelli regarded the commonwealth as plastic. We may compare the
whole of Guicciardini's elaborate essay 'Del Reggimento di Firenze' (*Op.
Ined.* vol. ii.), as well as the 'Discourses' addressed by Alessandro de'
Pazzi, Francesco Vettori, Ruberto Acciaiuoli, Francesco Guicciardini, and
Luigi Guicciardini, to the Cardinal Giulio de' Medici, on the settlement
of the Florentine Constitution in 1522 (*Arch. Stor.* vol. i.). Not one of
these men doubted that his nostrum would effect the cure of the republic
undermined by slow consumption.

selfish rivals, then such a constitution might have been im-posed on it with profit. But to expect that a city dominated by ancient prejudices, connected by a thousand subtle ties not only with the rest of Italy but also with the states of Europe, and rotten to the core in many of its most important members, could be restored to pristine vigour by a doctrinaire however able, was chimerical. The course of events contradicted this vain expectation. Meanwhile a few clear-headed and positive observers were dimly conscious of the instability of merely speculative constitution-making. Varchi, in a weighty passage on the defects of the Florentine republic, points out that its weakness arose partly from the violence of factions, but also in a great measure from the implicit faith reposed in doctors of the law.[1] The history of the Florentine Constitution, he says, is the history of changes effected by successions of mutually hostile parties, each in its own interest subverting the work of its predecessor, and each in turn relying on the theories of jurists, who without practical genius for politics make arbitrary rules for the control of state affairs. Yet even Varchi shares the prevailing conviction that the proper method is first to excogitate a perfect political system, and then to impress that like a stamp upon the material of the commonwealth. His criticism is directed against lawyers, not against philosophers and practical diplomatists.

In this sense and to this extent were the republics of Italy the products of constructive skill; and great was the political sagacity educed among the Italians by this state of things. The citizens reflected on the past, compared their institutions with those of neighbouring states, studied antiquity, and applied the whole of their intelligence to the one aim of giving a certain defined form to the commonwealth. Prejudice and passion distorted their schemes, and each successive modifica-tion of the government was apt to have a merely temporary

[1] *St. Fior.* lib. vi. cap. 4; vol. i. p. 294.

object. Thus the republics, as I have already hinted, lacked that safeguard which the Greek states gained by clinging each to its own character. The Greeks were no less self-conscious in their political practice and philosophy : but after the age of the Nomothetæ, when they had experienced nearly every phase through which a commonwealth can pass, they recognised the importance of maintaining the traditional character of their constitutions inviolate. Sparta adhered with singular tenacity to the code of Lycurgus ; and the Athenians, while they advanced from step to step in the development of a democracy, were bent on realising the ideal they had set before them.

Religion, which in Greece, owing to its local and genealogical character, was favourable to this stability, proved in Italy one of the most potent causes of disorder. The Greek city grew up under the protection of a local deity, whose blood had been transmitted in many instances to the chief families of the burgh. This ancestral god gave independence and autonomy to the state ; and when the Nomothetes appeared, he was understood to have interpreted and formulated the inherent law that animated the body politic. Thus the commonwealth was a divinely founded and divinely directed organism, self-sufficing, with no dependence upon foreign sanction, with no question of its right. The Italian cities, on the contrary, derived their law from the common *jus* of the Imperial system, their religion from the common fount of Christianity. They could not forget their origin, wrung with difficulty from existing institutions which preceded them and which still remained ascendent in the world of civilised humanity. The self-reliant autonomy of a Greek state, owing allegiance only to its protective deity and its inherent Nomos, had no parallel in Italy outside Venice. All the other republics were conscious of dependence on external power, and regarded themselves as *ab initio* artificial rather than natural creations.

Long before a true constitutional complexion had been given to any Italian state but Venice, parties had sprung up, and taken such firm root that the subsequent history of the republics was the record of their factions. To this point I have already alluded; but it is too important to be passed by without further illustration. The great division of Guelf and Ghibelline introduced a vital discord into each section of the people, by establishing two antagonistic theories respecting the right of supreme government. Then followed subordinate quarrels of the nobles with the townsfolk, schisms between the wealthier and poorer burghers, jealousies of the artisans and merchants, and factions for one or other eminent family. These different elements of discord succeed each other with astonishing rapidity; and as each gives place to another, it leaves a portion of its mischief rankling in the body politic, until at last there remains no possibility of self-government.[1] The history of Florence, or Genoa, or Pistoja would supply us with ample illustrations of each of these obstacles to the formation of a solid political temperament. But Siena furnishes perhaps the best example of the extent to which such feuds could disturb a state. The way in which this city conducted its government for a long course of years justified Varchi in calling it ' a jumble, so to speak, and chaos of republics, rather than a well-ordered and disciplined commonwealth.'[2] The discords of Siena were wholly internal. They proceeded from the wrangling of five successive factions, or Monti, as the people of Siena called them. The first of these was termed

[1] Machiavelli, in spite of his love of freedom, says (*St. Fior.* lib. vii. 1): ' Coloro che sperano che una repubblica possa essere unita, assai di questa speranza s' ingannano.'

[2] Vol. i. pp. 324–30. See, too, Segni, p. 213, and Giannotti, vol. i. p. 341. De Comines describes Siena thus: 'La ville est de tout temps en partialité, et se gouverne plus follement que ville d'Italie.'

the *Monte de' Nobili*; for Siena, like all Italian free burghs, had originally been controlled by certain noble families, who formed the people and excluded the other citizens from offices of state. In course of time the plebeians acquired wealth, and the nobles split into parties among themselves. To such a pitch were the quarrels of these nobles carried, that at last they found it impossible to conduct the government, and agreed to relinquish it for a season to nine plebeian families chosen from among the richest and most influential. This gave rise to the *Monte de' Nove*, who were supposed to hold the city in commission for the nobles, while the latter devoted themselves to the prosecution of their private animosities. Weakened by feuds, the patricians fell a prey to their own creatures, the *Monte de' Nove*, who in their turn ruled Siena like oligarchs, refusing to give up the power which had been entrusted to them. In time, however, their insolence became insufferable. The populace rebelled, deposed the *Nove*, and invested with supreme authority twelve other families of mixed origin. The *Monte de' Dodici*, created after this fashion, ran nearly the same course as their predecessors, except that they appear to have administered the city equitably. Getting tired of this form of government, the people next superseded them by sixteen men, chosen from the dregs of the plebeians, who assumed the title of *Riformatori*. This new *Monte de' Sedici* or *de' Riformatori* showed much integrity in their management of affairs, but, as is the wont of red republicans, they were not averse to bloodshed. Their cruelty caused the people, with the help of the surviving patrician houses, together with the *Nove* and the *Dodici*, to rise and shake them off. The last governing body formed in this diabolical five-part fugue of crazy statecraft received the name of *Monte del Popolo*, because it included all who were then eligible to the Great Council of the State. Yet the factions of the elder *Monti* still survived; and to what extent they had absorbed the population may be gathered from the fact that, on the defeat of the *Riformatori*, 4,500 of the Sienese were exiled. It must be borne in mind that with the creation of each new *Monte* a new party formed itself in the city, and the traditions of these parties were handed down from generation to generation. At last in the beginning of the sixteenth century, Pandolfo Petrucci, who belonged to the *Monte de' Nove*, made himself in reality, if not in name, the master of Siena, and the Duke of Florence later on in the same century extended his dominion over the republic.[1] There is something almost grotesque in the bare recital of these successive factions ; yet we must remember that beneath their dry names they conceal all elements of class and party discord.

What rendered the growth of parties still more pernicious, as already mentioned, was the smallness of Italian republics. Varchi reckoned 10,000 *fuochi* in Florence, 50,000 *bocche* of seculars, and 20,000 *bocche* of religious. According to Zuccagni Orlandini there were 90,000 Florentines in 1495, of whom only 3,200 were burghers. Venice, according to Giannotti, counted at about the same period 20,000 *fuochi*, each of which supplied the state with two men fit to bear arms. These calculations, though obviously rough and based upon no accurate returns, show that a republic of 100,000 souls, of whom 5,000 should be citizens, would have taken distinguished rank among Italian cities.[2] In a state of this size, divided by feuds of every kind, from the highest political antagonism down to the meanest

[1] Siena capitulated, in 1555, to the Spanish troops, who resigned it to Duke Cosmo I. in 1557.

[2] It may be worth while to compare the accurate return of the Venetian population in 1581 furnished by Yriarte (*Vie d'un Patricien de Venise*, p. 96). The whole number of the inhabitants was 134,600. Of these 1,843 were adult patricians ; 4,309 women and children of the patrician class ; Cittadini of all ages and both sexes, 3,553 ; monks, nuns, and priests, 3,969 ; Jews, 1,043 ; beggars, 187.

personal antipathy, changes were very easily effected. The slightest disturbance of the equilibrium in any quarter made itself felt throughout the city.[1] The opinions of each burgher were known and calculated. Individuals, by their wealth, their power of aiding or of suppressing poorer citizens, and the force of their personal ability, acquired a perilous importance. At Florence the political balance was so nicely adjusted that the ringing of the great bell in the Palazzo meant a revolution, and to raise the cry of *Palle* in the streets was tantamount to an outbreak in the Medicean interest. To call aloud *Popolo e libertà* was nothing less than riot punishable by law. Segni tells how Jacopino Alamanni, having used these words near the statue of David on the Piazza in a personal quarrel, was beheaded for it the same day.[2] The secession of three or four families from one faction to another altered the political situation of a whole republic, and led perhaps to the exile of a sixth part of the enfranchised population.[3] After this would follow the intrigues of the outlaws eager to return, including negotiations with lukewarm party-leaders in the city, alliances with hostile states, and contracts which compromised the future conduct of the commonwealth in the interest of a few revengeful citizens. The biographies of such men as Cosimo de' Medici the elder and Filippo Strozzi

[1] We might mention, as famous instances, the Neri and Bianchi factions introduced into Pistoja in 1296 by a quarrel of the Cancellieri family, the dismemberment of Florence in 1215 by a feud between the Buondelmonti and Amidei, the tragedy of Imelda Lambertazzi, which upset Bologna in 1273, the student riot which nearly delivered Bologna into the hands of Roméo de' Pepoli in 1321, the whole action of the Strozzi family at the period of the extinction of Florentine liberty, the petty jealousies of the Cerchi and Donati detailed by Dino Compagni, in 1294.

[2] Segni, *St. Fior.* p. 53.

[3] As an instance, take what Marco Foscari reported in 1527 to the Venetian Senate respecting the parties in Florence *Rel. Ven.* série ii. vol. i. p. 70). The *Compagnacci*, one of the three *great* parties, only numbered 800 persons.

throw the strongest light upon these delicacies and complexities of party politics in Florence.

In addition to the evils of internal factions we must reckon all the sources of mutual mistrust to which the republics were exposed. As the Italians had no notion of representative government, so they never conceived a confederation. The thirst for autonomy in each state was as great as of old among the cities of Greece. To be independent of a sister republic, though such freedom were bought at the price of the tyranny of a native family, was the first object of every commonwealth. At the same time this passion for independence was only equalled by the greed of foreign usurpation. The second object of each republic was to extend its power at the expense of its neighbours. As Pisa swallowed Amalfi, so Genoa destroyed Pisa, and Venice did her best to cripple Genoa. Florence obliterated the rival burgh of Semifonte, and Milan twice reduced Piacenza to a wilderness. The notion that the great maritime powers of Italy or the leading cities of Lombardy should permanently cooperate for a common purpose was never for a moment entertained. Such leagues as were formed were understood to be temporary. When their immediate object had been gained, the members returned to their old local rivalries. Milan, when, on the occasion of Filippo Maria Visconti's death, she had a chance of freedom, refused to recognise the liberties of the Lombard cities, and fell a prey to Francesco Sforza. Florence, under the pernicious policy of Cosimo de' Medici, helped to enslave Milan and Bologna instead of entering into a republican league against their common foes, the tyrants. Pisa, Arezzo, and the other subject cities of Tuscany were treated by her with such selfish harshness that they proved her chiefest peril in the hour of need.[1] Com-

[1] See the instructions furnished to Averardo dei Medici, quoted by Von Reumont in his *Life of Lorenzo*, vol. ii. p. 122, German edition.

dread long before this epoch : when she became aggressive, she was recognised as a common and intolerable enemy.

The external security of Venice was equalled by her internal repose. Owing to continued freedom from party quarrels, the Venetians were able to pursue a consistent course of constitutional development. They in fact alone of the Italian cities established and preserved the character of their state. Having originally founded a republic under the presidency of a Doge, who combined the offices of general and judge, and ruled in concert with a representative council of the chief citizens (697–1172), the Venetians by degrees caused this form of government to assume a strictly oligarchical character. They began by limiting the authority of the Doge, who, though elected for life, was in 1032 forbidden to associate his son in the supreme office of the state. In 1172 the election of the Doge was transferred from the people to the Grand Council, who, as a co-opting body, tended to become a close aristocracy. In 1179 the Ducal power was still further restricted by the creation of a senate called the Quarantia for the administration of justice ; while in 1229 the Senate of the Pregadi, interposed between the Doge and the Grand Council, became an integral part of the constitution. To this latter Senate were assigned all deliberations upon peace and war, the voting of supplies, the confirmation of laws. Both the Quarantia and the Pregadi were elected by the Consiglio Grande, which by this time had become the virtual sovereign of the State of Venice. It is not necessary here to mention the further checks imposed upon the power of the Doges by the institution of officials named Correttori and Inquisitori, whose special business it was to see that the coronation oaths were duly observed, or by the regulations which prevented the supreme magistrate from taking any

subjected him and his son Jacopo to the most frightfully protracted martyrdom that a relentless oligarchy has ever inflicted [1445–57].

important action except in concert with carefully selected
colleagues.   Enough has been said to show that the constitution of Venice w. s a pyramid resting upon the basis of the
Grand Council and rising to an ornamented apex, through
the Senate, and the College, in the Doge.   But in adopting
this old simile—originally the happy thought of Donato
Giannotti, it is said [1]—we must not forget that the vital force
of the Grand Council was felt throughout the whole of this
elaborate system, and that the same individuals were con-
stantly appearing in different capacities.   It is this which
makes the great event of the years 1297–1319 so all-important for the future destinies of Venice.   At this period the
Grand Council was restricted to a certain number of noble
families who had henceforth the hereditary right to belong to
it.   Every descendant of a member of the Grand Council could
take his seat there at the age of twenty-five ; and no new
families, except upon the most extraordinary occasions, were
admitted to this privilege.[2]   By the Closing of the Grand
Council, as the ordinances of this crisis were termed, the

---

[1] Vol. ii. of his works, p. 37.   On p. 29 he describes the population
of Venice as divided into ‘Popolari,’ or plebeians, exercising small
industries, and so forth ; ‘Cittadini,’ or the middle class, born in the
state, and of more importance than the plebeians ; ‘Gentiluomini,’ or
masters of Venice by sea and land, about 3,000 in number, corresponding
to the burghers of Florence.   What he says about the Constitution
refers solely to this upper class.   The elaborate work of M. Yriarte, *La
Vie d'un Patricien de Venise au Seizième Siècle*, Paris, 1874, contains a
complete analysis of the Venetian state-machine.   See in particular
what he says about the helplessness of the Doges, ch. xiii.   ‘Rex in
foro, senator in curiâ, captivus in aulâ,’ was a current phrase which
expressed the contrast between their dignity of parade and real servitude.   They had no personal freedom, and were always ruined by office.
It was necessary to pass a law compelling the Doge elect to accept the
onerous distinction thrust upon him.   The Venetian oligarchs argued
that it was good that one man should die for the people.

[2] See Giannotti, vol. ii. p. 55, for the mention of fifteen, admitted on
the occasion of Baiamonte Tiepolo's conspiracy, and of thirty ennobled
during the Genoese war.

administration of Venice was vested for perpetuity in the hands of a few great houses. The final completion was given to the oligarchy in 1311 by the establishment of the celebrated Council of Ten,[1] who exercised a supervision over all the magistracies, constituted the Supreme Court of judicature, and ended by controlling the whole foreign and internal policy of Venice. The changes which I have thus briefly indicated are not to be regarded as violent alterations in the constitution, but rather as successive steps in its development. Even the Council of Ten, which seems at first sight the most tyrannous state-engine ever devised for the enslavement of a nation, was in reality a natural climax to the evolution which had been consistently advancing since the year 1172. Created originally during the troublous times which succeeded the closing of the Grand Council, for the express purpose of curbing unruly nobles and preventing the emergence of conspirators like Tiepolo, the Council of Ten were specially designed to act as a check upon the several orders in the state and to preserve its oligarchical character inviolate. They were elected by the Consiglio Grande, and at the expiration of their office were liable to render strict account of all that they had done. Nor was this magistracy coveted by the Venetian nobles. On the contrary, so burdensome were its duties, and so great was the odium which from time to time the Ten incurred in the discharge of their functions, that it was not always found easy to fill up their vacancies. A law had even to be passed that the Ten had not completed their magistracy before their successors were appointed.[2] They may therefore be regarded as a select committee of the citizens, who voluntarily delegated dictatorial powers to this small body in order to maintain their own ascendency, to

---

[1] The actual number of this Council was seventeen, for the Ten were associated with the Signoria, which consisted of the Doge and six Councillors.   [2] Giannotti, vol. ii. p. 123.

centralise the conduct of important affairs, to preserve secrecy
in the administration of the republic, and to avoid the criticism to which the more public government of states like
Florence was exposed.[1] The weakness of this portion of the
state machinery was this : created with ill-defined and almost
unlimited authority,[2] designed to supersede the other public
functionaries on occasions of great moment, and composed of
men whose ability placed them in the very first rank of
citizens, the Ten could scarcely fail, as time advanced, to
become a permanently oppressive power—a despotism within
the bosom of an oligarchy. Thus in the whole mechanism
of the state of Venice we trace the action of a permanent
aristocracy tolerating, with a view to its own supremacy, an
amount of magisterial control which in certain cases, like
that of the two Foscari, amounted to the sternest tyranny.
By submitting to the Council of Ten the nobility of Venice
secured its hold upon the people and preserved unity in its
policy.

No State has ever exercised a greater spell of fascination
over its citizens than Venice. Of treason against the Republic
there was little. Against the decrees of the Council, arbitrary
though they might be, no one sought to rebel. The Venetian
bowed in silence and obeyed, knowing that all his actions were
watched, that his government had long arms in foreign lands,
and that to arouse revolt in a body of burghers so thoroughly
controlled by common interests would be impossible. Further
security the Venetians gained by their mild and beneficent
administration of subject cities, and by the prosperity in which
their population flourished. When, during the war of the
League of Cambray, Venice gave liberty to her towns upon

[1] The diplomatic difficulties of a popular government, a 'governo
largo,' as opposed to a 'governo stretto,' are set forth with great acumen
by Guicciardini, *Op. Ined.* vol. ii. p. 84. Cf. vol. iii. p. 272.

[2] 'è la sua autorità parì a quella del Consiglio de' Pregati e di tutta
la città,' says Giannotti, vol. ii. p. 120.

the mainland, they voluntarily returned to her allegiance. At home, the inhabitants of the lagoons, who had never seen a hostile army at their gates, and whose taxes were light in comparison with those of the rest of Italy, regarded the nobles as the authors of their unexampled happiness. Meanwhile, these nobles were merchants. Idleness was unknown in Venice. Instead of excogitating new constitutions or planning vengeance against hereditary foes, the Venetian attended to his commerce on the sea, swayed distant provinces, watched the interests of the state in foreign cities, and fought the naval battles of the republic. It was the custom of Venice to employ her patricians only on the sea as admirals, and never to entrust her armies to the generalship of burghers. This policy had undoubtedly its wisdom ; for by these means the nobles had no opportunity of intriguing on a large scale in Italian affairs, and never found the chance of growing dangerously powerful abroad. But it pledged the State to that system of paid condottieri and mercenary troops, jealously watched and scarcely ever trustworthy, which proved nearly as ruinous to Venice as it did to Florence.

It is difficult to imagine a greater contrast than that which is presented by Florence to Venice. While Venice pursued one consistent course of gradual growth, and seemed immovable, Florence remained in perpetual flux, and altered as the strength of factions or of party leaders varied.[1] When the strife of Guelfs and Ghibellines, Neri and Bianchi, had exhausted her in the fourteenth century, she submitted for a while to the indirect ascendency of the kings of Naples, who were recognised as Chiefs of the Guelf Party. Thence she passed for a few months into the hands of a Despot in the person of the Duke of Athens (1342–43). After the confirmation of

---

[1] 'Nunquam in eodem statu permanserunt,' says Marco Foscari (as quoted above, p. 42 of his report). The flux of Florence struck a Venetian profoundly.

her republican liberty followed a contest between the proletariat and the middle classes (Ciompi, 1378). During the
fifteenth century she was kept continually disturbed by the
rivalry of her great merchant families. The rule of the Albizzi,
who fought the Visconti and extended the Florentine territory
by numerous conquests, was virtually the despotism of a close
oligarchy. This phase of her career was terminated by the
rise of the Medici, who guided her affairs with a show of constitutional equity for four generations. In 1494 this state of
things was violently shaken. The Florentines expelled the
Medici, who had begun to throw off their mask and to assume
the airs of sovereignty. Then they reconstituted their Commonwealth as nearly as they could upon the model of Venice,
and to this new form of government Savonarola gave a quasi-
theocratic complexion by naming Christ the king of Florence.[1]
But the internal elements of discord were too potent for the
maintenance of this régime. The Medici were recalled ; and
this time Florence fell under the shadow of Church rule, being
controlled by Leo X. and Clement VII., through the hands of
prelates whom they made the guardians and advisers of their
nephews. In 1527 a final effort for liberty shed undying
lustre on the noblest of Italian cities. The sack of Rome had
paralysed the Pope. His family were compelled to quit the
Medicean palace. The Grand Council was restored ; a Gonfalonier was elected ; Florence suffered the hardships of her
memorable siege. At the end of her trials, menaced alike by
Pope and Emperor, who shook hands over her prostrate corpse,

[1] The Gonfalonier Capponi put up a tablet on the Public Palace,
in 1528, to this effect : ' Jesus Christus Rex Florentini Populi S. F. decreto electus.' This inscription is differently given. See Varchi, vol. i.
p. 266; Segni, p. 46. Nothing is more significant of the difference
between Venice and Florence than the political idealism implied in this
religious consecration of the republic by statute. In my essay on
' Florence and the Medici ' (*Sketches and Studies in Italy*) I have
attempted to condense the internal history of the Republic and to analyse
the statecraft of the Medici.

betrayed by her general, the infamous Malatesta Baglioni, and sold by her own selfish citizens, she had to submit to the hereditary sovereignty of the Medici. It was in vain that Lorenzino of that House pretended to play Brutus, and murdered his cousin the Duke Alessandro in 1536. Cosimo succeeded in the same year, and won the title of Grand Duke, which he transmitted to a line of semi-Austrian princes.

Throughout all these vicissitudes every form and phase of republican government was advocated, discussed, and put in practice by the Florentines. All the arts of factions, all the machinations of exiles, all the skill of demagogues, all the selfishness of party-leaders, all the learning of scholars, all the cupidity of subordinate officials, all the daring of conspirators, all the ingenuity of theorists, and all the malice of traitors, were brought successively or simultaneously into play by the burghers, who looked upon their State as something they might mould at will. One thing at least is clear amid so much apparent confusion, that Florence was living a vehemently active and self-conscious life, acknowledging no principle of stability in her constitution, but always stretching forward after that ideal *Reggimento* which was never realised.[1]

It is worth while to consider more in detail the different magistracies by which the government of Florence was conducted between the years 1250 and 1531, and the gradual changes in the constitution which prepared the way for the Medicean tyranny.[2] It is only thus that an accurate concep-

[1] In his 'Proemio' to the *Trattato del Reggimento di Firenze* Guicciardini thus describes the desideratum: 'introdurre in Firenze un governo onesto, bene ordinato, e che veramente si potesse chiamare libero, il che dalla sua prima origine insino a oggi non è mai stato cittadino alcuno che abbia saputo o potuto fare.'

[2] I will place in an appendix (No. ii.) translations of Varchi, book iii. sections 20–22, and Nardi, book i. cap. 4, which give complete and clear accounts of the Florentine Constitution after 1292.

tion of the difference between the republican systems of Venice
and of Florence can be gained.   Before the date 1282, which
may be fixed as the turning point in Florentine history, we
hear of twelve Anziani, two chosen for each Sestiere of the
city, acting in concert with a foreign Podestà, and a Captain
of the People charged with military authority.   At this time
no distinction was made between nobles and plebeians ; and
the town, though Guelf, had not enacted rigorous laws against
the Ghibelline families.   Towards the end of the thirteenth
century, however, important changes were effected in the very
elements of the commonwealth.   The Anziani were superseded by the Priors of the Arts.   Eight Priors, together with
a new officer called the Gonfalonier of Justice, formed the
Signoria, dwelling at public charge in the Palazzo and holding
office only for two months.[1]   No one who had not been matriculated into one of the Arti or commercial guilds could henceforth bear office in the state.   At the same time severe measures, called Ordinanze della Giustizia, were passed, by which
the nobles were for ever excluded from the government, and
the Gonfalonier of Justice was appointed to maintain civil
order by checking their pride and turbulence.[2]   These modifications of the constitution, effected between 1282 and 1292,
gave its peculiar character to the Florentine republic.   Hence-
forward Florence was governed solely by merchants.   Both
Varchi and Machiavelli have recorded unfavourable opinions
of the statute which reduced the republic of Florence to a
commonwealth of shop-keepers.[3]   But when we read these

[1] See Machiavelli, *Ist. Fior.* lib. ii. sect. 11.   The number of the Priors
was first three, then six, and finally eight.   Up to 1282 the city had been
divided into Sestieri.   It was then found convenient to divide it into
quarters, and the numbers followed this alteration.

[2] Machiavelli, *Ist. Fior.* lib. ii. sect. 13, may be consulted for the
history of Giano della Bella and his memorable ordinance.   Dino
Compagni's *Chronicle* contains the account of a contemporary.

[3] See Varchi, vol. i. p. 169 ; Mach. *Ist. Fior.* end of book ii.

criticisms, we must bear in mind the internecine ferocity of party-strife at this period, and the discords to which a city divided between a territorial aristocracy and a commercial bourgeoisie was perpetually exposed. If anything could make the Ordinanze della Giustizia appear rational, it would be a cool perusal of the 'Chronicle' of Matarazzo, which sets forth the wretched state of Perugia owing to the feuds of its patrician houses, the Oddi and the Baglioni.[1] Peace for the republic was not, however, secured by these strong measures. The factions of the Neri and Bianchi opened the fourteenth century with battles and proscriptions; and in 1323 the constitution had again to be modified. At this date the Signoria of eight Priors with the Gonfalonier of Justice, the College of the twelve Buonuomini, and the sixteen Gonfaloniers of the companies—called collectively *i tre maggiori*, or the three superior magistracies—were rendered eligible only to Guelf citizens of the age of thirty, who had qualified in one of the seven Arti Maggiori, and whose names were drawn by lot. This mode of election, the most democratic which it is possible to adopt, held good through all subsequent changes in the state. Its immediate object was to quiet discontent and to remove intrigue by opening the magistracies to all citizens alike. But, as Nardi has pointed out, it weakened the sense of responsibility in the burghers, who, when their names were once included in the bags kept for the purpose, felt sure of their election, and had no inducement to maintain a high standard of integrity. Sismondi also dates from this epoch the withdrawal of the Florentines from military service.[2] Nor, as the sequel shows, was the measure efficient as a check upon the personal ambition of encroaching party leaders. The *Squittino* and the *Borse* became instruments in the hands of

[1] *Archivio Storico*, vol. xvi. See also the article 'Perugia,' in my *Sketches in Italy and Greece*.

[2] Vol. iii. p. 347.

the Medici for the consolidation of their tyranny.[1] By the end of the fourteenth century (about 1378) the Florentines had to meet a new difficulty. The Guelf citizens began to abuse the so-called Law of Admonition, by means of which the Ghibellines were excluded from the government. This law had formed an essential part of the measures of 1323. In the intervening half century a new aristocracy, distinguished by the name of *nobili popolani*, had grown up and were now threatening the republic with a close oligarchy.[2] The discords which had previously raged between the people and the patricians were now transferred to this new aristocracy and the plebeians. It was found necessary to abolish the Admonition, which had been made a pretext of excluding all *novi homines* from the government, and to place the members of the inferior Arti on the same footing as those of the superior.[3] At this epoch the Medici, who neither belonged to the ancient aristocracy nor yet to the more distinguished houses of the *nobili popolani*, but rather to the so-called *gente grassa* or substantial tradesmen, first acquired importance. It was by a law of Salvestro de' Medici's in 1378 that the constitution received its final development in the direction of equality. Yet after all this levelling, and in spite of the vehement efforts made by the proletariat on the occasion of the Ciompi outbreak, the exclusive nature of the Florentine republic was maintained. The franchise was never extended to more than the burghers, and the matter in debate was always virtually, who shall be allowed to rank as citizen upon the register ?   In fact, by using the pregnant words of Machiavelli, we may sum up the history of Florence to this point in one sentence : 'Di

---

[1] See App. ii. for the phrases ' Squittino ' and ' Borse.'

[2] Of these new nobles the Albizzi and Ricci, deadly foes, were the most eminent. The former strove to exclude the Medici from the government.

[3] The number of the Arti varied at different times. Varchi treats of them as finally consisting of seven maggiori and fourteen minori.

Firenze in prima si divisono intra loro i nobili, dipoi i nobili e il popolo, e in ultimo il popolo e la plebe ; e molte volte occorse che una di queste parti rimasa superiore, si divise in due.' [1]

In the next generation the constitutional history of Florence exhibits a new phase. The equality which had been introduced into all classes of the commonwealth, combined with an absence of any state machinery like that of Venice, exposed Florence at this period to the encroachments of astute and selfish parvenus. The Medici, who had hitherto been nobodies, begin now to aspire to despotism. Partly by his remarkable talent for intrigue, partly by the clever use which he made of his vast wealth, and partly by espousing the plebeian cause, Cosimo de' Medici succeeded in monopolising the government. It was the policy of the Medici to create a party dependent for pecuniary aid upon their riches, and attached to their interests by the closest ties of personal necessity. At the same time they showed consummate caution in the conduct of the state, and expended large sums on works of public utility. There was nothing mean in their ambition ; and though posterity must condemn the arts by which they sought to sap the foundations of freedom in their native city, we are forced to acknowledge that they shared the noblest enthusiasms of their brilliant era. Little by little they advanced so far in the enslavement of Florence that the elections of all the magistrates, though still conducted by lot, were determined at their choice ; the names of none but men devoted to their interests were admitted to the bags from which the candidates for office were selected, while proscriptive measures of various degrees

---

[1] Proemio to *Storia Fiorentina*. ' In Florence the nobles first split up, then the nobles and the people, lastly the people and the multitude ; and it often happened that when one of these parties got the upper hand, it divided into two camps.' For the meaning of *Popolo* see above, p. 43.

of rigour excluded their enemies from participation in the government.[1] At length in 1480 the whole machinery of the republic was suspended by Lorenzo de' Medici in favour of the board of Seventy, whom he nominated, and with whom, acting like a Privy Council, he administered the state.[2] It is clear that this revolution could never have been effected without a succession of coups d'état. The instrument for their accomplishment lay ready to the hands of the Medicean party in the pernicious system of the Parlamento and Balia, by means of which the people, assembled from time to time in the public square, and intimidated by the reigning faction, entrusted full powers to a select committee nominated in private by the chiefs of the great house.[3] It is also clear that so

[1] What Machiavelli says (*Ist. Fior.* vii. 1) about the arts of Cosimo contains the essence of the policy by which the Medici rose. Compare v. 4 and vii. 4–6 for his character of Cosimo. Guicciardini (*Op. Ined.* vol. ii. p. 68) describes the use made of extraordinary taxation as a weapon of offence against his enemies, by Cosimo : ' usò le gravezze in luogo de' pugnali che communemente suole usare chi ha simili reggimenti nelle mani.' The Marchese Gino Capponi (*Arch. Stor.* vol. i. pp. 315–20) analyses the whole Medicean policy in a critique of great ability.

[2] Guicciardini (*Op. Ined.* vol. ii. pp. 35–49) exposes the principle and the *modus operandi* of this Council of Seventy, by means of which Lorenzo controlled the election of the magistracies, diverted the public moneys to his own use, and made his will law in Florence. The councils which he superseded at this date were the Consiglio del Popolo and the Consiglio del Comune, about which see Nardi, lib. i. cap. 4.

[3] For the operation of the Parlamento and Balia, see Varchi, vol. ii. p. 372 ; Segni, p. 199 ; Nardi, lib. vi. cap. 4. Segni says : ' The Parlamento is a meeting of the Florentine people on the Piazza of the Signory. When the Signory has taken its place to address the meeting, the piazza is guarded by armed men, and then the people are asked whether they wish to give absolute power (Balia) and authority to the citizens named, for their good. When the answer, yes, prompted partly by inclination and partly by compulsion, is returned, the Signory immediately retires into the palace. This is all that is meant by this Parlamento, which thus gives away the full power of effecting a change in the state.' The description given by Marco Foscari, p. 44 (loc. cit. supr.)

much political roguery could not have been successful without an extensive demoralisation of the upper rank of citizens.
The Medici in effect bought and sold the honour of the public
officials, lent money, jobbed posts of profit, and winked at
peculation, until they had created a sufficient body of *âmes
damnées*, men who had everything to gain by a continuance
of their corrupt authority. The party so formed, including
even such distinguished citizens as the Guicciardini, Baccio
Valori, and Francesco Vettori, proved the chief obstacle to
the restoration of Florentine liberty in the sixteenth
century.

This tyranny of a commercial family, swaying the republic
without the title and with but little of the pomp of princes,
subsisted until the hereditary presidency of the state was
conferred upon Alessandro de' Medici, Duke of Città di
Penna, in 1531. Cosimo, his successor, obtained the rank of
Grand Duke from Pius V. in 1569, and his son received the
imperial sanction to the title in 1575. The re-establishment
at two different periods of a free commonwealth upon the
sounder basis of the Consiglio Grande (1494–1512 and 1527–
30) formed but two episodes in the history of this masked
but tenacious despotism. Had Savonarola's constitution been
adopted in the thirteenth instead of at the end of the
fifteenth century, the stability of Florence might have been
secured. But at the latter date the roots of the Medicean
influence were too widely intertwined with private interests,
the jealousies of classes and of factions were too inveterate,

is to the same effect, but the Venetian exposes more clearly the despotic
nature of the institution in the hands of the Medici. It is well known
how hostile Savonarola was to an institution which had lent itself so
easily to despotism. This couplet he inscribed on the walls of the
Council Chamber, in 1495 :—

> 'E sappi che chi vuol parlamento
> Vuol torti dalle mani il reggimento.'

Compare the proverb, 'Chi disse parlamento disse guastamento.'

for any large and wholesome form of popular government to be universally acceptable. Besides, the burghers had been reduced to a nerveless equality of servitude, in which ambition and avarice took the place of patriotism; while the corruption of morals, fostered by the Medici for the confirmation of their own authority, was so widely spread as to justify Segni, Varchi, Giannotti, Guicciardini, and Machiavelli in representing the Florentines as equally unable to maintain their liberty and to submit to control.

The historical vicissitudes of Florence were no less remarkable than the unity of Venice. If in Venice we can trace the permanent and corporate existence of a state superior to the individuals who composed it, Florence exhibits the personal activity and conscious effort of her citizens. Nowhere can the intricate relations of classes to the commonwealth be studied more minutely than in the annals of Florence. In no other city have opinions had greater value in determining historical events; and nowhere was the influence of character in men of mark more notable. In this agitated political atmosphere the wonderful Florentine intelligence, which Varchi celebrated as the special glory of the Tuscan soil, and which Vasari referred to something felicitous in Tuscan air, was sharpened to the finest edge.[1] Successive generations of practical and theoretical statesmen trained the race to reason upon government, and to regard politics as a science. Men of letters were at the same time also prominent in public affairs. When, for instance, the exiles of 1529 sued Duke Alessandro before Charles V. at Naples, Jacopo Nardi drew up their pleas, and Francesco Guicciardini rebutted them in the interest of his master. Machiavelli learned his philosophy at the Courts of France and Germany and in the camp of Cesare Borgia. Segni shared the anxieties of Nicolo Capponi, when the Gonfalonier was

[1] Varchi, ix. 49 ; Vasari, xii. p. 158 ; Burckhardt, p. 270.

impeached for high treason to the state of Florence. This list might be extended almost indefinitely, with the object of proving the intimate connection which subsisted at Florence between the thinkers and the actors. No other European community of modern times has ever acquired so subtle a sense of its own political existence, has ever reasoned upon its past history so acutely, or has ever displayed so much ingenuity in attempting to control the future. Venice on the contrary owed but little to the creative genius of her citizens. In Venice the state was everything: the individual was almost nothing. We find but little reflection upon politics, and no speculative philosophy of history among the Venetians until the date of Trifone Gabrielli and Paruta. Their records are all positive and detailed. The generalisations and comparisons of the Florentines are absent; nor was it till a late date of the Renaissance that the Venetian history came to be written as a whole. It would seem as though the constitutional stability which formed the secret of the strength of Venice was also the source of comparative intellectual inertness. This contrast between the two republics displayed itself even in their art. Statues of Judith the tyrannicide, and of David the liberator of his country, adorned the squares and loggie of Florence. The painters of Venice represented their commonwealth as a beautiful queen receiving the homage of her subjects and the world. Florence had no mythus similar to that which made Venice the Bride of the Sea, and which justified the Doge in hailing Caterina Cornaro as daughter of S. Mark's (1471). It was in the personal courage and intelligence of individual heroes that the Florentines discovered the counterpart of their own spirit; whereas the Venetians personified their city as a whole, and paid their homage to the Genius of the State.

It is not merely fanciful to compare Athens, the city of self-conscious political activity, variable, cultivated, and ill-adapted by its very freedom for prolonged stability, with Florence ; Sparta, firmly based upon an ancient constitution, indifferent to culture, and solid at the cost of some rigidity, with Venice.   As in Greece the philosophers of Athens, especially Plato and Aristotle, wondered at the immobility of Sparta and idealised her institutions ; so did the theorists of Florence, Savonarola, Giannotti, Guicciardini, look with envy at the state machinery which secured repose and liberty for Venice.   The parallel between Venice and Sparta becomes still more remarkable when we inquire into the causes of their decay.   Just as the Ephors, introduced at first as a safeguard to the constitution, by degrees extinguished the influence of the royal families, superseded the Senate, and exercised a tyrannous control over every department of the state ; so the Council of Ten, dangerous because of its vaguely defined dictatorial functions, reduced Venice to a despotism.[1]   The gradual dwindling of the Venetian aristo-cracy, and the impoverishment of many noble families, which rendered votes in the Grand Council venal, and threw the power into the hands of a very limited oligarchy, complete the parallel.[2]   One of the chief sources of decay both to Venice and to Sparta was that shortsighted policy which prevented the nobles from recruiting their ranks by the admission of

[1] Aristotle terms the Spartan Ephoralty $\grave{\iota}\sigma o\tau\acute{\upsilon}\rho a\nu\nu o s$. Giannotti (vol. ii. p. 120) compares the Ten to dictators. We might bring the struggles of the Spartan kings with the Ephoralty into comparison with the attempts of the Doges Falieri and Foscari to make themselves the chiefs of the republic in more than name. Müller, in his *Dorians*, observes that ' the Ephoralty was the moving element, the principle of change, in the Spartan constitution, and, in the end, the cause of its dissolution.' Sismondi remarks that the precautions which led to the creation of the Council of Ten ' dénaturaient entièrement la constitution de l'état.'

[2] See what Aristotle in the *Politics* says about $\grave{o}\lambda\iota\gamma a\nu\theta\rho\omega\pi\acute{\iota}a$, and the unequal distribution of property. As to the property of the Venetian nobles, see Sanudo, *Vite dei Duchi*, Murat. xxii. p. 1194, who mentions the benevolences of the richer families to the poor. They built houses for aristocratic paupers to live in free of rent.

new families. The system again of secret justice, the espion-age, and the calculated terrorism, by means of which both the Spartan Ephoralty and the Venetian Council imposed their will upon the citizens, were stifling to the free life of a repub-lic.[1] Venice in the end became demoralised in politics and profligate in private life. Her narrowing oligarchy watched the national degeneration with approval, knowing that it is easier to control a vitiated populace than to curb a nation habituated to the manly virtues.

Between Athens and Florence the parallel is not so close. These two republics, however, resemble one another in the freedom and variety of their institutions. In Athens, as in Florence, there was constant change and a highly developed political consciousness. Eminent men played the same im-portant part in both. In both the genius of individuals was even stronger than the character of the state. Again, as Athens displayed more of a Panhellenic feeling than any other Greek city, so Florence was invariably more alive to the interests of Italy at large than any other state of the penin-sula. Florence, like Athens, was the centre of culture for the nation. Like Athens, she gave laws to her sister towns in language, in literature, in fine arts, poetry, philosophy, and history. Without Florence it is not probable that Italy would have taken the place of proud pre-eminence she held so long in Europe. Florence never attained to the material greatness of Athens, because her power, relatively to the rest of Italy, was slight, her factions were incessant, and her connection with the Papacy was a perpetual source of weakness. But

---

[1] A curious passage in Plutarch's *Life of Cleomenes* (Clough's Translation, vol. iv. p. 474) exactly applies to the Venetian state-craft :— ' They, the Spartans, worship Fear, not as they do supernatural powers which they dread, esteeming it hurtful, but thinking their polity is chiefly kept up by fear . . . . and therefore the Lacedæmonians placed the temple of Fear by the Syssitium of the Ephors, having raised that magistracy to almost regal authority.'

many of the causes which ruined Athens were in full operation at Florence. First and foremost was the petulant and
variable temper of a democracy, so well described by Plato,
and so ably analysed by Machiavelli. The want of agreement
among the versatile Florentines, fertile in plans but incapable
of concerted action, was a chief source of political debility.
Varchi and Segni both relate how, in spite of wealth, ability,
and formidable forces, the Florentine exiles under the
guidance of Filippo Strozzi (1533–37) became the laughing-
stock of Italy through their irresolution. The Venetian
ambassadors agree in representing the burghers of Florence
as timid from excess of intellectual mobility. And Dante,
whose insight into national characteristics was of the keenest,
has described in ever-memorable lines the temperament of
his fickle city (*Purg.* vi. 135–51).

Much of this instability was due to the fact that Florentine, like Athenian, intelligence was over-developed. It passed
into mere cleverness, and over-reached itself. Next we may
note the tyranny which both republics exercised over cities
that had once been free. Athens created a despotic empire
instead of forming an Ionian Confederation. Florence
reduced Pisa to the most miserable servitude, rendered herself
odious to Arezzo and Volterra, and never rested from attempts
upon the liberties of Lucca and Siena. All these states,
which as a Tuscan federation should have been her strength
in the hour of need, took the first opportunity of throwing off
her yoke and helping her enemies. What Florence spent in
recapturing Pisa, after the passage of Charles VIII. in 1494,
is incalculable. And no sooner was she in difficulties during
the siege of 1529, than both Arezzo and Pisa declared for
her foes.

It will not do to push historical parallels too far, interesting as it may be to note a repetition of the same phenomena
at distant periods and under varying conditions of society.

At the same time, to observe fundamental points of divergence is no less profitable. Many of the peculiarities of Greek history are attributable to the fact that a Greek commonwealth consisted of citizens living in idleness, supported by their slaves, and bound to the state by military service and by the performance of civic duties. The distinctive mark of both Venice and Florence, on the other hand, was that their citizens were traders. The Venetians carried on the commerce of the Levant; the Florentines were manufacturers and bankers: the one town sent her sons forth on the seas to barter and exchange; the other was full of speculators, calculating rates of interest and discount, and contracting with princes for the conduct of expensive wars. The mercantile character of these Italian republics is so essential to their history that it will not be out of place to enlarge a little on the topic. We have seen that the Florentines rendered commerce a condition of burghership. Giannotti, writing the life of one of the chief patriots of the republic,[1] says: Egli stette a bottega, come fanno la maggior parte de' nostri, cosi nobili come ignobili.' To quote instances in a matter so clear and obvious would be superfluous: else I might show how Bardi and Peruzzi, Strozzi, Medici, Pitti, and Pazzi, while they ranked with princes at the Courts of France, or Rome, or Naples, were moneylenders, mortgagees, and bill-discounters in every great city of Europe. The Palle of the Medici, which emboss the gorgeous ceilings of the Cathedral of Pisa, still swing above the pawnbroker's shop in London. And though great families like the Rothschilds in the most recent days have successfully asserted the aristocracy of wealth acquired by usury, it still remains a surprising fact that the daughter

---

[1] *Sulle azioni del Ferruccio*, vol. i. p. 44. The report of Marco Foscari on the state of Florence, already quoted more than once, contains a curious aristocratic comment upon the shop-life of illustrious Florentine citizens. See Appendix ii. Even Piero de' Medici refused a Neapolitan fief on the ground that he was a tradesman.

of the mediæval bankers should have given a monarch to the French in the sixteenth century.

A very lively picture of the modes of life and the habits of mind peculiar to the Italian burgher may be gained by the perusal of Agnolo Pandolfini's treatise, 'Del Governo della Famiglia.' This essay should be read side by side with Castiglione's 'Cortegiano,' by all who wish to understand the private life of the Italians in the age of the Renaissance.[1] Pandolfini lived at the time of the war of Florence with Filippo Visconti the exile, and the return of Cosimo de' Medici. He was employed by the republic on important missions, and his substance was so great that, on occasion of extraordinary aids, his contributions stood third or fourth upon the list. In the Councils of the Republic he always advocated peace, and in particular he spoke against the Impresa di Lucca. As age advanced, he retired from public affairs and devoted himself to study, religious exercises, and country excursions. He possessed a beautiful villa at Signa, notable for the splendour of its maintenance in all points which befit a gentleman. There he had the honour on various occasions of entertaining Pope Eugenius, King René, Francesco Sforza, and the Marchese Piccinino. His sons lived with him, and spent much of their spare time in hawking and the chase. They were three—Carlo, who rose to great dignity in the republic, Giannozzo, still more eminent as a public man, and Pandolfo, who died young. His wife,

---

[1] I ought to state that Pandolfini is at least a century earlier in date than Castiglione, and that he represents a more primitive condition of society. The facts I have mentioned about his life are given on the authority of Vespasiano da Bisticci. The references are made to the Milanese edition of 1802. It must also be added that there are strong reasons for assigning the treatise in question to Leo Battista Alberti. As it professes, however, to give a picture of Pandolfini's family, I have adhered to the old title. But the whole question of the authorship of the *Famiglia* is fully discussed in the last section of my book, which deals with Italian literature. Personally, I accept the theory of Alberti's authorship.

one of the Strozzi, died while Agnolo was between thirty and forty ; but he never married again. He was a great friend of Lionardo Aretino, who published nothing without his approval. He lived to be upwards of eighty-five, and died in 1446. These facts sufficiently indicate what sort of man was the supposed author of the 'Essay on the Family,' proving, as they do, that he passed his leisure among princes and scholars, and that he played some part in the public affairs of the State of Florence. Yet his view of human life is wholly bourgeois, though by no means ignoble. In his conception, the first of all virtues is thrift, which should regulate the use not only of money but of all the gifts of nature and of fortune. The proper economy of the mind involves liberal studies, courteous manners, honest conduct and religion.[1] The right use of the body implies keeping it in good health by continence, exercise and diet.[2] The thrift of time consists in being never idle. Agnolo's sons, who are represented as talking with their father in this dialogue, ask him, in relation to the gifts of fortune, whether he thinks the honours of the state desirable. This question introduces a long and vehement invective against the life of a professional statesman, as of necessity fraudulent, mendacious, egotistic, cruel.[3] The private man of middle station is really happiest : and only a sense of patriotism should induce him, not seeking but when sought, to serve the state in public office. The really dear possessions of a man are his family, his wealth, his good repute, and his friendships. In order to be successful in the conduct of the family, a man must choose a large and healthy house, where the whole of his offspring, children and

[1] A beautiful description of the religious temper, p. 74.

[2] What Pandolfini says about the beauty of the body is worthy of a Greek : what he says about exercise might have been written by an Englishman, p. 77.

[3] Pp. 82–89 are very important as showing how low the art of politics had sunk in Italy.

grandchildren, may live together. He must own an estate
which will supply him with corn, wine, oil, wood, fowls, in
fact with all the necessaries of life, so that he may not need
to buy much. The main food of the family will be bread and
wine. The discussion of the utility of the farm leads Agnolo
to praise the pleasure and profit to be derived from life in the
Villa. But at the same time a townhouse has to be maintained ; and it is here that the sons of the family should be
educated, so that they may learn caution, and avoid vice by
knowing its ugliness. In order to meet expenses, some trade
must be followed, silk or wool manufacture being preferred ;
and in this the whole family should join, the head distributing
work of various kinds to his children, as he deems most fitting, and always employing them rather than strangers.
Thus we get the three great elements of the Florentine
citizen's life : the *casa*, or town-house, the *villa*, or country-
farm, and the *bottega*, or place of business. What follows is
principally concerned with the details of economy. Expenses
are of two sorts : necessary, for the repair of the house, the
maintenance of the farm, the stocking of the shop ; and
unnecessary, for plate, house decoration, horses, grand clothes,
entertainments. On this topic Agnolo inveighs with severity
against household parasites, bravi, and dissolute dependents.[1]
A little further on he indulges in another diatribe against great
nobles, *i signori*, from whom he would have his sons keep
clear at any cost.[2] It is the animosity of the industrious
burgher for the haughty, pleasure-loving, idle, careless man
of blood and high estate. In the bourgeois household described by Pandolfini no one can be indolent. The men have
to work outside and collect wealth, the women to stay at
home and preserve it. The character of a good housewife is
sketched very minutely. Pandolfini describes how, when
he was first married, he took his wife over the house, and

gave up to her care all its contents.   Then he went into their
bedroom, and made her kneel with him before Madonna, and
prayed God to give them wealth, friends, and male children.
After that he told her that honesty would be her great charm
in his eyes, as well as her chief virtue, and advised her to
forego the use of paints and cosmetics.   Much sound advice
follows as to the respective positions of the master and the
mistress in the household, the superintendence of domestics,
and the right ordering of the most insignificant matters.
The quality of the dress which will beseem the children of
an honoured citizen on various occasions, the pocket money
of the boys, the food of the common table, are all discussed
with some minuteness; and the wife is made to feel that she
must learn to be neither jealous nor curious about concerns
which her husband finds it expedient to keep private.

The charm of a treatise like that of Pandolfini on the
family evaporates as soon as we try to make a summary of its
contents.   Enough, however, has been quoted to show the
thoroughly bourgeois tone which prevailed among the citizens
of Florence in the fifteenth century.[1]   Very important results
were the natural issue of this commercial spirit in the State.
Talking of the Ordinanze di Giustizia, Varchi observes:
'While they removed in part the civil discords of Florence,
they almost entirely extinguished all nobility of feeling in the
Florentines, and tended as much to diminish the power and
haughtiness of the city as to abate the insolence of the
patriciate.'[2]   A little further on he says: 'Hence may all
prudent men see how ill-ordered in all things, save only in
the Grand Council, has been the commonwealth of Florence;
seeing that, to speak of nought else, that kind of men who in
a wisely constituted republic ought not to fulfil any magistracy

[1] Varchi (book x. cap. 69) quotes a Florentine proverb : 'Chiunque
non sta a bottega è ladro.'   See above, p. 187.
[2] *Ibid* vol. i. p. 168; compare vol. ii. p. 87, however.

whatever, the merchants and artisans of all sorts, are in Florence alone capable of taking office, to the exclusion of all others.' Machiavelli, less wordy but far more emphatic than Varchi, says of the same revolution : ' This caused the abandonment by Florence not only of arms, but of all nobility of soul.' [1] The most notable consequence of the mercantile temper of the republics was the ruinous system of mercenary warfare, with all its attendant evils of ambitious captains of adventure, irresponsible soldiery, and mock campaigns, adopted by the free Italian States. It is true that even if the Italians had maintained their national militias in full force, they might not have been able to resist the shock of France and Spain any better than the armies of Thebes, Sparta, and Athens averted the Macedonian hegemony. But they would at least have run a better chance, and not perhaps have perished so ignobly through the treason of an Alfonso d' Este (1527), of a Marquis of Pescara (1525), of a Duke of Urbino (1527), and of a Malatesta Baglioni (1530).[2] Machiavelli, in a weighty passage at the end of the first book of his Florentine History, sums up the various causes which contributed to the disuse of national arms among the Italians of the Renaissance. The fear of the despot for his subjects, the priest-rule of the Church, the jealousy of Venice for her own nobles, and

[1] *Ist. Fior.* lib. ii. end. Aristotle's contempt for the τεχνῖται emerges in these comments of the doctrinaires.

[2] To multiply the instances of fraud and treason on the part of Italian condottieri would be easy. I have only mentioned the notable examples which fall within a critical period of five years. The Marquis of Pescara betrayed to Charles V. the league for the liberation of Italy, which he had joined at Milan. The Duke of Ferrara received and victualled Bourbon's (then Frundsberg's) army on its way to sack Rome, because he spited the Pope, and wanted to seize Modena for himself. The Duke of Urbino, wishing to punish Clement VII. for personal injuries, omitted to relieve Rome when it was being plundered by the Lutherans, though he held the commission of the Italian League. Malatesta Baglioni sold Florence, which he had undertaken to defend, to the Imperial army under the Prince of Orange.

the commercial sluggishness of the Florentine burghers, caused each and all of these powers, otherwise so different, to entrust their armies to paid captains. 'Di questi adunque oziosi principi e di queste vilissime armi sarà piena la mia istoria,' is the contemptuous phrase with which he winds up his analysis.[1]

[1] 'With the records of these indolent princes and most abject armaments, my history will, therefore, be filled.' Compare the following passage in a letter from Machiavelli to Francesco Guicciardini (*Op.* vol. x. p. 255) : 'Comincio ora a scrivere di nuovo, e mi sfogo accusando i principi, the hanno fatto ogni cosa per condurci qui.'

CHAPTER V

THE FLORENTINE HISTORIANS

Florence, the City of Intelligence—Cupidity, Curiosity, and the Love of
Beauty—Florentine Historical Literature—Philosophical Study of
History—Ricordano Malespini—Florentine History compared with
the Chronicles of other Italian Towns—The Villani—The Date 1300
—Statistics—Dante's Political Essays and Pamphlets—Dino Com-
pagni—Latin Histories of Florence in Fifteenth Century—Lionardo
Bruni and Poggio Bracciolini—The Historians of the First Half of
the Sixteenth Century—Men of Action and Men of Letters: the
Doctrinaires—Florence between 1494 and 1537—Varchi, Segni, Nardi,
Pitti, Nerli, Guicciardini—The Political Importance of these Writers
—The Last Years of Florentine Independence, and the Siege of 1529
—State of Parties—Filippo Strozzi—Different Views of Florentine
Weakness taken by the Historians—Their Literary Qualities—
Francesco Guicciardini and Niccolo Machiavelli—Scientific Statists—
Discord between Life and Literature—The Biography of Guicciardini
—His 'Istoria d' Italia,' 'Dialogo del Reggimento di Firenze,' 'Storia
Fiorentina,' 'Ricordi '—Biography of Machiavelli—His Scheme of a
National Militia—Dedication of 'The Prince '—Political Ethics of
the Italian Renaissance—The 'Discorsi '—The Seven Books on the
Art of War and the 'History of Florence.'

FLORENCE was essentially the city of intelligence in modern
times.   Other nations have surpassed the Italians in their
genius—the quality which gave a superhuman power of insight
to Shakspere and an universal sympathy to Goethe.   But
nowhere else except at Athens has the whole population of a
city been so permeated with ideas, so highly intellectual by
nature, so keen in perception, so witty and so subtle, as at
Florence.   The fine and delicate spirit of the Italians existed
in quintessence among the Florentines.   And of this superiority
not only they, but the inhabitants also of Rome and Lom-

bardy and Naples, were conscious. Boniface VIII., when he received the ambassadors of the Christian powers in Rome on the occasion of the Jubilee in 1300, observed that all of them were citizens of Florence. The witticism which he is said to have uttered, *i Fiorentini essere il quinto elemento*, 'that the men of Florence form a fifth element,' passed into a proverb. The primacy of the Florentines in literature, the fine arts, law, scholarship, philosophy, and science was acknowledged throughout Italy.

When the struggle for existence has been successfully terminated, and the mere instinct of self-preservation no longer absorbs the activities of a people, then the three chief motive forces of civilisation begin to operate. These are cupidity, or the desire of wealth and all that it procures ; curiosity, or the desire to discover new facts about the world and man ; and the love of beauty, which is the parent of all art. Commerce, philosophy, science, scholarship, sculpture, architecture, painting, music, poetry, are the products of these ruling impulses—everything in fact which gives a higher value to the life of man. Different nations have been swayed by these passions in different degrees. The artistic faculty, which owes its energy to the love of beauty, has been denied to some ; the philosophic faculty, which starts with curiosity, to others ; and some again have shown but little capacity for amassing wealth by industry or calculation. It is rare to find a whole nation possessed of all in an equal measure of perfection. Such, however, were the Florentines.[1] The mere sight of the city and her monuments would suffice to prove this. But we are not reduced to the necessity of divining what Florence was by the inspection of her churches, palaces, and pictures. That marvellous intelligence which was her

[1] Since the Greeks, no people have combined curiosity and the love of beauty, the scientific and the artistic sense, in the same proportions as the Florentines.

pride burned brightly in a long series of historians and annalists, who have handed down to us the biography of the city in volumes as remarkable for penetrative acumen as for definite delineation and dramatic interest. We possess picture-galleries of pages in which the great men of Florence live again and seem to breathe and move, epics of the commonwealth's vicissitudes from her earliest commencement, detailed tragedies and highly finished episodes, studies of separate characters, and idylls detached from the main current of her story. The whole mass of this historical literature is instinct with the spirit of criticism and vital with experience. The writers have been either actors or spectators of the drama. Trained in the study of antiquity, as well as in the council-chambers of the republic and in the courts of foreign princes, they survey the matter of their histories from a lofty vantage ground, fortifying their speculative conclusions by practical knowledge, and purifying their judgment of contemporary events with the philosophy of the past. Owing to this rare mixture of qualities, the Florentines deserve to be styled the discoverers of the historic method for the modern world. They first perceived that it is unprofitable to study the history of a state in isolation, that not wars and treaties only, but the internal vicissitudes of the commonwealth, form the real subject matter of inquiry,[1] and that the smallest details, biographical, economical, or topographical, may have the greatest value. While the rest of Europe was ignorant of statistics, and little apt to pierce below the surface of events to the secret springs of conduct, in Florence a body of scientific historians had gradually been formed, who recognised the necessity of basing their investigations upon a diligent

[1] See Machiavelli's critique of Lionardo d' Arezzo and Messer Poggio, in the Proemio to his *Florentine History*. His own conception of history, as the attempt to delineate the very spirit of a nation, is highly philosophical.

study of public records, state-papers, and notes of contemporary observers.[1] The same men prepared themselves for the task of criticism by a profound study of ethical and political philosophy in the works of Aristotle, Plato, Cicero, and Tacitus.[2] They examined the methods of classical historians, and compared the annals of Greece, Rome, and Palestine with the chronicles of their own country. They attempted to divine the genius and to characterise the special qualities of the nations, cities, and individuals of whom they had to treat.[3] At the same time they spared no pains in seeking out persons possessed of accurate knowledge in every branch of inquiry that came beneath their notice, so that their treatises have the freshness of original documents and the charm of personal memoirs. Much, as I have elsewhere noted, was due to the peculiarly restless temper of the Florentines, speculative, variable, unquiet in their politics. The very qualities which exposed the commonwealth to revolu-

[1] The high sense of the requirements of scientific history attained by the Italians is shown by what Giovio relates of Gian Galeazzo's archives (*Vita di Gio. Galeazzo*, p. 107). After describing these, he adds: 'talche, chi volesse scrivere un' historia giusta non potrebbe desiderare altronde nè più abbondante nè più certa materia; perciocchè da questi libri facilissimamente si traggono le cagioni delle guerre, i consigli, e i successi dell' imprese.' The Proemio to Varchi's *Storie Fiorentine* (vol. i. pp. 42–44), which gives an account of his preparatory labours, is an unconscious treatise on the model historian. Accuracy, patience love of truth, sincerity in criticism, and laborious research, have all their proper place assigned to them. Compare Guicciardini, *Ricordi*, No. cxliii., for sound remarks upon the historian's duty of collecting the statistics of his own age and country.

[2] The prefaces to Giannotti's critiques of Florence and of Venice show how thoroughly his mind had been imbued with the *Politics* of Aristotle. Varchi acknowledges the direct influence of Polybius and Tacitus. Livy is Machiavelli's favourite.

[3] On this point the Relazioni of Italian ambassadors are invaluable. What drily philosophical compendia are the notes of Machiavelli upon the French court and Cesare Borgia! How astute are the Venetian letters on the opinions and qualities of the Roman prelates!

tions developed the intelligence of her historians ; her want
of stability was the price she paid for intellectual versatility
and acuteness unrivalled in modern times. '" *O ingenia
magis acria quam matura*," said Petrarch, and with truth,
about the wits of the Florentines ; for it is their property by
nature to have more of liveliness and acumen than of maturity
or gravity.' [1]

The year 1300 marks the first development of historical
research in Florence. Two great writers, Dante Alighieri
and Giovanni Villani, at this epoch pursued different lines of
study, which determined the future of this branch of literature
for the Italians. It is not uncharacteristic of Florentine genius
that while the chief city of Tuscany was deficient in historians
of her achievements before the date which I have mentioned,
her first essays in historiography should have been monu-
mental and standard-making for the rest of Italy. Just as the
great burghs of Lombardy obtained municipal independence
somewhat earlier than those of Tuscany, so the historic sense
developed itself in the valley of the Po at a period when the
valley of the Arno had no chronicler. Sire Raul and Ottone
Morena, the annalists of Milan, Fra Salimbene, the sagacious
and comprehensive historian of Parma, Rolandino, to whom
we owe the chronicle of Ezzelino and the tragedy of the
Trevisan Marches, have no rivals south of the Apennines in
the thirteenth century. Even the Chronicle of the Malespini
family, written in the vulgar tongue from the beginning of
the world to the year 1281, which occupies 146 columns
of Muratori's Collection, and which used to be the pride of
Tuscan antiquaries, has recently been shown to be in all
probability a compilation based upon the Annals of Villani.[2]

---

[1] Guicc. *Ricordi*, cciii.   *Op. Ined.* vol. i. p. 229.
[2] See Paul Scheffer-Boichorst, *Florentiner Studien*, Leipzig, 1874.
Carl Hegel, in his defence of Compagni, *Die Chronik des Dino
Compagni, Versuch einer Rettung*, Leipzig, 1875, admits the proof of

This makes the clear emergence of a scientific sense for history in the year 1300 at Florence all the more remarkable. In order to estimate the high quality of the work achieved by the Villani it is only necessary to turn the pages of some early chronicles of sister cities which still breathe the spirit of un-intelligent mediæval industry, before the method of history had been critically apprehended. The naïveté of these records may be appreciated by the following extracts. A Roman writes [1]: 'I Lodovico Bonconte Monaldeschi was born in Orvieto, and was brought up in the city of Rome, where I have resided. I was born in the year 1327, in the month of June, at the time when the Emperor Lodovico came. Now I wish to relate the whole history of my age, seeing that I lived one hundred and fifteen years without illness, except that when I was born I fainted, and I died of old age, and remained in bed twelve months on end.' Burigozzo's Chronicle of Milan, again, concludes with these words: [2] 'As you will see in the Annals of my son, inasmuch as the death which has overtaken me prevents my writing more.' Chronicles conceived and written in this spirit are diaries of

spuriousness. See the preface, p. v. The point, however, is still disputed by Florentine scholars of high authority. Gino Capponi, in his *Storia della Repubblica di Firenze* (vol. i. Appendix, final note), observes that while the Villani are popular in tone the Malespini Chronicle is feudal. Adolfo Bartoli (*Storia della Lett. It.* vol. iii. p. 155) treats the question as still open. The custom of preserving brief *fasti* in the archives of great houses rendered such compilations as the Malespini Chronicle is now supposed to have been both easy and attractive. The Christian name *Ricordano* given to the first Malespini annalist does not exist. It has been suggested that it is due to a misreading of an initial sentence, *Ricordano i Malespini*.

[1] Muratori, vol. xii. p. 529.

[2] *Arch. Stor.* vol. iii. p. 552. Both Monaldeschi and Burigozzo appear to mention their own death. The probability is that their annals, as we have them, have been freely dealt with by transcribers or continuators adopting the historic 'I' after the decease of the titular authors.

events, repertories of strange stories, and old wives' tales, without a deep sense of personal responsibility, devoid alike of criticism and artistic unity. Very different is the character of the historical literature which starts into being in Florence at the opening of the fourteenth century.

Giovanni Villani relates how, having visited Rome on the occasion of the Jubilee, when 200,000 pilgrims crowded the streets of the Eternal City, he was moved in the depth of his soul by the spectacle of the ruins of the discrowned mistress of the world.[1] 'When I saw the great and ancient monuments of Rome, and read the histories and the great deeds of the Romans, written by Virgil, and by Sallust, and by Lucan, and by Livy, and by Valerius, and Orosius, and other masters of history, who related small as well as great things of the acts and doings of the Romans, I took style and manner from them, though, as a learner, I was not worthy of so vast a work.' Like our own Gibbon, musing upon the steps of Ara Celi, within sight of the Capitol, and within hearing of the monks at prayer, he felt the *genius loci* stir him with a mixture of astonishment and pathos. Then 'reflecting that our city of Florence, the daughter and the creature of Rome, was in the ascendant toward great achievements, while Rome was on the wane, I thought it seemly to relate in this new Chronicle all the doings and the origins of the town of Florence, as far as I could collect and discover them, and to continue the acts of the Florentines and other notable things of the world in brief onwards so long as it shall be God's pleasure, hoping in Whom by His grace I have done the work rather than by my poor knowledge ; and therefore in the year 1300, when I returned from Rome, I began to compile this book, to the reverence of God and Saint John and the praise of this our city Florence.' The key-note is struck in these passages. Admiration for the past mingles with prescience of the future. The artist and

[1] Lib. viii. cap. 36.

the patriot awake together in Villani at the sight of Rome and the thought of Florence.

The result of this visit to Rome in 1300 was the Chronicle which Giovanni Villani carried in twelve books down to the year 1346. In 1348 he died of the plague, and his work was continued on the same plan by his brother Matteo. Matteo in his turn died of the plague in 1362, and left the Chronicle to his son Filippo, who brought it down to the year 1365. Of the three Villani, Giovanni is the greatest, both as a master of style and as an historical artist. Matteo is valuable for the general reflections which form exordia to the eleven books that bear his name. Filippo was more of a rhetorician. He is known as the public lecturer upon the Divine Comedy, and as the author of some interesting but meagre lives of eminent Florentines, his predecessors or contemporaries.

The Chronicle of the Villani is a treasure-house of clear and accurate delineations rather than of profound analysis. Not only does it embrace the whole affairs of Europe in annals which leave little to be desired in precision of detail and brevity of statement; but what is more to our present purpose, it conveys a lively picture of the internal condition of the Florentines and the statistics of the city in the fourteenth century. We learn, for example, that the ordinary revenues of Florence amounted to about 300,000 golden florins,[1] levied chiefly by way of taxes—90,200 proceeding from the octroi, 58,300 from the retail wine trade, 14,450 from the salt duties, and so on through the various imposts, each of which is carefully calculated. Then we are informed concerning the ordinary expenditure of the Commune—15,240 lire for the Podestà and his establishment, 5,880 lire for the Captain of the People and his train, 3,600 for the maintenance of the Signory in the Palazzo, and so on down to a sum of

[1] xi. 62.

2,400 for the food of the lions, for candles, torches, and bonfires. The amount spent publicly in almsgiving; the salaries of ambassadors and governors; the cost of maintaining the state armoury; the pay of the night-watch; the money spent upon the yearly games when the palio was run; the wages of the city trumpeters; and so forth, are all accurately reckoned. In fact the ordinary Budget of the Commune is set forth. The rate of extraordinary expenses during war-time is estimated on the scale of sums voted by the Florentines to carry on the war with Martino della Scala in 1338. At that time they contributed 25,000 florins monthly to Venice, maintained full garrisons in the fortresses of the republic, and paid as well for upwards of 1,000 men-at-arms. In order that a correct notion of these balance-sheets may be obtained, Villani is careful to give particulars about the value of the florin and the lira, and the number of florins coined yearly. In describing the condition of Florence at this period, he computes the number of citizens capable of bearing arms, between the ages fifteen and seventy, at 25,000; the population of the city at 90,000, not counting the monastic communities, nor including the strangers, who are estimated at about 15,000. The country districts belonging to Florence add 80,000 to this calculation. It is further noticed that the excess of male births over female was between 300 and 500 yearly in Florence; that from 8,000 to 10,000 boys and girls learned to read; that there were six schools, in which from 10,000 to 12,000 children learned arithmetic; and four high schools, in which from 550 to 600 learned grammar and logic. Then follows a list of the religious houses and churches: among the charitable institutions are reckoned 30 hospitals capable of receiving more than 1,000 sick people. Here too it may be mentioned that Villani reckons the beggars of Florence at 17,000, with the addition of 4,000 paupers and sick persons and religious mendicants.[1] These mendicants were not all Florentines, but received relief from the city charities. The big wool factories are numbered at upwards of two hundred; and it is calculated that from sixty to eighty thousand pieces of cloth were turned out yearly, to the value in all of about 1,200,000 florins. More than 30,000 persons lived by this industry. The *calimala* factories, where foreign cloths were manufactured into fine materials, numbered about twenty. These imported some 10,000 pieces of cloth yearly, to the value of 300,000 florins. The exchange offices are estimated at about eighty in number. The fortunes made in Florence by trade and by banking were colossal for those days. Villani tells us that the great houses of the Bardi and Peruzzi lent to our King Edward III. more than 1,365,000 golden florins.[2] 'And mark this,' he continues, 'that these moneys were chiefly the property of persons who had given it to them on deposit.' This debt was to have been recovered out of the wool revenues and other income of the English; in fact, the Bardi and Peruzzi had negotiated a national loan, by which they hoped to gain a superb percentage on their capital. The speculation, however, proved unfortunate; and the two houses would have failed, but for their enormous possessions in Tuscany. We hear, for example, of the Bardi buying the villages of Vernia and Mangona in 1337.[3] As it was, their credit received a shock from which it never thoroughly recovered; and a little later on, in 1342, after the ruinous wars with the La Scala family and Pisa, and after the loss of Lucca, they finally stopped payment and declared themselves bankrupt.[4] The shock communicated by this failure to the whole commerce of Christendom is well described by Villani.[5]

[1] x. 162.   [2] xi. 88.
[3] xi. 74. On this occasion a law was passed forbidding citizens to become lords of districts within the territory of Florence.
[4] xi. 38.   [5] xi. 88.

The enormous wealth amassed by Florentine citizens in commerce may be still better imagined when we remember that
the Medici, between the years 1434 and 1471, spent some
663,755 golden florins upon alms and public works, of which
400,000 were supplied by Cosimo alone.   But to return
to Villani : not content with the statistics which I have
already extracted, he proceeds to calculate how many bushels
of wheat, hogsheads of wine, and head of cattle were consumed
in Florence by the year and the week.[1] We are even told
than in the month of July 1280, 40,000 loads of melons
entered the gate of San Friano and were sold in the city.
Nor are the manners and the costume of the Florentines
neglected : the severe and decent dress of the citizens in the
good old times (about 1260) is contrasted with the new-
fangled fashions introduced by the French in 1342.[2]   In
addition to all this miscellaneous information may be mentioned what we learn from Matteo Villani concerning the
foundation of the Monte or Public Funds of Florence in
the year 1345,[3] as well as the remarkable essay upon the
economical and other consequences of the plague of 1348,
which forms the prelude to the continuation of his brother's
Chronicle.[4]

In his survey of the results of the Black Death, Matteo
notices not only the diminution of the population, but the
alteration in public morality, the displacement of property,
the increase in prices, the diminution of labour, and the
multiplication of lawsuits, which were the consequences direct
or indirect of the frightful mortality.   Among the details
which he has supplied upon these topics deserve to be com-
memorated the enormous bequests to public charities in
Florence—350,000 florins to the Society of Orsammichele,
25,000 to the Compagnia della Misericordia, and 25,000 to

---

[1] xi. 94.   [2] vi. 69 ; xii. 4.   [3] iii. 1.   [4] i. 1-8.

the Hospital of Santa Maria Nuova. The poorer population had been almost utterly destroyed by the plague; so that these funds were for the most part wasted, misapplied, and preyed upon by maladministrators.[1] The foundation of the University of Florence is also mentioned as one of the extraordinary consequences of this calamity.

The whole work of the Villani remains a monument, unique in mediæval literature, of statistical patience and economical sagacity, proving how far in advance of the other European nations were the Italians at this period.[2] Dante's aim is wholly different. Of statistics and of historical detail we gain but little from his prose works. His mind was that of a philosopher who generalises, and of a poet who seizes salient characteristics, not that of an annalist who aims at scrupulous fidelity in his account of facts. I need not do more than mention here the concise and vivid portraits, which he has sketched in the Divine Comedy, of all the chief cities of Italy; but in his treatise 'De Monarchiâ' we possess the first attempt at political speculation, the first essay in constitutional philosophy, to which the literature of modern Europe gave birth; while his letters addressed to the princes of Italy, the cardinals, the emperor, and the republic of Florence, are in like manner the first instances of political pamphlets setting forth a rationalised and consistent system of the rights and duties of nations. In the 'De Monarchiâ' Dante bases a theory of universal government upon a definite conception of the nature and the destinies of humanity. Amid the anarchy and discord of Italy, where selfishness was everywhere predominant, and where the factions of the Papacy and Empire were but cloaks for party strife, Dante endeavours to

[1] Matteo Villani expressly excepts the Hospital of S. Maria Nuova, which seems to have been well managed.
[2] We must remember that our own annalists, Holinshed and Stow, were later by two centuries than the Villani.

bring his countrymen back to a sublime ideal of a single
monarchy, a true *imperium*, distinct from the priestly authority
of the Church, but not hostile to it—nay, rather seeking
sanction from Christ's Vicar upon earth and affording protection to the Holy See, as deriving its own right from the same
Divine source.   Political science in this essay takes rank as
an independent branch of philosophy, and the points which
Dante seeks to establish are supported by arguments implying
much historical knowledge, though quaintly scholastic in their
application.   The Epistles contain the same thoughts : peace,
mutual respect, and obedience to a common head, the duty of
the chief to his subordinates and of the governed to their lord,
are urged with no less force, but in a more familiar style and
with direct allusion to the events which called each letter
forth.   They are in fact political brochures addressed by a
thinker from his solitude to the chief actors in the drama of
history around him.   Nor would it here be right to omit some
notice of the essay 'De Vulgari Eloquio,' which, considering
the date of its appearance, is no less original and indicative
of a new spirit in the world than the treatise ' De Monarchiâ.'
It is an attempt to write the history of Italian as a member
of the Romance Languages, to discuss the qualities of its
several dialects, and to prove the advantages to be gained by
the formation of a common literary tongue for Italy.   Though
Dante was of course devoid of what we now call comparative
philology, and had but little knowledge of the first beginnings
of the languages which he discusses, yet it is not more than
the truth to say that this essay applies the true method of
critical analysis for the first time to the subject, and is the
first attempt to reason scientifically upon the origin and nature
of a modern language.

While discussing the historical work of Dante and the
Villani, it is impossible that another famous Florentine should
not occur to our recollection, whose name has long been

connected with the civic contests that resulted in the exile of
Italy's greatest poet from his native city. Yet it is not easy
for a foreign critic to deal with the question of Dino Compagni's
Chronicle—a question which for years has divided Italian
students into two camps, which has produced a voluminous
literature of its own, and which still remains undecided. The
point at issue is by no means insignificant. While one party
contends that we have in this Chronicle the veracious record
of an eye-witness, the other asserts that it is the impudent
fabrication of a later century, composed on hints furnished by
Dante, and obscure documents of the Compagni family, and
expressed in language that has little of the fourteenth century.
The one regards it as a faithful narrative, deficient only in
minor details of accuracy. The other stigmatises it as a
wholly untrustworthy forgery, and calls attention to numberless mistakes, confusions, misconceptions, and misrepresenta-
tions of events, which place its genuineness beyond the pale
of possibility. After a careful consideration of Scheffer's,
Fanfani's, Gino Capponi's, and Isidoro del Lungo's arguments,
it seems to me clearly established that the Chronicle of Dino
Compagni can no longer be regarded as a perfectly genuine
document of fourteenth-century literature. In the form in
which we now possess it, we are rather obliged to regard it as
a *rifacimento* of some authentic history, compiled during the
course of the fifteenth century in a prose which bears traces
of the post-Boccaccian style of composition.[1] Yet the authority

[1] The first critic to call Compagni's authenticity in question was
Pietro Fanfani, in an article of *Il Pievano Arlotto*, 1858. The cause
was taken up, shortly after this date, by an abler German authority,
P. Scheffer-Boichorst. The works which I have studied on this subject
are: 1. *Florentiner Studien*, von P. Scheffer-Boichorst, Leipzig, Hirzel,
1874. 2. *Dino Compagni vendicato dalla Calunnia di Scrittore della
Cronica*, di Pietro Fanfani, Milano, Carrara, 1875. 3. *Die Chronik des
Dino Compagni, Versuch einer Rettung*, von Dr. Carl Hegel, Leipzig,
Hirzel, 1875. 4. *Die Chronik des Dino Compagni, Kritik der
Hegelschen Schrift* von P. Scheffer-Boichorst, Leipzig, Hirzel, 1875.

of Dino Compagni has long been such, and such is still the
literary value of the monograph which bears his name, that
it would be impertinent to dismiss the Chronicle unceremo-
niously as a mere fiction.   I propose, therefore, first to give
an account of the book on its professed merits, and then to
discuss, as briefly as I can, the question of its authenticity.

The year 1300, which Dante chose for the date of his
descent with Virgil to the nether world, and which marked
the beginning of Villani's Chronicle, is also mentioned by
Dino Compagni in the first sentence of the preface to his
work. ' The recollections of ancient histories,' he says, ' have
a long while stirred my mind to writing the perilous and
ill-fated events which the noble city, daughter of Rome, has
suffered many years, and especially at the time of the Jubilee
in the year 1300.'   Dino Compagni, whose Chronicle
embraces the period between 1280 and 1312, took the popular
side in the struggles of 1282, sat as Prior in 1289 and in 1301,
and was chosen Gonfalonier of Justice in 1293.   He was,
therefore, a prominent actor in the drama of those troublous
times.   He died in 1324, two years and four months after the
date of Dante's death, and was buried in the church of Santa
Trinità.   He was a man of the same stamp as Dante; [1]
burning with love for his country, but still more a lover of
the truth ; severe in judgment, but beyond suspicion of mere
partisanship ; brief in utterance, but weighty with personal
experience, profound conviction, prophetic intensity of feeling,

5. The note appended to Gino Capponi's *Storia della Repubblica di
Firenze*. 6. *Dino Compagni e la sua Chronica*, per Isidoro del Lungo,
Firenze, Le Monnier.   Unluckily, the last-named work, though it
consists already of two bulky volumes in large 8vo, is not yet complete ;
and the part which will treat of the question of authorship and MS.
authority has not appeared.

[1] The apostrophes to the citizens of Florence at large, and the
imprecations on some of the worst offenders among the party-leaders
(especially in book ii. on the occasion of the calamities of 1301), are
conceived and uttered in the style of Dante.

sincerity, and justice.   As a historian, he narrowed his labours
to the field of one small but highly finished picture.   He
undertook to narrate the civic quarrels of his times, and to
show how the commonwealth of Florence was brought to ruin
by the selfishness of her own citizens ; nor can his Chronicle,
although it is by no means a masterpiece of historical accuracy or of lucid arrangement, be surpassed for the liveliness of
its delineation, the graphic clearness of its characters, the
earnestness of its patriotic spirit, and the acute analysis which
lays bare the political situation of a republic torn by factions,
during the memorable period which embraced the revolution
of Giano della Bella and the struggles of the Neri and Bianchi.
The comparison of Dino Compagni with any contemporary
annalist in Italy shows that here again, in these pages, a new
spirit has arisen.   Muratori, proud to print them for the first
time in 1726, put them on a level with the ' Commentaries ' of
Cæsar ; Giordani welcomed their author as a second Sallust.
The political sagacity and scientific penetration, possessed in
so high a degree by the Florentines, appear in full maturity.
Compagni's Chronicle heads a long list of similar mono-
graphs, unique in the literature of a single city.[1]

The arguments against the authenticity of Dino Com-

[1] Among these I may mention here Gino Capponi's history of the
Ciompi Rebellion, Giovanni Cavalcanti's memoirs of the period between
1420 and 1452, Leo Battista Alberti's narrative of Porcari's attempt
upon the life of Nicholas V., Vespasiano's Biographies, and Poliziano's
' Essay on the Pazzi Conspiracy.'   Gino Capponi, born about 1350,
was Prior in 1396, and Gonfalonier of Justice in 1401 and 1418; he
died in 1421.   Giovanni Cavalcanti was a zealous admirer of Cosimo
de' Medici ; he composed his Chronicle in the prison of the Stinche,
where he was unjustly incarcerated for a debt to the Commune of
Florence.   Vespasiano da Bisticci contributed a series of most valuable
portraits to the literature of Italy : all the great men of his time are
there delineated with a simplicity that is the sign of absolute sincerity.
Poliziano was present at the murder of Giuliano de' Medici in the
Florentine Duomo.   The historians of the sixteenth century will be
noticed together further on.

pagni's Chronicle may be arranged in three groups. The *first* concerns the man himself. It is urged that, with the exception of his offices as Prior and Gonfalonier, we have no evidence of his political activity, beyond what is furnished by the disputed Chronicle. According to his own account, Dino played a part of the first importance in the complicated events of 1280–1312. Yet he is not mentioned by Giovanni Villani, by Filippo Villani, or by Dante. There is no record of his death, except a MS. note in the Magliabecchian Codex of his Chronicle of the date 1514.[1] He is known in literature as the author of a few lyrics and an oration to Pope John XXII., the style of which is so rough and mediæval as to make it incredible that the same writer should have composed the masterly paragraphs of the Chronicle.[2] The *second* group of arguments affects the substance of the Chronicle itself. Though Dino was Prior when Charles of Valois entered Florence, he records that event under the date of Sunday the fourth of November, whereas Charles arrived on the first of November, and the first Sunday of the month was the fifth. He differs from the concurrent testimony of other historians in making the affianced bride of Buondelmonte dei Buondelmonti a Giantruffetti instead of an Amidei, and the Bishop of Arezzo a Pazzi instead of an Ubertini. He reckons the Arti at twenty-four, whereas they numbered twenty-one. He places the Coronation of Henry VII. in

[1] This is Isidoro del Lungo's Codex A. The note occurs also in the Ashburnham MS. which Del Lungo refers to the fifteenth century.

[2] On this point it is worth mentioning that some good critics refer the poems to an elder Dino Compagni, who sat as Ancient in 1251. See the discussion of this question, as also of the authorship of the *Intelligenza*, claimed by Isidoro del Lungo for the writer of the Chronicle, in Borgognini's Essays (*Scritti Vari*, Bologna, Romagnoli, 1877, vol. i.). With regard to the oration to Pope John XXII. date 1326, it must be noted that this performance was first printed by Anton Francesco Doni in 1547, and that its genuineness may be disputed. See Carl Hegel, op. cit. pp. 18–22.

August, instead of June, 1312. He seems to refer to the
Palace of the Signory, which could not have been built at the
date in question. He asserts that a member of the Benivieni
family was killed by one of the Galligai, whereas the murderer
was of the blood of the Galli. He represents himself as
having been the first Gonfalonier of Justice who destroyed
the houses of rebellious nobles, while Baldo de' Ruffoli, who
held the office before him, had previously carried out the
Ordinances. Speaking of Guido Cavalcanti about the year
1300, he calls him 'uno giovane gentile;' and yet Guido
had married the daughter of Farinata degli Uberti in 1266,
and certainly did not survive 1300 more than a few months.
The peace with Pisa, which was concluded during Compagni's
tenure of the Gonfalonierate, is not mentioned, though this
must have been one of the most important public events with
which he was concerned. Chronology is hopelessly and in-
extricably confused; while inaccuracies and difficulties of
the kind described abound on every page of the Chronicle,
rendering the labour of its last commentator and defender
one of no small difficulty. The *third* group of arguments
assails the language of the Chronicle and its MS. authority.
Fanfani, who showed more zeal than courtesy in his destructive criticism, undertook to prove that Dino's style in general
is not distinguished for the 'purity, simplicity, and propriety'
of the trecento[1]; that it abounds in expressions of a later
period, such as *armata* for *oste*, *marciare* for *andare*, *acciò* for
acciocchè, *onde* for *affinchè*; that numerous imitations of

[1] The most important of Fanfani's numerous essays on the Compagni
controversy, together with minor notes by his supporters, are collected
in the book quoted above, Note to p. 207. Fanfani exceeds all bounds
of decency in the language he uses, and in his arrogant claims to be
considered an unique judge of fourteenth-century style. These claims
he bases in some measure upon the fact that he deceived the Della
Crusca by a forgery of his own making, which was actually accepted
for the *Archivio Storico*. See op. cit. p. 181.

Dante can be traced in it ; and that to an acute student of early Italian prose its palpable *quattrocentismo* is only slightly veiled by a persistent affectation of fourteenth-century archaism. This argument from style seems the strongest that can be brought against the genuineness of the Chronicle; for while it is possible that Dino may have made innumerable blunders about the events in which he took a part, it is incredible that he should have anticipated the growth of Italian by at least a century. Yet judges no less competent than Fanfani in this matter of style, and far more trust-worthy as witnesses, Vincenzo Nannucci, Gino Capponi, Isidoro del Lungo, are of opinion that Dino's Chronicle is a masterpiece of Italian fourteenth-century prose ; and till Italian experts are agreed, foreign critics must suspend their judgment. The analysis of style receives a different develop-ment from Scheffer-Boichorst. In his last essay he undertakes to show that many passages of the Chronicle, especially the important one which refers to the ' Ordinamenti della Giustizia,' have been borrowed from Villani.[1] This critical weapon is difficult to handle, for it almost always cuts both ways. Yet the German historian has made out an un-doubtedly good case by proving Villani's language closer to the original ' Ordinamenti ' than Compagni's. With regard to MS. authority, the codices of Dino's Chronicle extant in Italy are all of them derived from a MS. transcribed by Noferi Busini and given by him to Giovanni Mazzuoli, surnamed Lo Stradino, who was a member of the Florentine Academy and a greedy collector of antiquities. This MS. bears the date 1514. The recent origin of this parent codex, and the questionable character of Lo Stradino, gave rise to not un-reasonable suspicions.   Fanfani roundly asserted that the Chronicle must have been fabricated as a hoax upon the uncritical antiquary, since it suddenly appeared without a

[1] *Die Chronik*, &c., pp. 53–57.

pedigree, at a moment when such forgeries were not uncommon. Scheffer-Boichorst, in his most recent pamphlet, committed himself to the opinion that either Lo Stradino himself, nicknamed *Cronaca Scorretta* by his Florentine cronies, or one of his contemporaries, was the forger.[1] An Italian impugner of the Chronicle, Giusto Grion of Verona, declared for Antonfrancesco Doni as the fabricator.[2] These hypotheses, however, are, to say the least, unlucky for their suggestors, and really serve to weaken rather than to strengthen the destructive line of argument. There exists an elder codex of which Fanfani and his followers were ignorant. It is a MS. of perhaps the middle of the fifteenth century, which was purchased for the Ashburnham Library in 1846. This MS. has been minutely described by Professor Paul Meyer; and Isidoro del Lungo publishes a facsimile specimen of one of its pages.[3] By some unaccountable negligence this latest and most determined defender of Compagni has failed to examine the MS. with his own eyes.

Thus stands the question of Dino Compagni's Chronicle. The defenders of its authenticity, forced to admit Compagni's glaring inaccuracies, fall back upon arguments deduced from the internal spirit of the author, from the difficulties of fabricating a personal narrative instinct with the spirit of the fourteenth century, from the hypotheses of a copyist's errors or of a thoroughgoing literary process of re-writing at a later date, from the absence of any positive evidence of forgery, and from general considerations affecting the validity of destructive criticism. One thing has been clearly proved in the course of the controversy: that the book can have but little

---

[1] *Die Chronik*, &c., p. 39. [2] See Hegel, op. cit. p. 6.

[3] See Del Lungo, op. cit. vol. ii. pp. 19-23, and facsimile, to face p. 1. This MS. was bought by G. Libri from the Pucci family in 1840, and sold to Lord Ashburnham. Del Lungo identifies it with a MS. which Braccio Compagni in the seventeenth century spoke of as 'la copia più antica, appresso il Signor senatore Pandolfini.'

historical value when not corroborated. Still there is a wide gap between inaccuracy and wilful fabrication. Until the best judges of Italian style are agreed that the Chronicle could not have been written in the second decade of the fourteenth century, the arguments adduced from an examination of the facts recorded in it are not strong enough to demonstrate a forgery. There is the further question of *cui bono* ? which in all problems of literary forgery must first receive some probable solution. What proof is there that the vanity or the cupidity of any parties was satisfied by its production? A book exists in a MS. of about 1450, acquires some notice in a MS. of 1514, but is not published to the world until 1726. Supposing it to have been a forgery, the labour of concocting it must have been enormous. With all its defects, the Chronicle would still remain a masterpiece of historical research, imagination, sympathy with bygone modes of feeling, dramatic vigour, and antiquarian command of language. But who profited by that labour? Not the author of the forgery, since he was dead or buried more than two centuries before his fabrication became famous. Not the Compagni family; for there is no evidence to show that they had piqued themselves upon being the depositaries of their ancestor's masterpiece, nor did they make any effort at a period when the printing press was very active, to give this jewel of their archives to the public. If it be objected that, on the hypothesis of genuineness, the MS. of the Chronicle must have been divulged before the beginning of the sixteenth century, we can adduce two plausible answers. In the first place, Dino was the partisan of a conquered cause; and his family had nothing to gain by publishing an acrimonious political pamphlet during the triumph of his antagonists. In the second place, MSS. of greater literary importance disappeared in the course of the fourteenth century, to be reproduced when their subjects again excited interest in the literary

world. The history of Dante's treatise ' De Vulgari Eloquio' is
a case in point. With regard to style, no foreigner can pretend
to be a competent judge. Reading the celebrated description
of Florence at the opening of Dino's Chronicle, I seem
indeed, for my own part, to discern a post-Boccaccian artifi-
ciality of phrase. Still there is nothing to render it impossible
that the Chronicle, as we possess it, in the texts of 1450 (?)
and 1514, may be a *rifacimento* of an elder and simpler work.
In that section of my history which deals with Italian literature of the fifteenth century, I shall have occasion to show
that such remodelling of ancient texts to suit the fashion of
the time was by no means unfrequent. The curious discre-
pancies between the 'Trattato della Famiglia' as written by
Alberti, and as ascribed to *Pandolfini*, can only be explained
upon the hypothesis of such *rifacimento*. If the historical
inaccuracies in which the Chronicle abounds are adduced
as convincing proof of its fabrication, it may be replied that
the author of so masterly a romance would naturally have
been anxious to preserve a strict accordance with documents
of acknowledged validity. Consequently, these very blunders
might not unreasonably be used to combat the hypothesis of
deliberate forgery. It is remarkable, in this connection, that
only one meagre reference is made to Dante by the Chronicler,
who, had he been a literary forger, would scarcely have
omitted to enlarge upon this theme. Without, therefore,
venturing to express a decided opinion on a question which
still divides the most competent Italian judges, I see no reason
to despair of the problem being ultimately solved in a way
less unfavourable to Dino Compagni than Scheffer-Boichorst
and Fanfani would approve of. Considered as the fifteenth-
century *rifacimento* of an elder document, the Chronicle
would lose its historical authority, but would still remain
an interesting monument of Florentine literature, and would
certainly not deserve the unqualified names of 'forgery'

and 'fabrication' that have been unhesitatingly showered upon it.[1]

The two chief Florentine historians of the fifteenth century are Lionardo Bruni, of Arezzo, and Poggio Bracciolini, each of whom, in his capacity of Chancellor to the Republic, undertook to write the annals of the people of Florence from the earliest date to his own time. Lionardo Aretino wrote down to the year 1404, and Poggio Bracciolini to the year 1455. Their histories are composed in Latin, and savour much of the pedantic spirit of the age in which they were projected.[2] Both of them deserve the criticism of Machiavelli, that they filled their pages too exclusively with the wars and foreign affairs in which Florence was engaged, failing to perceive that the true object of the historian is to set forth the life of a commonwealth as a continuous whole, to draw the portrait of a state with due regard to its especial physiognomy.[3] To this critique we may add that both Lionardo and Poggio were led astray by the false taste of the earlier Renaissance. Their admiration for Livy and the pedantic proprieties of a laboured Latinism made them pay more attention to rhetoric than to the substance of their work.[4]

[1] It is to be hoped that the completion of Del Lungo's work may put an end to the Compagni controversy, either by a solid vindication of the Chronicle, or by so weak a defence as to render further partisanship impossible. So far as his book has hitherto appeared, it contains no signs of an ultimate triumph. The weightiest point contained in it is the discovery of the Ashburnham MS. If Del Lungo fails to prove his position, we shall be left to choose between Scheffer-Boichorst's absolute scepticism or the modified view adopted by me in the text.

[2] Poggio's *Historia Populi Florentini* is given in the XXth volume of Muratori's collection. Lionardo's *Istoria Fiorentina*, translated into Italian by Donato Acciajuoli, has been published by Le Monnier (Firenze, 1861). The high praise which Ugo Foscolo bestowed upon the latter seems due to a want of familiarity.

[3] See the preface to the *History of Florence*, by Machiavelli.

[4] Lionardo Bruni, for example, complains in the preface to his history that it is impossible to accommodate the rude names of his personages to a polished style.

We meet with frigid imitations and bombastic generalities, where concise details and graphic touches would have been acceptable. In short, these works are rather studies of style in an age when the greatest stylists were but bunglers and beginners, than valuable histories. The Italians of the fifteenth century, striving to rival Cicero and Livy, succeeded only in becoming lifeless shadows of the past. History dictated under the inspiration of pedantic scholarship, and with the object of reproducing an obsolete style, by men of letters who had played no prominent part in the Commonwealth,[1] cannot pretend to the vigour and the freshness that we admire so much in the writings of men like the Villani, Gino Capponi, Giovanni Cavalcanti, and many others. Yet even after making these deductions, it may be asserted with truth that no city of Italy at this period of the Renaissance, except Florence, could boast historiographers so competent. Vespasiano at the close of his biography of Poggio estimates their labour in sentences which deserve to be remembered : 'Among the other singular obligations which the city of Florence owes to Messer Lionardo and to Messer Poggio, is this, that except the Roman Commonwealth no republic or free state in Italy has been so distinguished as the town of Florence, in having had two such notable writers to record its doings as Messer Lionardo and Messer Poggio ; for up to the time of their histories everything was in the greatest obscurity. If the republic of Venice, which can show so many wise citizens, had the deeds which they have done by sea and land committed to writing, it would be far more illustrious even than it is now. And Galeazzo Maria, and Filippo Maria, and all the Visconti—their actions would also be more famous than they are. Nay, there is not any republic that ought not to give every reward to writers who should com-

---

[1] Both Poggio and Lionardo began life as Papal secretaries ; the latter was not made a citizen of Florence till late in his career.

memorate its doings. We see at Florence that from the foundation of the city to the days of Messer Lionardo and Messer Poggio there was no record of anything that the Florentines had done, in Latin, or history devoted to themselves. Messer Poggio follows after Messer Lionardo, and writes like him in Latin. Giovanni Villani, too, wrote an universal history in the vulgar tongue of whatsoever happened in every place, and introduces the affairs of Florence as they happened. The same did Messer Filippo Villani, following after Giovanni Villani. These are they alone who have distinguished Florence by the histories that they have written.'[1] The pride of the citizen and a just sense of the value of history, together with sound remarks upon Venice and Milan, mingle curiously in this passage with the pedantry of a fifteenth-century scholar.

The historians of the first half of the sixteenth century are a race apart. Three generations of pedantic erudition and of courtly or scholastic trifling had separated the men of letters from the men of action, and had made literature a thing of curiosity. Three generations of the masked Medicean despotism had destroyed the reality of freedom in Florence, and had corrupted her citizens to the core. Yet, strange to say, it was at the end of the fifteenth century that the genius of the thirteenth revived. Italian literature was cultivated for its own sake under the auspices of Lorenzo de' Medici. The year 1494 marks the resurrection of the spirit of old liberty beneath the trumpet-blast of Savonarola's oratory. Amid the universal corruption of public morals, from the depth of sloth and servitude, when the reality of liberty was lost, when fate and fortune had combined to render constitutional reconstruction impossible for the shattered republics of Italy, the intellect of the Florentines displayed itself with more than its old vigour in a series of

---

[1] *Vite di Uomini Illustri.* Barbèra, 1859; p. 425.

the most brilliant political writers who have ever illustrated
one short but eventful period in the life of a single nation.
That period is marked by the years 1494 and 1537. It
embraces the two final efforts of the Florentines to shake off
the Medicean yoke, the disastrous siege at the end of which
they fell a prey to the selfishness of their own party-leaders,
the persecution of Savonarola by Pope Alexander, the Church-
rule of Popes Leo and Clement, the extinction of the elder
branch of the Medici in its two bastards (Ippolito, poisoned
by his cousin Alessandro, and Alessandro poignarded by his
cousin Lorenzino), and the final eclipse of liberty beneath
the Spanish-appointed dynasty of the younger Medicean line
in Duke Cosimo. The names of the historians of this period
are Niccolo Machiavelli, Jacopo Nardi, Francesco Guicciardini, Filippo Nerli, Donato Giannotti, Benedetto Varchi,
Bernardo Segni, and Jacopo Pitti.[1] In these men the mental
qualities which we admire in the Villani, Dante, and Compagni reappear, combined, indeed, in different proportions,
tempered with the new philosophy and scholarship of the
Renaissance, and permeated with quite another morality.
In the interval of two centuries freedom has been lost. It is
only the desire for freedom that survives. But that, after the
apathy of the fifteenth century, is still a passion. The recti-
tude of instinct and the intense convictions of the earlier age
have been exchanged for a scientific clairvoyance, a 'stoic-
epicurean acceptance' of the facts of vitiated civilisation,

[1] The dates of these historians are as follows:—

				BORN	DIED
Machiavelli	.	.	.	1469	1527
Nardi	.	.	.	1476	1556
Guicciardini	.	.	.	1482	1540
Nerli	.	.	.	1485	1536
Giannotti	.	.	.	1492	1572
Varchi	.	.	.	1502	1565
Segni	.	.	.	1504	1558
Pitti	.	.	.	1519	1589

which in men like Guicciardini and Machiavelli is absolutely appalling. Nearly all the authors of this period bear a double face. They write one set of memoirs for the public, and another set for their own delectation. In their inmost souls they burn with the zeal for liberty : yet they sell their abilities to the highest bidder—to Popes whom they despise, and to Dukes whom they revile in private. What makes the literary labours of these historians doubly interesting is that they were carried on for the most part independently ; for though they lived at the same time, and in some cases held familiar conversation with each other, they gave expression to different shades of political opinion, and their histories remained in manuscript till some time after their death.[1] The student of the Renaissance has, therefore, the advantage of comparing and confronting a whole band of independent witnesses to the same events. Beside their own deliberate criticism of the drama in which all played some part as actors or spectators, we can use the not less important testimony they afford unconsciously, according to the bias of private or political interest by which they are severally swayed.

The 'Storia Fiorentina' of Varchi extends from the year 1527 to the year 1538; that of Segni from 1527 to 1555 ; that of Nardi from 1494 to 1552 ; that of Pitti from 1494 to 1529 ; that of Nerli from 1494 to 1537 ; that of Guicciardini from 1420 to 1509. The prefatory chapters, which in most cases introduce the special subject of each history, contain a series of retrospective surveys over the whole history of Florence extremely valuable for the detailed information they contain, as well as for the critical judgments of men whose acumen had been sharpened to the utmost by their practical

[1] Varchi, it is true, had Nardi's *History of Florence* and Guicciardini's *History of Italy* before him while he was compiling his *History of Florence*. But Segni and Nerli were given for the first time to the press in the last century; Pitti in 1842, and Guicciardini's *History of Florence* in 1859.

participation in politics. It will not, perhaps, be superfluous to indicate the different parts played by these historians in the events of their own time. Guicciardini, it is well known, had governed Bologna and Romagna for the Medicean Popes. He too was instrumental in placing Duke Cosimo at the head of the republic in 1536. At Naples, in 1535, he pleaded the cause of Duke Alessandro against the exiles before Charles V. Nardi on this occasion acted as secretary and advocate for Filippo Strozzi and the exiles; his own history was composed in exile at Venice, where he died. Segni was nephew of the Gonfalonier Capponi, and shared the anxieties of the moderate liberals during the siege of Florence. Pitti was a member of the great house who contested the leadership of the republic with the Medici in the fifteenth century; his zeal for the popular party and his hatred of the Palleschi may still perhaps be tinctured with ancestral animosity. Giannotti, in whose critique of the Florentine republic we trace a spirit no less democratic than Pitti's, was also an actor in the events of the siege, and afterwards appeared among the exiles. In the attempt made by the Cardinal Salviati (1537) to reconcile Duke Cosimo and the adherents of Filippo Strozzi, Giannotti was chosen as the spokesman for the latter. He wrote and died in exile at Venice. Nerli again took part in the events of those troublous times, but on the wrong side, by mixing himself up with the exiles and acting as a spy upon their projects. All the authors I have mentioned were citizens of Florence, and some of them were members of her most illustrious families. Varchi, in whom the flame of Florentine patriotism burns brightest, and who is by far the most copious annalist of the period, was a native of Montevarchi. Yet, as often happens, he was more Florentine than the Florentines; and of the events which he describes, he had for the most part been witness. Duke Cosimo employed him to write the history; it is a credit both to the prince and to the author that its chapters should be full of criticisms so outspoken, and of aspirations after liberty so vehement. On the very first page of his preface Varchi dares to write these words respecting Florence—' divenne, dico, di stato piuttosto corrotto e licenzioso, tirannide, che di sana e moderata repubblica, principato[1]; ' in which he deals blame with impartial justice all round. It must, however, be remembered that at the time when Varchi wrote the younger branch of the Medici were firmly established on the throne of Florence. Between this branch and the elder line there had always been a coldness. Moreover, all parties had agreed to accept the duchy as a divinely appointed instrument for rescuing the city from her factions and reducing her to tranquillity.[2]

It would be beyond the purpose of this chapter to enter into the details of the history of Florence between 1527 and 1531—those years of her last struggle for freedom, which have been so admirably depicted by her great political annalists. It is rather my object to illustrate the intellectual qualities of philosophical analysis and acute observation for which her citizens were eminent. Yet a sketch of the situation is necessary in order to bring into relief the different points of view maintained by Segni, Nardi, Varchi, Pitti, and Nerli respectively.

At the period in question Florence was, according to the universal testimony of these authors, too corrupt for real liberty and too turbulent for the tranquil acceptance of a despotism. The yoke of the Medici had destroyed the sense of honour and the pride of the old noble families ; while the policy pursued by Lorenzo and the Popes had created a class of greedy professional politicians. The city was not content

[1] 'It passed, I say, from the condition of a corrupt and ill-conducted commonweath to tyranny, rather than from a healthy and well-tempered republic to principality.'
[2] See *Arch. Stor.* vol. i. p. xxxv.

with slavery; but the burghers, eminent for wealth or ability, were egotistical, vain, and mutually jealous. Each man sought advantage for himself. Common action seemed impossible. The Medicean party, or Palleschi, were either extreme in their devotion to the ruling house, and desirous of establishing a tyranny; or else they were moderate and anxious to retain the Medici as the chiefs of a dominant oligarchy. The point of union between these two divisions of the party was a prejudice in favour of class rule, a hope to get power and wealth for themselves through the elevation of the princely family. The popular faction on the other hand agreed in wishing to place the government of the city upon a broad republican basis. But the leaders of this section of the citizens favoured the plebeian cause from different motives. Some sought only a way to riches and authority, which they could never have opened for them under the oligarchy contemplated by the Palleschi. Others, styled Frateschi or Piagnoni, clung to the ideas of liberty which were associated with the high morality and impassioned creed of Savonarola. These were really the backbone of the nation, the class which might have saved the state if salvation had been possible. Another section, steeped in the study of ancient authors and imbued with memories of Roman patriotism, thought it still possible to secure the freedom of the state by liberal institutions. These men we may call the Doctrinaires. Their panacea was the establishment of a mixed form of government, such as that which Giannotti so learnedly illustrated. To these parties must be added the red republicans or Arrabbiati—a name originally reserved for the worst adherents of the Medici, but now applied to fanatics of Jacobin complexion—and the Libertines, who only cared for such a form of government as should permit them to indulge their passions.

Amid this medley of interests there resulted, as a matter

of fact, two policies at the moment when the affairs of
Florence, threatened by Pope and Emperor in combination,
and deserted by France and the rest of Italy, grew desperate.
One was that of the Gonfalonier Capponi, who advocated
moderate counsels and an accommodation with Clement VII.
The other was that of the Gonfalonier Carducci, who pushed
things to extremities and used the enthusiasm of the Frateschi
for sustaining the spirit of the people in the siege.[1] The latter
policy triumphed over the former.   Its principles were an
obstinate belief in Francis, though he had clearly turned a
deaf ear to Florence; confidence in the generals Baglioni
and Colonna, who were privately traitors to the cause they
professed to defend; and reliance on the prophecies of Savonarola, supported by the preaching of the Friars Foiano,
Bartolommeo, and Zaccaria. Ill founded as it was in fact,
the policy of Carducci had on its side all that was left of
nobility, patriotism, and the fire of liberty among the Florentines. In spite of the hopelessness of the attempt, we cannot
now read without emotion how bravely and desperately those
last champions of freedom fought, to maintain the independence of their city at any cost, and in the teeth of overwhelming opposition. The memory of Savonarola was the
inspiration of this policy. Ferrucci was its hero. It failed.
It was in vain that the Florentines had laid waste Valdarno,

---

[1] Guicciardini, writing his *Ricordi* during the first months of the
siege, remarks upon the power of faith (*Op. Ined.* vol. i. p. 83.
Compare p. 134): ' Esemplo a' dì nostri ne è grandissimo questa
ostinazione de' Fiorentini, che essendosi contro a ogni ragione del
mondo messi a aspettare la guerra del papa e imperadore, senza
speranza di alcuno soccorso di altri, disuniti e con mille difficoltà,
hanno sostenuto in quelle mura già sette mesi gli eserciti, e quali non
sì sarebbe creduto che avessino sostenuti sette dì ; e condotto le cose
in luogo che se vincessino, nessuno più se ne maraviglierebbe, dove
prima da tutti erano giudicati perduti ; e questa ostinazione ha causata
in gran parte la fede di non potere perire, secondo le predicazioni di Fra
Jeronimo da Ferrara.'

destroyed their beautiful suburbs, and levelled their crown of
towers.   It was in vain that they had poured forth their
treasures to the uttermost farthing, had borne plague and
famine without a murmur, and had turned themselves at
the call of their country into a nation of soldiers.   Charles,
Clement, the Palleschi, and Malatesta Baglioni—enemies
without the city walls and traitors within its gates—were too
powerful for the resistance of burghers who had learned but
yesterday to handle arms and to conduct a war on their own
account.[1] Florence had to capitulate.   The venomous Palleschi, Francesco Guicciardini and Baccio Valori, by proscription, exile, and taxation, drained the strength and broke the
spirit of the state.   Cæsar and Christ's Vicar, a new Herod
and a new Pilate, embraced and made friends over the prostrate
corpse of sold and slaughtered liberty.   Florence was paid as
compensation for the insult offered to the Pontiff in the sack
of Rome.

The part played by Filippo Strozzi in this last drama of
the liberties of Florence is feeble and discreditable, but at the
same time historically instructive, since it shows to what a
point the noblest of the Florentines had fallen.   All Pitti's
invectives against the Ottimati, bitter as they may be, are
justified by the unvarnished narrative we read in the pages
of Varchi and Segni concerning this most vicious, selfish,
vain, and brilliant hero of historical romance.   Married to
Clarice de' Medici, by whom he had a splendid family of
handsome and vigorous sons, he was more than the rival of
his wife's princely relatives by his wealth.   Yet though he
made a profession of patriotism, Filippo failed to use this
great influence consistently as a counterpoise to the Medicean
authority.   It was he, for instance, who advised Lorenzo the
younger to make himself Duke of Florence.   Distinguished, as
he was, above all men of his time for wit, urbanity, accom-

---

[1] See above, p. 187, for what Giannotti says of the heroic Ferrucci.

plishments, and splendid living, his want of character neutralised these radiant gifts of nature. His private morals were infamous. He encouraged by precept and example the worst vices of his age and nation, consorting with young men whom he instructed in the arts of dissolute living, and to whom he communicated his own selfish Epicureanism. To him in a great measure may be attributed the corruption of the Florentine aristocracy in the sixteenth century. In his public action he was no less vacillating than unprincipled in private life. After prevailing upon Ippolito and Alessandro de' Medici to leave Florence in 1527, he failed to execute his trust of getting Pisa from their grasp (moved, it is said, by a guilty fondness for the young and handsome Ippolito), nor did he afterwards share any of the hardships and responsibilities of the siege. Indeed, he then found it necessary to retire into exile in France, on the excuse of superintending his vast commercial affairs at Lyons. After the restoration of the Medici he returned to Florence as the courtier of Duke Alessandro, whom he aided and abetted in his juvenile debaucheries. Quarrelling with Alessandro on the occasion of an insult offered to his daughter Luisa, and the accusation of murder brought against his son Piero, he went into opposition and exile, less for political than for private reasons. After the murder of Alessandro, he received Lorenzo de' Medici, the fratricide, with the title of 'Second Brutus' at Venice. Meanwhile it was he who paid the dowry of Catherine de' Medici to the Duke of Orleans, helping thus to strengthen the house of princes against whom he was plotting, by that splendid foreign alliance which placed a descendant of the Florentine bill-brokers on the throne of France. After all these vicissitudes Filippo Strozzi headed an armed attack upon the dominions of Duke Cosimo, was taken in the battle of Montemurlo, and finally was murdered in that very fortress, outside the Porto a Faenza, which he had counselled Alessandro to construct for the intimidation of the Florentines.[1] The historians with the exception of Nerli agree in describing him as a pleasure-loving and self-seeking man, whose many changes of policy were due, not to conviction, but to the desire of gaining the utmost license of disorderly living. At the same time we cannot deny him the fame of brilliant mental qualities, a princely bearing, and great courage.

The moral and political debility which proved the real source of the ruin of Florence is accounted for in different ways by the historians of the siege. Pitti, whose insight into the situation is perhaps the keenest, and who is by far the most outspoken, does not refer the failure of the Florentines to the cowardice or stupidity of the popular party, but to the malignity of the Palleschi, the double-dealing and egotism of the wealthy nobles, who to suit their own interests favoured now one and now another of the parties. These Ottimati—as he calls them, by a title borrowed from classical phraseology— whether they professed the Medicean or the popular cause, were always bent on self-aggrandisement at the expense of the people or their princes.[2] The sympathies of Pitti were on the side of the plebeians, whose policy during the siege was carried out by the Gonfalonier Carducci. At the same time he admitted the feebleness and insufficiency of many of these men, called from a low rank of life and from mechanical trades to

[1] See Varchi, vol. iii. p. 61, for the first stone laid of this castle. It should be said that accounts disagree about Filippo's death. Nerli very distinctly asserts that he committed suicide. Segni inclines to the belief that he was murdered by the creatures of Duke Cosimo.

[2] He goes so far as to assert that Leo X. and Clement VII. wished to give a liberal constitution to Florence, but that their plans were frustrated by the avarice and jealousy of the would-be oligarchs. See *Arch. Stor.* vol. i. pp. 121, 131. The passages quoted from his 'Apologia de' Cappucci,' relative to Machiavelli, Filippo Strozzi, and Francesco Guicciardini (*Arch. Stor.* vol. i. pp. xxxix. xxxviii.), are very instructive; with such greedy self-seeking oligarchs, it was impossible for the Medicean Popes to establish any government but a tyranny in Florence.

the administration of the commonwealth. The state of Florence under Piero Soderini—that 'non mai abbastanza lodato cavaliere,' as he calls him—was the ideal to which he reverted with longing eyes. Segni, on the other hand, condemns the ambition of the plebeian leaders, and declares his opinion that the State could only have been saved by the more moderate among the influential citizens. He belonged in fact to that section of the Medicean party which Varchi styles the Neutrals. He had strong aristocratic leanings, and preferred a government of nobles to the popular democracy which flourished under Francesco Carducci. While he desired the liberty of Florence, Segni saw that the Republic could not hold its own against both Pope and Emperor, at a crisis when the King of France, who ought to have rendered assistance in the hour of need, was bound by the treaty of Cambray, and by the pledges he had given to Charles in the persons of his two sons. The policy of which Segni approved was that which Niccolo Capponi had prepared before his fall—a reconciliation with Clement through the intervention of the Emperor, according to the terms of which the Medici should have been restored as citizens of paramount authority, but not as sovereigns. Varchi, while no less alive to the insecurity of Carducci's policy, was animated with a more democratic spirit. He had none of Segni's Whig leanings, but shared the patriotic enthusiasm which at that supreme moment made the whole state splendidly audacious in the face of insurmountable difficulties. Both Segni and Varchi discerned the exaggerated and therefore baneful influence of Savonarola's prophecies over the populace of Florence. In spite of continued failure, the people kept trusting to the monk's prediction that, after her chastisement, Florence would bloom forth with double lustre, and that angels in the last resort would man her walls and repel the invaders. There is something pathetic in this delusion of a great city, trusting with infantine pertinacity to the promises of the man whom they had seen burned as an impostor, when all the while their statesmen and their generals were striking bargains with the foe. Nardi is more sincerely Piagnone than either Segni or Varchi. Yet, writing after the events of the siege, his faith is shaken; and while he records his conviction that Savonarola was an excellent Nomothetes, he questions his prophetic mission, and deplores the effect produced by his vain promises. Nerli, as might have been expected from a noble married to Caterina Salviati, the niece of Leo and the aunt of Cosimo, who had himself been courtier to Clement and privy councillor to Alessandro, sustains the Medicean note throughout his commentaries.

Thus from these five authors, writing from different points of view, we gain a complete insight into the complicated politics of Florence, at a period when her vitality was still vigorous, but when she had lost all faculty for centralised or concerted action. In sagacity, in the power of analysis with which they pierce below the surface, trace effects to causes, discern character, and regard the facts of history as the proper subject-matter of philosophical reflection, they have much in common. He who has seen Rembrandt's painting of the dissecting-room might construct for himself another picture, in which the five grave faces of these patient observers should be bent above the dead and diseased body of their native city. Life is extinct. Nothing is left for science but, scalpel in hand, to lay bare the secret causes of dissolution. Each anatomist has his own opinion to deliver upon the nature of the malady. Each records the facts revealed by the autopsy according to his own impressions.

The literary qualities of these historians are very different, and seem to be derived from essential differences in their characters. Pitti is by far the most brilliant in style, concentrated in expression to the point of epigram, and weighty in judgment. Nardi, though deficient in some of the most

attractive characteristics of the historian, is invaluable for
sincerity of intention and painstaking accuracy. The philosophical, rhetorical, and dramatic passages which add so much
splendour to the works of Guicciardini are absent from the
pages of Nardi. He is anxious to present a clear picture of
what happened ; but he cannot make it animated, and he
never reflects at length upon the matter of his history. At
the same time he lacks the *naïveté* which makes Corio, Allegretti, Infessura, and Matarazzo so amusing. He gossips as
little as Machiavelli, and has no profundity to make up for
the want of piquancy. The interest of his chronicle is greatest
in the part which concerns Savonarola, though even here the
peculiarly reticent and dubitative nature of the man is obvious.
While he sympathises with Savonarola's political and moral
reforms, he raises a doubt about his inner sincerity, and does
not approve of the attitude of the Piagnoni.[1] In his estima-
tion of men Nardi was remarkably cautious, preferring always
to give an external relation of events, instead of analysing
motives or criticising character.[2] He is in especial silent
about bad men and criminal actions. Therefore, when he
passes an adverse judgment (as, for instance, upon Cesare
Borgia), or notes a dark act (as the *stuprum* committed
upon Astorre Manfredi), his corroboration of historians more
addicted to scandal is important. Segni is far more lively
than Nardi, while he is not less painstaking to be accurate.
He shows a partisan feeling, especially in his admiration for
Niccolo Capponi and his prejudice against Francesco Carducci,

[1] Book ii. cap. 16.
[2] See lib. ii. cap. 34 : ' Nel nostro scrivere non intendiamo far giudizio
delle cose incerte, e massimamente della intenzione e animo segreto
degli uomini, che non apparisce chiara se non per congettura e riscontro
delle cose esteriori. E però stando fermo il primo proposito, vogliamo
raccontare quanto più possibile ci sia, la verità delle cose fatte, più
tosto che delle pensate o immaginate.' This is dignified and noble
language in an age which admired the brilliant falsehoods of Giovio.

which gives the relish of personality that Nardi's cautiously dry chronicle lacks. Rarely have the entangled events of a specially dramatic period been set forth more lucidly, more succinctly, and with greater elegance of style. Segni is deficient, when compared with Varchi, only perhaps in volume, minuteness, and that wonderful mixture of candour, enthusiasm, and zeal for truth which makes Varchi incomparable. His sketches of men, critiques, and digressions upon statistical details are far less copious than Varchi's. But in idiomatic purity of language he is superior. Varchi had been spoiled by academic habits of composition. His language is diffuse and lumbering. He lacks the vivacity of epigram, selection, and pointed phrase. But his 'Storia Fiorentina' remains the most valuable repertory of information we possess about the later vicissitudes of the republic, and the charm of detail compensates for the lack of style. Nerli is altogether a less interesting writer than those that have been mentioned; yet some of the particulars which he relates, about Savonarola's reform of manners, for example, and the literary gatherings in the Rucellai gardens, are such as we find nowhere else.

Many of my readers will doubtless feel that too much time has been spent in the discussion of these annalists of the siege of Florence. Yet for the student of history they have a value almost unique. They suggest the possibilities of a true science of comparative history, and reveal a vivacity of the historic consciousness which can be paralleled by no other nation. How different might be our conception of the vicissitudes of Athens between 404 and 338 B.C. if we possessed a similar Pleiad of contemporary Greek authors !

Having traced the development of historical research and political philosophy in Florence from the year 1300 to the fall of the Republic, it remains to speak of the two greatest masters of practical and theoretical statecraft—Francesco

Guicciardini and Niccolo Machiavelli. These two writers combine all the distinctive qualities of the Florentine historiographers in the most eminent perfection. At the same time they are, not merely as authors but also as men, mirrors of the times in which they both played prominent parts. In their biographies and in their works we trace the spirit of an age devoid of moral sensibility, penetrative in analysis, but deficient in faith, hope, enthusiasm, and stability of character. The dry light of the intellect determined their judgment of men, as well as their theories of government. On the other hand, the sordid conditions of existence to which they were subjected as the servants of corrupt states, or the instruments of wily princes—as diplomatists intent upon the plans of kings like Ferdinand or adventurers like Cesare Borgia, privy councillors of such Popes as Clement VII. and such tyrants as Duke Alessandro de' Medici—distorted their philosophy and blunted their instincts. For the student of the sixteenth century they remain riddles, the solution of which is difficult, because by no strain of the imagination is it easy to place ourselves in their position. One half of their written utterances seem to be at variance with the other half. Their actions often contradict their most brilliant and emphatic precepts ; while contemporaries disagree about their private character and public conduct. All this confusion, through which it is now perhaps impossible to discern what either Guicciardini or Machiavelli really was, and what they really felt and thought, is due to the anomaly of consummate ability and unrivalled knowledge of the world existing without religious or political faith, in an age of the utmost depravity of public and private morals. No criticism could be more stringent upon the contemporary disorganisation of society in Italy than is the silent witness of these men, sublimely great in all mental qualities, but helplessly adrift upon a sea of contradictions and of doubts, ignorant of the real nature of mankind in spite of all their science, because they leave both goodness and beauty out of their calculations.

Francesco Guicciardini was born in 1482. In 1505, at the age of twenty-three, he had already so distinguished himself as a student of law that he was appointed by the Signoria of Florence to read the Institutes in public. However, as he preferred active to professorial work, he began at this time to practise at the bar, where he soon ranked as an able advocate and eloquent. speaker. This reputation, together with his character for gravity and insight, determined the Signoria to send him on an embassy to the Court of Ferdinand of Aragon in 1512. Thus Guicciardini entered on the real work of his life as a diplomatist and statesman. We may also conclude with safety that it was at the court of that crowned hypocrite and traitor to all loyalty of soul that he learned his first lessons in political cynicism. The court of Spain under Ferdinand the Catholic was a perfect school of perfidy, where even an Italian might discern deeper reaches of human depravity and formulate for his own guidance a philosophy of despair. It was whispered by his enemies that here, upon the threshold of his public life, Guicciardini sold his honour by accepting a bribe from Ferdinand.[1] Certain it is that avarice was one of his besetting sins, and that from this time forward he preferred expediency to justice, and believed in the policy of supporting force by clever dissimulation.[2] Returning to Florence, Guicciardini was, in 1515, deputed to meet Leo X. on the part of the Republic at Cortona. Leo, who had the faculty of discerning able men and making use of them, took him into favour, and three years later appointed him Governor of Reggio and Modena. In 1521 Parma was

---

[1] See the 'Apologia de' Cappucci,' *Arch. Stor.* vol. iv. part 2, p. 318.

[2] For the avarice of Guicciardini, see Varchi, vol. i. p. 318. His *Ricordi Politici* amply justify the second, though not the first, clause of this sentence.

added to his rule. Clement VII. made him Viceroy of
Romagna in 1523, and in 1526 elevated him to the rank of
Lieutenant-General of the Papal army. In consequence of
this high commission, Guicciardini shared in the humiliation
attaching to all the officers of the League who, with the Duke of
Urbino at their head, suffered Rome to be sacked and the
Pope to be imprisoned in 1527. The blame of this con-
temptible display of cowardice or private spite cannot, how-
ever, be ascribed to him : for he attended the armies of the
League not as general, but as counsellor and chief reporter.
It was his business not to control the movements of the army
so much as to act as referee in the Pope's interest, and to
keep the Vatican informed of what was stirring in the camp.
In 1531 Guicciardini was advanced to the governorship of
Bologna, the most important of all the Papal lord-lieutenan-
cies. This post he resigned in 1534 on the election of
Paul III., preferring to follow the fortunes of the Medicean
princes at Florence. In this sketch of his career I must not
omit to mention that Guicciardini was declared a rebel in
1527 by the popular government on account of his well-known
Medicean prejudices, and that in 1530 he had been appointed
by Clement VII. to punish the rebellious citizens. On the
latter occasion he revenged himself for the insult offered him
in 1527 by the cruelty with which he pushed proscription to
the utmost limits, relegating his enemies to unhealthy places
of exile, burdening them with intolerable fines, and using all
the indirect means which his ingenuity could devise for
forcing them into outlawry and contumacy.[1] Therefore when
he returned to inhabit Florence, he did so as the creature of
the Medici, sworn to maintain the bastard Alessandro in his
power. He was elected a member of the Senate of eighty;

[1] See Varchi, book xii. (and especially cap. xxv.), for these arts ; he
says, 'Nel che messer Francesco Guicciardini si scoperse più crudele e
più appassionato degli altri.'

and so thoroughly did he espouse the cause of his new master, that he had the face to undertake the Duke's defence before Charles V. at Naples in 1535. On this occasion Alessandro, who had rendered himself unbearable by his despotic habits, and in particular by the insults which he offered to women of all ranks and conditions in Florence, was arraigned by the exiles before the bar of Cæsar. Guicciardini won the cause of his client, and restored Alessandro with an Imperial confirmation of his despotism to Florence. This period of his political career deserves particular attention, since it displays a glaring contradiction between some of his unpublished compositions and his actions, and confirms the accusations of his enemies.[1] That he should have preferred a government of Ottimati, or wealthy nobles, to a more popular constitution, and that he should have adhered with fidelity to the Medicean faction in Florence, is no ground for censure.[2] But when we find him in private unmasking the artifices of the Despots by the most relentless use of frigid criticism, and advocating a mixed government upon the type of the Venetian Constitution, we are constrained to admit with Varchi and Pitti that his support of Alessandro was prompted less by loyalty than by a desire to gratify his own ambition and avarice under the protective shadow of the Medicean tyranny.[3] He belonged

[1] Knowing what sort of a tyrant Alessandro was, and remembering that Guicciardini had written (*Ricordi*, No. ccxlii.): 'La calcina con che si murano gli stati de' tiranni è il sangue de' cittadini: però doverebbe sforzarsi ognuno che nella città sua non s' avessino a murare tali palazzi,' it is very difficult to approve of his advocacy of the Duke.

[2] Though even here the selfish ambition of the man was apparent to contemporaries: 'egli arebbe voluto uno stato col nome d' Ottimati, ma in fatti de' Pochi, nel quale larghissima parte, per le sue molte e rarissime qualità, meritissimamente gli si venia.'—Varchi, vol. i. p. 318.

[3] Guicciardini's *Storia Fiorentina* and *Reggimento di Firenze* (*Op. Ined.* vols. i. and iii.) may be consulted for his private critique of the Medici. What was the judgment passed upon him by contemporaries may be gathered from Varchi, vols. i. pp. 238, 318; ii. 410; iii. 204. Segni, pp. 219, 332. Nardi, vol. ii. p. 287. Pitti, quoted in *Arch. Stor.*

in fact to those selfish citizens whom Pitti denounces, diplomatists and men of the world, whose thirst for power induced
them to play into the hands of the Medici, wishing to suck
the state[1] themselves, and to hold the prince in the leading-
strings of vice and pleasure for their own advantage.[2] After
the murder of Alessandro, it was principally through Guicciardini's influence that Cosimo was placed at the head of
the Florentine Republic with the title of Duke.   Cosimo was
but a boy, and much addicted to field sports. Guicciardini therefore reckoned that, with an assured income of 12,000 ducats,
the youth would be contented to amuse himself, while he left
the government of Florence in the hands of his Vizier.[3]   But
here the wily politician overreached himself. Cosimo wore
an old head on his young shoulders.   With decent modesty
and a becoming show of deference, he used Guicciardini as

vol. i. p. xxxviii, and the 'Apologia de' Cappucci ' (*Arch. Stor.* vol. iv. pt. 2).
It is, however, only fair to Guicciardini to record here his opinion,
expressed in *Ricordi*, Nos. ccxx. and cccxxx., that it was the duty of
good citizens to seek to guide the tyrant : ' Credo sia uficio di buoni
cittadini, quando la patria viene in mano di tiranni, cercare d' avere
luogo con loro per potere persuadere il bene, e detestare il male ; e
certo è interesse della città che in qualunque tempo gli uomini da bene
abbino autorità ; e ancora che gli ignoranti e passionati di Firenze
l' abbino sempre intesa altrimenti, si accorgerebbero quanto pestifero
sarebbe il governo de' Medici, se non avessi intorno altri che pazzi e
cattivi.'

[1] See Varchi, vol. iii. p. 204. ' Che Cosimo . . . *succiarsi lo stato.*'

[2] Pitti dips his pen in gall when he describes these citizens : ' Cotesti
vogliosi Ottimati ; i quali non hanno saputo mai ritrovare luogo che
piaccia loro, sottomettendosi ora a' Medici per l' ingorda avarizia ; ora
gittandosi al popolo, per non potere a modo loro tiranneggiare ; ora
rivendendolo a' Medici, vedutisi scoperti e raffrenati da lui ; e sempre
mai con danno della Repubblica, e di ciascuna parte, inquieti, insaziabili
e fraudolenti.'—' Apologia de' Cappucci,' *Arch. Stor.* iv. pt. ii. p. 215.

[3] Here is a graphic touch in Varchi's *History*, vol. iii. p. 202.
Guicciardini is discussing the appointment of Cosimo de' Medici : ' Gli
dovessero esser pagati per suo piatto ogn' anno 12,000 fiorini d' oro, e
non più, avendo il Guicciardino, *abbassando il viso e alzando gli occhi,*
detto : " Un 12,000 fiorini d' oro è—un bello spendere." '

his ladder to mount the throne by, and then kicked the ladder away. The first days of his administration showed that he intended to be sole master in Florence. Guicciardini, perceiving that his game was spoiled, retired to his villa in 1537 and spent the last years of his life in composing his histories. The famous 'Istoria d' Italia' was the work of one year of this enforced retirement. The question irresistibly rises to our mind, whether some of the severe criticisms passed upon the Medici in his unpublished compositions were the fruit of these same bitter leisure hours.[1] Guicciardini died in 1540 at the age of fifty-eight, without male heirs.

Turning now from the statesman to the man of letters, we find in Guicciardini one of the most consummate historians of any nation or of any age. The work by which he is best known, the 'Istoria d' Italia,' is one that can scarcely be surpassed for masterly control of a very intricate period, for subordination of the parts to the whole, for calmness of judgment, and for philosophic depth of thought. Considering that Guicciardini in this great work was writing the annals of his own times, and that he had to disentangle the ravelled skein of Italian politics in the sixteenth century, these qualities are most remarkable. The whole movement of the history recalls the pomp and dignity of Livy, while a series of portraits sketched from life with the unerring hand of an anatomist and artist add something of the vivid force of Tacitus. Yet Guicciardini in this work deserves less com-

---

[1] Pitti seems to have taken this view: see 'Apologia de' Cappucci' (*Arch. Stor.* vol. iv. part ii. p. 329) : 'Tosto che 'l duca Cosimo lo pose a sedere insieme con certi altri suoi colleghi, si adirò malamente ; e se la disputa della provvisione non l' avesse ritenuto, sarebbe ito a servire papa Pagolo terzo. Onde, restato confuso e disperato, si tratteneva alla sua villa di Santa Margarita a Montici ; dove transportato dalla stizza ritoccò in molte parti la sua Istoria, per mostrare di non essere stato della setta Pallesca ; e dove potette, accattò l' occasione di parere istrumento della Repubblica.' Guicciardini's own apology for his treatment of the Medici, in the proemio to the treatise *Del Reggimento di Firenze*, deserves also to be read.

mendation as a writer than as a thinker. There is a manifest straining to secure style, by manipulation and rehandling, which contrasts unfavourably with the unaffected ease, the pregnant spontaneity, of his unpublished writings. His periods are almost interminable, and his rhetoric is prolix and monotonous. We can trace the effort to emulate the authors of antiquity without the ease which is acquired by practice or the taste that comes with nature.

The transcendent merit of the history is this—that it presents us with a scientific picture of politics and of society during the first half of the sixteenth century. The picture is set forth with a clairvoyance and a candour that are almost terrible. The author never feels enthusiasm for a moment : no character, however great for good or evil, rouses him from the attitude of tranquil disillusioned criticism. He utters but few exclamations of horror or of applause. Faith, religion, conscience, self-subordination to the public good, have no place in his list of human motives ; interest, ambition, calculation, envy, are the forces which, according to his experience, move the world. That the strong should trample on the weak, that the wily should circumvent the innocent, that hypocrisy and fraud and dissimulation should triumph, seems to him but natural. His whole theory of humanity is tinged with the sad grey colours of a stolid, cold-eyed, ill-contented, egotistical indifference. He is not angry, desperate, indignant, but phlegmatically prudent, face to face with the ruin of his country. For him the world was a game of intrigue, in which his friends, his enemies, and himself played parts, equally sordid, with grave faces and hearts bent only on the gratification of mean desires. Accordingly, though his mastery of detail, his comprehension of personal motives, and his analysis of craft are alike incomparable, we find him incapable of forming general views with the breadth of philosophic insight or the sagacity of a frank and indepen-

dent nature.   The movements of the eagle and the lion must
be unintelligible to the spider or the fox.   It was impossible
for Guicciardini to feel the real greatness of the century, or
to foresee the new forces to which it was giving birth.   He
could not divine the momentous issues of the Lutheran
schism; and though he perceived the immediate effect upon
Italian politics of the invasion of the French, he failed to
comprehend the revolution marked out for the future in the
shock of the modern nations.   While criticising the papacy,
he discerned the pernicious results of nepotism and secular
ambition : but he had no instinct for the necessity of a
spiritual and religious regeneration.   His judgment of the
political situation led him to believe that the several units
of the Italian system might be turned to profit and account by
the application of superficial remedies,—by the development
of despotism, for example, or of oligarchy,—when in reality
the disease of the nation was already past all cure.

Two other masterpieces from Guicciardini's pen, the 'Dialogo del Reggimento di Firenze ' and the ' Storia Fiorentina,'
have been given to the world during the last twenty years.
To have published them immediately after their author's
death would have been inexpedient, since they are far too
candid and outspoken to have been acceptable to the Medicean dynasty.   Yet in these writings we find Guicciardini at
his best.   Here he has not yet assumed the mantle of the
rhetorician, which in the ' Istoria d' Italia ' sits upon him somewhat cumbrously.   His style is more spontaneous ; his
utterances are less guarded.   Writing for himself alone, he
dares to say more plainly what he thinks and feels.   At the
same time the political sagacity of the statesman is revealed
in all its vigour.   I have so frequently used both of these
treatises that I need not enter into a minute analysis of their
contents.   It will be enough to indicate some of the passages
which display the literary style and the scientific acumen of

Guicciardini at their best. The 'Reggimento di Firenze' is an essay upon the form of government for which Florence was best suited. Starting with a discussion of Savonarola's constitution, in which ample justice is done to the sagacity and promptitude by means of which he saved the commonwealth at a critical juncture (pp. 27–30), the interlocutors pass to an examination of the Medicean tyranny (pp. 34–49). This is one of the masterpieces of Guicciardini's analysis. He shows how the administration of justice, the distribution of public honours, and the foreign policy of the republic were perverted by this family. He condemns Cosimo's tyrannical application of fines and imposts (p. 68), Piero the younger's insolence (p. 46), and Lorenzo's appropriation of the public moneys to his private use (p. 43). Yet while setting forth the vices of this tyranny in language which even Sismondi would have been contented to translate and sign, Guicciardini shows no passion. The Medici were only acting as befitted princes eager for power, although they crushed the spirit of the people, discouraged political ardour, extinguished military zeal, and did all that in them lay to enervate the nation they governed. The scientific statist acknowledges no reciprocal rights and duties between the governor and the governed. It is a trial of strength. If the tyrant gets the upper hand, the people must expect to be oppressed. If, on the other side, the people triumph, they must take good care to exterminate the despotic brood : 'The one true remedy would be to destroy and extinguish them so utterly that not a vestige should remain, and to employ for this purpose the poignard or poison, as may be most convenient; otherwise the least surviving spark is certain to cause trouble and annoyance for the future' (p. 215). The same precise criticism lays bare the weakness of democracy. Men, says Guicciardini, always really desire their own power more than the freedom of the state (p. 50), and the motives

even of tyrannicides are very rarely pure (pp. 53-54). The
governments established by the liberals are full of defects.
The Consiglio Grande, for example, of the Florentines is
ignorant in its choice of magistrates, unjust in its apportion-
ment of taxes, scarcely less prejudiced against individuals than
a tyrant would be, and incapable of diplomatic foreign policy
(pp. 58-69). Then follows a discussion of the relative merits
of the three chief forms of government—the Governo dell'
Uno, the Governo degli Ottimati, and the Governo del Popolo
(p. 129). Guicciardini has already criticised the first and the
third.[1] He now expresses a strong opinion that the second
is the worst which could be applied to the actual conditions
of the Florentine Republic (p. 130). His panegyric of the
Venetian constitution (pp. 139-41) illustrates his plan for
combining the advantages of the three species and obviating
their respective evils. In fact he declares for that Utopia of
the sixteenth century—the Governo Misto—a political invention which fascinated the imagination of Italian statesmen
much in the same way as the theory of perpetual motion
attracted scientific minds in the last century.[2] What follows

[1] Cf. *Ricordi*, cxl.: 'Chi disse uno popolo, disse veramente uno
animale pazzo, pieno di mille errori, di mille confusioni, sanza gusto,
sanza diletto, sanza stabilità.' It should be noted that Guicciardini
here and elsewhere uses the term *Popolo* in its fuller democratic sense.
The successive enlargements of the burgher class in Florence, together
with the study of Greek and Latin political philosophy, had introduced
the modern connotation of the term.

[2] A lucid criticism of the three forms of government is contained in
Guicciardini's Comment on the second chapter of the first book of
Machiavelli's *Discorsi* (*Op. Ined.* vol. i. p. 6): 'E non è dubio che il
governo misto delle tre spezie, principi, ottimati e popolo, è migliore e
più stabile che uno governo semplice di qualunque delle tre spezie, e
massime quando è misto in modo che di qualunque spezie è tolto il
buono e lasciato indietro il cattivo.' Machiavelli had himself, in the
passage criticised, examined the three simple governments and declared
in favour of the mixed as that which gave stability to Sparta, Rome,
and Venice. The same line of thought may be traced in the political
speculations of both Plato and Aristotle. The Athenians and Florentines

is an elaborate scheme for applying the principles of the Governo Misto to the existing state of things in Florence. This lucid and learned disquisition is wound up (p. 188) with a mournful expression of the doubt which hung like a thick cloud over all the political speculations of both Guicciardini and Machiavelli: 'I hold it very doubtful, and I think it much depends on chance whether this disorganised constitution will ever take new shape or not . . . and as I said yesterday, I should have more hope if the city were but young; seeing that not only does a state at the commencement take form with greater facility than one that has grown old under evil governments, but things always turn out more prosperously and more easily while fortune is yet fresh and has not run its course,' &c.[1] In reading the 'Dialogue on the Constitution of Florence' it must finally be remembered that Guicciardini has thrown it back into the year 1494, and that he speaks through the mouths of four interlocutors. Therefore we may presume that he intended his readers to regard it as a work of speculative science rather than of practical political philosophy. Yet it is not difficult to gather the drift of his own meaning.

The 'Istoria Fiorentina' is a succinct narrative of the events of Italian History, especially as they concerned Florence, between the years 1378 and 1509. In other words, it relates the vicissitudes of the Republic under the Medici, and the administration of the Gonfalonier Soderini. This masterpiece of historical narration sets forth with brevity and

felt the superior stability of the Spartan and Venetian forms of government, just as a French theorist might idealise the English constitution. The essential element of the Governo Misto, which Florence had lost beyond the possibility of regaining it, was a body of hereditary and patriotic patricians. This gave its strength to Venice; and this is that which hitherto has distinguished the English nation.

[1] Compare *Ricordi Politici e Civili*, No. clxxxix., for a lament of this kind over the decrepitude of kingdoms, almost sublime in its stoicism.

frankness the whole series of events which are rhetorically and cautiously unfolded in the 'Istoria d' Italia.' Most noticeable are the characters of Lorenzo de' Medici (cap. ix.), of Savonarola (cap. xvii.), and of Alexander VI. (cap. xxvii.) The immediate consequences of the French invasion have never been more ably treated than in Chapter xi., while the whole progress of Cesare Borgia in his career of villany is analysed with exquisite distinctness in Chapter xxvi. The wisdom of Guicciardini nowhere appears more ripe, or his intellect more elastic, than in the 'Istoria Fiorentina.' Students who desire to gain a still closer insight into the working of Guicciardini's mind should consult the 403 'Ricordi Politici e Civili' collected in the first volume of his 'Opere Inedite.' These have all the charm which belongs to occasional utterances, and are fit, like proverbs, to be worn for jewels on the finger of Time.

The biography of Niccolo Machiavelli consists for the most part of a record of his public services to the State of Florence. He was born on May 3, 1469, of parents who belonged to the prosperous middle class of Florentine citizens. His ancestry was noble ; for the old tradition which connected his descent with the feudal house of Montespertoli has been confirmed by documentary evidence.[1] His forefathers held offices of high distinction in the commonwealth ; and though their wealth and station had decreased, Machiavelli inherited a small landed estate. His family, who were originally settled in the Val di Pesa, owned farms at San Casciano and in other villages of the Florentine dominion, a list of which may be seen in the return presented by his father Bernardo to the revenue office in 1498.[2] Their wealth

[1] See Villari's *Machiavelli*, vol. i. p. 303. Ed. Le Monnier.
[2] See vol. i. of the edition of Machiavelli, by Mess. Fanfani and Passerini, Florence, 1873 ; p. lv. Villari's *Machiavelli*, ib. p. 306. The income is estimated at about 180*l*.

was no doubt trivial in comparison with that which citizens amassed by trade in Florence ; for it was not the usage of those times to draw more than the necessaries of life from the Villa : all superfluities were provided by the Bottega in the town.[1]   Yet there can be no question, after a comparison of Bernardo Machiavelli's return of his landed property with Niccolo Machiavelli's will,[2] that the illustrious war secretary at all periods of his life owned just sufficient property to maintain his family in a decent, if not a dignified, style. About his education we know next to nothing.   Giovio[3] asserts that he possessed but little Latin, and that he owed the show of learning in his works to quotations furnished by Marcellus Virgilius.   This accusation, which, whether it be true or not, was intended to be injurious, has lost its force in an age that, like ours, values erudition less than native genius. It is certain that Machiavelli knew quite enough of Latin and Greek literature to serve his turn ; and his familiarity with some of the classical historians and philosophers is intimate. There is even too much parade in his works of illustrations borrowed from Polybius, Livy, and Plutarch : the only question is whether Machiavelli relied upon translations rather than originals.   On this point, it is also worthy of remark that his culture was rather Roman than Hellenic.   Had he at any period of his life made as profound a study of Plato's political dialogues as he made of Livy's histories, we cannot but feel that his theories both of government and statecraft might have been more concordant with a sane and normal humanity.

In 1494, the date of the expulsion of the Medici, Machiavelli was admitted to the Chancery of the Commune as a clerk ; and in 1498 he was appointed to the post of chancellor

[1] See Pandolfini, *Trattato del Governo della Famiglia.*
[2] Fanfani and Passerini's edition, vol. i. p. xcii.
[3] Elogia, cap. 87.

and secretary to the *Dieci di libertà e pace.* This place he held for the better half of fifteen years ; that is to say, during the whole period of Florentine freedom. His diplomatic missions undertaken at the instance of the Republic were very numerous. Omitting those of less importance, we find him at the camp of Cesare Borgia in 1502, in France in 1504, with Julius II. in 1506, with the Emperor Maximilian in 1507, and again at the French Court in 1510.[1] To this department of his public life belong the despatches and Relazioni which he sent home to the Signory of Florence, his Monograph upon the Massacre of Sinigaglia, his treatises upon the method of dealing with Pisa, Pistoja, and Valdichiana, and those two remarkable studies of foreign nations which are entitled 'Ritratti delle Cose dell' Alemagna' and 'Ritratti delle Cose di Francia.' It was also in the year 1500 that he laid the first foundations of his improved military system. The political sagacity and the patriotism for which Machiavelli has been admired are nowhere more conspicuous than in the discernment which suggested this measure, and in the indefatigable zeal with which he strove to carry it into effect. Pondering upon the causes of Italian weakness when confronted with nations like the French, and comparing contemporary with ancient history, Machiavelli came to the conclusion that the universal employment of mercenary troops was the chief secret of the insecurity of Italy. He therefore conceived a plan for establishing a national militia, and for placing the whole male population at the service of the state in times of war. He had to begin cautiously in bringing this scheme before the public ; for the stronghold of the mercenary system was the sloth and luxury of the burghers. At first he induced the *Dieci di libertà e pace,* or war office, to require

[1] Machiavelli never bore the title of Ambassador on these missions. He went as Secretary. His pay was miserable. We find him receiving one ducat a day for maintenance.

the service of one man per house throughout the Florentine dominion; but at the same time he caused a census to be taken of all men capable of bearing arms. His next step was to carry a law by which the permanent militia of the state was fixed at 10,000. Then in 1503, having prepared the way by these preliminary measures, he addressed the Council of the Burghers in a set oration, unfolding the principles of his proposed reform, and appealing not only to their patriotism but also to their sense of self-preservation. It was his aim to prove that mercenary arms must be exchanged for a national militia, if freedom and independence were to be maintained. The Florentines allowed themselves to be convinced, and, on the recommendation of Machiavelli, they voted in 1506 a new magistracy, called the *Nove dell' Ordinanza e Milizia*, for the formation of companies, the discipline of soldiers, and the maintenance of the militia in a state of readiness for active service.[1] Machiavelli became the secretary of this board; and much of his time was spent thenceforth in the levying of troops and the practical development of his system. It requires an intimate familiarity with the Italian military system of the fourteenth and fifteenth centuries to understand the importance of this reform. We are so accustomed to the systems of Militia, Conscription, and Landwehr, by means of which military service has been nationalised among the modern races, that we need to tax our imagination before we can place ourselves at the point of view of men to whom Machiavelli's measure was a novelty of genius.[2]

[1] Documents relating to the institution of the *Nove dell' Ordinanza e Milizia*, and to its operations between December 6, 1506, and August 6, 1512, from the pen of Machiavelli, will be found printed by Signor Canestrini in *Arch. Stor.* vol. xv. pp. 377 to 453. Machiavelli's treatise *De re militari*, or *I libri sull' arte della guerra*, was the work of his later life; it was published in 1521 at Florence.

[2] Though Machiavelli deserves the credit of this military system

It must be admitted that the new militia proved ineffectual in the hour of need. To revive the martial spirit of a nation, enervated by tyranny and given over to commerce, merely by a stroke of genius, was beyond the force of even Machiavelli. When Prato had been sacked in 1512, the Florentines, destitute of troops, divided among themselves, and, headed by the excellent but hesitating Piero Soderini, threw their gates open to the Medici. Giuliano, the brother of Pope Leo, and Lorenzo, his nephew, whose statues sit throned in the immortality of Michael Angelo's marble upon their tombs in San Lorenzo, disposed of the Republic at their pleasure. Machiavelli, as War Secretary of the anti-Medicean government, was of course disgraced and deprived of his appointments. In 1513 he was suspected of complicity in the conjuration of Pietropaolo Boscoli and Agostino Capponi, was imprisoned in the Bargello, and tortured to the extent of four turns of the rack. It seems that he was innocent. Leo X. released him by the act of amnesty passed upon the event of his assuming the tiara; and Machiavelli immediately retired to his farm near San Casciano.

Since we are now approaching the most critical passage of Machiavelli's biography, it may be well to draw from his private letters a picture of the life to which this statesman of the restless brain was condemned in the solitude of the

the part of Antonio Giacomini in carrying it into effect must not be forgotten. Pitti, in his 'Life of Giacomini' (*Arch. Stor.* vol. iv. pt. ii. p. 241), says: 'Avendo per dieci anni continovi fatto prova nelle fazioni e nelle battaglie de' fanti del dominio e delli esterni, aveva troppo bene conosciuto con quanta più sicurezza si potesse la repubblica servire de' suoi propri che delli istranieri.' Machiavelli had gone as Commissary to the camp of Giacomini before Pisa in August 1505; there the man of action and the man of theory came to an agreement: both found in the Gonfalonier Soderini a chief of the Republic capable of entering into their views.

country.[1] Writing on December 10 to his friend Francesco Vettori, he says, 'I am at my farm; and, since my last misfortunes, have not been in Florence twenty days. I rise with the sun, and go into a wood of mine that is being cut, where I remain two hours inspecting the work of the previous day and conversing with the woodcutters, who have always some trouble on hand among themselves or with their neighbours. When I leave the wood, I proceed to a well, and thence to the place which I use for snaring birds, with a book under my arm—Dante, or Petrarch, or one of the minor poets, like Tibullus or Ovid. I read the story of their passions, and let their loves remind me of my own, which is a pleasant pastime for a while. Next I take the road, enter the inn door, talk with the passers-by, inquire the news of the neighbourhood, listen to a variety of matters, and make note of the different tastes and humours of men. This brings me to dinner-time, when I join my family and eat the poor produce of my farm. After dinner I go back to the inn, where I generally find the host and a butcher, a miller, and a pair of bakers. With these companions I play the fool all day at cards or backgammon : a thousand squabbles, a thousand insults and abusive dialogues take place, while we haggle over a farthing, and shout loud enough to be heard from San Casciano. But when evening falls I go home and

[1] This letter may be compared with others of about the same date. In one (Aug. 3, 1514) he says : 'Ho lasciato dunque i pensieri delle cose grandi e gravi ; non mi diletta più leggere le cose antiche, nè ragionare delle moderne ; tutte si son converse in ragionamenti dolci,' &c. Again he writes (Dec. 4, 1514) : 'Quod autem ad me pertinet, si quid agam scire cupis, omnem meae vitae rationem ab eodem Tafano intelliges, quam sordidam ingloriamque, non sine indignatione, si me ut soles amas, cognosces.' Later on, we may notice the same language. Thus (Feb. 5, 1515), 'Sono diventato inutile a me, a' parenti ed agli amici,' and (June 8, 1517) 'Essendomi io ridotto a stare in villa per le avversità che io ho avuto ed ho, sto qualche volta un mese che non mi ricordo di me.

enter my writing-room. On the threshold I put off my country habit, filthy with mud and mire, and array myself in royal courtly garments; thus worthily attired, I make my entrance into the ancient courts of the men of old, where they receive me with love, and where I feed upon that food which only is my own and for which I was born. I feel no shame in conversing with them and asking them the reason of their actions. They, moved by their humanity, make answer; for four hours' space I feel no annoyance, forget all care; poverty cannot frighten, nor death appal me. I am carried away to their society. And since Dante says "that there is no science unless we retain what we have learned," I have set down what I have gained from their discourse, and composed a treatise, "De Principatibus," in which I enter as deeply as I can into the science of the subject, with reasonings on the nature of principality, its several species, and how they are acquired, how maintained, how lost. If you ever liked any of my scribblings, this ought to suit your taste. To a prince, and especially to a new prince, it ought to prove acceptable. Therefore I am dedicating it to the Magnificence of Giuliano.'

Further on in the same letter he writes: 'I have talked with Filippo Casavecchia about this little work of mine, whether I ought to present it or not; and if so, whether I ought to send or take it myself to him. I was induced to doubt about presenting it at all by the fear lest Giuliano should not even read it, and that this Ardinghelli should profit by my latest labours. On the other hand, I am prompted to present it by the necessity which pursues me, seeing that I am consuming myself in idleness, and I cannot continue long in this way without becoming contemptible through poverty. I wish these Signori Medici would begin to make some use of me, if it were only to set me to the work of rolling a stone.[1]   If I did not win them over to me afterwards, I should only complain of myself.   As for my book, if they read it, they would perceive that the fifteen years I have spent in studying statecraft have not been wasted in sleep or play ; and everybody ought to be glad to make use of a man who has so filled himself with experience at the expense of others.   About my fidelity they ought not to doubt.   Having always kept faith, I am not going to learn to break it now. A man who has been loyal and good for forty-three years, like me, is not likely to change his nature ; and of my loyalty and goodness my poverty is sufficient witness to them.'

This letter, invaluable to the student of Machiavelli's work, is prejudicial to his reputation.   It was written only ten months after he had been imprisoned and tortured by the Medici, just thirteen months after the Republic he had served so long had been enslaved by the princes before whom he was now cringing.   It is true that Machiavelli was not wealthy ; his habits of prodigality made his fortune insufficient for his needs.[2]   It is true that he could ill bear the enforced idleness of country life, after being engaged for fifteen years in the most important concerns of the Florentine Republic.   But neither his poverty, which, after all, was but comparative, nor his inactivity, for which he found relief in study, justifies the tone of the conclusion to this letter.   When we read it, we cannot help remembering the language of another exile, who while he tells us—

> come sa di sale
> Lo pane altrui, e com' è duro calle
> Lo scendere e 'l salir per l' altrui scale.

---

[1] Compare the letter, dated June 10, 1514, to Fr. Vettori: 'Starommi dunque così tra i miei cenci, senza trovare uomo che della mia servitù si ricordi, o che creda che io possa esser buono a nulla.   Ma egli è impossibile che io possa star molto così, perchè io mi logoro,' &c. Again, Dec. 20, 1514 : ' E se la fortuna avesse voluto che i Medici, o in cosa di Firenze o di fuora, o in cose loro particolari o in pubbliche, mi avessino una volta comandato, io sarei contento.'

[2] See familiar letter, June 10, 1514.

—can yet refuse the advances of his factious city thus : 'If Florence cannot be entered honourably, I will never set foot within her walls. And what ? Shall I not be able from any angle whatsoever of the earth to gaze upon the sun and stars ? shall I not beneath whatever region of the heavens have power to meditate the sweetest truths, unless I make myself ignoble first, nay ignominious, in the face of Florence and her people? Nor will bread, I warrant, fail me !' If Machiavelli, who in this very letter to Vettori quoted Dante, had remembered these words, they ought to have fallen like drops of molten lead upon his soul. But such was the debasement of the century that probably he would have only shrugged his shoulders and sighed, 'Tempora mutantur, nos et mutamur in illis.'

In some respects Dante, Machiavelli, and Michael Angelo Buonarroti may be said to have been the three greatest intellects produced by Florence. Dante, in exile and in opposition, would hold no sort of traffic with her citizens. Michael Angelo, after the siege, worked at the Medici tombs for Pope Clement, as a makepeace offering for the fortification of Samminiato ; while Machiavelli entreats to be put *to roll a stone by these Signori Medici,* if only he may so escape from poverty and dulness. Michael Angelo, we must remember, owed a debt of gratitude as an artist to the Medici for his education in the gardens of Lorenzo. Moreover, the quatrain which he wrote for his statue of the Night justifies us in regarding that chapel as the cenotaph designed by him for murdered Liberty. Machiavelli owed nothing to the Medici, who had disgraced and tortured him, and whom he had opposed in all his public action during fifteen years. Yet what was the gift with which he came before them as a suppliant, crawling to the footstool of their throne? A treatise 'De Principatibus;' in other words, the celebrated 'Principe;' which, misread it as Machiavelli's apologists may choose to do, or explain it as the rational historian is bound to do, yet carries venom in its pages. Remembering the circumstances under which it was composed, we are in a condition to estimate the proud humility and prostrate pride of the dedication. 'Niccolo Machiavelli to the Magnificent Lorenzo, son of Piero de' Medici:' so runs the title. 'Desiring to present myself to your Magnificence with some proof of my devotion, I have not found among my various furniture aught that I prize more than the knowledge of the actions of great men acquired by me through a long experience of modern affairs and a continual study of ancient. These I have long and diligently revolved and examined in my mind, and have now compressed into a little book which I send to your Magnificence. And though I judge this work unworthy of your presence, yet I am confident that your humanity will cause you to value it when you consider that I could not make you a greater gift than this of enabling you in a few hours to understand what I have learned through perils and discomforts in a lengthy course of years.' 'If your Magnificence will deign, from the summit of your height, some time to turn your eyes to my low place, you will know how unjustly I am forced to endure the great and continued malice of fortune.' The work so dedicated was sent in MS. for the Magnificent's private perusal. It was not published until 1532, by order of Clement VII., after the death of Machiavelli.

I intend to reserve the 'Principe,' considered as the supreme expression of Italian political science, for a separate study; and after the introduction to Macaulay's Essay on Machiavelli, I need hardly enter in detail into a discussion of the various theories respecting the intention of this treatise.[1] Yet this is

[1] Macaulay's essay is, of course, brilliant and comprehensive. I do not agree with his theory of the Italian Despot, as I have explained on pp. 98, 99 of this volume. Sometimes, too, he indulges in rhetoric that is merely sentimental, as when he says about the dedication of the Florentine History to Clement: 'The miseries and humiliations of

the proper place for explaining my view about Machiavelli's writings in relation to his biography, and for attempting to connect them into such unity as a mind so strictly logical as his may have designed.

With regard to the circumstances under which the 'Prince' was composed, enough has already been said. Machiavelli's selfish purpose in putting it forth seems to my mind apparent. He wanted employment: he despaired of the Republic: he strove to furnish the princes in power with a convincing proof of his capacity for great affairs. Yet it must not on this account be concluded that the 'Principe' was merely a cheap bid for office. On the contrary, it contained the most mature and the most splendid of Machiavelli's thoughts, accumulated through his long years of public service; and, strange as it may seem, it embodied the dream of a philosophical patriot for the restitution of liberty to Italy. Florence, indeed, was lost. 'These Signori Medici' were in power. But could not even they be employed to purge the sacred soil of Italy from the Barbarians?

If we can pretend to sound the depths of Machiavelli's mind at this distance of time, we may conjecture that he had come to believe the free cities too corrupt for independence. The only chance Italy had of holding her own against the great powers of Europe was by union under a prince. At the same time the Utopia of this union, with which he closes the 'Principe,' could only be realised by such a combination as would either neutralise the power of the Church, or else gain the Pope for an ally by motives of interest. Now at the

dependence, the bread which is more bitter than every other food, the stairs which are more painful than every other ascent, had not broken the spirit of Machiavelli. *The most corrupting post in a corrupting profession had not depraved the generous heart of Clement.*' The sentence I have printed in italics may perhaps tell the truth about the Church and Popes in general; but the panegyric of Clement is preposterous. Macaulay must have been laughing in his sleeve.

period of the dedication of the 'Principe' to Lorenzo de' Medici,
Leo X. was striving to found a principality in the States of the
Church.[1]   In 1516 he created his nephew Duke of Urbino,
and it was thought that this was but a prelude to still further
greatness.   Florence in combination with Rome might do
much for Italy.   Leo meanwhile was still young, and his participation in the most ambitious schemes was to be expected.
Thus the moment was propitious for suggesting to Lorenzo
that he should put himself at the head of an Italian kingdom,
which, by its union beneath the strong will of a single prince,
might suffice to cope with nations more potent in numbers
and in arms.[2]   The 'Principe' was therefore dedicated in good
faith to the Medici, and the note on which it closes was not
false.   Machiavelli hoped that what Cesare Borgia had but
just failed in accomplishing, Lorenzo de' Medici, with the
assistance of a younger Pope than Alexander, a firmer basis
to his princedom in Florence, and a grasp upon the States of
the Church made sure by the policy of Julius II., might effect.
Whether so good a judge of character as Machiavelli expected
really much from Lorenzo may be doubted.

These circumstances make the morality of the book the
more remarkable.   To teach political science denuded of commonplace hypocrisies was a worthy object.   But while seeking
to lay bare the springs of action, and to separate statecraft
from morals, Machiavelli found himself impelled to recognise
a system of inverted ethics.   The abrupt division of the two
realms, ethical and political, which he attempted, was mon-

[1] We are, however, bound to remember that Leo was only made
Pope in March 1513, and that the *Principe* was nearly finished in the
following December.   Machiavelli cannot therefore be credited with
knowing as well as we do now to what length the ambition of the
Medici was about to run when he composed his work.   He wrote in the
hope that it might induce them to employ him.

[2] The two long letters to Fr. Vettori (Aug. 26, 1513) and to Piero
Soderini (no date) should be studied side by side with the *Principe* for
the light they throw on Machiavelli's opinions there expressed.

strous; and he ended by substituting inhumanity for human nature. Unable to escape the logic which links morality of some sort with conduct, he gave his adhesion to the false code of contemporary practice. He believed that the right way to attain a result so splendid as the liberation of Italy was to proceed by force, craft, bad faith, and all the petty arts of a political adventurer. The public ethics of his day had sunk to this low level. Success by means of plain dealing was impossible. The game of statecraft could only be carried on by guile and violence. Even the clear genius of Machiavelli had been obscured by the muddy medium of intrigue in which he had been working all his life. Even his keen insight was dazzled by the false splendour of the adventurer Cesare Borgia.

To have formulated the ethics of the 'Principe' is not diabolical. There is no inventive superfluity of naughtiness in the treatise. It is simply a handbook of princecraft, as that art was commonly received in Italy, where the principles of public morality had been translated into terms of material aggrandisement, glory, gain, and greatness. No one thought of judging men by their motives but by their practice; they were not regarded as moral but as political beings, responsible, that is to say, to no law but the obligation of success. Crimes which we regard as horrible were then commended as magnanimous, if it could be shown that they were prompted by a firm will and had for their object a deliberate end. Machiavelli and Paolo Giovio, for example, both praise the massacre at Sinigaglia as a masterstroke of art, without uttering a word in condemnation of its perfidy. Machiavelli sneers at Gianpaolo Baglioni because he had not the courage to strangle his guest Julius II. and to crown his other crimes with this signal act of magnanimity. What virtue had come to mean in the Italian language we have seen already. The one quality which every one despised was simplicity, however this might be combined with lofty genius and noble aims. It was because Soderini was simple and had a good heart that Machiavelli wrote the famous epigram—

> La notte che morì Pier Soderini,
> L' alma n' andò dell' inferno alla bocca;
> E Pluto le gridò : Anima sciocca,
> Che inferno ? va nel limbo de' bambini.

> The night that Peter Soderini died,
> His soul flew down unto the mouth of hell:
> 'What? Hell for you? You silly spirit!' cried
> The fiend: 'your place is where the babies dwell.'

As of old in Corcyra, so now in Italy, 'guilelessness, which is the principal ingredient of genuine nobleness, was laughed down, and disappeared.'[1] What men feared was not the moral verdict of society, pronouncing them degraded by vicious or violent acts, but the intellectual estimate of incapacity and the stigma of dulness. They were afraid of being reckoned among feebler personalities ; and to escape from this contempt, by the commission even of atrocities, had come to be accounted manly. The truth, missed almost universally, was that the supreme wisdom, the paramount virility, is law-abiding honesty, the doing of right because right is right, in scorn of consequence. Nothing appears more clearly in the memoirs of Cellini than this point, while the Italian novels are full of matter bearing on the same topic. It is therefore ridiculous to assume that an Italian judged of men or conduct in any sense according to our standards. Pinturicchio and Perugino thought it no shame to work for princes like the Baglioni and for Popes like Alexander VI. Lionardo da Vinci placed his talents as an engineer at the service of Cesare Borgia, and employed his genius as a musician and a painter for the amusement of the Milanese Court, which must have been, according to Corio's account, flagrantly and shamelessly

---

[1] Thuc. iii. 83. The whole of the passage about Corcyra in the third book of Thucydides (chs. 82 and 83) applies literally to the moral condition of Italy at this period.

corrupt.   Leo Battista Alberti, one of the most charming
and the most gentle spirits of the earlier Renaissance, in like
manner lent his architectural ability to the vanity of the in-
iquitous Sigismondo Malatesta.   No: the 'Principe' was not
inconsistent with the general tone of Italian morality; and
Machiavelli cannot be fairly taxed with the discovery of a
new infernal method.   The conception of politics as a bare
art of means to ends had grown up in his mind by the study
of Italian history and social customs.   His idealisation of
Cesare Borgia and his romance of 'Castruccio' were the first
products of the theory he had formed by observation of the
world he lived in.   The 'Principe' revealed it fully organised.
But to have presented such an essay in good faith to the
Despots of his native city, at that particular moment in his
own career, and under the pressure of trivial distress, is a real
blot upon his memory.

We learn from Varchi that Machiavelli was execrated in
Florence for his 'Principe,' the poor thinking it would teach
the Medici to take away their honour, the rich regarding it
as an attack upon their wealth, and both discerning in it
a death-blow to freedom.[1]   Machiavelli can scarcely have
calculated upon this evil opinion, which followed him to the
grave: for though he showed some hesitation in his letter to
Vettori about the propriety of presenting the essay to the
Medici, this was only grounded on the fear lest a rival should
get the credit of his labours.   Again, he uttered no syllable
about its being intended for a trap to catch the Medici, and
commit them to unpardonable crimes.   We may therefore
conclude that this explanation of the purpose of the 'Principe'
(which, strange to say, has approved itself to even recent
critics) was promulgated either by himself or by his friends,
as an afterthought, when he saw that the work had missed
its mark, and at the time when he was trying to suppress the

[1] *Storia Fior.* lib. iv. cap. 15.

MS.[1] Bernardo Giunti in the dedication of the edition of 1532, and Reginald Pole in 1535, were, I believe, the first to put forth this fanciful theory in print. Machiavelli could not before 1520 have boasted of the patriotic treachery with which he was afterwards accredited, so far, at any rate, as to lose the confidence of the Medicean family; for in that year the Cardinal Giulio de' Medici commissioned him to write the history of Florence.

The 'Principe,' after its dedication to Lorenzo, remained in MS., and Machiavelli was not employed, in spite of the continual solicitations of his friend Vettori.[2] Nothing remained for him but to seek other patrons, and to employ his leisure in new literary work. Between 1516 and 1519, therefore, we find him taking part in the literary and philosophical discussions of the Florentine Academy, which assembled at that period in the Rucellai Gardens.[3] It was here that he read his 'Discourses on the First Decade of Livy'—a series of profound essays upon the administration of the State, to which the sentences of the

[1] See Varchi, loc. cit. The letter written by Machiavelli to Fr. Guicciardini from Carpi, May 17, 1521, should be studied in this connection. It is unfortunately too mutilated to be wholly intelligible. After explaining his desire to be of use to Florence, but not after the manner most approved of by the Florentines themselves, he says: 'Io credo che questo sarebbe il vero modo di andare in Paradiso, imparare la via dell' Inferno per fuggirla.'

[2] The political letters addressed to Francesco Vettori, at Rome, and intended probably for the eye of Leo X., were written in 1514. The discourse addressed to Leo, *sulla riforma dello stato di Firenze*, may be referred perhaps to 1519.

[3] Of these meetings Filippo de' Nerli writes in the Seventh Book of his Commentaries, p. 138: 'Avendo convenuto assai tempo nell' orto de' Rucellai una certa scuola di giovani letterati e d' elevato ingegno, infra quali praticava continuamente Niccolò Machiavelli (ed io ero di Niccolò e di tutti loro amicissimo, e molto spesso con loro conversavo), s' esercitavano costoro assai, mediante le lettere, nelle lezioni dell' istorie, e sopra di esse, ed a loro istanza compose il Machiavello quel suo libro de' discorsi sopra Tito Livio, e anco il libro di que' trattati e ragionamenti sopra la milizia.'

Roman historian serve as texts. Having set forth in the 'Principe' the method of gaining or maintaining sovereign power, he shows in the 'Discorsi' what institutions are necessary to preserve the body politic in a condition of vigorous activity. We may therefore regard the 'Discorsi' as in some sense a continuation of the 'Principe.' But the wisdom of the scientific politician is no longer placed at the disposal of a sovereign. He addresses himself to all the members of a State who are concerned in its prosperity. Machiavelli's enemies have therefore been able to insinuate that, after teaching tyranny in one pamphlet, he expounded the principles of opposition to a tyrant in the other, shifting his sails as the wind veered.[1] The truth here also lies in the critical and scientific quality of Machiavelli's method. He was content to lecture either to princes or to burghers upon politics, as an art which he had taken great pains to study, while his interest in the demonstration of principles rendered him in a measure indifferent to their application.[2] In fact, to use the pithy words of Macaulay, 'the "Prince" traces the progress of an ambitious man, the "Discourses" the progress of an ambitious people. The same principles on which, in the former work, the elevation of an individual is explained, are applied in the latter to the longer duration and more complex interest of a society.'

The Seven Books on the Art of War may be referred with certainty to the same period of Machiavelli's life. They were probably composed in 1520. If we may venture to connect the works of the historian's leisure, according to the plan above suggested, this treatise forms a supplement to the 'Principe' and the 'Discorsi.' Both in his analysis of the

---

[1] See Pitti, 'Apologia de' Cappucci,' *Arch. Stor.* vol. iv. pt. ii. p. 294.

[2] The dedication of the *Discorsi* contains a phrase which recalls Machiavelli's words about the *Principe*: 'Perche in quello io ho espresso quanto io so, e quanto io ho imparato per una lunga pratica e continua lezione delle cose del mondo.'

successful tyrant and in his description of the powerful commonwealth he had insisted on the prime necessity of warfare, conducted by the people and their rulers in person. The military organisation of a great kingdom is here developed in a separate essay, and Machiavelli's favourite scheme for nationalising the militia of Italy is systematically expounded. Giovio's flippant objection, that the philosopher could not in practice manœuvre a single company, is no real criticism on the merit of his theory.

By this time the Medici had determined to take Machiavelli into favour ; and since he had expressed a wish to be set at least to rolling stones, they found for him a trivial piece of work. The Franciscans at Carpi had to be requested to organise a separate Province of their Order in the Florentine dominion ; and the conduct of this weighty matter was entrusted to the former secretary at the Courts of Maximilian and Louis. Several other missions during the last years of his life devolved upon Machiavelli ; but none of them were of much importance : nor, when the popular government was instituted in 1527, had he so far regained the confidence of the Florentines as to resume his old office of war secretary. This post, considering his recent alliance with the Medicean party, he could hardly have expected to receive ; and therefore it is improbable that the news of Giannotti's election at all contributed to cause his death.[1]   Disappointment he may indeed have felt : for his moral force had been squandered during fifteen years in the attempt to gain the favour of princes who were now once more regarded as the enemies of their country. When the republic was at last restored, he found himself in neither camp. The overtures which he had made to the Medici had been but coldly received ; yet they were sufficiently notorious to bring upon him the suspicion of the patriots. He had not sincerely acted up to the precept

[1] See Varchi, loc. cit.

of Polonius : 'This above all,—to thine own self be true.'
His intellectual ability, untempered by sufficient political
consistency or moral elevation, had placed him among the
outcasts :—

> che non furon ribelli,
> Nè fur fedeli a Dio, ma per sè foro.

The great achievement of these years was the composition
of the 'Istorie Fiorentine.' The commission for this work he
received from Giulio de' Medici through the Officiali dello
Studio in 1520, with an annual allowance of 100 florins. In
1527, the year of his death, he dedicated the finished History
to Pope Clement VII. This masterpiece of literary art,
though it may be open to the charges of inaccuracy and
superficiality,[1] marks an epoch in the development of modern
historiography. It must be remembered that it preceded the
great work of Guicciardini by some years, and that before
the date of its appearance the annalists of Italy had been
content with records of events, personal impressions, and
critiques of particular periods. Machiavelli was the first to
contemplate the life of a nation in its continuity, to trace the
operation of political forces through successive generations,
to contrast the action of individuals with the evolution of
causes over which they had but little control, and to bring
the salient features of the national biography into relief by
the suppression of comparatively unimportant details. By
thus applying the philosophical method to history, Machiavelli
enriched the science of humanity with a new department.
There is something in his view of national existence beyond
the reach of even the profoundest of the classical historians.
His style is adequate to the matter of his work. Never were
clear and definite thoughts expressed with greater precision
in language of more masculine vigour. We are irresistibly

[1] See the criticisms of Ammirato and Romagnosi, quoted by Cantù,
Letteratura Italiana, p. 187.

compelled, while characterising this style, to think of the spare sinews of a trained gladiator. Though Machiavelli was a poet, he indulges in no ornaments of rhetoric.[1] His images, rare and carefully chosen, seem necessary to the thoughts they illustrate. Though a philosopher, he never wanders into speculation. Facts and experience are so thoroughly compacted with reflection in his mind, that his widest generalisations have the substance of realities. The element of unreality, if such there be, is due to a misconception of human nature. Machiavelli seems to have only studied men in masses, or as political instruments, never as feeling and thinking personalities.

Machiavelli, according to the letter addressed by his son Pietro to Francesco Nelli, died of a dose of medicine taken at the wrong time. He was attended on his deathbed by a friar, who received his confession. His private morality was but indifferent. His contempt for weakness and simplicity was undisguised. His knowledge of the world and men had turned to cynicism. The frigid philosophy expressed in his political Essays, and the sarcastic speeches in which he gave a vent to his soured humours, made him unpopular. It was supposed that he had died with blasphemy upon his lips, after turning all the sanctities of human nature into ridicule. Through these myths, as through a mist, we may discern the bitterness of that great disenchanted, disappointed soul. The desert in which spirits of the stamp of Machiavelli wander is too arid and too aerial for the gross substantial bugbears of the vulgar conscience to inhabit. Moreover, as Varchi says, ' In his conversation Machiavelli was pleasant, serviceable to his friends, a friend of virtuous men, and, in a word, worthy of having received from nature either less genius or a better mind.'

---

[1] I shall have to speak elsewhere of Machiavelli's comedies, occasional poems, novel of *Belphegor*, &c.

CHAPTER VI

'THE PRINCE' OF MACHIAVELLI

AFTER what has been already said about the circumstances under which Machiavelli composed the 'Principe,' we are justified in regarding it as a sincere expression of his political philosophy. The intellect of its author was eminently analytical and positive; he knew well how to confine himself within the strictest limits of the subject he had chosen. In the 'Principe' it was not his purpose to write a treatise of morality, but to set forth with scientific accuracy the arts which he considered necessary to the success of an absolute ruler. We may therefore accept this essay as the most profound and lucid exposition of the principles by which Italian statesmen were guided in the sixteenth century. That Machiavellism existed before Machiavelli has now become a

truism. Gian Galeazzo Visconti, Louis XI. of France,
Ferdinand the Catholic, the Papal Curia, and the Venetian
Council had systematically pursued the policy laid down in
the chapters of the 'Prince.' But it is no less true that
Machiavelli was the first in modern times to formulate a
theory of government in which the interests of the ruler are
alone regarded, which assumes a separation between statecraft and morality, which recognises force and fraud among
the legitimate means of attaining high political ends, which
makes success alone the test of conduct, and which presupposes the corruption, venality, and baseness of mankind at
large. It was this which aroused the animosity of Europe
against Machiavelli, as soon as the 'Prince' attained wide
circulation. Nations accustomed to the Monarchical rather
than the Despotic form of government resented the systematic
exposition of an art of tyranny which had long been practised
among the Italians. The people of the North, whose moral
fibre was still vigorous, and who retained their respect for
established religion, could not tolerate the cynicism with
which Machiavelli analysed his subject from the merely
intellectual point of view. His name became a byword.
'Am I Machiavel?' says the Host in the 'Merry Wives of
Windsor.' Marlowe makes the ghost of the great Florentine
speak prologue to the ' Jew of Malta ' thus—

> I count religion but a childish toy,
> And hold there is no sin but ignorance.

When the Counter-Reformation had begun in Italy, and
desperate efforts were being made to check the speculative
freedom of the Renaissance, the 'Principe' was condemned
by the Inquisition. Meanwhile it was whispered that the
Spanish princes, and the sons of Catherine de' Medici upon
the throne of France, conned its pages just as a manual of
toxicology might be studied by a Marquise de Brinvilliers.
Machiavelli became the scapegoat of great political crimes ;

and during the religious wars of the sixteenth century there were not wanting fanatics who ascribed such acts of atrocity as the Massacre of S. Bartholomew to his venomous influence. Yet this book was really nothing more or less than a critical compendium of facts respecting Italy, a highly condensed abstract of political experience. In it as in a mirror we may study the lineaments of the Italian Despot who by adventure or by heritage succeeded to the conduct of a kingdom. At the same time the political principles here established are those which guided the deliberations of the Venetian Council and the Papal Court, no less than the actions of a Sforza or a Borgia upon the path to power. It is therefore a document of the very highest value for the illustration of the Italian conscience in relation to political morality.

The 'Principe' opens with the statement that all forms of government may be classified as republics or as principalities. Of the latter some are hereditary, others acquired. Of the principalities acquired in the lifetime of the ruler some are wholly new, like Milan under Francesco Sforza; others are added to hereditary kingdoms, like Naples to Spain. Again, such acquired states have been previously accustomed either to the rule of a single man or to self-government. Finally they are won either with the conqueror's own or with borrowed armies, either by fortune or by ability.[1] Thus nine conditions under which principalities may be considered are established at the outset.

The short chapter devoted by Machiavelli to hereditary principalities may be passed over as comparatively unimportant. It is characteristic of Italian politics that the only instance he adduces of this form of government in Italy is

[1] The word Virtù, which I have translated ability, is almost equivalent to the Greek ἀρετή before it had received a moral definition, or to the Roman Virtus. It is very far, as will be gathered from the sequel of the *Principe*, from denoting what we mean by Virtue.

the Duchy of Ferrara. States and cities were so frequently shifting owners in the sixteenth century that the scientific politician was justified in confining his attention to the method of establishing and preserving principalities acquired by force. When he passes to the consideration of this class, Machiavelli enters upon the real subject of his essay. The first instance he discusses is that of a prince who has conquered a dominion which he wishes to unite as firmly as possible to his hereditary states. The new territory may either belong to the same nationality and language as the old possession, or may not. In the former case it will be enough to extinguish the whole line of the ancient rulers, and to take care that neither the laws nor the imposts of the province be materially altered. It will then in course of time become by natural coalition part of the old kingdom. But if the acquired dominion be separate in language, customs, and traditions from the old, then arises a real difficulty for the conqueror. In order to consolidate his empire and to accustom his new subjects to his rule, Machiavelli recommends that he should either take up his residence in the subjugated province, or else plant colonies throughout it, but that he should by no means trust merely to garrisons. 'Colonies,' he remarks, 'are not costly to the prince, are more faithful, and cause less offence to the subject states; those whom they may injure, being poor and scattered, are prevented from doing mischief. For it should be observed that men ought either to be caressed or trampled out, seeing that small injuries may be avenged, whereas great ones destroy the possibility of retaliation; and so the damage that has to be inflicted ought to be such that it need involve no fear of vengeance.' I quote this passage as a specimen of Machiavelli's direct and scientific handling of the most inhuman necessities of statecraft, as conceived by him.[1]

[1] It is fair to call attention to the strong expressions used by Machiavelli in the *Discorsi*, lib. i. cap. 18 and cap. 26, on the infamies and inhumanities to which the aspirant after tyranny is condemned.

He uses no hypocritical palliation to disguise the egotism of the conqueror. He does not even pretend to take into consideration any interests but those of the ambitious prince. He treats humanity as though it were the marble out of which the political artist should hew the form that pleased his fancy best. He calculates the exact amount of oppression which will render a nation incapable of resistance, and relieve the conqueror of trouble in his work of building up a puissant kingdom for his own aggrandisement.

What Machiavelli says about mixed principalities is pointed by a searching critique of the Italian policy of Louis XII. The French king had well-known claims upon the Duchy of Milan, which the Venetians urged him to make good. They proposed to unite forces and to divide the conquered province of Lombardy. Machiavelli does not blame Louis for accepting this offer and acting in concert with the Republic. His mistakes began the moment after he had gained possession of Milan, Genoa, and the majority of the North Italian cities. It was then his true policy to balance Venice against Rome, to assume the protectorate of the minor states, and to keep all dangerous rivals out of Italy. Instead of acting thus, he put Romagna into the hands of the Pope and divided Naples with the King of Spain. 'Louis indeed,' concludes Machiavelli, 'was guilty of five capital errors : he destroyed the hopes of his numerous and weak allies; he increased the power, already too great, of the Papacy; he introduced a foreign potentate; he neglected to reside in Italy; he founded no colonies for the maintenance of his authority. If I am told that Louis acted thus imprudently toward Alexander and Ferdinand in order to avoid a war, I answer that in each case the mistake was as bad as any war could be in its results. If I am reminded of his promise to the Pope, I reply that princes ought to know how and when to break their faith, as I intend to prove. When I was at

Nantes, the Cardinal of Rouen told me that the Italians did not know how to conduct a war : I retorted that the French did not understand statecraft, or they would not have allowed the Church to gain so much power in Italy. Experience showed that I was right ; for the French wrought their own ruin by aggrandising the Papacy and introducing Spain into the realm of Naples.'

This criticism contains the very essence of political sagacity. It lays bare the secret of the failure of the French under Charles, under Louis, and under Francis, to establish themselves in Italy. Expeditions of parade, however brilliant, temporary conquests, cross alliances, and bloody victories do not consolidate a kingdom. They upset states and cause misery to nations ; but their effects pass and leave the so-called conquerors worse off than they were before. It was the doom of Italy to be ravaged by these inconsequent marauders, who never attempted by internal organisation to found a substantial empire, until the mortmain of the Spanish rule was laid upon the peninsula, and Austria gained by marriages what France had failed to win by force of arms.

The fourth chapter of the ' Principe ' is devoted to a parallel between Monarchies and Despotisms which is chiefly interesting as showing that Machiavelli appreciated the stability of kingdoms based upon feudal foundations. France is chosen as the best example of the one and Turkey of the other. ' The whole empire of the Turk is governed by one Lord ; the others are his servants ; he divides his kingdom into satrapies, to which he appoints different administrators, whom he changes about at pleasure. But the King of France is placed in the centre of a time-honoured company of lords, acknowledged as such by their subjects and loved by them ; they have their own prerogatives, nor can the king deprive them of these without peril.' Hence it follows that the prince who has once dispossessed a Despot finds ready to his hand a machinery of government and a band of subservient ministers: while he who may dethrone a monarch has immediately to cope with a multitude of independent rulers, too numerous to extinguish and too proud to conciliate.

Machiavelli now proceeds to discuss the best method of subjugating free cities which have been acquired by a prince. There are three ways of doing it, he says. 'The first is to destroy them utterly; the second, to rule them in your own person; the third, to leave them their constitution under the conduct of an oligarchy chosen by yourself, and to be content with tribute. But, to speak the truth, the only safe way is to ruin them.' This sounds very much like the advice which an old spider might give to a young one: When you have caught a big fly, suck him at once; suck out at any rate so much of his blood as may make him powerless to break your web, and feed on him afterwards at leisure. Then he goes on to give his reasons. 'He who becomes the master of a city used to liberty, and does not destroy it, should be prepared to be undone by it himself, because that name of Liberty, those ancient usages of Freedom, which no length of years and no benefits can extinguish in the nation's mind, which cannot be uprooted by any forethought or by any pains, unless the citizens themselves be broken or dispersed, will always be a rallying-point for revolution when an opportunity occurs.' This terrific moral—through which, let it be said in justice to Machiavelli, the enthusiasm of a patriot transpires—is pointed by the example of Pisa. Pisa, held for a century beneath the heel of Florence—her ports shut up, her fields abandoned to marsh fever, her civic life extinguished, her arts and sciences crushed out—had yet not been utterly ruined in the true sense of depopulation or dismemberment. Therefore when Charles VIII. in 1494 entered Pisa, and Orlandi, the orator, caught him by the royal mantle, and besought him to restore her liberty, that word, the only word the crowd could

catch in his petition, inflamed a nation : the lions and lilies of
Florence were erased from the public buildings ; the Marzocco
was dashed from its column on the quay into the Arno ; and
in a moment the dead republic awoke to life.   Therefore,
argues Machiavelli, so tenacious is the vitality of a free state
that a prudent conqueror will extinguish it entirely or will
rule it in person with a rod of iron.   This, be it remembered,
is the advice of Machiavelli, the Florentine patriot, to Lorenzo
de' Medici, the Florentine tyrant, who has recently resumed
his seat upon the neck of that irrepressible republic.

Hitherto we have been considering how the state acquired
by a conqueror should be incorporated with his previous
dominions.   The next section of Machiavelli's discourse is by
far the most interesting.   It treats of principalities created by
the arms, personal qualities, and good fortune of adventurers.
Italy alone in the sixteenth century furnished examples of
these tyrannies : consequently that portion of the ' Principe '
which is concerned with them has a special interest for
students of the Renaissance.   Machiavelli begins with the
founders of kingdoms who have owed but little to fortune and
have depended on their own forces.   The list he furnishes,
when tested by modern notions of history, is to say the least
a curious one.   It contains Moses, Cyrus, Romulus, and
Theseus.   Having mentioned Moses first, Machiavelli proceeds to explain that, though we have to regard him as the
mere instrument of God's purpose, yet the principles on
which the other founders acted were ' not different from those
which Moses derived from so supreme a teacher.'   What these
men severally owed to fortune was but the occasion for the
display of the greatness that was in them.   Moses found the
people of Israel enslaved in Egypt.   Romulus was an exile
from Alba.   Cyrus had to deal with the Persian people tired
of the empire of effeminate Medes.   Theseus undertook to
unite the scattered elements of the Athenian nation.   Thus

each of these founders had an opening provided for him, by making use of which he was able to bring his illustrious qualities into play. The achievement in each case was afterwards due solely to his own ability, and the conquest which he made with difficulty was preserved with ease. This exordium is not without practical importance, as will be seen when we reach the application of the whole argument to the house of Medici at the conclusion of the treatise. The initial obstacles which an innovator has to overcome, meanwhile, are enormous. ' He has for passionate foes all such as flourish under the old order, for friends those who might flourish under the new; but these are lukewarm, partly from fear of their opponents, on whose side are established law and right, partly from the incredulity which prevents men from putting faith in what is novel and untried.' It therefore becomes a matter of necessity that the innovator should be backed up with force, that he should be in a position to command and not obliged to sue for aid. This is the reason why all the prophets who have used arms to enforce their revelations have succeeded, and why those who have only trusted to their personal ascendency have failed. Moses, of course, is an illustrious example of the successful prophet. Savonarola is adduced as a notable instance of a reformer ' who was ruined in his work of innovation as soon as the multitude lost their faith in him, since he had no means of keeping those who had believed firm, or of compelling faith from disbelievers.' In this critique Machiavelli remains true to his positive and scientific philosophy of human nature. He will not allow that there are other permanent agencies in the world than the calculating ability of resolute men and the might derived from physical forces.

Among the eminent examples of Italian founders who rose to princely power by their own ability or by availing themselves of the advantages which fortune put within their reach,

Machiavelli selects Francesco Sforza and Cesare Borgia.   The
former is a notable instance of success achieved by pure
virtù : ' Francesco, by using the right means, and by his own
singular ability, raised himself from the rank of a private man
to the Duchy of Milan, and maintained with ease the mastery
he had acquired with infinite pains.'   Cesare, on the other
hand, illustrates both the strength and the weakness of
fortuna : ' he acquired his dominion by the aid derived from
his father's position, and when he lost that he also lost his
power, notwithstanding that he used every endeavour and did
all that a prudent and able man ought to do in order to plant
himself firmly in those states which the arms and fortune of
others had placed at his disposal.'   It is not necessary to dwell
upon the career of Francesco Sforza.   Not he but Cesare
Borgia is Machiavelli's hero in this treatise, the example from
which he deduces lessons both of imitation and avoidance
for the benefit of Lorenzo de' Medici.   Lorenzo, it must be
remembered, like Cesare, would have the fortunes of the
Church to start with in that career of ambition to which
Machiavelli incites him.   Unlike Francesco Sforza, he was no
mere soldier of adventure, but a prince, born in the purple,
and bound to make use of those undefined advantages which
he derived from his position in Florence and from the countenance of his uncle, the Pope.   The Duke Valentino, therefore,
who is at one and the same time Machiavelli's ideal of
prudence and courage in the conduct of affairs, and also his
chief instance of the instability of fortune, supplies the
philosopher with all he needed for the guidance of his princely
pupil.   With the Duke Valentino Machiavelli had conversed
on terms of private intimacy, and there is no doubt that his
imagination had been dazzled by the brilliant intellectual
abilities of this consummate rogue.   Despatched in 1502 by
the Florentine Republic to watch the operations of Cesare at
Imola, with secret instructions to offer the Duke false promises

in the hope of eliciting information that could be relied upon,
Machiavelli had enjoyed the rare pleasure of a game at
political écarté with the subtlest and most unscrupulous diplomatist of his age.   He had witnessed his terrible yet beneficial
administration of Romagna.   He had been present at his
murder of the chiefs of the Orsini faction at Sinigaglia.
Cesare had confided to him, or had pretended to confide, his
schemes of personal ambition, as well as the motives and the
measures of his secret policy.   On the day of the election of
Pope Julius II. he had laid bare the whole of his past history
before the Florentine secretary, and had pointed out the single
weakness of which he felt himself to have been guilty.   In
these trials of skill and this exchange of confidence it is impossible to say which of the two gamesters may have been the
more deceived.   But Machiavelli felt that the Borgia supplied
him with a perfect specimen for the study of the arts of statecraft : and so deep was the impression produced upon his mind,
that even after the utter failure of Cesare's designs he made
him the hero of the political romance before us.   His artistic
perception of the perfect and the beautiful, both in unscrupulous conduct and in frigid calculation of conflicting interests,
was satisfied by the steady selfishness, the persistent perfidy,
the profound mistrust of men, the self-command in the execution of perilous designs, the moderate and deliberate employment of cruelty for definite ends, which he observed in the
young Duke, and which he has idealised in his own ' Principe.'
That nature, as of a salamander adapted to its element of fire,
as of 'a resolute angel that delights in flame,' to which nothing
was sacred, which nothing could daunt, which never for a
moment sacrificed reason to passion, which was incapable of
weakness or fatigue, had fascinated Machiavelli's fancy.   The
moral qualities of the man, the base foundations upon which
he raised his power, the unutterable scandals of his private
life, and the hatred of all Christendom were as nothing in the

balance. Such considerations had, according to the conditions
of his subject, to be eliminated before he weighed the
intellectual qualities of the adventurer. 'If all the achievements of the Duke are considered'—it is Machiavelli speaking
—'it will be found that he built up a great substructure for
his future power ; nor do I know what precepts I could furnish
to a prince in his commencement better than such as are to
be derived from his example.' It is thus that Machiavelli,
the citizen, addresses Lorenzo, the tyrant of Florence. He
says to him : Go thou and do likewise. And what, then, is
this likewise ?

Cesare, being a Pope's son, had nothing to look to but the
influence of his father. At first he designed to use this influence in the Church ; but after murdering his elder brother,
he threw aside the Cardinal's scarlet and proclaimed himself
a political aspirant. His father could not make him lord
of any state, unless it were a portion of the territory of the
Church : and though, by creating, as he did, twelve Cardinals
in one day, he got the Sacred College to sanction his investiture
of the Duchy of Romagna, yet both Venice and Milan were
opposed to this scheme. Again there was a difficulty to be
encountered in the great baronial houses of Orsini and Colonna,
who at that time headed all the mercenary troops of Italy,
and who, as Roman nobles, had a natural hatred for the Pope.
It was necessary to use their aid in the acquisition of Cesare's
principality. It was no less needful to humour their animosity.
Under these circumstances Alexander thought it best to invite the French king into Italy, bargaining with Louis that he
would dissolve his marriage in return for protection awarded
to Cesare. The Colonna faction meanwhile was to be crushed,
and the Orsini to be flattered. Cesare, by the help of his
French allies and the Orsini captains, took possession of Imola
and Faenza, and thence proceeded to overrun Romagna. In
this enterprise he succeeded to the full. Romagna had been,

from the earliest period of Italian history, a nest of petty tyrants who governed badly and who kept no peace in their dominions. Therefore the towns were but languid in their opposition to Cesare, and were soon more than contented with a conqueror who introduced a good system for the administration of justice. But now two difficulties arose. The subjugation of Romagna had been effected by the help of the French and the Orsini. Cesare as yet had formed no militia of his own, and his allies were becoming suspicious. The Orsini had shown some slackness at Faenza; and when Cesare proceeded to make himself master of Urbino, and to place a foot in Tuscany by the capture of Piombino—which conquests he completed during 1500 and 1501—Louis began to be jealous of him. The problem for the Duke was how to disembarrass himself of the two forces by which he had acquired a solid basis for his future principality. His first move was to buy over the Cardinal d'Amboise, whose influence in the French Court was supreme, and thus to keep his credit for awhile afloat with Louis. His second was to neutralise the power of the Orsini, partly by pitting them against the Colonnesi, and partly by superseding them in their command as captains. For the latter purpose he became his own Condottiere, drawing to his standard by the lure of splendid pay all the minor gentry of the Roman Campagna. Thus he collected his own forces, and was able to dispense with the unsafe aid of mercenary troops. At this point of his career the Orsini, finding him established in Romagna, in Urbino, and in part of Tuscany, while their own strength was on the decline, determined if possible to check the career of this formidable tyrant by assassination. The conspiracy known as the 'Diet of La Magione' was the consequence. In this conjuration the Cardinal Orsini, Paolo Orsini, his brother and head of the great house, together with Vitellozzo Vitelli, lord of Città di Castello, the Baglione of Perugia, the Bentivoglio

of Bologna, Antonio da Venasso from Siena, and Oliverotto
da Fermo took each a part.   The result of their machinations
against the common foe was that Cesare for a moment lost
Urbino, and was nearly unseated in Romagna.   But the
French helped him, and he stood firm. Still it was impossible
to believe that Louis XII. would suffer him to advance unchecked in his career of conquest; and as long as he continued
between the French and the Orsini his position was of necessity insecure.   The former had to be cast off; the latter to be
extirpated: and as yet he had not force enough to play an
open game.   'He therefore,' says Machiavelli, 'turned to
craft, and displayed such skill in dissimulation that the Orsini
through the mediation of Paolo became his friends again.'
The cruelty of Cesare Borgia was only equalled by his craft;
and it was by a supreme exercise of his power of fascination
that he lured the foes who had plotted against him at La
Magione into his snare at Sinigaglia. Paolo Orsini, Francesco
Orsini, duke of Gravina, Vitellozzo Vitelli, and Oliverotto da
Fermo were all men of arms, accustomed to intrigue and to
bloodshed, and more than one of them were stained with
crimes of the most atrocious treachery.   Yet such were the
arts of Cesare Borgia that in 1502 he managed to assemble
them, apart from their troops, in the castle of Sinigaglia,
where he had them strangled.   Having now destroyed the
chiefs of the opposition and enlisted their forces in his own
service, Cesare, to use the phrase of Machiavelli, 'had laid
good foundations for his future power.'   He commanded a
sufficient territory; he wielded the temporal and spiritual
power of his father; he was feared by the princes and respected
by the people throughout Italy; his cruelty and perfidy and
subtlety and boldness caused him to be universally admired.
But as yet he had only laid foundations.   The empire of Italy
was still to win; for he aspired to nothing else, and it is
even probable that he entertained a notion of secularising the

Papacy. France was the chief obstacle to his ambition. The alarm of Louis had at last been roused. But Louis' own mistake in bringing the Spaniards into Naples afforded Cesare the means of shaking off the French control. He espoused the cause of Spain, and by intriguing now with the one power and now with the other made himself both formidable and desirable to each. His geographical position between Milan and Naples enforced this policy. Another difficulty against which he had to provide was in the future rather than the present. Should his father die, and a new Pope adverse to his interests be elected, he might lose not only the support of the Holy See, but also his fiefs of Romagna and Urbino. To meet this contingency he took four precautions, mentioned with great admiration by Machiavelli. In the first place he systematically murdered the heirs of the ruling families of all the cities he acquired—as for example three Varani at Camerino, two Manfredi at Faenza, the Orsini and Vitelli at Sinigaglia, and others whom it would be tedious to mention. By this process he left no scion of the ancient houses for a future Pope to restore. In the second place he attached to his person, by pensions, offices, and emoluments, all the Roman gentry, so that he might be able to keep the new Pope a prisoner and unarmed in Rome. Thirdly, he reduced the College of Cardinals, by bribery, terrorism, poisoning, and packed elections, to such a state that he could count on the creation of a Pope, if not his nominee, at least not hostile to his interests. Fourthly, he lost no time, but pushed his plans of conquest on with the utmost speed, so as, if possible, to command a large territory at the time of Alexander's death. Machiavelli, who records these four points with approbation, adds: 'He, therefore, who finds it needful in his new authority to secure himself against foes, to acquire allies, to gain a point by force or fraud, &c., &c., could not discover an ensample more vigorous and blooming than that of Cesare.'

Such is the panegyric which Machiavelli, writing, as it seems to me, in all good faith and innocence, records of a man who, taken altogether, is perhaps the most selfish, perfidious, and murderous of adventurers on record. The only fault for which he blames him is that he did not prevent the election of Pope Julius II. by concentrating his influence on either the Cardinal d'Amboise or a Spaniard.

It is curious to read the title of the chapter following that which criticises the action of Cesare Borgia : it runs thus, 'Concerning those who have attained to sovereignty by crimes.' Cesare was clearly not one of these men in the eyes of Machiavelli, who confines his attention to Agathocles of Syracuse, and to Oliverotto da Fermo, a brigand who acquired the lordship of Fermo by murdering his uncle and benefactor, Giovanni Fogliani, and all the chief men of the city at a banquet to which he had invited them. This atrocity, according to Machiavelli's creed, would have been justified, if Oliverotto had combined cruelty and subtlety in proper proportions. But his savagery was not sufficiently veiled ; a prince should never incur odium by crimes of violence, but only use them as the means of inspiring terror. Besides, Oliverotto was so simple as to fall at last into the snare of Cesare Borgia at Sinigaglia. Cesare himself supplies Machiavelli with a notable example of the way in which cruelty can be well used. Having found the cities of Romagna in great disorder, Cesare determined to quell them by the ferocity of a terrible governor. For this purpose he chose Messer Ramiro d' Orco, ' a man cruel and quick of action, to whom he gave the fullest power.' A story is told of Messer Ramiro which illustrates his temper in a very bizarre fashion : he one day kicked a clumsy page on to the fire, and held him there with a poker till he was burned up. Acting after this fashion, with plenipotentiary authority, Ramiro soon froze the whole province into comparative tranquillity. But it did not suit Cesare to incur the odium which the man's cruelty brought on his administration. Accordingly he had him decapitated one night and exposed to public view, together with the block and bloody hatchet, in the square at Cesena. Of the art with which Cesare first reduced Romagna to order by the cruelty of his agent, and then avoided the odium of this cruelty by using the wretched creature as an appalling example of his justice and his power, Machiavelli wholly approves. His theory is that cruelty should be employed for certain definite purposes, but that the prince should endeavour to shun as far as possible the hatred it inspires. In justice both to Machiavelli and to Cesare, it should be said that the administration of Romagna was far better under the Borgia rule than it had ever been before. The exhibition of savage violence of which Machiavelli approves was perhaps needed to cow so brutalised a population.

In those chapters which Machiavelli has devoted to the exposition of the qualities that befit a prince, it is clear that Cesare Borgia was not unfrequently before his eyes.[1] The worst thing that can be said about Italy of the sixteenth century is that such an analyst as Machiavelli should have been able to idealise an adventurer whose egotistic immorality was so undisguised. The ethics of this profound anatomist of human motives were based upon a conviction that men are altogether bad. When discussing the question whether it be better to be loved or feared, Machiavelli decides that 'it is far safer to be feared than loved, if you must choose; seeing that you may say of men generally that they are ungrateful and changeable, dissemblers, apt to shun danger, eager for gain; as long as you serve them, they offer you everything, down to their very children, if you have no need; but when you want help, they

---

[1] In a letter to Fr. Vettori (Jan. 31, 1514) he says: 'Il duca Valentino, l' opere del quale io imiterei sempre quando fossi principe nuovo.'

fail you. Therefore it is best to put no faith in their pretended love.' This is language which could only be used in a
country where loyalty was unknown and where all political
and social combinations were founded upon force or convenience. Princes must, however, be cautious not to injure
their subjects in their honour or their property—especially the
latter, since men 'forget the murder of their fathers quicker
than the loss of their money.' Under another heading
Machiavelli returns to the same topic, and lays it down as an
axiom that, since the large majority of men are bad, a prince
must learn in self-defence how to be bad, and must use this
science when and where he deems appropriate, endeavouring,
however, under all circumstances to pass for good.

He brings the same desperate philosophy of life, the same
bitter experience of mankind, to bear upon his discussion of
the faith of princes. The chapter which is entitled 'How
princes ought to keep their word' is one of the most brilliantly
composed and thoroughly Machiavellian of the whole treatise.
He starts with the assertion that to fight the battles of life in
accordance with law is human, to depend on force is brutal;
yet when the former method is insufficient, the latter must be
adopted. A prince should know how to combine the natures
of the man and of the beast; and this is the meaning of the
mythus of Cheiron, who was made the tutor of Achilles. He
should strive to acquire the qualities of the fox and of the
lion, in order that he may both avoid snares and guard
himself from wolves. A prudent prince cannot and must
not keep faith when it is harmful to do so, or when the occasion under which he promised has passed by. He will
always find colourable pretexts for breaking his word; and if
he learns well how to feign, he will have but little difficulty
in deceiving people. Among the innumerable instances of
successful hypocrites Machiavelli can think of none more
excellent than Alexander VI. 'He never did anything else

but deceive men, nor ever thought of anything but this, and always found apt matter for his practice. Never was there a man who had a greater force in swearing and tying himself down to his engagements, or who observed them less. Nevertheless his wiles were always successful in the way he wished, because he well knew that side of the world.' It is curious that Machiavelli should have forgotten that the whole elaborate life's policy of Alexander and his son was ruined precisely by their falling into one of their own traps, and that the mistake or treason of a servant upset the calculations of the two most masterly deceivers of their age.[1] Following out the same line of thought, which implies that in a bad world a prince cannot afford to be good, Machiavelli asserts: ' It is not necessary that a prince should be merciful, loyal, humane, religious, just : nay, I will venture to say, that if he had all these qualities and always used them, they would harm him. But he must *seem* to have them, especially if he be new in his principality, where he will find it quite impossible to exercise these virtues, since in order to maintain his power he will be often obliged to act contrary to humanity, charity, religion.' Machiavelli does not advise him to become bad for the sake of badness, but to know when to quit the path of virtue for the preservation of his kingdom. ' He must take care to say nothing that is not full of these five qualities, and must always appear all mercy, all loyalty, all humanity, all justice, all religion, especially the last.' On the advantage of a reputation for piety Machiavelli insists most strongly. He points out how Ferdinand the Catholic used the pretext of religious zeal in order to achieve the conquest of Granada, to invade Africa, to expel the Moors, and how his perfidies in Italy, his perjuries to France, were coloured with a sanctimonious decency.

[1] Perhaps this is an indirect argument against the legend of their death.

After reading these passages we feel that though it may be true that Machiavelli only spoke with scientific candour of the vices which were common to all statesmen in his age— though the Italians were so corrupt that it seemed hopeless to deal fairly with them—yet there was a radical taint in the soul of the man who could have the heart to cull these poisonous herbs of policy and distil their juices to a quint-essence for the use of the prince to whom he was confiding the destinies of Italy.[1] Almost involuntarily we remember the oath which Arthur administered to his knights, when he bade them 'never to do outrage nor murder, and always to flee treason; also by no means to be cruel, but to give mercy unto him that asked mercy, upon pain of forfeiture of their worship and lordship of King Arthur for evermore.' In a land where chivalry like this had ever taken root, either as an ideal or as an institution, the chapters of Machiavelli could scarcely have been published. The Italians lacked the virtues of knighthood. It was possible among them for the philosophers to teach the princes that success purchased at the expense of honour, loyalty, humanity, and truth might be illustrious.

It is refreshing to turn from those chapters in which Machiavelli teaches the prince how to cope with the world by using the vices of the wicked, to his exposition of the military organisation suited to the maintenance of a great kingdom. Machiavelli has no mean or humble ambition for his prince : 'double will his glory be, who has founded a new realm, and fortified and adorned it with good laws, good arms, good friends, and good ensamples.' What the enterprise to which he fain would rouse Lorenzo really is, will appear in

[1] In the *Discorsi*, lib. i. cap. 55, he calls Italy 'la corruttela del mondo,' and judges that her case is desperate; 'non si può sperare nelle provincie che in questi tempi si veggono corrotte, come è l' Italia sopra tutte le altre.'

the conclusion. Meanwhile he encourages him by the example of Ferdinand the Catholic to gird his loins up for great enterprises. He bids him be circumspect in his choice of secretaries, seeing that 'the first opinion formed of a prince and of his capacity is derived from the men whom he has gathered round him.' He points out how he should shun flattery and seek respectful but sincere advice. Finally he reminds him that a prince is impotent unless he can command obedience by his arms. Fortresses are a doubtful source of strength; against foreign foes they are worse than useless; against subjects they are worthless in comparison with the goodwill of the people : ' the best fortress possible is to escape the hatred of your subjects.' Everything therefore depends upon the well-ordering of a national militia. The neglect of that ruined the princes of Italy and enabled Charles VIII. to conquer the fairest of European kingdoms with wooden spurs and a piece of chalk.[1]

In his discourse on armies Machiavelli lays it down that the troops with which a prince defends his state are either his own, or mercenaries, or auxiliaries, or mixed. 'Mercenary and auxiliary forces are both useless and perilous, and he who founds the security of his dominion on the former will never be established firmly : seeing that they are disunited, ambitious, and undisciplined, without loyalty, truculent to their friends, cowardly among foes; they have no fear of God, no faith with men; you are only safe with them before they are attacked; in peace they plunder you; in war you are the prey of your enemies. The cause of this is that they have no other love nor other reason to keep the field beyond a little pay, which is far from sufficient to make them wish to die for you. They are willing enough to be your soldiers so long as you are at peace, but when war comes

---

[1] The references in this paragraph are made to chapters xx.–xxiv. and chapter xii. of the *Principe*.

their impulse is to fly or sneak away.   It ought to be easy to
establish the truth of this assertion, since the ruin of Italy
is due to nothing else except this, that we have now for many
years depended upon mercenary arms.'[1]   Here he touches the
real weakness of the Italian States.   Then he proceeds to
explain further the rottenness of the Condottiere system.
Captains of adventure are either men of ability or not.   If
they are, you have to fear lest their ambition prompt them to
turn their arms against yourself or your allies.   This happened to Queen Joan of Naples, who was deserted by Sforza
Attendolo in her sorest need ; to the Milanese, when Francesco
Sforza made himself their Despot ; to the Venetians, who
were driven to decapitate Carmagnuola because they feared
him.   The only reason why the Florentines were not enslaved
by Sir John Hawkwood was that, though an able general,
he achieved no great successes in the field.   In the same way
they escaped by luck from Sforza, who turned his attention to
Milan, and from Braccio, who formed designs against the
Church and Naples.   If Paolo Vitelli had been victorious
against Pisa (1498), he would have held them at discretion.
In each of these cases it was only the good fortune of the
republic which saved it from a military despotism.   If, on the
other hand, the mercenary captains are men of no capacity,
you are defeated in the field.   Proceeding to the historical
development of this bad system, Machiavelli points out how,
after the decline of the Imperial authority in Italy, the Papacy
and the republics got the upper hand.   Priests and merchants
were alike unwilling to engage in war.   Therefore they took
mercenary troops into their pay.   The companies of the
Sforzeschi and Bracceschi were formed ; and 'after these
came all those others who have ruled this sort of warfare
down to our own days.   The consequence of their valour is
that Italy has been harried by Charles, plundered by Louis,

' See chapter xii. of the *Principe*.

forced by Ferdinand, insulted by the Swiss. Their method
has been to enhance the reputation of their cavalry by
depressing the infantry. Being without dominion of their
own, and making war their commerce, a few foot soldiers
brought them no repute, while they were unable to support
many. Therefore they confined themselves to cavalry, until
in a force of 20,000 men you could not number 2,000 infantry.
Besides this they employed all their ingenuity to relieve
themselves and their soldiers of fatigue and peril, by refrain-
ing from slaughter and from taking prisoners without ransom.
Night attacks and sorties were abandoned; stockades and
trenches in the camp were given up; no one thought of a
winter campaign. All these things were allowed, or rather
introduced, in order to avoid, as I have said, fatigue and
peril. Whereby they have reduced Italy to slavery and insult.'
Auxiliaries, such as the French troops borrowed by Cesare
Borgia, and the Spaniards engaged by Julius II., are even
worse. 'He who wants to be unable to win the game should
make use of these forces; for they are far more dangerous
than mercenaries, seeing that in them the cause of ruin is
ready made—they are united together, and inclined to obey
their own masters.' Machiavelli enforces this moral by one of
those rare but energetic figures which add virile dignity to his
discourse. He compares auxiliary troops to the armour of Saul,
which David refused, preferring to fight Goliath with his stone
and sling. 'In one word, arms borrowed from another either
fall from your back, or weigh you down, or impede your action.'
It remains for a prince to form his own troops and to take
the field in person, like Cesare Borgia, when he discarded his
French allies and the mercenary aid of the Orsini captains.
Republics should follow the same course, despatching, as the
Romans did, their own citizens to the war, and controlling by
law the personal ambition of victorious generals. It was thus
that the Venetians prospered in their conquests, before they

acquired their provinces in Italy and adopted the Condottiere system from their neighbours. 'A prince, therefore, should have but one object, one thought, one art—the art of war.' Those who have followed this rule have attained to sovereignty, like Francesco Sforza, who became Duke of Milan; those who have neglected it have lost even hereditary kingdoms, like the last Sforzas, who sank from dukedom into private life. Even amid the pleasures of the chase a prince should always be studying the geographical conformation of his country with a view to its defence, and should acquire a minute knowledge of such strategical laws as are everywhere applicable. He should read history with the same object, and should keep before his eyes the example of those great men of the past from whom he can learn lessons for his guidance in the present.

This brings us to the peroration of the 'Principe,' which contains the practical issue toward which the whole treatise has been tending, the patriotic thought that reflects a kind of lustre even on the darkest pages that have gone before. Like Thetis, Machiavelli has dipped his Achilles in the Styx of infernal counsels; like Cheiron, he has shown him how the human and the bestial natures should be combined in one who has to break the teeth of wolves and keep his feet from snares; like Hephaistos, he has forged for him invulnerable armour. The object toward which this preparation has been leading is the liberation of Italy from the barbarians. The slavery of Israel in Egypt, the oppression of the Persians by the Medes, the dispersion of the Athenians into villages, were the occasions which enabled Moses and Cyrus and Theseus to display their greatness. The new prince, who would fain win honour in Italy and confer upon his country untold benefits, finds her at the present moment 'more enslaved than the Hebrews, more downtrodden than the Persians, more disunited than the Athenians, without a chief, without order, beaten, despoiled, mangled, overrun, subject to every sort of desolation.' Fortune could not have offered him a nobler opportunity. 'See how she prays God to send her some one who should save her from these barbarous cruelties and insults! See her all ready and alert to follow any standard, if only there be a man to raise it!' Then Machiavelli addresses himself to the chief of the Medici in person. 'Nor is there at the present moment any place more full of hope for her than your illustrious House, which by its valour and its fortune, favoured by God and by the Church, whereof it is now the head, might take the lead in this delivery.' This is followed by one of the rare passages of courtly rhetoric which, when Machiavelli condescends to indulge in them, add peculiar splendour to his style. Then he turns again to speak of the means which should immediately be used. He urges Lorenzo above all things to put no faith in mercenaries or auxiliaries, but to raise his own forces, and to rely on the Italian infantry. If Italian armies have always been defeated in the field during the past twenty years, it is not due so much to their defective courage as to the weakness of their commanders. Lorenzo will have to raise a force capable of coping with the Swiss, the Spanish, and the French. The respect with which Machiavelli speaks at this supreme moment of these foreign troops, proves how great was their prestige in Italy; yet he ventures to point out that there are faults peculiar to each of them: the Spanish infantry cannot stand a cavalry charge, and the Switzers are liable to be disconcerted by the rapid attack of the wiry infantry of Spain. It is therefore necessary to train troops capable of resisting cavalry, and not afraid of facing any foot soldiers in the world. 'This opportunity, therefore, must not be suffered to slip by; in order that Italy may after so long a time at last behold her saviour. Nor can I find words to describe the love with which he would be hailed in all the provinces that have suffered

through these foreign deluges, the thirst for vengeance, the
stubborn fidelity, the piety, the tears, that he would meet.
What gates would be closed against him ?   What people
would refuse him allegiance ?   What jealousy would thwart
him ?   What Italian would be found to refuse him homage ?
This rule of the barbarians stinks in the nostrils of us all.
Then let your illustrious House assume this enterprise in
the spirit and the confidence wherewith just enterprises are
begun, that so, under your flag, this land of ours may be
ennobled, and under your auspices be brought to pass that
prophecy of Petrarch :—

> Lo, valour against rage
> Shall take up arms, nor shall the fight be long ;
> For that old heritage
> Of courage in Italian hearts is stout and strong.'

With this trumpet-cry of impassioned patriotism the 'Principe'
closes.

Hegel, in his 'Philosophy of History,' has recorded a
judgment of Machiavelli's treatise in relation to the political
conditions of Italy at the end of the mediæval period, which
might be quoted as the most complete apology for the author
to make.   'This book,' he says, 'has often been cast aside
with horror as containing maxims of the most revolting
tyranny ; yet it was Machiavelli's high sense of the necessity
of constituting a state which caused him to lay down the
principles on which alone states could be formed under the
circumstances.   The isolated lords and lordships had to be
entirely suppressed ; and though our idea of Freedom is incompatible with the means which he proposes both as the
only available and also as wholly justifiable—including, as
these do, the most reckless violence, all kinds of deception,
murder, and the like—yet we must confess that the Despots
who had to be subdued were assailable in no other way, inas-

much as indomitable lawlessness and perfect depravity were thoroughly engrained in them.'

Yet after the book has been shut and the apology has been weighed, we cannot but pause and ask ourselves this question: Which was the truer patriot—Machiavelli, systematising the political vices and corruptions of his time in a philosophical essay, and calling on the Despot to whom it was dedicated to liberate Italy; or Savonarola, denouncing sin and enforcing repentance—Machiavelli, who taught as precepts of pure wisdom those very principles of public immorality which lay at the root of Italy's disunion and weakness; or Savonarola, who insisted that without a moral reformation no liberty was possible? We shall have to consider the action of Savonarola in another place. Meanwhile, it is not too much to affirm that, with diplomatists like Machiavelli, and with princes like those whom he has idealised, Italy could not be free. Hypocrisy, treachery, dissimulation, cruelty are the vices of the selfish and the enslaved. Yet Machiavelli was led by his study of the past and by his experience of the present to defend these vices, as the necessary qualities of the prince whom he would fain have chosen for the saviour of his country. It is legitimate to excuse him on the ground that the Italians of his age had not conceived a philosophy of right which should include duties as well as privileges, and which should guard the interests of the governed no less than those of the governor. It is true that the feudal conception of Monarchy, so well apprehended by him in the fourth chapter of the 'Principe,' had nowhere been realised in Italy, and that therefore the right solution of the political problem seemed to lie in setting force against force, and fraud against fraud, for a sublime purpose. It may also be urged with justice that the historians and speculators of antiquity, esteemed beyond their value by the students of the sixteenth century, confirmed him in his application of a positive philosophy to statecraft. The success which attended the violence and dissimulation of the Romans, as described by Livy, induced him to inculcate the principles on which they acted. The scientific method followed by Aristotle in the 'Politics' encouraged him in the adoption of a similar analysis; while the close parallel between ancient Greece and mediæval Italy was sufficient to create a conviction that the wisdom of the old world would be precisely applicable to the conditions of the new. These, however, are exculpations of the man, rather than justifications of his theory. The theory was false and vicious. And the fact remains that the man, impregnated by the bad morality of the period in which he lived, was incapable of ascending above it to the truth, was impotent with all his acumen to read the deepest lessons of past and present history, and in spite of his acknowledged patriotism succeeded only in adding his conscious and unconscious testimony to the corruption of the country that he loved. The broad common-sense, the mental soundness, the humane instinct and the sympathy with nature, which give fertility and wholeness to the political philosophy of men like Burke, are absent in Machiavelli. In spite of its vigour, his system implies an inversion of the ruling laws of health in the body politic. In spite of its logical cogency, it is inconclusive by reason of defective premises. Incomparable as an essay in pathological anatomy, it throws no light upon the working of a normal social organism, and has at no time been used with profit even by the ambitious and unscrupulous.

CHAPTER VII

THE POPES OF THE RENAISSANCE

In the fourteenth and the first half of the fifteenth centuries the authority of the Popes, both as Heads of the Church and as temporal rulers, had been impaired by exile in France and by ruinous schisms. A new era began with the election of Nicholas V. in 1447, and ended during the pontificate of Clement VII. with the sack of Rome in 1527. Through the whole of this period the Popes acted more as monarchs than as pontiffs, and the secularisation of the See of Rome was carried to its utmost limits. The contrast between the sacerdotal pretensions and the personal immorality of the Popes was glaring; nor had the chiefs of the Church yet learned to regard the liberalism of the Renaissance with suspicion. About the middle of the sixteenth century the

Papal States had become a recognised kingdom ; while the Popes of this later epoch were endeavouring by means of the Inquisition and the educational orders to check the free spirit of Italy.

The history of Italy has at all times been closely bound up with that of the Papacy ; but at no period has this been more the case than during these eighty years of Papal worldliness, ambition, nepotism, and profligacy, which are also marked by the irruption of the European nations into Italy and by the secession of the Teutonic races from the Latin Church. In this short space of time a succession of Popes filled the Holy Chair with such dramatic propriety—displaying a pride so regal, a cynicism so unblushing, so selfish a cupidity, and a policy so suicidal as to favour the belief that they had been placed there in the providence of God to warn the world against Babylon. At the same time the history of the Papal Court reveals with peculiar vividness the contradictions of Renaissance morality and manners. We find in the Popes of this period what has been already noticed in the Despots—learning, the patronage of the arts, the passion for magnificence, and the refinements of polite culture, alternating and not unfrequently combined with barbarous ferocity of temper and with savage and coarse tastes. On the one side we observe a Pagan dissoluteness which would have scandalised the parasites of Commodus and Nero ; on the other, a seeming zeal for dogma worthy of S. Dominic. The Vicar of Christ is at one time worshipped as a god by princes seeking absolution for sins or liberation from burdensome engagements ; at another he is trampled under foot, in his capacity of sovereign, by the same potentates. Undisguised sensuality ; fraud cynical and unabashed ; policy marching to its end by murders, treasons, interdicts, and imprisonments ; the open sale of spiritual privileges ; commercial traffic in ecclesiastical emoluments ; hypocrisy and cruelty studied as fine arts ;

theft and perjury reduced to system—these are the ordinary
scandals which beset the Papacy. Yet the Pope is still a holy
being. His foot is kissed by thousands. His curse and
blessing carry death and life. He rises from the bed of harlots
to unlock or bolt the gates of heaven and purgatory. In the
midst of crime he believes himself to be the representative of
Christ on earth. These anomalies, glaring as they seem to us,
and obvious as they might be to deeper thinkers like Machiavelli or Savonarola, did not shock the mass of men who
witnessed them. The Renaissance was so dazzling by its
brilliancy, so confusing by its rapid changes, that moral
distinctions were obliterated in a blaze of splendour, an outburst of new life, a carnival of liberated energies. The
corruption of Italy was only equalled by its culture. Its
immorality was matched by its enthusiasm. It was not the
decay of an old age dying, so much as the fermentation of a
new age coming into life, that bred the monstrous paradoxes
of the fifteenth and the sixteenth centuries. The contrast
between mediæval Christianity and renascent Paganism—the
sharp conflict of two adverse principles, destined to fuse their
forces and to recompose the modern world—made the Renaissance what it was in Italy. Nowhere is the first effervescence
of these elements so well displayed as in the history of those
Pontiffs who, after striving in the Middle Ages to suppress
humanity beneath a cowl, are now the chief actors in the
comedy of Aphrodite and Priapus raising their foreheads once
more to the light of day.

The struggle carried on between the Popes of the thirteenth
century and the House of Hohenstauffen ended in the elevation
of the Princes of Anjou to the throne of Naples—the most
pernicious of all the evils inflicted by the Papal power on Italy.
Then followed the French tyranny, under which Boniface VIII.
expired at Anagni. Benedict XI. was poisoned at the instigation of Philip le Bel, and the Papal see was transferred

to Avignon.   The Popes lost their hold upon the city of
Rome and upon those territories of Romagna, the March, and
S. Peter's Patrimony which had been confirmed to them by
the grant of Rodolph of Hapsburg (1273).   They had to
govern their Italian dependencies by means of Legates, while,
one by one, the cities which had recognised their sway passed
beneath the yoke of independent princes.   The Malatesti
established themselves in Rimini, Pesaro, and Fano ; the
house of Montefeltro confirmed its occupation of Urbino ;
Camerino, Faenza, Ravenna, Forli, and Imola became the
appanages of the Varani, the Manfredi, the Polentani, the
Ordelaffi, and the Alidosi.[1]   The traditional supremacy of the
Popes was acknowledged in these tyrannies ; but the nobles I
have named acquired a real authority, against which Egidio
Albornoz and Robert of Geneva struggled to a great extent in
vain, and to break which at a future period taxed the whole
energies of Sixtus and of Alexander.

While the influence of the Popes was thus weakened in
their states beyond the Apennines, three great families, the
Orsini, the Savelli, and the Colonnesi, grew to princely
eminence in Rome and its immediate neighbourhood.   They
had been severally raised to power during the second half
of the thirteenth century by the nepotism of Nicholas III.,
Honorius IV., and Nicholas IV.   This nepotism bore baneful
fruits in the future ; for during the exile at Avignon the
houses of Colonna and Orsini became so overbearing as to
threaten the freedom and safety of the Popes.   It was again
reserved for Sixtus and Alexander to undo the work of their
predecessors and to secure the independence of the Holy See
by the coercion of these towering nobles.

In the States of the Church the temporal power of the
Popes, founded upon false donations, confirmed by tradition,
and contested by rival despots, was an anomaly.   In Rome

[1] See Mach. *Ist. Fior.* lib. i.

itself their situation, though different, was no less peculiar. While the factions of Orsini and Colonna divided the Campagna and wrangled in the streets of the city, Rome continued to preserve, in form at least, the old constitution of Caporioni and Senator. The Senator, elected by the people, swore, not to obey the Pope, but to defend his person. The government was ostensibly republican. The Pope had no sovereign rights, but only the ascendency inseparable from his wealth and from his position as Primate of Christendom. At the same time the spirit of Arnold of Brescia, of Brancaleone, and of Rienzi revived from time to time in patriots like Porcari and Baroncelli, who resented the encroachments of the Church upon the privileges of the city. Rome afforded no real security to the members of the Holy College. They commanded no fortress like the Castello of Milan, and had no army at their disposition. When the people or the nobles rose against them, the best they could do was to retire to Orvieto or Viterbo and to wait the passing of the storm.

Such was the position of the Pope, considered as one of the ruling princes of Italy, before the election of Nicholas V. His authority was wide but undefined, confirmed by prescription, but based on neither force nor legal right. Italy, however, regarded the Papacy as indispensable to her prosperity, while Rome was proud to be called the metropolis of Christendom, and ready to sacrifice the shadow of republican liberty for the material advantages which might accrue from the sovereignty of her bishop. How the Roman burghers may have felt upon this point we gather from a sentence of Leo Alberti's, referring to the administration of Nicholas : ' The city had become a city of gold through the jubilee ; the dignity of the citizens was respected ; all reasonable petitions were granted by the Pontiff. There were no exactions, no new taxes. Justice was fairly administered. It was the whole care of the Pontiff to adorn the city.'[1] The prosperity which the Papal Court brought to Rome was the main support of the Popes as princes, at a time when many thinkers looked with Dante's jealousy upon the union of temporal and spiritual functions in the Papacy.[2] Moreover, the whole of Italy, as we have seen in the previous chapters, was undergoing a gradual and instinctive change in politics : commonwealths were being superseded by tyrannies, and the sentiments of the race at large were by no means unfavourable to this revolution. Now was the proper moment, therefore, for the Popes to convert their ill-defined authority into a settled despotism, to secure themselves in Rome as sovereigns, and to subdue the States of the Church to their temporal jurisdiction.

The work was begun by Thomas of Sarzana, who ascended the Chair of S. Peter, as Nicholas V., in 1447. One part of his biography belongs to the history of scholarship, and need not here be touched upon. Educated at Florence, under the shadow of the house of Medici, he had imbibed those principles of deference to princely authority which were supplanting the old republican virtues throughout Italy. The schisms which had rent the Catholic Church were healed; and finding no opposition to his spiritual power, he determined to consolidate the temporalities of his See. In this purpose he was confirmed by the conspiracy of Stefano Porcari, a Roman noble who had endeavoured to rouse republican enthusiasm in the city at the moment of the Pope's election, and who subsequently plotted against his liberty, if not his life. Porcari and his associates were put to death in 1453, and by this act the

---

[1] See history of Porcari's Conspiracy (Muratori, vol. xxv.)

[2] Lorenzo Valla's famous declamation against the Donation of Constantine, which appeared during the pontificate of Nicholas, contained these reminiscences of the *De Monarchiâ*: ' Ut Papa tantum vicarius Christi sit et non etiam Cæsaris . . . tunc Papa et erit et dicetur pater sanctus, pater omnium, pater ecclesiæ.'

Pope proclaimed himself a monarch. The vast wealth which the jubilee of 1450 had poured into the Papal coffers [1] he employed in beautifying the city of Rome and in creating a stronghold for the Sovereign Pontiff. The mausoleum of Hadrian, used long before as a fortress in the Middle Ages, was now strengthened, while the bridge of S. Angelo and the Leonine city were so connected and defended by a system of walls and outworks as to give the key of Rome into the hands of the Pope. A new Vatican began to rise, and the foundations of a nobler S. Peter's Church were laid within the circuit of the Papal domain. Nicholas had, in fact, conceived the great idea of restoring the supremacy of Rome, not after the fashion of a Hildebrand, by enforcing the spiritual despotism of the Papacy, but by establishing the Popes as kings, by renewing the architectural magnificence of the Eternal City, and by rendering his court the centre of European culture. In the will which he recited on his death-bed to the princes of the Church, he set forth all that he had done for the secular and ecclesiastical architecture of Rome, explaining his deep sense of the necessity of securing the Popes from internal revolution and external force, together with his desire to exalt the Church by rendering her chief seat splendid in the eyes of Christendom. This testament of Nicholas remains a memorable document. Nothing illustrates more forcibly the transition from the Middle Ages to the worldliness of the Renaissance than the conviction of the Pontiff that the destinies of Christianity depended on the state and glory of the town of Rome. What he began was carried on amid crime, anarchy, and bloodshed by successive Popes of the Renaissance, until at last the troops of Frundsberg paved the way, in 1527, for the Jesuits of Loyola, and

[1] The bank of the Medici alone held 100,000 florins for the Pope. Vespasiano, *Vit. Nic. V.*

Rome, still the Eternal City, cloaked her splendour and her
scandals beneath the black pall of Spanish inquisitors. The
political changes in the Papacy initiated by Nicholas had been,
however, by that date fully accomplished, and for more than
three centuries the Popes have since held rank among the
kings of the earth.

Of Alfonso Borgia, who reigned for three years as Calixtus III., little need be said, except that his pontificate prepared
for the greatness of his nephew, Roderigo Lenzuoli, known as
Borgia in compliment to his uncle. The last days of Nicholas
had been embittered by the fall of Constantinople and the
imminent peril which threatened Europe from the Turks.
The whole energies of Pius II. were directed towards the
one end of uniting the European nations against the infidel.
Æneas Sylvius Piccolomini, as an author, an orator, a diplomatist, a traveller, and a courtier, bears a name illustrious in
the annals of the Renaissance. As a Pope, he claims attention
for the single-hearted zeal which he displayed in the vain
attempt to rouse the piety of Christendom against the foes of
civilisation and the faith. Rarely has a greater contrast been
displayed between the man and the pontiff than in the case
of Pius. The pleasure-loving, astute, free-thinking man of
letters and the world has become a Holy Father, jealous for
Christian proprieties, and bent on stirring Europe by an
appeal to motives which had lost their force three centuries
before. Frederick II. and S. Louis closed the age of the
Crusades, the one by striking a bargain with the infidel, the
other by snatching at a martyr's crown. Æneas Sylvius
Piccolomini was the mirror of his times—a humanist and
stylist, imbued with the rhetorical and pseudo-classic taste of
the earlier Renaissance. Pius II. is almost an anachronism.
The disappointment which the learned world experienced
when they discovered that the new Pope, from whom so much
had been expected, declined to play the part of their Mæcenas,

may be gathered from the epigrams of Filelfo upon his death[1] : —

> Gaudeat orator, Musæ gaudete Latinæ ;
>   Sustulit e medio quod Deus ipse Pium.
> Ut bene consuluit doctis Deus omnibus æque,
>   Quos Pius in cunctos se tulit usque gravem.
> Nunc sperare licet. Nobis Deus optime Quintum
>   Reddito Nicoleon Eugeniumve patrem.

and again :—

> Hac sibi quam vivus construxit clauditur arca
>   Corpore ; nam Stygios mens habet atra lacus.

Pius himself was not unconscious of the discrepancy between his old and his new self. *Æneam rejicite, Pium recipite*, he exclaims in a celebrated passage of his Retractation, where he declares his heartfelt sorrow for the irrevocable words of light and vain romance that he had scattered in his careless youth. Yet though Pius II. proved a virtual failure by lacking the strength to lead his age either backwards to the ideal of earlier Christianity or forwards on the path of modern culture, he is the last Pope of the Renaissance period whom we can regard with real respect. Those who follow, and with whose personal characters, rather than their action as Pontiffs, we shall now be principally occupied, sacrificed the interests of Christendom to family ambition, secured their sovereignty at the price of discord in Italy, transacted with the infidel, and played the part of Antichrist upon the theatre of Europe.

It would be possible to write the history of these priest-kings without dwelling more than lightly on scandalous circumstances, to merge the court-chronicle of the Vatican in a recital of European politics, or to hide the true features of high Papal dignitaries beneath the masks constructed for them by ecclesiastical apologists. That cannot, however, be the line adopted by a writer treating of civilisation in Italy during the fifteenth and sixteenth centuries. He must paint the Popes of the Renaissance as they appeared in the midst of society,

Rosmini, *Vita di Filelfo*, vol. ii. p. 321.

when Lorenzo de' Medici called Rome ' a sink of all the vices,' and observers so competent as Machiavelli and Guicciardini ascribed the moral depravity and political decay of Italy to their influence. It might be objected that there is now no need to portray the profligacy of that court which, by arousing the conscience of Northern Europe to a sense of intolerable shame, proved one of the main causes of the Reformation. But without reviewing those old scandals, a true under-standing of Italian morality, and a true insight into Italian social feeling as expressed in literature, are alike impossible. Nor will the historian of this epoch shrink from his task, even though the transactions he has to record seem to savour of legend rather than of simple fact.   No fiction contains matter more fantastic, no myth or allegory is more adapted to express a truth in figures of the fancy, than the authentic well-attested annals of this period of seventy years, from 1464 to 1534.

Paul II. was a Venetian named Pietro Barbi, who began life as a merchant. He had already shipped his worldly goods on board a trading vessel for a foreign trip, when news reached him that his uncle had been made Pope under the name of Eugenius IV. His call to the ministry consisted of the calculation that he could make his fortune in the Church with a Pope for uncle sooner than on the high seas by his wits. So he unloaded his bales, took to his book, became a priest, and at the age of forty-eight rose to the Papacy. Being a handsome man, he was fain to take the ecclesiastical title of Formosus ; but the Cardinals dissuaded him from this parade of vanity, and he assumed the tiara as Paul in 1464. A vulgar love of show was his ruling characteristic. He spent enormous sums in the collection of jewels, and his tiara alone was valued at 200,000 golden florins.   In all public ceremonies, whether ecclesiastical or secular, he was splendid, delighting equally to sun himself before the eyes of the Romans as the chief actor

in an Easter benediction or a Carnival procession. The poorer
Cardinals received subsidies from his purse in order that they
might add lustre to his pageants by their retinues. The arts
found in him a munificent patron. For the building of the
palace of S. Marco, which marks an abrupt departure from
the previous Gothic style in vogue, he brought architects of
eminence to Rome, and gave employment to Mino da Fiesole,
the sculptor, and to Giuliano da San Gallo, the wood-carver.
The arches of Titus and Septimius Severus were restored at
his expense, together with the statue of Marcus Aurelius and
the horses of Monte Cavallo. But Paul showed his connois-
seurship more especially in the collection of gems, medals,
precious stones, and cameos, accumulating rare treasures of
antiquity and costly masterpieces of Italian and Flemish gold-
work in his cabinets. This patronage of contemporary art, no
less than the appreciation of classical monuments, marked him
as a Mæcenas of the true Renaissance type.[1] But the qualities

[1] See *Les Arts à la Cour des Papes pendant le* xv *et le* xvi *Siècles*,
E. Müntz, Paris, Thorin, 2me Partie. M. Müntz has done good service
to æsthetic archæology by vindicating the fame of Paul II. as an em-
ployer of artists from the wholesale abuse heaped on him by Platina.
It may here be conveniently noticed that even the fierce Sixtus IV.
showed intelligence as a patron of arts and letters. He built the
Sistine Chapel, and brought the greatest painters of the day to Rome—
Signorelli, Perugino, Botticelli, Cosimo Rosselli, and Ghirlandajo.
Melozzo da Forlì worked for him. One of that painter's few remaining
masterpieces is the wall-picture, now in the Vatican, which represents
Sixtus among his Cardinals and Secretaries—a magnificent piece of
vivid portraiture. Sixtus again threw the Vatican library open to the
public, and in his days the Confraternity of S. Luke was founded for
the encouragement of design. Rome owes to him the hospital of
S. Spirito, a severe building, by Baccio Pontelli, and the churches of
S. Maria del Popolo and S. Maria della Pace. Innocent VIII. added
the Belvedere to the Vatican after Antonio del Pollajuolo's plan, and
commenced the Villa Magliana. Alexander VI. enriched the Vatican
with the famous Borgia apartments, decorated by Pinturicchio. He
also began the Palace of the University, and converted the Mausoleum
of Hadrian into the Castle of S. Angelo. These brief allusions must
suffice. It is not the object of the present chapter to treat of the Popes

of a dilettante were not calculated to shed lustre on a Pontiff who spent the substance of the Church in heaping up immensely valuable curiosities. His thirst for gold and his love of hoarding were so extreme that, when bishoprics fell vacant, he often refused to fill them up, drawing their revenues for his own use. His court was luxurious, and in private he was addicted to sensual lust.[1] This would not, however, have brought his name into bad odour in Rome, where the Holy Father was already regarded as an Italian Despot with certain sacerdotal additions. It was his prosecution of the Platonists which made him unpopular in an age when men had the right to expect that, whatever happened, learning at least would be respected. The example of the Florentine and Neapolitan academies had encouraged the Romans to found a society for the discussion of philosophical questions. The Pope conceived that a political intrigue was the real object of this club. Nor was the suspicion wholly destitute of colour. The conspiracy of Porcari against Nicholas, and the Catilinarian riots of Tiburzio which had troubled the pontificate of Pius, were still fresh in people's memories; nor was the position of the Pope in Rome as yet by any means secure. What increased Paul's anxiety was the fact that some scholars, appointed secretaries of the briefs (Abbreviatori) by Pius and deprived of office by himself, were members of the Platonic Society. Their animosity against him was both natural and ill-concealed. At the same time the bitter hatred avowed by

as patrons; but it should not be forgotten that, having accepted a place among the Despots of Italy, they strove to acquit their debt to art and learning in the spirit of contemporary potentates.

[1] Corio sums up his character thus: 'Fu costui uomo alla libidine molto proclivo; in grandissimo precio furono le gioie appresso di lui. Del giorno faceva notte, e la notte ispediva quanto gli occorreva.' Marcus Attilius Alexius says: 'Paulus II. ex concubinâ domum replevit, et quasi sterquilinium facta est sedes Barionis.' See Gregorovius, *Stadt Rom*, vol. vii. p. 215, for the latter quotation.

Laurentius Valla against the temporal power might in an age of conjurations have meant active malice. Leo Albèrti hints that Porcari had been supported by strong backers outside Rome; and one of the accusations against the Platonists was that Pomponius Lætus had addressed Platina as Holy Father. Now both Pomponius Lætus and Valla had influence in Naples, while Paul was on the verge of open rupture with King Ferdinand. He therefore had sufficient grounds for suspecting a Neapolitan intrigue, in which the humanists were playing the parts of Brutus and Cassius. Yet though we take this trouble to construct some show of reason for the panic of the Pope, the fact remains that he was really mistaken at the outset; and of the stupidity, cruelty, and injustice of his subsequent conduct there can be no doubt. He seized the chief members of the Roman Academy, imprisoned them, put them to the torture, and killed some of them upon the rack. 'You would have taken Castle S. Angelo for Phalaris' bull,' writes Platina; 'the hollow vaults did so resound with the cries of innocent young men.' No evidence of a conspiracy could be extorted. Then Paul tried the survivors for unorthodoxy. They proved the soundness of their faith to the satisfaction of the Pope's inquisitors. Nothing remained but to release them, or to shut them up in dungeons, in order that people might not say the Holy Father had arrested them without due cause. The latter course was chosen. Platina, the historian of the Popes, was one of the *abbreviatori* whom Paul had cashiered, and one of the Platonists whom he had tortured. The tale of Papal persecution loses, therefore, nothing in the telling; for if the humanists of the fifteenth century were powerful in anything, it was in writing innuendoes and invectives. Among other anecdotes, he relates how, while he was being dislocated on the rack, the inquisitors Vianesi and Sanga held a sprightly colloquy about a ring which the one said jestingly the other had received as a love-token from a girl. The whole situation is characteristic of Papal Rome in the Renaissance.

Paul did not live as long as his comparative youth led people to anticipate. He died of apoplexy in 1471, alone and suddenly, after supping on two huge water-melons, *duos prægrandes pepones.* His successor was a man of base extraction, named Francesco della Rovere, born near the town of Savona, on the Genoese Riviera. It was his whim to be thought noble ; so he bought the goodwill of the ancient house of Rovere of Türin by giving them two cardinals' hats, and proclaimed himself their kinsman. Theirs is the golden oak-tree on an azure ground which Michael Angelo painted on the roof of the Sistine Chapel in compliment to Sixtus and his nephew Julius. Having bribed the most venal members of the Sacred College, Francesco della Rovere was elected Pope, and assumed the name of Sixtus IV. He began his career with a lie ; for though he succeeded to the avaricious Paul, who had spent his time in amassing money which he did not use, he declared that he had only found 5,000 florins in the Papal treasury. This assertion was proved false by the prodigality with which he lavished wealth immediately upon his nephews. It is difficult even to hint at the horrible suspicions which were cast upon the birth of two of the Pope's nephews and upon the nature of his weakness for them. Yet the private life of Sixtus rendered the most monstrous stories plausible, while his public treatment of these men recalled to mind the partiality of Nero for Doryphorus.[1] We may, how-

[1] The infamous stories about Sixtus and Alexander may in part be fables, currently reported by the vulgar and committed to epigrams by scholars. Still the fact remains that Infessura, Burchard, and the Venetian ambassadors relate of these two Popes such traits of character and such abominable actions as render the worst calumnies probable. Infessura, though he expressed horror for the crimes of Sixtus, was yet a dry chronicler of daily events, many of which passed beneath his own eyes. Burchard was a frigid diarist of Court ceremonies, who reported the rapes, murders, and profligacies of Alexander with phlegmatic

ever, dwell upon the principal features of his nepotism; for
Sixtus was the first Pontiff who deliberately organised a
system for pillaging the Church in order to exalt his family to
principalities. The weakness of this policy has already been
exposed [1]; its justification, if there is any, lies in the exigencies of a dynasty which had no legitimate or hereditary succession. The names of the Pope's nephews were Lionardo,
Giuliano, and Giovanni della Rovere, the three sons of his
brother Raffaello; Pietro and Girolamo Riario, the two sons
of his sister Jolanda; and Girolamo, the son of another sister
married to Giovanni Basso. With the notable exception of
Giuliano della Rovere,[2] these young men had no claim to
distinction beyond good looks and a certain martial spirit
which ill suited with the ecclesiastical dignities thrust upon
some of them. Lionardo was made prefect of Rome and
married to a natural daughter of King Ferdinand of Naples.
Giuliano received a cardinal's hat, and, after a tempestuous
warfare with the intervening Popes, ascended the Holy Chair
as Julius II. Girolamo Basso was created Cardinal of San
Crisogono in 1477, and died in 1507. Girolamo Riario wedded
Catherine, a natural daughter of Galeazzo Sforza. For him
the Pope in 1473 bought the town of Imola with money of
the Church, and, after adding to it Forli, made Girolamo a
Duke. He was murdered by his subjects in the latter place in
1488, not, however, before he had founded a line of princes.
Pietro, another nephew of the Riario blood, or, as scandal

gravity. The evidence of these men, neither of whom indulges in satire
strictly so called, is more valuable than that of Tacitus or Suetonius to
the vices of the Roman emperors. The despatches of the Venetian
ambassadors, again, are trustworthy, seeing they were always written
with political intention and not for the sake of gossip.

[1] See ch. iii. p. 88.

[2] As Julius II., by far the greatest name in his age. Yet even
Giuliano did not at first impress men with his power. Jacobus
Volaterranus (Mur. xxiii. 107) writes of him: 'Vir est naturæ duriusculæ,
acuti ingenii, mediocris literaturæ.'

then reported and Muratori has since believed, a son of the Pope himself, was elevated at the age of twenty-six to the dignities of Cardinal, Patriarch of Constantinople, and Archbishop of Florence. He had no virtues, no abilities, nothing but his beauty, the scandalous affection of the Pope, and the extravagant profligacy of his own life to recommend him to the notice of posterity. All Italy during two years rang with the noise of his debaucheries. His official revenues were estimated at 60,000 golden florins; but in his short career of profligate magnificence he managed to squander a sum reckoned at not less than 200,000. When Leonora of Aragon passed through Rome on her way to wed the Marquis of Ferrara, this fop of a Patriarch erected a pavilion in the Piazza de' Santi Apostoli for her entertainment.[1] The square was partitioned into chambers communicating with the palace of the Cardinal. The ordinary hangings were of velvet and of white and crimson silk, while one of the apartments was draped with the famous tapestries of Nicholas V., which represented the Creation of the World. All the utensils in this magic dwelling were of silver—even to the very vilest. The air of the banquet-hall was cooled with punkahs; *tre mantici coperti, che facevano continoamente vento*, are the words of Corio; and on a column in the centre stood a living naked gilded boy, who poured forth water from an urn. The description of the feast takes up three pages of the history of Corio, where we find a minute list of the dishes—wild boars and deer and peacocks, roasted whole; peeled oranges, gilt and sugared; gilt rolls; rosewater for washing; and the tales of Perseus, Atalanta, Hercules, &c., wrought in pastry—*tutte in vivande*. We are also told how masques of Hercules, Jason and Phædra alternated with the story of Susannah and the Elders, played by Florentine actors, and with the Mysteries of *San Giovan Battista decapitato* and *quel Giudeo che rosti*

---

[1] For what follows read Corio, *Storia di Milano*, pp. 417-20.

il corpo di Cristo. The servants were arrayed in silk, and the seneschal changed his dress of richest stuffs and jewels four times in the course of the banquet. Nymphs and centaurs, singers and buffoons, drank choice wine from golden goblets. The most eminent and reverend master of the palace, meanwhile, moved among his guests 'like some great Cæsar's son.' The whole entertainment lasted from Saturday till Thursday, during which time Ercole of Este and his bride assisted at Church ceremonies in S. Peter's, and visited the notabilities of Rome in the intervals of games, dances, and banquets of the kind described. We need scarcely add that, in spite of his enormous wealth, the young Cardinal died 60,000 florins in debt. Happily for the Church and for Italy, he expired at Rome in January 1474, after parading his impudent debaucheries through Milan and Venice as the Pope's Legate. It was rumoured, but never well authenticated, that the Venetians helped his death by poison.[1] The sensual indulgences of every sort in which this child of the proletariat, suddenly raised to princely splendour, wallowed for twenty-five continuous months, are enough to account for his immature death without the hypothesis of poisoning. With him expired a plan which might have ended in making the Papacy a secular, hereditary kingdom. During his stay at Milan, Pietro struck a bargain with the Duke, by the terms of which Galeazzo Maria Sforza was to be crowned King of Lombardy, while the Cardinal Legate was to return and seize upon the Papal throne.[2] Sixtus, it is said, was willing to abdicate in his nephew's favour, with a view to the firmer establishment of his family in the tyranny of Rome. The scheme was a wild one, yet, considering the power and wealth of the Sforza family, not so wholly impracticable as might

[1] Mach. *Ist. Fior.* lib. vii.; Corio, p. 420.
[2] See Corio, p. 420. Corio hints that the Venetians poisoned the Cardinal for fear of this convention being carried out.

appear. The same dream floated, a few years later, before the imagination of the two Borgias; and Machiavelli wrote in his calm style that to make the Papal power hereditary was all that remained for nepotism in his days to do.[1] The opinion which had been conceived of the Cardinal of San Sisto during his two years of eminence may be gathered from the following couplets of an epigram placed, as Corio informs us, on his tomb:—

Fur, scortum, leno, mœchus, pedico, cynædus,
    Et scurra, et fidicen cedat ab Italiâ:
Namque illa Ausonii pestis scelerata senatûs,
    Petrus, ad infernas est modo raptus aquas.

After the death of Pietro, Sixtus took his last nephew, Giovanni della Rovere, into like favour. He was married to Giovanna, daughter of Federigo di Montefeltro, Duke of Urbino, and created Duke of Sinigaglia. Afterwards he became Prefect of Rome, upon the death of his brother Lionardo. This man founded the second dynasty in the Dukedom of Urbino. The plebeian violence of the della Rovere temper reached a climax in Giovanni's son, the Duke Francesco Maria, who murdered his sister's lover with his own hand when a youth of sixteen, stabbed the Papal Legate to death in the streets of Bologna at the age of twenty, and knocked Guicciardini, the historian, down with a blow of his fist during a council of war in 1526.

Sixtus, however, while thus providing for his family, could not enjoy life without some youthful protégé about his person. Accordingly in 1463 he made his valet, a lad of no education and of base birth, Cardinal and Bishop of Parma at the age of twenty. His merit was the beauty of a young Olympian. With this divine gift he luckily combined a harmless though stupid character.

With all these favourites to plant out in life, the Pope

[1] *Ist. Fior.* lib. i. vol. i. p. 38.

was naturally short of money. He relied on two principal
methods for replenishing his coffers. One was the public
sale of places about the Court at Rome, each of which had
its well-known price.[1] Benefices were disposed of with
rather more reserve and privacy, for simony had not yet
come to be considered venial. Yet it was notorious that
Sixtus held no privilege within his pontifical control on which
he was not willing to raise money : ' Our churches, priests,
altars, sacred rites, our prayers, our heaven, our very God,
are purchasable ! ' exclaims a scholar of the time ; while the
Holy Father himself was wont to say, ' A pope needs only
pen and ink to get what sum he wants.' [2] The second great
financial expedient was the monopoly of corn throughout the
Papal States. Fictitious dearths were created ; the value of
wheat was raised to famine prices ; good grain was sold out
of the kingdom, and bad imported in exchange ; while
Sixtus forced his subjects to purchase from his stores, and
made a profit by the hunger and disease of his emaciated
provinces. Ferdinand, the King of Naples, practised the
same system in the south. It is worth while to hear what
this bread was like from one of the men condemned to eat
it : ' The bread made from the corn of which I have spoken

[1] The greatest ingenuity was displayed in promoting this market.
Infessura writes : ' Multa et inexcogitata in Curiâ Romanâ officia
adinvenit et vendidit,' p. 1183.

[2] Baptista Mantuanus, *de Calamitatibus Temporum*, lib. iii.

Venalia nobis
Templa, sacerdotes, altaria, sacra, coronæ,
Ignes, thura, preces, cœlum est venale, Deusque.

Soriano, the Venetian ambassador, ap. Alberi ii. 3, p. 330, writes :
' Conviene ricordarsi quello che soleva dire Sisto IV., che il papa
bastava solo la mano con la penna e l' inchiostro, per avere quella
somma che vuole.' Cp. Æn. Sylv. Picc. *Ep.* i. 66 : ' Nihil est quod
absque argento Romana Curia dedat ; nam et ipsæ manus impositiones
et Spiritus Sancti dona venduntur, nec peccatorum venia nisi nummatis
impenditur '

was black, stinking, and abominable; one was obliged to
consume it, and from this cause sickness frequently took hold
upon the State.'[1]

But Christendom beheld in Sixtus not merely the spectacle
of a Pope who trafficked in the bodies of his subjects and
the holy things of God, to squander basely gotten gold upon
abandoned minions. The peace of Italy was destroyed by
desolating wars in the advancement of the same worthless
favourites. Sixtus desired to annex Ferrara to the dominions
of Girolamo Riario. Nothing stood in his way but the House
of Este, firmly planted for centuries, and connected by
marriage or alliance with all the chief families of Italy. The
Pope, whose lust for blood and broils was only equalled by his
avarice and his libertinism,[2] rushed with wild delight into a
project which involved the discord of the whole Peninsula.
He made treaties with Venice and unmade them, stirred up
all the passions of the Despots and set them together by the
ears, called the Swiss mercenaries into Lombardy, and when
finally, tired of fighting for his nephew, the Italian powers

---

[1] Infessura, *Eccardus*, vol. ii. p. 1941: 'Panis vero qui ex dicto
frumento fiebat, erat ater, fœtidus, et abominabilis; et ex necessitate
comedebatur, ex quo sæpenumero in civitate morbus viguit.'

[2] This phrase requires support. Infessura (loc. cit. p. 1941) relates
the savage pleasure with which Sixtus watched a combat 'a steccato
chiuso.' Hearing that a duel to the death was to be fought by two
bands of his body-guard, he told them to choose the Piazza of S. Peter
for their rendezvous. Then he appeared at a window, blessed the
combatants, and crossed himself as a signal for the battle to begin.
We who think the ring, the cockpit, and the bullfight barbarous, should
study Pollajuolo's engraving in order to imagine the horrors of a duel
'a steccato chiuso.' Of the inclination of Sixtus to sensuality, Infessura
writes: 'Hic, ut fertur vulgo, et experientia demonstravit, puerorum
amator et sodomita fuit.' After mentioning the Riarii and a barber's
son, aged twelve, he goes on: 'taceo nunc alia, quæ circa hoc possent
recitari, quia visa sunt de continuo.' It was not, perhaps, a wholly
Protestant calumny which accused Sixtus of granting private indulgences for the commission of abominable crimes in certain seasons of the
year.

concluded the peace of Bagnolo, he died of rage in 1484. The Pope did actually die of disappointed fury because peace had been restored to the country he had mangled for the sake of a favourite nephew.

The crime of Sixtus which most vividly paints the corruption of the Papacy in his age remains still to be told. This was the sanction of the Pazzi Conjuration against Giuliano and Lorenzo de' Medici. In the year 1477 the Medici, after excluding the merchant princes of the Pazzi family from the magistracy at Florence and otherwise annoying them, had driven Francesco de' Pazzi in disgust to Rome. Sixtus chose him for his banker in the place of the Medicean Company. He became intimate with Girolamo Riario, and was well received at the Papal Court. Political reasons at this moment made the Pope and his nephew anxious to destroy the Medici, who opposed Girolamo's schemes of aggrandisement in Lombardy. Private rancour induced Francesco de' Pazzi to second their views and to stimulate their passion. The three between them hatched a plot which was joined by Salviati, Archbishop of Pisa, another private foe of the Medici, and by Giambattista Montesecco, a captain well affected to the Count Girolamo. The first design of the conspirators was to lure the brothers Medici to Rome, and to kill them there. But the young men were too prudent to leave Florence. Pazzi and Salviati then proceeded to Tuscany, hoping either at a banquet or in church to succeed in murdering their two enemies together. Bernardo Bandini, a man of blood by trade, and Francesco de' Pazzi were chosen to assassinate Giuliano. Giambattista Montesecco undertook to dispose of Lorenzo.[1] The 26th of April, 1478 was finally fixed for the deed. The

---

[1] His ' Confession,' printed by Fabroni, *Lorenzi Medicis Vita*, vol. ii. p. 168, gives an interesting account of the hatching of the plot. It is fair to Sixtus to say that Montesecco exculpates him of the design to murder the Medici. He only wanted to ruin them.

place selected was the Duomo.[1] The elevation of the Host at Mass-time was to be the signal. Both the Medici arrived. The murderers embraced Giuliano and discovered that this timid youth had left his secret coat of mail at home. But a difficulty, which ought to have been foreseen, arose. Montesecco, cut-throat as he was, refused to stab Lorenzo before the high altar; at the last moment some sense of the *religio loci* dashed his courage. Two priests were then discovered who had no such silly scruples. In the words of an old chronicle, 'Another man was found, who, *being a priest*, was more accustomed to the place and therefore less superstitious about its sanctity.' This, however, spoiled all. The priests, though more sacrilegious than the bravos, were less used to the trade of assassination. They failed to strike home. Giuliano, it is true, was stabbed to death by Bernardo Bandini and Francesco de' Pazzi at the very moment of the elevation of Christ's body. But Lorenzo escaped with a slight flesh wound. The whole conspiracy collapsed. In the retaliation which the infuriated people of Florence took upon the murderers, the Archbishop Salviati, together with Jacopo and Francesco de' Pazzi and some others among the principal conspirators, were hanged from the windows of the Palazzo Pubblico. For this act of violence to the sacred person of a traitorous priest, Sixtus, who had upon his own conscience the

[1] It is curious to note how many of the numerous Italian tyrannicides took place in church. The Chiavelli of Fabriano were murdered during a solemn service in 1435; the sentence of the creed 'Et incarnatus est' was chosen for the signal. Gian Maria Visconti was killed in San Gottardo (1412), Galeazzo Maria Sforza in San Stefano (1484). Lodovico Moro only just escaped assassination in Sant' Ambrogio (1484). Machiavelli says that Lorenzo de' Medici's life was attempted by Battista Frescobaldi in the Carmine (see *Ist. Fior.* book viii. near the end). The Baglioni of Perugia were to have been massacred during the marriage festival of Astorre with Lavinia Colonna (1500). Stefano Porcari intended to capture Nicholas V. at the great gate of S. Peter's (1453). The only chance of catching cautious princes off their guard was when they were engaged in high solemnities. See above, pp. 131, 132.

crime of mingled treason, sacrilege, and murder, excommunicated Florence, and carried on for years a savage war with the
Republic. It was not until 1481, when the descent of the
Turks upon Otranto made him tremble for his own safety,
that he chose to make peace with these enemies whom he had
himself provoked and plotted against.

Another peculiarity in the Pontificate of Sixtus deserves
special mention. It was under his auspices in the year 1478
that the Inquisition was founded in Spain for the extermination of Jews, Moors, and Christians with a taint of heresy.
During the next four years 2,000 victims were burned in the
province of Castile. In Seville, a plot of ground, called the
Quemadero, or pla   of burning—a new Aceldama—was set
apart for executions; and here in one year 280 heretics were
committed to the flames, while 79 were condemned to perpetual
imprisonment, and 17,000 to lighter punishments of various
kinds. In Andalusia alone 5,000 houses were at once
abandoned by their inhabitants. Then followed in 1492 the
celebrated edict against the Jews. Before four months had
expired the whole Jewish population were bidden to leave
Spain, carrying with them nothing in the shape of gold or
silver. To convert their property into bills of exchange and
movables was their only resource. The market speedily was
glutted: a house was given for an ass, a vineyard for a suit
of clothes. Vainly did the persecuted race endeavour to purchase a remission of the sentence by the payment of an exor-
bitant ransom. Torquemada appeared before Ferdinand and
his consort, raising the crucifix, and crying: ' Judas sold
Christ for 30 pieces of silver; sell ye him for a larger sum,
and account for the same to God!' The exodus began.
Eight hundred thousand Jews left Spain[1]—some for the

---

[1] This number is perhaps exaggerated. Limborch in his *History of
the Inquisition* (p. 83) gives both 800,000 and 400,000; he also speaks
of 170,000 *families* as one calculation.

coast of Africa, where the Arabs ripped their bodies up in
search for gems or gold they might have swallowed, and deflowered their women—some for Portugal, where they bought
the right to exist for a large head-tax, and where they saw their
sons and daughters dragged away to baptism before their eyes.
Others were sold as slaves, or had to satisfy the rapacity of their
persecutors with the bodies of their children. Many flung
themselves into the wells, and sought to bury despair in suicide.
The Mediterranean was covered with famine-stricken and
plague-breeding fleets of exiles. Putting into the port of
Genoa, they were refused leave to reside in the city, and died
by hundreds in the harbour.[1] Their festering bodies bred a
pestilence along the whole Italian sea-board, of which at
Naples alone 20,000 persons died. Flitting from shore to
shore, these forlorn spectres, the victims of bigotry and avarice,
everywhere pillaged and everywhere rejected, dwindled away
and disappeared. Meanwhile the orthodox rejoiced. Pico
della Mirandola, who spent his life in reconciling Plato with the
Cabala, finds nothing more to say than this : ' The sufferings
of the Jews, in which the glory of the Divine justice delighted,
were so extreme as to fill us Christians with commiseration.'
With these words we may compare the following passage from
Senarega : ' The matter at first sight seemed praiseworthy,
as regarding the honour done to our religion ; yet it involved
some amount of cruelty, if we look upon them, not as beasts,
but as men, the handiwork of God.' A critic of this century
can only exclaim with stupefaction : *Tantum religio potuit
suadere malorum !* Thus Spain began to devour and depopu-
late herself. The curse which fell upon the Jew and Moor
descended next upon philosopher and patriot. The very life of
the nation, in its commerce, its industry, its free thought, its

[1] Senarega's account of the entry of the Jews into Genoa is truly
awful. He was an eye-witness of what he relates. The passage may
be read in Prescott's *Ferdinand and Isabella*, chapter 17.

energy of character, was deliberately and steadily throttled. And at no long interval of time the blight of Spain was destined to descend on Italy, paralysing the fair movements of her manifold existence to a rigid uniformity, shrouding the light and colour of her art and letters in the blackness of inquisitorial gloom.

Most singular is the attitude of a Sixtus—indulging his lust and pride in the Vatican, adorning the chapel called after his name with masterpieces,[1] rending Italy with broils for the aggrandisement of favourites, haggling over the prices to be paid for bishoprics, extorting money from starved provinces, plotting murder against his enemies, hounding the semi-barbarous Swiss mountaineers on Milan by indulgences, refusing aid to Venice in her championship of Christendom against the Turk—yet meanwhile thinking to please God by holocausts of Moors, by myriads of famished Jews, conferring on a faithless and avaricious Ferdinand the title of Catholic, endeavouring to wipe out his sins by the blood of others, to burn his own vices in the *autos de fé* of Seville, and by the foundation of that diabolical engine the Inquisition to secure the fabric his own infamy was undermining.[2] This is not the language of a Protestant denouncing the Pope. With all

[1] Musing beneath the Sibyls and before the Judgment of Michael Angelo, it is difficult not to picture to the fancy the arraignment of the Popes who built and beautified that chapel, when the Christ, whose blood they sold, should appear with His menacing right arm uplifted, and the prophets should thunder their denunciations: 'Howl, ye shepherds, and cry; and wallow yourselves in the ashes, ye principal of the flock, for the days of your slaughter and your dispersions are accomplished.'

[2] The same incongruity appears also in Innocent VIII., whose bull against witchcraft (1484) systematised the persecution directed against unfortunate old women and idiots. Sprenger, in the *Malleus Maleficarum*, mentions that in the first year after its publication forty-one witches were burned in the district of Como, while crowds of suspected women took refuge in the province of the Archduke Sigismond. Cantù's *Storia della Diocesi di Como* (Le Monnier, 2 vols.) may be consulted for the persecution of witches in Valtellina and Val Camonica. Cp. Folengo's *Maccaronea* for the prevalence of witchcraft in those districts.

respect for the Roman Church, that Alma Mater of the Middle Ages, that august and venerable monument of immemorial antiquity, we cannot close our eyes to the contradictions between practice and pretension upon which the History of the Italian Renaissance throws a light so lurid.

After Sixtus IV. came Innocent VIII. His secular name was Giambattista Cibo. The Sacred College, terrified by the experience of Sixtus into thinking that another Pope, so reckless in his creation of scandalous Cardinals, might ruin Christendom, laid the most solemn obligations on the Pope elect. Cibo took oaths on every relic, by every saint, to every member of the Conclave, that he would maintain a certain order of appointment and a purity of election in the Church. No Cardinal under the age of 30, not more than one of the Pope's own blood, none without the rank of Doctor of Theology or Law, were to be elected, and so forth. But as soon as the tiara was on his head, he renounced them all as inconsistent with the rights and liberties of S. Peter's Chair. Engagements made by the man might always be broken by the Pope. Of Innocent's Pontificate little need be said. He was the first Pope publicly to acknowledge his seven children, and to call them sons and daughters.[1] Avarice, venality, sloth, and the ascendency of base favourites made his reign loathsome without the blaze and splendour of the scandals of his fiery predecessor. In corruption he advanced a step even beyond Sixtus, by establishing a bank at Rome for the sale of pardons.[2] Each sin had its price, which might be paid at the convenience of

---

[1] 'Primus pontificum filios filiasque palam ostentavit, primus eorum apertas fecit nuptias, primus domesticos hymenæos celebravit.' Egidius of Viterbo, quoted by Greg. *Stadt Rom*, vol. vii. p. 274, note.

[2] Infessura says he heard the Vice-Chancellor, when asked why criminals were allowed to pay instead of being punished, answer: 'God wills not the death of a sinner, but rather that he should pay and live.' Dominico di Viterbo, Apostolic Scribe, forged bulls by which the Pope granted indulgences for the commission of the worst scandals. His father tried to buy him off for 5,000 ducats. Innocent replied that, as

the criminal : 150 ducats of the tax were poured into the Papal coffers ; the surplus fell to Franceschetto, the Pope's son. This insignificant princeling, for whom the county of Anguillara was purchased, showed no ability or ambition for aught but getting and spending money. He was small of stature and tame-spirited ; yet the destinies of an important house of Europe depended on him ; for his father married him to Maddalena, the daughter of Lorenzo de' Medici, in 1487. This led to Giovanni de' Medici receiving a cardinal's hat at the age of thirteen, and thus the Medicean interest in Rome was founded ; in the course of a few years the Medici gave two Popes to the Holy See, and by their ecclesiastical influence riveted the chains of Florence fast.[1] The traffic which Innocent and Franceschetto carried on in theft and murder filled the Campagna with brigands and assassins.[2] Travellers and pilgrims and ambassadors were stripped and murdered on their way to Rome ; and in the city itself more than two hundred people were publicly assassinated with impunity during the last months of the Pope's life. He was gradually dozing off into his last long sleep, and Franceschetto was planning how to carry off his ducats. While the Holy Father still hovered between life and death, a Jewish doctor proposed to reinvigorate him by the transfusion of young blood into his torpid veins. Three boys throbbing with the elixir of early youth were sacrificed in vain. Each boy, says Infessura, received one ducat. He adds, not without grim

his honour was concerned, he must have 6,000. The poor father could not scrape so much money together ; so the bargain fell through, and Dominico was executed. A Roman who had killed two of his own daughters bought his pardon for 800 ducats.

[1] Guicciardini, i. 1, points out that Lorenzo, having the Pope for his ally, was able to create that balance of power in Italy which it was his chief political merit to have maintained until his death.

[2] It is only by reading the pages of Infessura's Diary (Eccardus, vol. ii. pp. 2003-2005) that any notion of the mixed debauchery and violence of Rome at this time can be formed.

humour: 'Et paulo post mortui sunt; Judæus quidem
aufugit, et Papa non sanatus est.' The epitaph of this poor
old Pope reads like a rather clever but blasphemous witticism :
' Ego autem in Innocentiâ meâ ingressus sum.'

Meanwhile the Cardinals had not been idle. The tedious
leisure of Innocent's long lethargy was employed by them in
active simony. Simony, it may be said in passing, gave the
great Italian families a direct interest in the election of the
richest and most paying candidate. It served the turn of a
man like Ascanio Sforza to fatten the golden goose that laid
such eggs, before he killed it—in other words, to take the
bribes of Innocent and Alexander, while deferring for a future
time his own election. All the Cardinals, with the exception of
Roderigo Borgia,[1] were the creatures of Sixtus or of Innocent.
Having bought their hats with gold, they were now disposed
to sell their votes to the highest bidder. The Borgia was the
richest, strongest, wisest, and most worldly of them all. He
ascertained exactly what the price of each suffrage would be,
and laid his plans accordingly. The Cardinal Ascanio Sforza,
brother of the Duke of Milan, would accept the lucrative post
of Vice-Chancellor. The Cardinal Orsini would be satisfied
with the Borgia Palaces at Rome and the Castles of Monti-
cello and Saviano. The Cardinal Colonna had a mind for the
Abbey of Subbiaco with its fortresses. The Cardinal of S.
Angelo preferred the comfortable Bishopric of Porto with its
palace stocked with choice wines. The Cardinal of Parma
would take Nepi. The Cardinal of Genoa was bribable with
the Church of S. Maria in Via Lata. Less influential
members of the Conclave sold themselves for gold : to meet
their demands the Borgia sent Ascanio Sforza four mules
laden with coin in open day, requesting him to distribute it

---

[1] Roderigo was the son of Isabella Borgia, niece of Pope Calixtus III.,
by her marriage with Joffré Lenzuoli. He took the name of Borgia,
when he came to Rome to be made Cardinal, and to share in his uncle's
greatness.

in proper portions to the voters. The fiery Giuliano della Rovere remained implacable and obdurate. In the Borgia his vehement temperament perceived a fit antagonist. The armour which he donned in their first encounters he never doffed, but waged fierce war with the whole brood of Borgias at Ostia, at the French Court, in Romagna, wherever and whenever he found opportunity.[1] He and five other Cardinals —among them his cousin Raphael Riario—refused to sell their votes. But Roderigo Borgia, having corrupted the rest of the College, assumed the mantle of S. Peter in 1492, with the ever-memorable title of Alexander VI.

Rome rejoiced. The Holy City attired herself in festival array, exhibiting on every flag and balcony the Bull of the house of Borgia, and crying like the Egyptians when they found Apis :—

> Vive diu Bos ! Vive diu Bos ! Borgia vive !
> Vivit Alexander : Roma beata manet.

In truth there was nothing to convince the Romans of the coming woe, or to raise suspicion that a Pope had been elected who would deserve the execration of succeeding centuries. In Roderigo Borgia the people only saw, as yet, a man accomplished at all points, of handsome person, royal carriage, majestic presence, affable address. He was a brilliant orator, a passionate lover, a demigod of court pageantry and ecclesiastic parade—qualities which, though they do not suit our notions of a churchman, imposed upon the taste of the Renaissance. As he rode in triumph toward the Lateran, voices were loud in his praise. ‘He sits upon a snow-white horse,’ writes one of the humanists of the century,[2] ‘with serene forehead, with commanding dignity. As he distributes

[1] The marriage of his nephew Nicolo della Rovere to Laura, the daughter of Alexander VI. by Giulia Bella, in 1505, long after the Borgia family had lost its hold on Italy, is a curious and unexplained incident.
[2] See Michael Fernus, quoted by Greg. *Lucrezia Borgia*, p. 45.

his blessing to the crowd, all eyes are fixed upon him, and all hearts rejoice. How admirable is the mild composure of his mien! how noble his countenance! his glance how free! His stature and carriage, his beauty and the full health of his body, how they enhance the reverence which he inspires!' Another panegyrist[1] describes his 'broad forehead, kingly brow, free countenance full of majesty,' adding that 'the heroic beauty of his whole body' was given him by nature in order that he might 'adorn the seat of the Apostles with his divine form in the place of God.' How little in the early days of his Pontificate the Borgia resembled that Alexander with whom the legend of his subsequent life has familiarised our fancy, may be gathered from the following account:[2] 'He is handsome, of a most glad countenance and joyous aspect, gifted with honeyed and choice eloquence; the beautiful women on whom his eyes are cast he lures to love him, and moves them in a wondrous way, more powerfully than the magnet influences iron.' These, we must remember, are the testimonies of men of letters, imbued with the Pagan sentiments of the fifteenth century, and rejoicing in the advent of a Pope who would, they hoped, make Rome the capital of luxury and licence. Therefore they require to be received with caution. Yet there is no reason to suppose that the majority of the Italians regarded the elevation of the Borgia with peculiar horror. As a Cardinal he had given proof of his ability, but shown no signs of force or cruelty or fraud. Nor were his morals worse than those of his colleagues. If he was the father of several children, so was Giuliano della Rovere, and so had been Pope Innocent before him. This mattered but little in an age when the Primate of Christendom had come to be regarded as a secular potentate, less fortunate than other princes inasmuch as his rule was not hereditary, but more

[1] Jason Mainus, quoted by Greg. *Stadt Rom*, p. 314, note.
[2] Gasp. Ver., quoted by Greg. *Stadt Rom*, p. 208, note.

fortunate in so far as he could wield the thunders and dispense the privileges of the Church. A few men of discernment knew what had been done, and shuddered. ' The King of Naples,' says Guicciardini, ' though he dissembled his grief, told the queen, his wife, with tears—tears which he was wont to check even at the death of his own sons—that a Pope had been made who would prove most pestilent to the whole Christian commonwealth.' The young Cardinal Giovanni de' Medici, again, showed his discernment of the situation by whispering in the Conclave to his kinsman Cibo : ' We are in the wolf's jaws ; he will gulp us down, unless we make our flight good.' Besides, there was in Italy a widely spread repugnance to the Spanish intruders—Marrani, or renegade Moors, as they were popularly called—who crowded the Vatican and threatened to possess the land of their adoption like conquerors. ' Ten Papacies would not suffice to satiate the greed of all this kindred,' wrote Giannandrea Boccaccio to the Duke of Ferrara in 1492 : and events proved that these apprehensions were justified; for during the Pontificate of Alexander eighteen Spanish Cardinals were created, five of whom belonged to the house of the Borgias.

It is certain, however, that the profound horror with which the name of Alexander VI. strikes a modern ear was not felt among the Italians at the time of his election. The sentiment of hatred with which he was afterwards regarded arose partly from the crimes by which his Pontificate was rendered infamous, partly from the fear which his son Cesare inspired, and partly from the mysteries of his private life, which revolted even the corrupt conscience of the sixteenth century. This sentiment of hatred had grown to universal execration at the date of his death. In course of time, when the attention of the Northern nations had been directed to the iniquities of Rome, and when the glaring discrepancy between Alexander's pretension as a Pope and his conduct as a man had been apprehended, it inspired a legend which, like all legends, distorts the facts which it reflects.

Alexander was, in truth, a man eminently fitted to close an old age and to inaugurate a new, to demonstrate the paradoxical situation of the Popes by the inexorable logic of his practical impiety, and to fuse two conflicting world-forces in the cynicism of supreme corruption. The Emperors of the Julian house had exhibited the extreme of sensual insolence in their autocracy. What they desired of strange and sweet and terrible in the forbidden fruits of lust, they had enjoyed. The Popes of the Middle Ages—Hildebrand and Boniface— had displayed the extreme of spiritual insolence in their theocracy. What they desired of tyrannous and forceful in the exercise of an usurped despotism over souls, they had enjoyed. The Borgia combined both impulses toward the illimitable. To describe him as the Genius of Evil, whose sensualities, as unrestrained as Nero's, were relieved against the background of flame and smoke which Christianity had raised for fleshly sins, is justifiable. His spiritual tyranny, that arrogated Jus, by right of which he claimed the hemisphere revealed by Christopher Columbus, and imposed upon the press of Europe the censure of the Church of Rome, was rendered ten times more monstrous by the glare reflected on it from the unquenched furnace of a godless life. The universal conscience of Christianity is revolted by those unnameable delights, orgies of blood and festivals of lust, which were enjoyed in the plenitude of his green and vigorous old age by this versatile diplomatist and subtle priest, who controlled the councils of kings, and who chaunted the sacramental service for a listening world on Easter Day in Rome. Rome has never been small or weak or mediocre. And now in the Pontificate of Alexander 'that memorable scene' presented to the nations of the modern world a pageant of Antichrist and Antiphysis—the negation of the Gospel and of nature; a

glaring spectacle of discord between humanity as it aspires to
be at its best, and humanity as it is at its worst; a tragi-
comedy composed by some infernal Aristophanes, in which
the servant of servants, the anointed of the Lord, the
lieutenant upon earth of Christ, played the chief part. It
may be objected that this is the language not of history but
of the legend. I reply that there are occasions when the
legend has caught the spirit of the truth.

Alexander was a stronger and a firmer man than his
immediate predecessors. 'He combined,' says Guicciardini,
'craft with singular sagacity, a sound judgment with extraordinary powers of persuasion; and to all the grave affairs of
life he applied ability and pains beyond belief.'[1] His first
care was to reduce Rome to order. The old factions of
Colonna and Orsini, which Sixtus had scotched, but which
had raised their heads again during the dotage of Innocent,
were destroyed in his Pontificate. In this way, as Machiavelli observed,[2] he laid the real basis for the temporal power
of the Papacy. Alexander, indeed, as a sovereign, achieved
for the Papal See what Louis XI. had done for the throne of
France, and made Rome on its small scale follow the type of
the large European monarchies. The faithlessness and perjuries of the Pope, 'who never did aught else but deceive, nor
ever thought of anything but this, and always found occa-

[1] It is but fair to Guicciardini to complete his sentence in a note:
'These good qualities were far surpassed by his vices; private habits
of the utmost obscenity, no shame nor sense of truth, no fidelity to his
engagements, no religious sentiment; insatiable avarice, unbridled
ambition, cruelty beyond the cruelty of barbarous races, burning desire
to elevate his sons by any means: of these there were many, and among
them—in order that he might not lack vicious instruments for effecting
his vicious schemes—one not less detestable in any way than his father.'
St. d' It. vol. i. p. 9. I shall translate and put into the appendix Guicciardini's character of Alexander from the Storia di Firenze.

[2] In the sentences which close the 11th chapter of the Prince.

sion for his frauds,' [1] when combined with his logical intellect and persuasive eloquence, made him a redoubtable antagonist. All considerations of religion and morality were subordinated by him with strict impartiality to policy: and his policy he restrained to two objects—the advancement of his family, and the consolidation of the temporal power. These were narrow aims for the ambition of a potentate who with one stroke of his pen pretended to confer the new-found world on Spain. Yet they taxed his whole strength, and drove him to the perpetration of enormous crimes.

Former Pontiffs had raised money by the sale of benefices and indulgences: this, of course, Alexander also practised— to such an extent, indeed, that an epigram gained currency: 'Alexander sells the keys, the altars, Christ. Well, he bought them; so he has a right to sell them.' But he went further and took lessons from Tiberius. Having sold the scarlet to the highest bidder, he used to feed his prelate with rich benefices. When he had fattened him sufficiently, he poisoned him, laid hands upon his hoards, and recommenced the game. Paolo Capello, the Venetian Ambassador, wrote in the year 1500: 'Every night they find in Rome four or five murdered men, Bishops and Prelates and so forth.' Panvinius mentions three Cardinals who were known to have been poisoned by the Pope; and to their names may be added those of the Cardinals of Capua and of Verona.[2] To be a prince of the Church was dangerous in those days; and if the Borgia had not at last poisoned himself by mistake, he must in the long run have had to pay people to accept so perilous a privilege. His traffic in Church dignities was carried on upon a grand scale: twelve Cardinals' hats, for example, were put up to auction in a

---

[1] Mach. *Prince*, ch. xvii. In the Satires of Ariosto (Satire i. 208–27) there is a brilliant and singularly outspoken passage on the nepotism of the Popes and its ruinous results for Italy.

[2] See the authorities in Burckhardt, pp. 93, 94.

single day in 1500.[1] This was when he wished to pack the Conclave with votes in favour of the cession of Romagna to Cesare Borgia, as well as to replenish his exhausted coffers. Forty-three Cardinals were created by him in eleven promotions : each of these was worth on an average 10,000 florins ; while the price paid by Francesco Soderini amounted to 20,000, and that paid by Domenico Grimani reached the sum of 30,000.

Former Popes had preached crusades against the Turk, languidly or energetically according as the coasts of Italy were threatened. Alexander frequently invited Bajazet to enter Europe and relieve him of the princes who opposed his intrigues in the favour of his children. The fraternal feeling which subsisted between the Pope and the Sultan was to some extent dependent on the fate of Prince Djem, a brother of Bajazet and son of the conqueror of Constantinople, who had fled for protection to the Christian powers, and whom the Pope kept prisoner, receiving 40,000 ducats yearly from the Porte for his jail fee. Innocent VIII. had been the first to snare this lucrative guest in 1489. The Lance of Longinus was sent him as a token of the Sultan's gratitude, and Innocent, who built an altar for the relique, caused his own tomb to be raised closed close by. His effigy in bronze by Pollajuolo still carries in its hand this blood-gift from the infidel to the High Priest of Christendom. Djem meanwhile remained in Rome, and held his Moslem Court side by side with the Pontiff in the Vatican. Despatches are extant in which Alexander and Bajazet exchange terms of the warmest friendship, the Turk imploring his Greatness—so he addressed the Pope—to put an end to the unlucky Djem, and promising as the price of this assassination a sum of 300,000 ducats and the tunic worn by Christ, presumably that very seamless coat

---

[1] Guicc. *St. d' It.* vol. iii. p. 15.

over which the soldiers of Calvary had cast their dice.[1] The money and the relique arrived in Italy and were intercepted by the partisans of Giuliano della Rovere. Alexander, before the bargain with the Sultan had been concluded by the murder of Djem, was forced to hand him over to the French king. But the unlucky Turk carried in his constitution the slow poison of the Borgias, and died in Charles's camp between Rome and Naples. Whatever crimes may be condoned in Alexander, it is difficult to extenuate this traffic with the Turks. By his appeal from the powers of Europe to the Sultan, at a time when the peril to the Western world was still most serious, he stands attainted for high treason against Christendom, of which he professed to be the chief; against civilisation, which the Church pretended to protect; against Christ, whose vicar he presumed to style himself.

Like Sixtus, Alexander combined this deadness to the spirit and the interests of Christianity with zeal for dogma. He never flinched in formal orthodoxy, and the measures which he took for riveting the chains of superstition on the people were calculated with the military firmness of a Napoleon. It was he who established the censure of the press, by which printers were obliged, under pain of excommunication, to submit the books they issued to the control of the Archbishops and their delegates. The Brief of June 1, 1501, which contains this order, may be reasonably said to have retarded civilisation, at least in Italy and Spain.

Carnal sensuality was the besetting vice of this Pope throughout his life.[2] This, together with his almost insane

[1] See the letters in the 'Preuves et Observations,' printed at the end of the *Mémoires de Comines*.

[2] Guicciardini (*St. Fior.* cap. 27) writes : 'Fu lussoriosissimo nell' uno e nell' altro sesso, tenendo publicamente femine e garzoni, ma più ancora nelle femine.' A notion of the public disorders connected with his dissolute life may be gained from this passage in Sanudo's Diary (Gregorovius, *Lucrezia Borgia*, p. 88) : 'Da Roma per le lettere del orator nostro se intese et etiam de private persone cossa assai abominevole in le

weakness for his children, whereby he became a slave to the terrible Cesare, caused all the crimes which he committed. At the same time, though sensual, Alexander was not gluttonous. Boccaccio, the Ferrarese Ambassador, remarks: 'The Pope eats only of one dish. It is, therefore, disagreeable to have to dine with him.' In this respect he may be favourably contrasted with the Roman prelates of the age of Leo. His relations to Vannozza Catanei, the titular wife first of Giorgio de Croce, and then of Carlo Canale, and to Giulia Farnese,[1] surnamed La Bella, the titular wife of Orsino Orsini, were open and acknowledged. These two sultanas ruled him during the greater portion of his career, conniving meanwhile at the harem, which, after truly Oriental fashion, he maintained in the Vatican. An incident which happened during the French invasion of 1494 brings the domestic circumstances of a Pope of the Renaissance vividly before us. Monseigneur d'Allegre caught the ladies Giulia and Girolama Farnese, together with the lady Adriana de Mila, who was employed as their duenna, near Capodimonte, on November 29, and carried them to Montefiascone. The sum fixed for their ransom was 3,000 ducats. This the Pope paid, and on December 1 they were released. Alexander met them outside Rome, attired like a layman in a black jerkin trimmed with gold brocade,

chiesa di Dio, che al papa erra nato un fiolo di una dona romana maritata, ch' el padre l' havea rufianata, e di questa il marito invitò il suocero a la vigna e lo uccise tagliandoli el capo, ponendo quello sopra uno legno con letere che diceva questo è il capo de mio suocero che a rufianato sua fiola al papa, et che inteso questo il papa fece metter el dito in exilio di Roma con taglia. Questa nova venne per letere particular; etiam si godea con la sua spagnola menatali per suo fiol duca di Gandia novamente li venuto.'

[1] Her brother Alexander, afterwards Paul III., owed his promotion to the purple to this liaison, which was, therefore, the origin of the greatness of the Farnesi. The tomb of Paul III. in the Tribune of S. Peter's has three notable family portraits—the Pope himself in bronze; his sister Giulia, naked in marble, as Justice, and their old mother, Giovanna Gaetani, the bawd, as Prudence.

and fastened round his waist by a Spanish girdle, from which hung his dagger. Lodovico Sforza, when he heard what had happened, remarked that it was weak to release these ladies, who were 'the very eyes and heart' of his Holiness, for so small a ransom—if 50,000 ducats had been demanded, they would have been paid. This and a few similar jokes, uttered at the Pope's expense, make us understand to what extent the Italians were accustomed to regard their high priest as a secular prince. Even the pageant of Alexander seated in S. Peter's, with his daughter Lucrezia on one side of his throne and his daughter-in-law Sancia upon the other, moved no moral indignation; nor were the Romans astonished when Lucrezia was appointed Governor of Spoleto, and plenipotentiary Regent of the Vatican in her father's absence. These scandals, however, created a very different impression in the north, and prepared the way for the Reformation.

The nepotism of Sixtus was like water to the strong wine of Alexander's paternal ambition. The passion of paternity, exaggerated beyond the bounds of natural affection, and scandalous in a Roman Pontiff, was the main motive of the Borgia's action. Of his children by Vannozza, he caused the eldest son to be created Duke of Gandia; the youngest he married to Donna Sancia, a daughter of Alfonso of Aragon, by whom the boy was honoured with the Dukedom of Squillace. Cesare, the second of this family, was appointed Bishop of Valentia, and Cardinal. The Dukedoms of Camerino and Nepi were given to another John, whom Alexander first declared to be his grandson through Cesare, and afterwards acknowledged as his son. This John may possibly have been Lucrezia's child. The Dukedom of Sermoneta, wrenched for a moment from the hands of the Gaetani family, who still own it, was conferred upon Lucrezia's son, Roderigo. Lucrezia, the only daughter of Alexander by Vannozza, took three husbands in succession, after having been formally betrothed to

two Spanish nobles, Don Cherubino Juan de Centelles, and
Don Gasparo da Procida, son of the Count of Aversa.   These
contracts, made before her father became Pope, were annulled
as not magnificent enough for the Pontiff's daughter.   In
1492 she was married to Giovanni Sforza, Lord of Pesaro.
But in 1497 the pretensions of the Borgias had outgrown this
alliance, and their public policy was inclining to relations with
the Southern Courts of Italy.   Accordingly she was divorced
and given to Alfonso, Prince of Biseglia, a natural son of the
King of Naples.   When this man's father lost his crown, the
Borgias, not caring to be connected with an ex-royal family,
caused Alfonso to be stabbed on the steps of S. Peter's in 1501;
and while he lingered between life and death, they had him
strangled in his sick-bed, by Michellozzo, Cesare's assassin in
chief.   Finally Lucrezia was wedded to Alfonso, crown-prince
of Ferrara, in 1502.[1]   The proud heir of the Este dynasty
was forced by policy, against his in lination, to take to his
board and bed a Pope's bastard, twice divorced, once severed
from her husband by murder, and soiled, whether justly or
not, by atrocious rumours, to which her father's and her
brother's conduct gave but too much colour.   She proved a
model princess after all, and died at last in childbirth, after
having been praised by Ariosto as a second Lucrece, brighter
for her virtues than the star of regal Rome.

History has at last done justice to the memory of this
woman, whose long yellow hair was so beautiful, and whose
character was so colourless.   The legend which made her a
poison-brewing Mænad has been proved a lie—but only at the
expense of the whole society in which she lived.   The simple
northern folk, familiar with the tales of Chriemhild, Brynhild,
and Gudrun, who helped to forge this legend, could not

[1] Her dowry was 300,000 ducats, besides wedding presents, and
certain important immunities and privileges granted to Ferrara by the
Pope.

understand that a woman should be irresponsible for all the crimes and scandals perpetrated in her name. Yet it seems now clear enough that not hers, but her father's and her brother's, were the atrocities which made her married life in Rome a byword. She sat and smiled through all the tempests which tossed her to and fro, until she found at last a fair port in the Duchy of Ferrara. Nursed in the corruption of Papal Rome, which Lorenzo de' Medici described to his son Giovanni as 'a sink of all the vices,' consorting habitually with her father's concubines, and conscious that her own mother had been married for show to two successive husbands, it is not possible that Lucrezia ruled her conduct at any time with propriety. It is even probable that the darkest tales about her are true. The Lord of Pesaro, we must remember, told his kinsman, the Duke of Milan, that the assigned reasons for his divorce were false, and that the fact was what can scarcely be recorded.[1] Still, there is no ground for supposing that, in the matter of her first husband's divorce and the second's

[1] The whole question of Lucrezia's guilt has been ably investigated by Gregorovius (*Lucrezia Borgia*, pp. 101, 159–64). Charity suggests that the dreadful tradition of her relation to her father and brothers is founded less upon fact than upon the scandals current after her divorce. What Giovanni Sforza said was this: '*anzi haverla conosciuta infinite volte, ma chel Papa non gelha tolta per altro se non per usare con lei.*' This confession of the injured husband went the round of all the Courts of Italy, was repeated by Malipiero and Paolo Capello, formed the substance of the satires of Sannazaro and Pontano, crept into the chronicle of Matarazzo, and survived in the histories of Machiavelli and Guicciardini. There was nothing in his words to astonish men who were cognisant of the acts of Gianpaolo Baglioni and Sigismondo Malatesta; while the frantic passion of Alexander for his children, closely allied as this feeling was in him to excessive sensuality, gave them confirmation. Were they, however, true; or were they a malevolent lie? That is the real point at issue. Psychological speculation will help but little here. It is true that Lucrezia in after-life showed all the signs of a clear conscience. But so also did Alexander, whose buoyancy of spirits lasted till the very day of his death. Yet he was stained with crimes foul enough to darken the conscience of any man, at any period of life, and in any position.

murder, she was more than a passive agent in the hands of Alexander and Cesare. The pleasure-loving, careless woman of the Renaissance is very different from the Medea of Victor Hugo's romance; and what remains most revolting to the modern conscience in her conduct is complacent acquiescence in scenes of debauchery devised for her amusement.[1] Instead of viewing her with dread as a potent and malignant witch, we have to regard her with contempt as a feeble woman, soiled with sensual foulness from the cradle. It is also due to truth to remember that at Ferrara she won the esteem of a husband who had married her unwillingly, attached the whole state to her by her sweetness of temper, and received the panegyrics of the two Strozzi, Bembo, Ariosto, Aldo Manuzio, and many other men of note. Foreigners who saw her surrounded by her brilliant Court exclaimed, like the French biographer of Bayard: 'J'ose bien dire que, de son temps, ni beaucoup avant, il ne s'est point trouvé de plus triomphante princesse; car elle était belle, bonne, douce, et courtoise à toutes gens.'

Yet even at Ferrara tragedies which might remind her of the Vatican continued to surround her path. Alfonso, rude in manners and devoted to gun-foundry, interfered but little with the life she led among the wits and scholars who surrounded her. One day, however, in 1508, the poet Ercole Strozzi, who had sung her praises, was found dead, wrapped in his mantle, and pierced with two and twenty wounds. No judicial inquiry into this murder was made. Rumour credited both Alfonso and Lucrezia with the deed—Alfonso, because he might be jealous of his wife; Lucrezia, because her poet had recently married Barbara Torelli. Two years earlier another dark crime at Ferrara brought the name of Borgia before the public. One of Lucrezia's ladies, Angela Borgia, was courted by both Giulio d' Este and the Cardinal Ippolito. The girl

[1] See Burchard, ed. Leibnitz, pp. 77 and 78.

praised the eyes of Giulio in the hearing of the Cardinal, who forthwith hired assassins to mutilate his brother's face. Giulio escaped from their hands with the loss of one of his eyes, and sought justice from the Duke against the Cardinal in vain. Thereupon he vowed to be revenged on both Ippolito and Alfonso. His plot was to murder them, and to place Ferdinand of Este on the throne. The treason was discovered; the conspirators appeared before Alfonso: he rushed upon Ferdinand, and with his dagger stabbed him in the face. Both Giulio and Ferdinand were thrown into the dungeons of the palace at Ferrara, where they languished for years, while the Duke and Lucrezia enjoyed themselves in its spacious halls and sunny loggie among their courtiers. Ferdinand died in prison, aged sixty-three, in 1540. Giulio was released in 1559 and died, aged eighty-three, in 1561. These facts deserve to be recorded in connection with Lucrezia's married life at Ferrara, lest we should pay too much attention to the flatteries of Ariosto. At the same time her history as Duchess consists, for the most part, in the record of the birth of children. Like her mother Vannozza, she gave herself, in the decline of life, to works of charity and mercy. After this fashion the bright and baleful dames of the Renaissance saved their souls.

But to return to the domestic history of Alexander. The murder of the Duke of Gandia brings the whole Borgia family upon the scene. It is related with great circumstantiality and with surprising sangfroid by Burchard, the Pope's Master of the Ceremonies. The Duke with his brother Cesare, then Cardinal Valentino, supped one night at the house of their mother Vannozza. On their way home the Duke said that he should visit a lady of their acquaintance. He parted from Cesare and was never seen again alive. When the news of his disappearance spread abroad, a boatman of the Tiber deposed to having watched the body of a man thrown into the river on the night of the Duke's death, the 14th of June; he had not thought it worth while to report this fact, for he had seen 'a hundred bodies in his day thrown into the water at the said spot, and no questions asked about them afterwards.' The Pope had the Tiber dragged for some hours, while the wits of Rome made epigrams upon this true successor of S. Peter, this new fisher of men. At last the body of the Duke of Gandia was hauled up: nine wounds, one in the throat, the others in the head and legs and trunk, were found upon the corpse. From the evidence accumulated on the subject of the murder it appeared that Cesare had planned it; whether, as some have supposed, out of a jealousy of his brother too dreadful to describe, or, as is more probable, because he wished to take the first place in the Borgia family, we do not know exactly. The Pontiff in his rage and grief was like a wild beast driven to bay. He shut himself up in a private room, refused food, and howled with so terrible a voice that it was heard in the streets beyond his palace. When he rose up from this agony, remorse seemed to have struck him. He assembled a Conclave of the Cardinals, wept before them, rent his robes, confessed his sins, and instituted a commission for the reform of the abuses he had sanctioned in the Church. But the storm of anguish spent its strength at last. A visit from Vannozza, the mother of his children, wrought a sudden change from fury to reconcilement. What passed between them is not known for certain; Vannozza is supposed, however, to have pointed out, what was indisputably true, that Cesare was more fitted to support the dignity of the family by his abilities than had been the weak and amiable Duke of Gandia. The miserable father rose from the earth, dried his eyes, took food, put from him his remorse, and forgot together with his grief for Absalom the reforms which he had promised for the Church.

Henceforth he devoted himself with sustained energy to

building up the fortunes of Cesare, whom he released from
all ecclesiastical obligations, and to whose service he seemed
bound by some mysterious power.   Nor did he even resent the
savageness and cruelty which this young hell-cat vented in
his presence on the persons of his favourites.   At one time
Cesare stabbed Perotto, the Pope's minion, with his own
hand, when the youth had taken refuge in Alexander's arms ;
the blood spirted out upon the priestly mantle, and the young
man died there.[1]   At another time he employed the same
diabolical temper for the delectation of his father.   He turned
out some prisoners sentenced to death in a courtyard of the
palace, arrayed himself in fantastic clothes, and amused the
papal party by shooting the unlucky criminals.   They ran
round and round the court crouching and doubling to avoid
his arrows.   He showed his skill by hitting each where he
thought fit.   The Pope and Lucrezia looked on applaudingly.
Other scenes, not of bloodshed, but of grovelling sensuality,
devised for the entertainment of his father and his sister,
though described by the dry pen of Burchard, can scarcely be
transferred to these pages.

The history of Cesare's attempt to found a principality
belongs properly to another chapter.[2]   But the assistance
rendered by his father is essential to the biography of Alexander.   The vision of an Italian sovereignty which Charles of
Anjou, Gian Galeazzo Visconti, and Galeazzo Maria Sforza
had successively entertained, now fascinated the imagination
of the Borgias.   Having resolved to make Cesare a prince,
Alexander allied himself with Louis XII. of France, promising
to annul his first marriage and to sanction his nuptials with
Anne of Brittany, if he would undertake the advancement of
his son.   This bribe induced Louis to create Cesare Duke of
Valence and to confer on him the hand of Charlotte of Navarre.

---

[1] The account is given by Capello, the Venetian envoy.
[2] See Chapter VI.

He also entered Italy and with his arms enabled Cesare to subdue Romagna. The system adopted by Alexander and his son in their conquests was a simple one. They took the capitals and murdered the princes. Thus Cesare strangled the Varani at Camerino in 1502, and the Vitelli and Orsini at Sinigaglia in the same year: by his means the Marescotti had been massacred wholesale in Bologna; Pesaro, Rimini, and Forli had been treated in like manner; and after the capture of Faenza in 1501, the two young Manfredi had been sent to Rome, where they were exposed to the worst insults, and then drowned or strangled.[1] A system of equal simplicity kept their policy alive in foreign Courts. The Bishop of Cette in France was poisoned for hinting at a secret of Cesare's (1498); the Cardinal d'Amb   was bribed to maintain the credit of the Borgias with Louis XII.; the offer of a red hat to Briçonnet saved Alexander from a general council in 1494. The historical interest of Alexander's method consists of its deliberate adaptation of all the means in his power to one end—the elevation of his family. His spiritual authority, the wealth of the Church, the honours of the Holy College, the arts of an assassin, the diplomacy of a despot, were all devoted systematically and openly to the purpose in view. Whatever could be done to weaken Italy by foreign invasions and internal discords, so as to render it a prey for his poisonous son, he

[1] Their father, Galeotto Manfredi, had been murdered in 1488 by their mother, Francesca Bentivogli. Of Astorre's death Guicciardini writes: 'Astorre, che era minore di diciotto anni e di forma eccellente . . . . . condotto a Roma, saziata prima (secondo che si disse) la libidine di qualcuno, fu occultamente insieme con un suo fratello naturale privato della vita.' Nardi (*Storie Fiorentine*, lib. iv. 13) credits Cesare with the violation and murder of the boy. How far, we may ask, were these dark crimes of violence actuated by astrological superstition? This question is raised by Burckhardt (p. 363) apropos of Sigismondo Malatesta's assault upon his son, and Pier Luigi Farnese's violation of the Bishop of Fano. To a temperament like Alexander's, however, mere lust enhanced by cruelty, and seasoned with the joy of insult to an enemy, was a sufficient motive for the commission of monstrous crime.

attempted.   When Louis XII. made his infamous alliance
with Ferdinand the Catholic for the spoliation of the house of
Aragon in Naples, the Pope gladly gave it his sanction.   The
two kings quarrelled over their prey : then Alexander fomented
their discord in order that Cesare might have an opportunity
of carrying on his operations in Tuscany unchecked.   Patriotism in his breast, whether the patriotism of a born Spaniard
or the patriotism of an Italian potentate, was as dead as
Christianity.   To make profit for the house of Borgia by fraud,
sacrilege, and the dismemberment of nations, was the Papal
policy.

It is wearisome to continue to the end the catalogue of his
misdoings.   We are relieved when at last the final crash
arrives.   The two Borgias, so runs the legend of their downfall, invited themselves to dine with the Cardinal Adriano of
Corneto in a vineyard of the Vatican belonging to their host.
Thither by the hands of Alexander's butler they previously
conveyed some poisoned wine.   By mistake, or by the contriv-
ance of the Cardinal, who may have bribed this trusted agent,
they drank the death-cup mingled for their victim.   Nearly all
contemporary Italian annalists, including Guicciardini, Paolo
Giovio, and Sanudo, gave currency to this version of the
tragedy, which became the common property of historians,
novelists, and moralists.[1]   Yet Burchard, who was on the spot,
recorded in his diary that both father and son were attacked
by a malignant fever ; and Giustiniani wrote to his masters
in Venice that the Pope's physician ascribed his illness to
apoplexy.[2]   The season was remarkably unhealthy, and deaths

[1] The story is related by Cinthio in his *Ecatommithi*, Dec. 9,
Nov. 10.

[2] The various accounts of Alexander's death have been epitomised by
Gregorovius (*Stadt Rom*, vol. vii.), and have been discussed by Villari in
his edition of the Giustiniani Despatches, 2 vols. Florence, Le Monnier.
Gregorovius thinks the question still open.   Villari decides in favour of
fever against poison.

from fever had been frequent. A circular letter to the German Princes, written probably by the Cardinal of Gurk, and dated August 31, 1503, distinctly mentioned fever as the cause of the Pope's sudden decease, *ex hoc seculo horrendâ febrium incensione absorptum.*[1] Machiavelli, again, who conversed with Cesare Borgia about this turning-point in his career, gave no hint of poison, but spoke only of son and father being simultaneously prostrated by disease.

At this distance of time, and without further details of evidence, we are unable to decide whether Alexander's death was natural, or whether the singularly circumstantial and commonly accepted story of the poisoned wine contained the truth. On the one side, in favour of the hypothesis of fever, we have Burchard's testimony, which does not, however, exactly agree with Giustiniani's, who reported apoplexy to the Venetian Senate as the cause of death, and whose report, even at Venice, was rejected by Sanudo for the hypothesis of poison. On the other side, we have the consent of all contemporary historians, with the single and, it must be allowed, remarkable exception of Machiavelli. Paolo Giovio goes even so far as to assert that the Cardinal Corneto told him he had narrowly escaped from the effects of antidotes taken in his extreme terror to counteract the possibility of poison.

Whatever may have been the proximate cause of his sickness, Alexander died, a black and swollen mass, hideous to contemplate, after a sharp struggle with the venom he had absorbed.[2] 'All Rome,' says Guicciardini, 'ran with indescribable gladness to view the corpse. Men could not satiate their eyes with feeding on the carcase of the serpent who, by

---

[1] Reprinted by R. Garnett in *Athenæum*, Jan. 16, 1875.

[2] 'Morto chel fu, il corpo comincio a bollire, e la bocca a spumare come faria uno caldaro al focho, assì perseverò mentre che fu sopra terra ; divenne anchor ultra modo grosso in tanto che in lui non apparea forma di corpo humano, ne dala larghezza ala lunghezza del corpo suo era differenzia alcuna' (letter of Marquis of Mantua).

his unbounded ambition and pestiferous perfidy, by every demonstration of horrible cruelty, monstrous lust, and unheard-of avarice, selling without distinction things sacred and profane, had filled the world with venom.' Cesare languished for some days on a sick bed : but in the end, by the aid of a powerful constitution, he recovered, to find his claws cut and his plans in irretrievable confusion. 'The state of the Duke of Valence,' says Filippo Nerli,[1] 'vanished even as smoke in air, or foam upon the water.'

The moral sense of the Italians expressed itself after Alexander's death in the legend of a devil, who had carried off his soul. Burchard, Giustiniani, Sanudo, and others mention this incident with apparent belief. But a letter from the Marquis of Mantua to his wife, dated September 22, 1503, gives the fullest particulars : 'in his sickness the Pope talked in such a way that those who did not know what was in his mind thought him wandering, though he spoke with great feeling, and his words were : *I will come ; it is but right ; wait yet a little while.* Those who were privy to his secret thought explained that, after the death of Innocent, while the Conclave was sitting, he bargained with the devil for the Papacy at the price of his soul : and among the agreements was this, that he should hold the See twelve years, which he did, with the addition of four days ; and some attest they saw seven devils in the room at the moment that he breathed his last.' Mere old wives' tales ; yet they mark the point to which the credit of the Borgia had fallen, even in Italy, since the hour when the humanists had praised his godlike carriage and heroic mien upon the day of his election.

Thus, overreaching themselves, ended this pair of villains —the most notable adventurers who ever played their part upon the stage of the great world. The fruit of so many crimes and such persistent effort was reaped by their enemy,

[1] *Commentari*, lib. v.

Giuliano della Rovere, for whose benefit the nobles of the Roman state and the despots of Romagna had been extirpated.[1] Alexander had proved the old order of Catholicity to be untenable. The Reformation was imperiously demanded. His very vices spurred the spirit of humanity to freedom. Before a saintly Pontiff the new age might still have trembled in superstitious reverence. The Borgia to all logical intellects rendered the pretensions of a Pope to sway the souls of men ridiculous. This is an excuse for dwelling so long upon the spectacle of his enormities. Better than any other series of facts, they illustrate, not only the corruption of society, and the separation between morality and religion in Italy, but also the absurdity of that Church policy which in the age of the Renaissance confined the action of the head of Christendom to the narrow interests of a brood of parvenus and bastards.

Of Pius III., who reigned for a few days after Alexander, no account need be taken. Giuliano della Rovere was made Pope in 1503. Whatever opinion may be formed of him considered as the high-priest of the Christian faith, there can be no doubt that Julius II. was one of the greatest figures of the Renaissance, and that his name, instead of that of Leo X., should by right be given to the golden age of letters and of arts in Rome. He stamped the century with the impress of a powerful personality. It is to him we owe the most splendid of Michael Angelo's and Raphael's masterpieces. The Basilica of S. Peter's, that materialised idea, which remains to symbolise the transition from the Church of the Middle Ages to the modern semi-secular supremacy of Papal Rome, was his thought. No nepotism, no loathsome sensuality, no flagrant violation of ecclesiastical justice, stain his pontificate. His one purpose was to secure and extend the temporal

---

[1] Cesare, it must be remembered, had ostensibly reduced the cities of Lombardy, Romagna, and the March, as Gonfalonier of the Church.

authority of the Popes; and this he achieved by curbing the
ambition of the Venetians, who threatened to absorb Romagna, by reducing Perugia and Bologna to the Papal sway,
by annexing Parma and Piacenza, and by entering on the
heritage bequeathed to him by Cesare Borgia. At his death
he transmitted to his successors the largest and most solid
sovereignty in Italy. But restless, turbid, never happy unless
fighting, Julius drowned the peninsula in blood. He has
been called a patriot, because from time to time he raised the
cry of driving the barbarians from Italy : it must, however,
be remembered that it was he, while still Cardinal di San
Pietro in Vincoli, who finally moved Charles VIII. from
Lyons ; it was he who stirred up the League of Cambray
against Venice, and who invited the Swiss mercenaries into
Lombardy ; in each case adding the weight of the Papal
authority to the forces which were enslaving his country.
Julius, again, has been variously represented as the saviour
of the Papacy and as the curse of Italy.[1] He was emphati-
cally both. In those days of national anarchy it was perhaps
impossible for Julius to magnify the Church except at the
expense of the nation, and to achieve the purpose of his life
without inflicting the scourge of foreign war upon his
countrymen. The powers of Europe had outgrown the Papal
discipline. Italian questions were being decided in the
cabinets of Louis, Maximilian, and Ferdinand. Instead of
controlling the arbiters of Italy, a Pope could only play off
one against another.

Leo X. succeeded Julius in 1513, to the great relief of
the Romans, wearied with the continual warfare of the old
Pontifice terribile. In the gorgeous pageant of his triumphal
procession to the Lateran, the streets were decked with

---

[1] 'Fatale instrumento e allora e prima e poi de' mali d' Italia,' says
Guicciardini, *Storia d' Italia*, vol. i. p. 84. 'Der Retter des Papst-
thums,' says Burckhardt, p 95.

arches, emblems, and inscriptions. Among these may be
noticed the couplet emblazoned by the banker Agostino Chigi
before his palace :

> Olim habuit Cypris sua tempora ; tempora Mavors
> Olim habuit ; sua nunc tempora Pallas habet,

' Venus ruled here with Alexander ; Mars with Julius ; now
Pallas enters on her reign with Leo.' To this epigram the
goldsmith Antonio di San Marco answered with one pithy
line :

> Mars fuit ; est Pallas ; Cypria semper ero :

'Mars reigned : Pallas reigns ; Venus' own I shall always be.'

This first Pope of the house of Medici enjoyed at Rome
the fame of his father Lorenzo the Magnificent at Florence.
Extolled as an Augustus in his lifetime, he has given his
name to what is called the golden age of Italian culture. As
a man, he was well qualified to represent the neo-pagan
freedom of the Renaissance. Saturated with the spirit of his
period, he had no sympathy with religious earnestness, no
conception of moral elevation, no aim beyond a superficial
polish of the understanding and the taste. Good Latinity
seemed to him of more importance than true doctrine :
Jupiter sounded better in a sermon than Jehovah : the
immortality of the soul was an open topic for debate. At the
same time he was extravagantly munificent to men of culture,
and hearty in his zeal for the diffusion of liberal knowledge.
But what was reasonable in the man was ridiculous in the
pontiff. There remained an irreconcilable incongruity between
his profession of the Primacy of Christianity and his easy
epicurean philosophy.

Leo, like all the Medici after the first Cosimo, was a bad
financier. His reckless expenditure contributed in no small
measure to the corruption of Rome and to the ruin of the
Latin Church, while it won the praises of the literary world.

Julius, who had exercised rigid economy, left 700,000 ducats
in the coffers of S. Angelo.   The very jewels of Leo's tiara
were pledged to pay his debts, when he died suddenly in 1521.
During the heyday of his splendour he spent 8,000 ducats
monthly on presents to his favourites and on his play-
debts.   His table, which was open to all the poets, singers,
scholars, and buffoons of Rome, cost half the revenues of
Romagna and the March.   He founded the knightly Order of
S. Peter to replenish his treasury, and turned the conspiracy
of the Cardinal Petrucci against his life to such good account
—extorting from the Cardinal Riario a fine of 5,000 ducats,
and from the Cardinals Soderini and Hadrian the sum of
125,000—that Von Hutten was almost justified in treating
the whole of that dark business as a mere financial speculation.   The creation of thirty-nine Cardinals in 1517 brought
him in above 500,000 ducats.   Yet, in spite of these expedients for getting gold, the bankers of Rome were half ruined
when he died.   The Bini had lent him 200,000 ducats ; the
Gaddi, 32,000 ; the Ricasoli, 10,000 ; the Cardinal Salviati
claimed a debt of 80,000 ; the Cardinals Santi Quattro and
Armellini, each 150,000.[1]   These figures are only interesting
when we remember that the mountains of gold which they
denote were squandered in æsthetic sensuality.

'When the Pope was made, he said to Giuliano (Duke of
Nemours) : Let us enjoy the Papacy since God has given it us
—*godiamoci il Papato, poichè Dio ce l' ha dato.*'[2]   It was in
this spirit that Leo administered the Holy See.   The keynote
which he struck dominated the whole society of Rome.   At
Agostino Chigi's banquets, prelates of the Church and Apostolic
secretaries sat side by side with beautiful Imperias and smooth-
cheeked singing-boys ; fishes from Byzantium and ragoûts of

[1] See Gregorovius, *Stadt Rom*, book xiv. ch. 3.
[2] 'Relazione di Marino Giorgi,' March 17, 1517.   Alberi, ser. ii. vol.
iii. p. 51.

parrots' tongues were served on golden platters, which the guests threw from the open windows into the Tiber. Masques and balls, comedies and carnival processions filled the streets and squares and palaces of the Eternal City with a mimicry of pagan festivals, while art went hand in hand with luxury. It seemed as though Bacchus and Pallas and Priapus would be reinstated in their old realm, and yet Rome had not ceased to call herself Christian. The hoarse rhetoric of friars in the Coliseum, and the drone of pifferari from the Ara Cœli, mingled with the Latin declamations of the Capitol and the twang of lute-strings in the Vatican. Meanwhile, amid crowds of Cardinals in hunting-dress, dances of half-naked girls, and masques of Carnival Bacchantes, moved pilgrims from the North with wide, astonished, woeful eyes—disciples of Luther, in whose soul, as in a scabbard, lay sheathed the sword of the Spirit, ready to flash forth and smite.

A more complete conception may be formed of Leo by comparing him with Julius. Julius disturbed the peace of Italy with a view to establishing the temporal power of his see. Leo returned to the old nepotism of the previous Popes, and fomented discord for the sake of the Medici. It was at one time his project to secure the kingdom of Naples for his brother Giuliano, and a Milanese sovereignty for his nephew Lorenzo. On the latter he succeeded in conferring the Duchy of Urbino, to the prejudice of its rightful owners.[1] With Florence in their hands and the Papacy under their control, the Medici might have swayed all Italy. Such plans, however, in the days of Francis I. and Charles V. had become impracticable; nor had any of the Medicean family stuff to undertake more than the subjugation of their native city. Julius was violent in temper, but observant of his promises. Leo

[1] He would have given it to Giuliano, but Giuliano was an honest man and remembered what he owed to the Della Rovere family. See the 'Relazione' of Marino Giorgi (Rel. Ven. ser. ii. vol. iii. p. 51).

was suave and slippery. He lured Gianpaolo Baglioni to
Rome by a safe-conduct, and then had him imprisoned and
beheaded in the Castle of S. Angelo. Julius delighted in war
and was never happier than when the cannons roared around
him at Mirandola. Leo vexed the soul of his master of the
ceremonies because he would ride out a-hunting in topboots.
Julius designed S. Peter's and comprehended Michael Angelo.
Leo had the wit to patronise the poets, artists and historians
who added lustre to his Court ; but he brought no new great
man of genius to the front. The portraits of the two Popes,
both from the hand of Raphael, are exceedingly characteristic.
Julius, bent and emaciated, has the nervous glance of a
passionate and energetic temperament ; though the brand is
hoar with ashes and more than half burned out, it glows and
can inflame a conflagration. Leo, heavy-jawed, dull-eyed,
with thick lips and a brawny jowl, betrays the coarser fibre of
a sensualist.

It has often been remarked that both Julius and Leo
raised money by the sale of indulgences with a view to the
building of S. Peter's, thus aggravating one of the chief
scandals which provoked the Reformation. In that age of
maladjusted impulses the desire to execute a great work of
art, combined with the cynical resolve to turn the superstitions
of the people to account, forced rebellion to a head. Leo was
unconscious of the magnitude of Luther's movement. If he
thought at all seriously of the phenomenon, it stirred his
wonder. Nor did he feel the necessity of reformation in the
Church of Italy. The rich and many-sided life of Rome and
the diplomatic interests of Italian despotism absorbed his
whole attention. It was but a small matter what barbarians
thought or did.

The sudden death of Leo threw the Holy College into
great perplexity. To choose the new Pope without reference
to political interests was impossible ; and these were divided

between Charles V. and Francis I. After twelve days spent
by the Cardinals in conclave, the result of their innumerable
schemes and counter-schemes was the election of the Cardinal
of Tortosa. No one knew him; and his elevation to the
Papacy, due to the influence of Charles, was almost as great a
surprise to the electors as to the Romans. In their rage and
horror at having chosen this barbarian, the College began to
talk about the inspiration of the Holy Ghost, seeking the most
improbable of all excuses for the mistake to which intrigue
had driven them. 'The courtiers of the Vatican and chief
officers of the Church,' says an eyewitness, 'wept and
screamed and cursed and gave themselves up to despair.'
Along the blank walls of the city was scrawled : 'Rome to let.'
Sonnets fell in showers, accusing the Cardinals of having delivered over ' the fair Vatican to a German's fury.' [1] Adrian VI.
came to Rome for the first time as Pope.[2] He knew no
Italian, and talked Latin with an accent unfamiliar to southern
ears. His studies had been confined to scholastic philosophy
and theology. With courts he had no commerce ; and he was
so ignorant of the state a Pope should keep in Rome, that he
wrote beforehand requesting that a modest house and garden
might be hired for his abode. When he saw the Vatican, he
exclaimed that here the successors, not of Peter, but of Constantine should dwell. Leo kept one hundred grooms for the
service of his stable ; Adrian retained but four. Two Flemish
valets sufficed for his personal attendance, and to these he
gave each evening one ducat for the expenses of the next day's
living. A Flemish serving woman cooked his food, made his

---

[1] See Greg. *Stadt Rom*, vol. viii. pp. 382, 383. The details about
Adriano are chiefly taken from the *Relazioni* of the Venetian ambassadors,
series ii. vol. iii. pp. 75–120.

[2] His father's name was Florus or Florentius, of the Flemish family,
it is supposed, of Dedel. Berni calls him a carpet-maker. Other accounts
represent him as a ship's carpenter. The Pope's baptismal name was
Adrian.

bed, and washed his linen. Rome, with its splendid immorality, its classic art and pagan culture, made the same impression on him that it made on Luther. When his courtiers
pointed to the Laocoon as the most illustrious monument of
ancient sculpture, he turned away with horror, murmuring:
'Idols of the Pagans!' The Belvedere, which was fast becoming the first statue-gallery in Europe, he walled up and
never entered. At the same time he set himself with earnest
purpose, so far as his tied hands and limited ability would go,
to reform the more patent abuses of the Church. Leo had
raised about three million ducats by the sale of offices, which
represented an income of 348,000 ducats to the purchasers, and
provided places for 2,550 persons. By a stroke of his pen Adrian
cancelled these contracts and threw upon the world a crowd
of angry and defrauded officials. It was but poor justice to
remind them that their bargain with his predecessor had been
illegal. Such attempts, however, at a reformation of ecclesiastical society were as ineffectual as pin-pricks in the cure of a
fever which demands blood-letting. The real corruption of
Rome, deeply seated in high places, remained untouched.
Luther meanwhile had carried all before him in the North,
and accurate observers in Rome itself dreaded some awful
catastrophe for the guilty city. 'This state is set upon the
razor-edge of peril; God grant we have not soon to take flight
to Avignon or to the ends of the ocean. I see the downfall of
this spiritual monarchy at hand. Unless God help, it is all
over with us.'[1] Adrian met the emergency, and took up arms
against the sea of troubles by expressing his horror of simony,
sensuality, thievery, and so forth. The result was that he was
simply laughed at. Pasquin made so merry with his name
that Adrian vowed he would throw the statue into the Tiber;
whereupon the Duke of Sessa wittily replied : 'Throw him to

---

[1] See the passage quoted from the *Lettere de' Principi*, Rome,
March 17, 1523, by Burckhardt, p. 99, note.

the bottom, and, like a frog, he'll go on croaking.' Berni,
again, wrote one of his cleverest Capitoli upon the dunce who
could not comprehend his age; and when he died, his doctor's
door was ornamented with this inscription: *Liberatori patriæ
Senatus Populusque Romanus.*

Great was the rejoicing when another Medici was made
Pope in 1523. People hoped that the merry days of Leo
would return. But things had gone too far toward dissolution.
Clement VII. failed to give satisfaction to the courtiers whom
his more genial cousin had delighted: even the scholars and
the poets grumbled.[1] His rule was weak and vacillating, so
that the Colonna faction raised its head again and drove him
to the Castle of S. Angelo. The political horizon of Italy
grew darker and more sullen daily, as before some dreadful
storm. Over Rome itself impended ruin—

> as when God
> Will o'er some high-viced city hang his poison
> In the sick air.[2]

At last the crash came. Clement by a series of treaties,
treacheries, and tergiversations had deprived himself of every
friend and exasperated every foe. Italy was so worn out with
warfare, so accustomed to the anarchy of aimless revolutions
and to the trampling to and fro of stranger squadrons on her
shores, that the news of a Lutheran troop, levied with the
express object of pillaging Rome, and reinforced with Spanish
ruffians and the scum of every nation, scarcely roused her
apathy. The so-called army of Frundsberg—a horde of
robbers held together by the hope of plunder—marched without difficulty to the gates of Rome. So low had the honour
of Italian princes fallen that the Duke of Ferrara, by direct

---

[1] See, for instance, Berni's sonnets. In one of these, Berni very
powerfully describes the vacillation and irresolution of Clement's state-
policy.

[2] See Varchi's picture of the state of Rome, *St. Fior.* ii. 16.

aid given, and the Duke of Urbino, by counter-force withheld, opened the passes of the Po and of the Apennines to these marauders. They lost their general in Lombardy. The Constable Bourbon, who succeeded him, died in the assault of the city. Then Rome for nine months was abandoned to the lust, rapacity, and cruelty of some 30,000 brigands without a leader. It was then discovered to what lengths of insult, violence. and bestiality the brutal barbarism of Germans and the avarice of Spaniards could be carried. Clement, beleaguered in the Castle of S. Angelo, saw day and night the smoke ascend from desolated palaces and desecrated temples, heard the wailing of women and the groans of tortured men mingle with the jests of Lutheran drunkards and the curses of Castilian bandits. Roaming its galleries and leaning from its windows he exclaimed with Job:[1] '*Quare de vulvâ eduxisti me? qui utinam consumptus essem, ne oculus me videret.*' What the Romans, emasculated by luxury and priest rule, what the Cardinals and prelates, lapped in sensuality and sloth, were made to suffer during this long agony can scarcely be described. It is too horrible. When at last the barbarians, sated with blood, surfeited with lechery, glutted with gold, and decimated by pestilence, withdrew Rome raised her head a widow. From the shame and torment of that sack she never recovered, never became again the gay licentious lovely capital of arts and letters, the glittering gilded Rome of Leo. But the kings of the earth took pity on her desolation. The treaty of Amiens (August 18, 1527), concluded between Francis I. and Henry VIII. against Charles V., in whose name this insult had been offered to the Holy City of Christendom, together with Charles's own tardy willingness to make amends, restored the Papacy to the respect of Europe.

It is well known that at this crisis the Emperor seriously thought of putting an end to the State of the Church. His

[1] So Luigi Guicciardini, in his account of the sack of Rome, relates.

councillors advised him to restore the Pope to his original rank of Bishop, and to make Rome again the seat of empire.[1] But to have done this would have been impossible under the political conditions of the sixteenth century and in the face of Christendom still Catholic. His deliberations, therefore, cost Rome the miseries of the sack; but they were speedily superseded by the determination to strengthen the Papal by means of the Imperial authority in Italy. Florence was given as a makepeace offering to the contemptible Medici; and it remains the worst shame of Clement that he used the dregs of the army that had sacked Rome for the enslavement of his mother-city.

Internally, the Papal State had learned by its misfortunes the necessity of a reform. Sadoleto, writing in the September of that memorable year to Clement, reminds him that the sufferings of Rome have satisfied the wrath of God, and that the way was now open for an amelioration of manners and laws.[2] No force of arms could prevent the Holy City from returning to a better life, and proving that the Christian priesthood was not a mere mockery and sham.[3] In truth the Counter-Reformation may be said to date historically from 1527.

[1] See the authorities in Greg. *Stadt Rom*, vol. viii. pp. 569, 575.

[2] It was universally recognised in Italy that the sack of Rome was a punishment inflicted by Providence upon the godless city. Without quoting great authorities like Sadoleto or the Bishop of Fossombrone, one of whose letters gives a really awful picture of Roman profligacy (*Opere di M. G. Guidiccioni*, Barbera, vol. i. p. 193), we find abundant testimony to this persuasion regarding the intolerable vice of Rome, even in men devoid of moral conscience. Aretino (*La Cortigiana*, end of Act i. Sc. xxiii.) writes: 'Io mi credeva che il castigo, che l' ha dato Cristo per mano degli Spagnuoli, l' avesse fatta migliore, et è più scellerata che mai.' Bandello (*Novelle*, Parte ii. xxxvi), alluding to the sack, remarks in a parenthesis, 'benche i peccati di quella città meritassero esser castigati.' After adducing two such witnesses, it would weaken the case to cite Trissino or Vettori, both of whom expressed themselves with force upon the iniquities of Papal Rome.

[3] Compare *Lettere de' Princ.* ii. 77; Cardinal Cajetanus, and other testimonies quoted by Greg. *Stadt Rom*, vol. viii. pp. 568, 578.

CHAPTER VIII

THE CHURCH AND MORALITY

Corruption of the Church—Degradation and Division of Italy—Opinions of Machiavelli, Guicciardini, and King Ferdinand of Naples—Incapacity of the Italians for thorough Reformation—The Worldliness and Culture of the Renaissance—Witness of Italian Authors against the Papal Court and the Convents—Superstitious Respect for Relics—Separation between Religion and Morality—Mixture of Contempt and Reverence for the Popes—Gianpaolo Baglioni—Religious Sentiments of the Tyrannicides—Pietro Paolo Boscoli—Tenacity of Religions—The direct Interest of the Italians in Rome—Reverence for the Sacraments of the Church—Opinions pronounced by Englishmen on Italian Immorality—Bad Faith and Sensuality—The Element of the Fancy in Italian Vice—The Italians not Cruel, or Brutal, or Intemperate by Nature—Domestic Murders—Sense of Honour in Italy—Onore and Onestà—General Refinement—Good Qualities of the People—Religious Revivalism.

THE corruption of the Papal Court involved a corresponding moral weakness throughout Italy. This makes the history of the Popes of the Renaissance important precisely in those details which formed the subject of the preceding chapter. Morality and religion suffered an almost complete separation in the fifteenth century. The chiefs of the Church with cynical effrontery violated every tradition of Christ and the Apostles, so that the example of Rome was in some sense the justification of fraud, violence, lust, filthy living, and ungodliness to the whole nation.

The contradiction between the spiritual pretensions of the Popes and their actual worldliness was not so glaring to the men of the Renaissance, accustomed by long habit to the spectacle of this anomaly, as it is to us. Nor would it be scientific to imagine that any Italian in that age judged by moral standards similar to ours. Æsthetic propriety rather than strict conceptions of duty ruled the conduct even of the best, and it is wonderful to observe with what artless simplicity the worst sinners believed they might make peace in time of need with heaven. Yet there were not wanting profound thinkers who traced the national decay of the Italians to the corruption of the Church. Among these Machiavelli stands foremost. In a celebrated passage of the 'Discorsi,' [1] after treating the whole subject of the connection between good government and religion, he breaks forth into this fiery criticism of the Papacy: 'Had the religion of Christianity been preserved according to the ordinances of its founder, the states and commonwealths of Christendom would have been far more united and far happier than they are. Nor is it possible to form a better estimate of its decay than by observing that, in proportion as we approach nearer to the Roman Church, the head of this religion, we find less piety prevail among the nations. Considering the primitive constitution of that Church, and noting how diverse are its present customs, we are forced to judge that without doubt either ruin or a scourge is now impending over it. And since some men are of opinion that the welfare of Italy depends upon the Church, I wish to put forth such arguments as occur to my mind to the contrary; and of these I will adduce two, which, as I think, are irrefutable. The first is this: that owing to the evil ensample of the Papal Court, Italy has lost all piety and all religion: whence follow infinite troubles and disorders; for as religion implies all good, so its absence implies the contrary. Consequently, to the Church and priests of Rome we Italians owe this obligation first—that we have become void of religion and corrupt. But we also owe them another, even greater,

[1] Lib. i. cap. 12.

which is the cause of our ruin. I mean that the Church has
maintained and still maintains Italy divided. Of a truth no
province ever was united and prosperous, unless it were reduced
beneath the sway of one republic or one monarch, as is the case
with France and Spain. And the reason why Italy is not in
this condition, but has neither commonwealth nor monarch
for head, is none other than the Church : for the Church,
established in our midst and exercising a temporal authority,
has never had the force or vigour to extend its sway over the
whole country and to become the ruling power in Italy. Nor
on the other hand has it been so feeble as not to be able,
when afraid of losing its temporalities, to call in a foreign
potentate, as a counterpoise in its defence against those powers
which threatened to become supreme. Of the truth of this,
past history furnishes many instances ; as when, by the help
of Charlemagne, the Popes expelled the Lombards; and when
in our own days they humbled Venice by the aid of France,
and afterwards drove out the French by calling in the Swiss.
So then the Church, being on the one hand too weak to grasp
the whole of Italy, and at the same time too jealous to allow
another power to do so, has prevented our union beneath one
head, and has kept us under scattered lords and princes.
These have caused so much discord and debility that Italy
has become the prey not only of powerful barbarians, but also
of every assailant. And this we owe solely and entirely to
the Church. In order to learn by experience the truth of
what I say, one ought to be able to send the Roman Court,
armed with like authority to that it wields in Italy, to take
up its abode among the Swiss, who at the present moment
are the only nation living, as regards religion and military
discipline, according to the antique fashion ; he would
then see that the evil habits of that Court would in no
long space of time create more disorders than any other misfortune that could arise there in any period whatever.' In

this scientific and deliberate opinion pronounced by the profoundest thinker of the sixteenth century, the Papacy is
accused of having caused both the moral depravation and the
political disunion of Italy.   The second of these points, which
belongs to the general history of the Italian nation, might be
illustrated abundantly: but one other sentence from the pen
of Machiavelli exposes the ruinous and selfish policy of the
Church more forcibly than could be done by copious examples: [1] 'In this way the Pontiffs at one time by love of their
religion, at other times for the furtherance of their ambitious
schemes, have never ceased to sow the seeds of disturbance
and to call foreigners into Italy, spreading wars, making and
unmaking princes, and preventing stronger potentates from
holding the province they were too feeble to rule.'

Guicciardini, commenting upon the 'Discorsi' of Machiavelli,
begins his gloss upon the passage I have just translated with
these emphatic words: [2] 'It would be impossible to speak so
ill of the Roman Court but that more abuse would not be
merited, seeing it is an infamy, an example of all the shames
and scandals of the world.'   He then proceeds to argue, like
Machiavelli, that the greatness of the Church prevented Italy
from becoming a nation under one head, showing, however,
at the same time that the Italians had derived much benefit
from their division into separate states. [3]   To the concurrent

---

[1] *Ist. Fior.* lib. i.

[2] Guicc. *Op. Ined.* vol. i. p. 27.

[3] In another place (*Op. Ined.* vol. i. p. 104) Guicciardini describes
the rule of priests as founded on violence of two sorts; 'perchè ci
sforzano con le armi temporali e con le spirituali.'   It may be well to
collect the chief passages in Machiavelli and Guicciardini, besides those
already quoted, which criticise the Papacy in relation to Italian politics.
The most famous is at the end of the fourth book of the *Istoria d'Italia*
(Edn. Rosini, vol. ii. pp. 218–30).   Next may be placed the sketch of
Papal History in Machiavelli's *Istorie Fiorentine* (lib. i. cap. 9–25).   The
eleventh chapter of the *Principe* gives a short sketch of the growth of
the temporal power, so framed as to be acceptable to the Medici, but

testimony of these great philosophic writers may be added
the evidence of a practical statesman, Ferdinand, king of
Naples, who in 1493 wrote as follows: [1] 'From year to year
up to this time we have seen the Popes seeking to hurt and
hurting their neighbours, without having to act on the
defensive or receiving any injury. Of this we are ourselves
the witness, by reason of the things they have done and
attempted against us through their inborn ambition; and of
the many misfortunes which have happened of late in Italy it
is clear that the Popes are authors.'

It is not so much, however, with the political as with
the moral aspect of the Church that we are at present
concerned: and on the latter point Guicciardini may once
more be confronted with his illustrious contemporary.
In his aphorisms he says: [2] 'No man hates the ambition,
avarice, and effeminacy of the priests more than I do; for
these vices, odious in themselves, are most unseemly in men
who make a profession of living in special dependence on the
Deity. Besides, they are so contradictory that they cannot
be combined except in a very extraordinary subject. My
position under several Popes has compelled me to desire their
aggrandisement for the sake of my own profit.[3] Otherwise,
I should have loved Martin Luther like myself—not that I
might break loose from the laws which Christianity, as it is
usually interpreted and comprehended, imposes on us, but that
I might see that horde of villains reduced within due limits,
and forced to live either without vices or without power.'

steeped in the most acid irony. See, in particular, the sentence
'Costoro solo hanno stati e non li difendono, hanno sudditi e non li
governano,' &c.

[1] See the despatch quoted by Gregorovius, *Stadt Rom*, vol. vii. p. 7,
note.

[2] *Op. Ined. Ricordi* No. 28. Compare Ariosto, Satire i. 208–27.

[3] Guicciardini had been secretary and vicegerent of the Medicean
Popes. See back, p. 233.

These utterances are all the more remarkable because they
do not proceed from the deep sense of holiness which animated
reformers like Savonarola.   Machiavelli was not zealous for
the doctrines of Christianity so much as for the decencies of
an established religion. In one passage of the 'Discorsi' he even
pronounces his opinion that the Christian faith, compared
with the creeds of antiquity, had enfeebled national spirit.[1]
Privately, moreover, he was himself stained with the moral
corruption which he publicly condemned.   Guicciardini,
again, in the passage before us, openly avows his egotism.
Keen-sighted as they were in theory, these politicians suffered
in their own lives from that gangrene which had penetrated
the upper classes of Italy to the marrow.   Their patriotism
and their desire for righteousness were not strong enough to
make them relinquish the pleasure and the profit they derived
from the existing state of things.   Nor had they the energy
or the opportunity to institute a thorough revolution.   Italy,
as Machiavelli pointed out in another passage of the ' Discorsi,'
had become too prematurely decrepit for reinvigorating
changes; [2] and the splendid appeal with which the ' Principe '
is closed must even to its author have sounded like a flourish
of rhetorical trumpets.

Moreover, it seemed impossible for an Italian to rise above
the conception of a merely formal reformation, or to reach
that higher principle of life which consists in the enuncia-
tion of a new religious truth.   The whole argument in the
' Discorsi ' which precedes the chapter I have quoted, treats
of religion not in its essence as pure Christianity, but as a state
engine for the maintenance of public order and national well-
being.[3]   That Milton and Cromwell may have so regarded

[1] *Discorsi*, ii. 2, iii. 1. These chapters breathe the bitterest contempt
for Christianity, the most undisguised hatred for its historical
development, the intensest rancour against Catholic ecclesiastics.

[2] *Discorsi*, i. 55.

[3] Mach. *Disc.* i. 12, after exposing the shams on which, as he

religion is true : but they had, besides, a personal sense of the necessity of righteousness, the fear of God, at the root of their political convictions.   While Machiavelli and Guicciardini wished to deprive the Popes of temporal sovereignty, in order that the worst scandals of their Court might be suppressed, and that the peace of Italy might be secured, Savonarola desired to purge the Church of sin, but to retain its hierarchy and its dogmas inviolate.   Neither the politicians nor the prophet had discerned, what Luther and the nations of the North saw clearly, that a fresh element of spiritual vitality was necessary for the regeneration of society ; or, in other words, that good government presupposes living religion, and not that religion should be used as an engine for the consolidation of empire over the people.[1]

The inherent feebleness of Italy in this respect proceeded from an intellectual apathy toward religious questions, produced partly by the stigma attaching to unorthodoxy, partly by the absorbing interests of secular culture, partly by the worldliness of the Renaissance, partly by the infamy of the ecclesiastics, and partly by the enervating influence of tyrannies.   However bold a man might be, he dreaded the name of heretic ; the term *paterino*, originally applied to religious innovators, had become synonymous in common phraseology with rogue.   It was a point of good society and refined taste to support the Church.   Again, the mental faculties of Italy had for three centuries been taxed to the utmost in studies wide apart from the field of religious faith.

believed, the religious institutions of Numa rested, asserts that, however much governors may be persuaded of the falseness of religions, it is their duty to maintain them : 'e debbono . . . come che le giudicassero false, favorirle e accrescerle.'

[1] Yet read the curious passage (*Disc.* iii. 1) in which Machiavelli discusses the regeneration of religion by a return to its vital principle, and shows how S. Francis and S. Dominic had done this in the thirteenth century.   It was precisely what Luther was designing while Machiavelli was writing.

Art, scholarship, philosophy, and meditation upon politics had given a definite direction to the minds of thinking men, so that little energy was left for those instinctive movements of the spirit which produced the German Reformation. The great work of Italy had been the genesis of the Renaissance, the development of modern culture. And the tendencies of the Renaissance were worldly : its ideal of human life left no room for a pure and ardent intuition into spiritual truth. Scholars occupied with the interpretation of classic authors, artists bent upon investing current notions with the form of beauty, could hardly be expected to exclaim : ' The fear of the Lord, that is wisdom ; and to depart from evil, that is under-standing.'[1] Materialism ruled the speculations no less than the conduct of the age. Pamponazzo preached an atheistic doctrine, with the plausible reservation of *Salva Fide*, which then covered all. The more delicate thinkers, Pico and Ficino, sought to reconcile irreconcilables by fusing philo-sophy and theology, while they distinguished truths of science from truths of revelation. It seems meanwhile to have occurred to no one in Italy that the liberation of the reason necessitated an abrupt departure from Catholicism. They did not perceive that a power antagonistic to mediæval orthodoxy had been generated. This was in great measure due to indif-ference ; for the Church herself had taught her children by

[1] It is well known that Savonarola's objection to classic culture was based upon his perception of its worldliness. It is very remarkable to note the feeling on this point of some of the greatest northern scholars. Erasmus, for example, writes : ' Unus adhuc scrupulus habet animum meum, ne sub obtentu priscæ literaturæ renascentis caput erigere conetur Paganismus, ut sunt inter Christianos qui titulo pæne duntaxat Christum agnoscunt, ceterum intus Gentilitatem spirant '—Letter 207 (quoted by Milman in his *Quarterly* article on Erasmus). Ascham and Melanchthon passed similar judgments upon the Italian scholars. The nations of the North had the Italians at a disadvantage, for they entered into their labours, and all the dangerous work of sympathy with the ancient world, upon which modern scholarship was based, had been done in Italy before Germany and England came into the field.

example to regard her dogmas and her discipline as a convenient convention. It required all the scourges of the Inquisition to flog the nation back, not to lively faith, but to hypocrisy. Furthermore, the political conditions of Italy were highly unfavourable to a profound religious revolution. The thirst for national liberty which inspired England in the sixteenth century, impelling the despotic Tudors to cast off the yoke of Rome, arming Howard the Catholic against the holy fleet of Philip, and joining prince and people in one aspiration after freedom, was impossible in Italy. The tone of Machiavelli's 'Principe,' the whole tenor of Castiglione's 'Cortigiano,' prove this without the need of further demonstration.

Few things are more difficult than to estimate the exact condition of a people at any given period with regard to morality and religion. And this difficulty is increased tenfold when the age presents such rapid transitions and such bewildering complexities as mark the Renaissance. Yet we cannot omit to notice the attitude of the Italians at large in relation to the Church, and to determine in some degree the character of their national morality. Against the corruption of Rome one cry of hatred and contempt arises from a crowd of witnesses. Dante's fiery denunciations, Jacopone's threats the fierce invectives of Petrarch, and the thundering prophecies of Joachim lead the chorus. Boccaccio follows with his scathing irony. 'Send the most obstinate Jew to Rome,' he says, 'and the profligacy of the Papal Court will not fail to convert him to the faith that can resist such obloquy.' [1] Another glaring scandal was the condition of the convents. All novelists combine in painting the depravity of the religious

[1] We may compare this Umbrian Rispetto for the opposite view :—

A Roma Santa ce so gito anch' io,
E ho visto co' miei occhi il fatto mio :
E quando a Roma ce s' è posto il piede,
Resta la rabbia e se ne va la fede.

houses as a patent fact in social life. Boccaccio, Sacchetti, Bandello, and Masuccio may be mentioned in particular for their familiar delineation of a profligacy which was interwoven with the national existence.[1] The comic poets take the same course, and delight in ridiculing the gross manners of the clergy. Nor do the ecclesiastics spare themselves. Poggio, the author of the 'Facetiæ,' held benefices and places at the Papal Court. Bandello was a Dominican and nephew of the General of his order. Folengo was a Benedictine. Bibbiena became a Cardinal. Berni received a Canonry in the Cathedral of Florence. Such was the open and acknowledged immorality of the priests in Rome that more than one Papal edict was issued forbidding them to keep houses of bad repute or to act as panders.[2] Among the aphorisms of Pius II. is recorded

[1] It may not be out of place to collect some passages from Masuccio's *Novelle* on the Clergy, premising that what he writes with the fierceness of indignation is repeated with the cynicism of indulgence by contemporary novelists. Speaking of the Popes, he says (ed. Napoli, Morano, 1874): 'me tacerò non solo de loro scelesti ed enormissimi vizi e pubblici e occulti adoperati, e de li officii, de beneficii, prelature, i vermigli cappelli, che all' incanto per loro morte vendono, ma del camauro del principe San Pietro che ne è gia stato fatto pattuito baratto non farò alcuna mentione.' Descending to prelates, he uses similar language (p. 64) : 'Non possa mai pervenire ad alcun grado di prelatura se non col favore del maestro della zecca, e quelle conviensela comprare all' incanto come si fa dei cavalli in fiera.' A priest is (p. 31) 'il venerabile lupo.' The members of religious orders are (p. 534) 'ministri de satanasso . . . soldati del gran diavolo:' (p. 25) 'più facilmente tra cento soldati se ne trovarebbero la metà buoni, che tra tutto un capitolo de frati ne fosse uno senza bruttissima macchia.' It is perilous to hold any communication with them (p. 39) : 'Con loro non altri che usurai, fornicatori, e omini di mala sorte conversare si vedeno.' Their sins against nature (p. 65), the secret marriages of monks and nuns (p. 83), the 'fetide cloache di monache,' choked with the fruits of infanticide (p. 84), not to mention their avarice (p. 55) and gross impiety (p. 52), are described with a naked sincerity that bears upon its face the stamp of truth.

[2] A famous passage from Agrippa (*De Vanitate Scientiarum*) deserves a place here. After alluding to Sixtus IV. he says that many state officers 'in civitatibus suis lupanaria construunt foventque,

the saying that if there were good reasons for enjoining
celibacy on the clergy, there were far better and stronger
arguments for insisting on their marriage.[1]

Some of the contempt and hatred expressed by the Italian
satirists for the two great orders of S. Francis and S. Dominic
may perhaps be due to an ancient grudge against them as a
Papal police founded in the interests of orthodoxy. But the
chief point aimed at is the mixture of hypocrisy with immorality, which rendered them odious to all classes of society. At
the same time the Franciscans embraced among their lay
brethren nearly all the population of Italy, and to die in the
habit of the order was thought the safest way of cheating the
devil of his due. Corruption had gone so far and deep that it
was universally recognised and treated with the sarcasm of
levity. It roused no sincere reaction, and stimulated no persistent indignation. Everyone acknowledged it; yet everyone continued to live indolently according to the fashion of
his forefathers, acting up to Ovid's maxim—

> Pro magnâ parte vetustas
> Creditur ; acceptam parce movere fidem.

It is only this incurable indifference that renders Machiavelli's

nonnihil ex meretricio questu etiam ærario suo accumulantes
emolumenti; quod quidem in Italiâ non rarum est, ubi etiam Romana
scorta in singulas hebdomadas Julium pendent Pontifici, qui census
annuus nonnunquam viginti millia ducatos excedit, adeoque Ecclesiæ
procerum id munus est, ut una cum Ecclesiarum proventibus etiam
lenociniorum numerent mercedem. Sic enim ego illos supputantes
aliquando audivi : Habet, inquientes, ille duo beneficia, unum curatum
aureorum viginti, alterum prioratum ducatorum quadraginta, et tres
putanas in burdello, quæ reddunt singulis hebdomadibus Julios Viginti.'

[1] Very few ecclesiastics of high rank escaped the contagion of Roman
society. It was fashionable for men like Bembo and La Casa to form
connections with women of the *demi-monde* and to recognise their
children, whose legitimation they frequently procured. The Capitoli of
the burlesque poets show that this laxity of conduct was pardonable,
when compared with other laughingly avowed and all but universal
indulgences. Once more, compare Guidiccioni's letter to M. Giamb.
Bernardi, *Opp.* vol. i. p. 193.

comic portraits of Fra Alberigo and Fra Timoteo at all intelligible. They are neither satires nor caricatures, but simple pictures drawn for the amusement of contemporaries and the stupefaction of posterity.

The criticism of the Italian writers, so far as we have yet followed it, was directed against two separate evils—the vicious worldliness of Rome, and the demoralisation of the clergy both in their dealings with the people and in their conventual life. Contempt for false miracles and spurious reliques, and the horror of the traffic in indulgences, swelled the storm of discontent among the more enlightened. But the people continued to make saints, to adore wonder-working shrines, and to profit by the spiritual advantages which could be bought. Pius II., mindful of the honour of his native city, canonised S. Bernardino and S. Catherine of Siena. Innocent VIII. consecrated a chapel for the Lance of Longinus, which he had received from the Turk as part-payment for the guardianship of Djem. The Venetian Senate offered 10,000 ducats for the seamless coat of Christ (1455). The whole of Italy was agitated by the news that S. Andrew's head had arrived from Patras (1462). The Pope and his Cardinals went forth to meet it near the Milvian bridge. There Pius II. pronounced a Latin speech of welcome, while Bessarion delivered an oration when the precious member was deposited in S. Peter's. In this passion for reliques two different sentiments seem to have been combined—the merely superstitious belief in the efficacy of charms, which caused the Venetians to guard the body of S. Mark so jealously, and the Neapolitans to watch the liquefaction of the blood of S. Januarius with a frenzy of excitement—and that nobler respect for the persons of the mighty dead which induced Sigismondo Malatesta to transport the body of Gemistus Pletho to Rimini, and which rendered the supposed coffin of Aristotle at Palermo an object of admiration to Mussulman and Christian alike. The bones

of Virgil, it will be remembered, had been built into the walls
of Naples, while those of Livy were honoured with splendid
sepulture at Padua.

Owing to the separation between religion and morality
which existed in Italy under the influence of Papal and
monastic profligacy, the Italians saw no reason why spiritual
benefits should not be purchased from a notoriously rapacious
Pontiff, or why the penalty of hell should not depend upon
the mere word of a consecrated monster. The Pope as successor of S. Peter, and the Pope as Roman sovereign, were
two separate beings. Many curious indications of the mixed
feeling of the people upon this point, and of the advantage
which the Pope derived from his anomalous position, may be
gathered from the historians of the period. Machiavelli, in
his narrative of the massacre at Sinigaglia, relates that Vitellozzo Vitelli, while being strangled by Cesare Borgia's assassin,
begged hard that the father of his murderer, the horrible
Alexander, might be entreated to pronounce his absolution.
The same Alexander was nearly suffocated in the Vatican by
the French soldiers who crowded round to kiss his mantle,
and who had made him tremble for his life a few days previously. Cellini on his knees implored Pope Clement to ab-
solve him from the guilt of homicide and theft, yet spoke of
him as 'transformed to a savage beast' by a sudden access of
fury. At one time he trembled before the awful majesty of
Christ's Vicar, revealed in Paul III.; at another he reviled
him as a man 'who neither believed in God nor in any other
article of religion.' A mysterious sanctity environed the person of the Pontiff. When Gianpaolo Baglioni held Julius II.
in his power in Perugia, he respected the Pope's freedom,
though he knew that Julius would overthrow his tyranny.
Machiavelli condemns this as cowardice, but it was wholly
consistent with the sentiment of the age. 'It cannot have
been goodness or conscience which restrained nim,' writes the

philosopher of Florence, 'for the heart of a man who cohabited with his sister, and had massacred his cousins and his nephews, could not have harboured any piety. We must conclude that men know not how to be either guilty in a noble manner, or entirely good. Although crime may have a certain grandeur of its own, or at least a mixture of more generous motives, they do not attain to this. Gianpaolo, careless though he was about incest and parricide, could not, or dared not, on a just occasion, achieve an exploit for which the whole world would have admired his spirit, and by which he would have won immortal glory: for he would have been the first to show how little prelates, living and ruling as they do, deserve to be esteemed, and would have done a deed superior in its greatness to all the infamy, to all the peril, that it might have brought with it.' [1] It is difficult to know which to admire most, the superstition of Gianpaolo, or the cynicism of the commentary, the spurious piety which made the tyrant miss his opportunity, or the false standard of moral sublimity by which the half-ironical critic measures his mistake. In combination they produce a lively impression of the truth of what I have attempted to establish—that in Italy at this period religion survived as superstition even among the most depraved, and that the crimes of the Church had produced a schism between this superstition and morality.

While the Church was thus gradually deviating more and

---

[1] *Discorsi*, i. 27. This episode in Gianpaolo Baglioni's life may be illustrated by the curious story told about Gabrino Fondulo, the tyrant of Cremona. The Emperor Sigismund and Pope John XXIII. were his guests together in the year 1414. Part of their entertainment consisted in visiting the sights of Cremona with their host, who took them up the great Tower (396 feet high) without any escort. They all three returned safely, but when Gabrino was executed at Milan in 1425, he remarked that he only regretted one thing in the course of his life—namely, that he had not pitched Pope and Emperor together from the Torazzo. What a golden opportunity to have let slip! The story is told by Antonio Campo, *Historia di Cremona* (Milan, 1645), p. 114.

more directly from the Christian ideal, and was exhibiting to Italy an ensample of worldliness and evil living, the Italians, earlier than any other European nation, had become imbued with the spirit of the ancient world. Instead of the Gospel and the Lives of the Saints, men studied Plutarch and Livy with avidity. The tyrannicides of Greece and the suicides of the Roman Empire, patriots like Harmodius and Brutus, philosophers like Seneca and Pætus Thrasea, seemed to the humanists of the fifteenth century more admirable than the martyrs and confessors of the faith. Pagan virtues were strangely mingled with confused and ill-assimilated precepts of the Christian Church, while pagan vices wore a halo borrowed from the lustre of the newly found and passionately welcomed poets of antiquity. Blending the visionary intuitions of the Middle Ages with the positive and mundane ethics of the ancients, the Italians of the Renaissance strove to adopt the sentiments and customs of an age long dead and not to be resuscitated. At the same time the rhetorical taste of the nation inclined the more adventurous and passionate natures to seek glory by dramatic exhibitions of personal heroism. The Greek ideal of τὸ καλὸν, the Roman conception of *Virtus*, agitated the imagination of a people who had been powerfully influenced by professors of eloquence, by public orators, by men of letters, masters in the arts of style and of parade. Painting and sculpture, and that magnificence of public life which characterised the fifteenth century, contributed to the substitution of æsthetic for moral or religious standards. Actions were estimated by the effect which they produced ; and to sin against the laws of culture was of more moment than to transgress the code of Christianity. Still, the men of the Renaissance could not forget the creed which they had drawn in with their mothers' milk, but which the Church had not adjusted to the new conditions of the growing

age. The result was a wild phantasmagoric chaos of con-
used and clashing influences.

Of this peculiar moral condition the records of the
umerous tyrannicides supply many interesting examples.[1]
Girolamo Olgiati offered prayers to S. Ambrose for protection
before he stabbed the Duke of Milan in S. Stephen's Church.[2]
The Pazzi conspirators, intimidated by the sanctity of the
Florentine Duomo, had to employ a priest to wield the
sacrilegious dagger.[3]   Pietro Paolo Boscoli's last confession,
after the failure of his attempt to assassinate the Medici in
1513, adds further details in illustration of the mixture of
religious feeling with patriotic paganism.   Luca della Robbia,
the nephew of the great sculptor of that name, and himself
no mean artist, visited his friend Boscoli on the night of his
execution, and wrote a minute account of their interview.
Both of these men were members of the Confraternità de'
Neri, who assumed the duty of comforting condemned
prisoners with spiritual counsel, prayer, and exhortation.
The narrative, dictated in the choicest vernacular Tuscan, by
an artist whose charity and beauty of soul transpire in every
line in contrast with the fiercer fortitude of Boscoli, is one of
the most valuable original documents for this period which
we possess.[4]   What is most striking is the combination of
deeply rooted and almost infantine piety with antique heroism
in the young patriot.   He is greatly concerned because,
ignorant of his approaching end, he had eaten a hearty
supper: 'Son troppo carico di cibo, et ho mangiato cose
insalate; in modo che non mi pare poter unir lo spirito a
Dio . . . Iddio abbi di me misericordia, che costoro m' hanno
carico di cibo.   Oh indiscrezione!'[5]   Then he expresses a

[1] For the Italian ethics of tyrannicide, see back, pp. 132, 133.
[2] See p. 130.   [3] See p. 312.
[4] It is printed in *Arch. Stor.* vol. i.
[5] 'I am over-burdened with food, and I have eaten salt meats: so that
I do not seem able to join my spirit to God. . . . God have pity on me,

vehement desire for the services of a learned confessor, to
resolve his intellectual doubts, pleading with all the earnestness of desperate conviction that the salvation of his soul
must depend upon his orthodoxy at the last. He complains
that he ought to have been allowed at least a month's
seclusion with good friars before he was brought face to face
with death. At another time he is chiefly anxious to free
himself from classic memories : ' Deh ! Luca, cavatemi della
testa quel Bruto, acciò ch' io faccia questo passo interamente
da Cristiano.' [1] Then again it grieves him that the tears of
compunction, which he has been taught to regard as the true
sign of a soul at one with God, will not flow. About the
mere fact of dying he has no anxiety. The philosophers have
strengthened him upon that point. He is only eager to die
piously. When he tries to pray, he can barely remember the
Paternoster and the Ave Maria. That reminds him how
easy it would have been to have spent his time better, and he
bids Luca remember that the mind a man makes for himself
in life, will be with him in death. When they bring him a
picture of Christ, he asks whether he needs *that* to fix his
soul upon his Saviour. Throughout this long contention of
so many varying thoughts, he never questions the morality of
the act for which he is condemned to die. Luca, how
has his doubts, and privately asks the confessor whether
Thomas Aquinas had not discountenanced tyrannicide. ' Yes,
answers the monk, ' in case the people have elected their own
tyrant, but not when he has imposed himself on them by
force.' This casuistical answer satisfies Luca that his friend
may reasonably be held blameless. After confessing, Boscoli
received the sacrament with great piety, and died bravely.

for they have burdened me with food. Oh, how thoughtless of them !'
His words cannot be translated. Naïf in the extreme, they become
ludicrous in English.

[1] ' Ah, Luca, turn that Brutus out of my head, in order that I may
take this last step wholly as a Christian man ! '

The confessor told Luca, weeping, that he was sure the young man's soul had gone straight to Paradise, and that he might be reckoned a real martyr. His head after death was like that of an angel; and Luca was, we know, a connoisseur in angels' heads. Boscoli was only thirty-two years of age; he had light hair, and was short-sighted.

To this narrative might be added the apology written by Lorenzino de' Medici, after the murder of his cousin Alessandro in 1536.[1] He relies for his defence entirely upon arguments borrowed from Pagan ethics, and by his treatment of the subject vindicates for himself that name of Brutus with which Filippo Strozzi in person at Venice, and Varchi and Molsa in Latin epigrams, saluted him. There is no trace of Christian feeling in this strong and splendid display of rhetorical ability; nor does any document of the age more forcibly exhibit the extent to which classical studies had influenced the morality of the Renaissance. Lorenzino, however, when he wrote it, was not, like Boscoli, upon the point of dying.

The last thing to perish in a nation is its faith. The whole history of the world proves that no anomalies are so glaring, no inconsistencies so paradoxical, as to sap the credit of a religious system which has once been firmly rooted in the habits, instincts, and traditions of a race: and what remains longest is often the least rational portion. Religions from the first are not the product of logical reflection or experiment, but of sentiment and aspiration. They come into being as simple intuitions, and afterwards invade the province of the reason and assimilate the thought of centuries to their own conceptions. This is the secret of their strength as well as the source of their weakness. It is only a

---

[1] It is printed at the end of the third volume of Varchi, pp. 283-95; compare p. 210. A medal in honour of Lorenzino's tyrannicide was struck with a profile copied from Michael Angelo's bust of Brutus.

stronger enthusiasm, a new intuition, a fresh outburst of
emotional vitality, that can supplant the old :—

> ' Cotal rimedio ha questo aspro furore,
>   Tale acqua suole spegner questo fuoco,
>   Come d' asse si trae chiodo con chiodo.'

Criticism from without, internal corruption, patent absurdity,
are comparatively powerless to destroy those habits of belief
which once have taken hold upon the fancy and the feeling
of a nation. The work of dissolution proceeds in silence
and in secret. But the established order subsists until the
moment comes for a new synthesis. And in the sixteenth
century the necessary impulse of regeneration was to come,
not from Italy, satisfied with the serenity of her art, preoccupied with her culture, and hardened to the infamy of
her corruption, but from the Germany of the barbarians she
despised.

These considerations will help to explain how it was that
the Church, in spite of its corruption, stood its ground and
retained the respect of the people in Italy. We must moreover bear in mind that, bad as it was, it still to some extent
maintained the Christian verity. Apart from the Roman
Curia and the Convents, there existed a hierarchy of able and
God-fearing men, who by the sanctity of their lives, by the
gravity of their doctrine, by the eloquence of their preaching,
by their ministration to the sick, by the relief of the poor, by
the maintenance of hospitals, Monti di Pietà, schools and
orphanages, kept alive in the people of Italy the ideal at least
of a religion pure and undefiled before God.[1] In the tottering
statue of the Church some true metal might be found between
the pinchbeck at the summit and the clay of the foundation.

It must also be remembered how far the worldly interests
and domestic sympathies of the Italians were engaged in
the maintenance of their Church system. The fibres of the

---

[1] See the life of S. Antonino, the good Archbishop of Florence.

Church were intertwined with the very heartstrings of the people. Few families could not show one or more members who had chosen the clerical career, and who looked to Rome for patronage, employment, and perhaps advancement to the highest honours. The whole nation felt a pride in the Eternal City : patriotic vanity and personal interest were alike involved in the maintenance of the metropolis of Christendom, which drew the suites of ambassadors, multitudes of pilgrims, and the religious traffic of the whole of Europe to the shores of Italy. It was easy for Germans and Englishmen to reason calmly about dethroning the Papal hierarchy. Italians, however they might loathe the temporal power, could not willingly forego the spiritual primacy of the civilised world.

Moreover, the sacraments of the Church, the absolutions, consecrations, and benedictions which priests dispensed or withheld at pleasure, had by no means lost their power. To what extent even the nations of the North still clung to them is proved by our own Liturgy, framed in the tumult of war with Rome, yet so worded as to leave the utmost resemblance to the old ritual consistent with the spirit of the Reformation. Far more imposing were they in their effect upon the imagination of Italians, who had never dreamed of actual rebellion, who possessed the fountain of Apostolical privileges in the person of the Pope, and whose southern temperament inclined them to a more sensuous and less metaphysical conception of Christianity than the Germans or the English. The dread of the Papal Interdict was still a reality. Though the clergy of Florence, roused to retaliative fury, might fling back in the teeth of Sixtus such words as *leno matris suæ, adulterorum minister, diaboli vicarius*, yet the people could not long endure ' the niggardly and imperfect rites, the baptism sparingly administered, the extreme unction or the last sacrament coldly vouchsafed to the chosen few, the churchyard closed against the dead,' which, to quote the energetic language of

Dean Milman,[1] were the proper fruits of the Papal ban, however unjustly issued and however manfully resisted.

The history of the Despots and the Popes, together with the analysis of Machiavelli's political ethics, prove the demoralisation of a society in which crimes so extravagant could have their origin, and cynicism so deliberate could be accepted as a system. Yet it remains in estimating the general character of Italian morality to record the judgment passed upon it by foreign nations of a different complexion. The morality of races, as of individuals, is rarely otherwise than mixed—virtue balancing vice and evil vitiating goodness. Still the impression produced by Renaissance Italy upon observers from the North was almost wholly bad. Our own ancestors returned from their Italian travels either horrified with what they had witnessed, or else contaminated. Ascham writes : [2] 'I was once in Italy myself ; but I thank God my abode there was but nine days ; and yet I saw in that little time, in one city, more liberty to sin than ever I heard tell of in our noble city of London in nine years. I saw it was there as free to sin, not only without all punishment, but also without any man's marking, as it is free in the City of London to choose without all blame whether a man lust to wear shoe or pantofle.' Robert Greene, who did so much to introduce the novels of Italy into England, confesses that during his youthful travels in the South he ' saw and practised

---

[1] *Latin Christianity*, vol. vi. p. 361.

[2] *The Schoolmaster*, edn. 1863, p. 87. The whole discourse on Italian travelling and Italian influence is very curious, when we reflect that at this time contact with Italy was forming the chief culture of the English in literature and social manners. The ninth satire in Marston's *Scourge of Villanie* contains much interesting matter on the same point. Howell's *Instructions for forreine travell* furnishes the following illustration : ' And being in Italy, that great limbique of working braines, he must be very circumspect in his carriage, for she is able to turne a Saint into a devill, and deprave the best natures, if one will abandon himself, and become a prey to dissolute courses and wantonnesse.'

such villany as it is abominable to declare.'[1] The whole of
our dramatic literature corroborates these witnesses, while
the proverb, *Inglese Italianato è un diavolo incarnato*, quoted
by Sidney, Howell, Parker, Ascham, shows how pernicious to
the coarser natures of the North were the refined vices of the
South. What principally struck our ancestors in the morality
of the Italians was the license allowed in sensual indulgences,
and the bad faith which tainted all public and private dealings.
In respect to the latter point, what has already been said about
Machiavelli is enough.[2] Loyalty was a virtue but little
esteemed in Italy ; engagements seemed made to be broken :
even the crime of violence was aggravated by the crime of
perfidy, a bravo's stiletto or a slow poison being reckoned
among the legitimate means for ridding men of rivals or for
revenging a slight. Yet it must not be forgotten that the
commercial integrity of the Italians ranked high. In all
countries of Europe they carried on the banking business of
monarchs, cities, and private persons.

With reference to carnal vice, it cannot be denied that the
corruption of Italy was shameful. Putting aside the profligacy of the convents, the city of Rome in 1490 is reported to
have held as many as 6,800 public prostitutes, besides those
who practised their trade under the cloak of concubinage.[3]

---

[1] *The Repentance of Robert Greene*, quoted in the memoir to Dyce's
edition of his Dramatic Works.

[2] See Chapter V.

[3] Infessura, p. 1997. He adds : ' Consideratur modo qualiter vivatur
Romæ ubi caput fidei est.' From what Parent Duchâtelet (*Prostitution
dans la Ville de Paris*, p. 27) has noted concerning the tendency to
exaggerate the numbers of prostitutes in any given town, we have every
reason to regard the estimate of Infessura as excessive. In Paris, in
1854, there were only 4,206 registered ' filles publiques,' when the
population of the city numbered 1,500,000 persons ; while those who
exercised their calling clandestinely were variously computed at 20,000
or 40,000 and upwards to 60,000. Accurate statistics relating to the
population of any Italian city in the fifteenth century de not, unfortunately, exist.

These women were accompanied by confederate ruffians, ready to stab, poison, and extort money; thus violence and lust went hand in hand, and to this profligate lower stratum of society may be ascribed the crimes of lawlessness which rendered Rome under Innocent VIII. almost uninhabitable. Venice, praised for its piety by De Comines,[1] was the resort of all the debauchees of Europe who could afford the time and money to visit this modern Corinth. Tom Coryat, the eccentric English traveller, gives a curious account of the splendour and refinement displayed by the demi-monde of the lagoons, and Marston describes Venice as a school of luxury in which the monstrous Aretine played professor.[2] Of the state of morals in Florence Savonarola's sermons give the best picture.

But the characteristic vice of the Italian was not coarse sensuality. He required the fascination of the fancy to be added to the allurement of the senses.[3] It is this which makes the Capitoli of the burlesque poets, of men of note like Berni, La Casa, Varchi, Mauro, Molsa, Dolce, Bembo, Firenzuola, Bronzino, Aretino, and de' Medici, so amazing. The crudest forms of debauchery receive the most refined and

[1] *Memoirs*, lib. vii. 'C'est la plus triomphante cité que j'ai jamais vue, et qui plus fait d'honneur à ambassadeurs et étrangers, et qui plus sagement se gouverne, *et où le service de Dieu est le plus solemnellement faict*.' The prostitutes of Venice were computed to number 11,654 so far back as the end of the fourteenth century. See Filiasi, quoted by Mutinelli in his *Annali urbani di Venezia*.

[2] *Satires*, ii.

[3] Much might be written about the play of the imagination which gave a peculiar complexion to the profligacy, the jealousy, and the vengeance of the Italians. I shall have occasion elsewhere to maintain that in their literature at least the Italians were not a highly imaginative race; nor were they subject to those highly wrought conditions of the brooding fancy, termed by the northern nations Melancholy, which Dürer has personified in his celebrated etching, and Burton has described in his *Anatomy*. But in their love and hatred, their lust and their cruelty, the Italians required an intellectual element which brought the imaginative faculty into play.

highly finished treatment in poems which are as remarkable for their wit as for their cynicism. A like vein of elaborate innuendo runs through the 'Canti Carnascialeschi' of Florence, proving that, however profligate the people might have been, they were not contented with grossness unless seasoned with wit. The same excitement of the fancy, playing freely in the lawlessness of sensual self-indulgence and heightening the consciousness of personal force in the agent, rendered the exercise of ingenuity or the avoidance of peril an enhancement of pleasure to the Italians. This is perhaps one of the reasons why all the imaginative compositions of the Renaissance, especially the *Novelle*, turn upon adultery. Judging by the majority of these romances, by the comedies of the time, and by the poetry of Ariosto, we are compelled to believe that such illicit love was merely sensual, and owed its principal-attractions to the scope it afforded for whimsical adventures. Yet Bembo's 'Asolani,' Castiglione's panegyric of Platonic Love, and much of the lyrical poetry in vogue warn us to be cautious. The old romantic sentiment expressed by the Florentines of the thirteenth century still survived to some extent, adding a sort of dignity in form at least to these affections.

It was due again in a great measure to their demand for imaginative excitement in all matters of the sense, to their desire for the extravagant and extraordinary as a seasoning of pleasure, that the Italians came to deserve so terrible a name among the nations for unnatural passions.[1] This is a

---

[1] Italian literature is loud-voiced on this topic. The concluding stanzas of Poliziano's *Orfeo*, recited before the Cardinal of Mantua, the Capitoli of Berni, Bronzino, La Casa, and some of the *Canti Carnascialeschi*, might be cited. We might add Varchi's express testimony as to the morals of Filippo Strozzi, Lorenzino de' Medici, Pier Luigi Farnese, and Clement VII. What Segni (lib. x. p. 409) tells us about the brave Giovanni Bandini is also very significant. In the Life of San Bernardino of Siena, Vespasiano (*Vite di Illustri Uomini*, p. 186) writes: 'L' Italia, ch' era piena di queste tenebre, e aveva lasciata ogni norma di buoni

subject which can hardly be touched in passing; yet the opinion may be recorded that it belongs rather to the science of psychopathy than to the chronicle of vulgar lusts. English poets have given us the right key to the Italian temperament, on this as on so many other points. Shelley in his portrait of Francesco Cenci has drawn a man in whom cruelty and incest have become appetites of the distempered soul; the love of Giovanni and Annabella in Ford's tragedy is rightly depicted as more imaginative than sensual. It is no excuse for the Italians to say that they had spiritualised abominable vices. What this really means is that their immorality was nearer that of devils than of beasts. But in seeking to distinguish its true character, we must take notice of the highly wrought phantasy which seasoned both their luxury and their jealousy, their vengeance and their lust.

The same is to some extent true of their cruelty. The really cruel nation of the Renaissance was Spain, not Italy.[1] The Italians, as a rule, were gentle and humane, especially in warfare.[2] No Italian army would systematically have

costumi, e non era più chi conoscesse Iddio. Tanto erano sommersi e sepulti ne' maladetti e abbominevoli vizi nefandi! Gli avevano in modo messi in uso, che non temevano nè Iddio nè l' onore del mondo. Maladetta cecità! In tanto eccesso era venuto ogni cosa, che gli scellerati ed enormi vizi non era più chi gli stimasse, per lo maladetto uso che n' avevano fatto . . . massime il maladetto e abominando e detestando peccato della sodomia. Erano in modo stracorsi in questa recità, che bisognava che l' onnipotente Iddio facesse un' altra volta piovere dal cielo zolfo e fuoco come egli fece a Sodoma e Gomorra.' Compare Savonarola passim, the inductions to the *Sacre Rappresentazioni*, the familiar letters of Machiavelli, and the statute of Cosimo against this vice (year 1542, Sabellii Summa. Venice, 1715; vol. v. p. 287).

[1] Those who wish to gain a lively notion of Spanish cruelty in Italy should read, besides the accounts of the Sacco di Roma by Guicciardini and Buonaparte, the narrative of the Sacco di Prato in the *Archivio Storico Italiano*, vol. i., and Cagnola's account of the Spanish occupation of Milan, ib. vol. iii.

[2] De Comines more than once notices the humanity shown by the Italian peasants to the French army.

tortured the whole population of a captured city day after day for months, as the Spaniards did in Rome and Milan, to satisfy their avarice and glut their stolid appetite for blood. Their respect for human life again was higher than that of the French or Swiss. They gave quarter to their foes upon the battle-field, and were horrified with the massacres in cold blood perpetrated at Fivizzano and Rapallo by the army of Charles VIII. But when the demon of cruelty possessed the imagination of an Italian, when, like Gian Maria Visconti, he came to relish the sight of torment for its own sake, or when he sought to inspire fear by the spectacle of pain, then no Spaniard surpassed him in the ingenuity of his devices. In gratifying his thirst for vengeance he was never contented with mere murder. To obtain a personal triumph at the expense of his enemy by the display of superior cunning, by rendering him ridiculous, by exposing him to mental as well as physical anguish, by wounding him through his affections or his sense of honour, was the end which he pursued. This is why so many acts of violence in Italy assumed fantastic forms. Even the country folk showed an infernal art in the execution of their *vendette*. To serve the flesh of children up to their fathers at a meal of courtesy is mentioned, for example, as one mode of wreaking vengeance in country villages. Thus the high culture and æsthetic temperament of the Italians gave an intellectual quality to their vices. Crude lust and bloodshed were insipid to their palates : they required the pungent sauce of a melodramatic catastrophe.

The drunkenness and gluttony of northern nations for a like reason found no favour in Italy. It disgusted the Romans beyond measure to witness the swinish excesses of the Germans. Their own sensuality prompted them to a refined Epicureanism in food and drink ; on this point, however, it must be admitted that the prelates, here as elsewhere foremost in profligacy, disgraced the age of Leo with banquets

worthy of Vitellius.[1]   We trace the same play ot the fancy,
the same promptitude to quicken and intensify the immediate
sense of personality at any cost of after-suffering, in another
characteristic vice of the Italians.   Gambling among them
was carried further and produced more harm than it did in
the transalpine cities.   This we gather from Savonarola's
denunciations, from the animated pictures drawn by Alberti
in his 'Trattato della Famiglia' and 'Cena della Famiglia'
and also from the inductions to many of the 'Sacre Rappresentazioni.'[2]

Another point which struck a northern visitor in Italy was
the frequency of private and domestic murders.[3]   The Italians
had and deserved a bad reputation for poisoning and assassination.   To refer to the deeds of violence in the history of
a single family, the Baglioni of Perugia, as recorded by their
chronicler Matarazzo; to cite the passages in which Varchi
relates the deaths by poison of Luisa Strozzi, Cardinal
Ippolito de' Medici, and Sanga; or to translate the pages of
annalists, who describe the palaces of nobles swarming with
bravi, would be a very easy task.[4]   But the sketch of Benvenuto
Cellini's autobiography, which will be found in a subsequent
volume, gives so lively a picture of this aspect of Italian life,
that there is no reason to enlarge upon the topic now.   It is
enough to observe that, in their employment of poison and of

[1] See Gregorovius, Stadt Rom, vol. viii. p. 225 : ' E li cardinali
comenzarono a vomitar e cussi li altri,' quoted from Sanudo.

[2] One of the excellent characteristics of Alfonso the Great (Vespasiano, p. 49) was his abhorrence of gambling.

[3] See Guicc. St. It. vol. i. p. 101, for the impression produced upon
the army of Charles by the murder by poison of Gian Galeazzo Sforza.

[4] A vivid illustration of the method adopted by hired assassins in
tracking and hunting down their victims is presented by Francesco
Bibboni's narrative of his murder of Lorenzino dei Medici at Venice.
It casts much curious light, moreover, on the relations between paid
bravi and their employers, the esteem in which professional cut-throats
were held, and their connection with the police of the Italian towns.
It is published in a tract concerning Lorenzino, Milano, Daelli, 1862.

paid assassins, the Italians were guided by those habits of calculation which distinguished their character.[1] They thought
nothing of removing an enemy by craft or violence : but they
took no pleasure in murder for its own sake.[2] The object
which they had in view prompted them to take a man's life ;
the mere delight in brawls and bloodshed of Switzers,
Germans, and Spaniards offended their taste.

While the imagination played so important a part in the
morality of the Italians, it must be remembered that they
were deficient in that which is the highest imaginative safeguard against vice, a scrupulous sense of honour. It is true
that the Italian authors talk much about *Onore*. Pandolfini
tells his sons that *Onore* is one of the qualities which require
the greatest thrift in keeping, and Machiavelli asserts that it
is almost as dangerous to attack men in their *Onore* as in
their property. But when we come to analyse the word, we
find that it means something different from that mixture of
conscience, pride, and self-respect which makes a man true
to a high ideal in all the possible circumstances of life. The
Italian *Onore* consisted partly of the credit attaching to public
distinction, and partly of a reputation for *Virtù*, understanding
that word in its Machiavellian usage, as force, courage,
ability, virility. It was not incompatible with craft and
dissimulation, or with the indulgence of sensual vices.
Statesmen like Guicciardini, who, by the way, has written a
fine paragraph upon the very word in question,[3] did not
think it unworthy of their honour to traffic in affairs of state

[1] See the instructions given by the Venetian government to their
agents for the purchase of poison and the hiring of secret murderers.
See also the Maxims laid down by Sarpi.

[2] This at least was accounted eccentric and barbarous in the extreme.
See Pontano, *de Immanitate*, vol. i. p. 326, concerning Niccolo Forti-
braccio, Antonio Pontadera, and Riccio Montechiaro, who stabbed and
strangled for the pleasure of seeing men die. I have already discussed
the blood-madness of some of the Despots.

[3] *Ricordi politici e civili*, No. 118 *Op. Ined.* vol. i.

for private profit. Machiavelli not only recommended breaches of political faith, but sacrificed his principles to his pecuniary interests with the Medici. It would be curious to inquire how far the obtuse sensibility of the Italians on this point was due to their freedom from vanity.[1] No nation is perhaps less influenced by mere opinion, less inclined to value men by their adventitious advantages: the Italian has the courage and the independence of his personality. It is, however, more important to take notice that Chivalry never took a firm root in Italy ; and honour, as distinguished from vanity, *amour propre*, and credit, draws its life from that ideal of the knightly character which Chivalry established. The true knight was equally sensitive upon the point of honour, in all that concerned the maintenance of an unsullied self, whether he found himself in a king's court or a robber's den. Chivalry, as epitomised in the celebrated oath imposed by Arthur on his peers of the Round Table, was a northern, a Teutonic, institution. The sense of honour which formed its very essence was further developed by the social atmosphere of a monarch's court. It became the virtue of the nobly born and chivalrously nurtured, as appears very remarkably in this passage from Rabelais[2] : ' En leur reigle n'estoit que ceste clause ; Fay ce que vouldras. Parce que gens liberes, bien nayz, bien instruictz, conversans en compaignies honnesties, ont par nature ung instinct et aguillon qui toujours les poulse à faitctz vertueux, et retire de vice : lequel ils nommoyent honneur.' Now in Italy not only was Chivalry as an institution weak ; but the feudal courts in which it produced its

[1] See De Stendhal, *Histoire de la peinture en Italie*, pp. 285–91, for a curious catalogue of examples. The modern sense of honour is based, no doubt, to some extent on a delicate *amour propre*, which makes a man desirous of winning the esteem of his neighbours for its own sake. Granting that conscience, pride, vanity, and self-respect are all constituents of honour, we may, perhaps, find more pride in the Spanish, more *amour propre* in the French, and more conscience in the English.

[2] Gargantua, lib. i. ch. 57.

fairest flower, the knightly sense of honour, did not exist.[1] Instead of a circle of peers gathered from all quarters of the kingdom round the fount of honour in the person of the sovereign, commercial republics, forceful tyrannies, and the Papal Curia gave the tone to society. In every part of the peninsula rich bankers who bought and sold cities, adventurers who grasped at principalities by violence or intrigue, and priests who sought the aggrandisement of a sacerdotal corporation, were brought together in the meshes of diplomacy. The few noble families which claimed a feudal origin carried on wars for pay by contract in the interest of burghers, popes, or despots. Of these conditions not one was conducive to the sense of honour as conceived in France or England. Taken altogether and in combination, they could not fail to be eminently unfavourable to its development. In such a society Bayard and Sir Walter Manny would have been out of place; the motto *noblesse oblige* would have had but little meaning.[2] Instead of Honour, *Virtù* ruled the world in Italy. The moral atmosphere again was critical and highly intellectualised. Mental ability combined with personal daring gave rank. But the very subtlety and force of mind which formed the strength of the Italians proved hostile to any delicate sentiment of honour. Analysis enfeebles the tact and spontaneity of feeling which constitute its strongest safeguard. All this is obvious in the ethics of the ‘Principe.’ What most astounds us in that treatise is the assumption that no men will be bound by laws of honour when utility or the object in view require their sacrifice. In conclusion: although the Italians were not lacking in integrity, honesty, probity, or

[1] See, however, what I have already said about Castiglione and his ideal of the courtier in Chapter III. We must remember that he represents a late period of the Renaissance.

[2] It is curious to compare, for example, the part played by Italians, especially by Venice, Pisa, Genoa, Amalfi, as contractors and merchants in the Crusades, with the enthusiasm of the northern nations.

pride, their positive and highly analytical genius was out little influenced by that chivalrous honour which was an enthusiasm and a religion to the feudal nations, surviving the decay of Chivalry as a preservative instinct more undefinable than absolute morality. Honour with the northern gentry was subjective; with the Italians *Onore* was objective—an addition conferred from without, in the shape of reputation, glory, titles of distinction, or offices of trust.[1]

With the Italian conception of *Onore* we may compare their view of *Onestà* in the female sex. This is set forth plainly by Piccolomini in 'La Bella Creanza delle Donne.'[2] As in the case of *Onore*, we have here to deal, not with an exquisite personal ideal, but with something far more material and external. The *onestà* of a married woman is compatible with secret infidelity, provided she does not expose herself to ridicule and censure by letting her amour be known. Here, again, therefore, the proper translation of the word seems to be credit. Finally, we may allude to the invective against honour which Tasso puts into the mouths of his shepherds in 'Aminta.'[3] Though at this period the influence of France

---

[1] In confirmation of this view I may call attention to Giannotti's critique of the Florentine constitution (Florence, 1850, vol. i. pp. 15 and 156), and to what Machiavelli says about Gianpaolo Baglioni (*Disc.* i. 27), 'Gli uomini non sanno essere *onorevolmente* tristi;' men know not how to be bad with credit to themselves. The context proves that Gianpaolo failed to win the honour of a signal crime. Compare the use of the word *onore* in Lorenzino de' Medici's *Apologia*.

[2] *La Raffaella, ovvero Della bella Creanza delle Donne* (Milano, Daelli). Compare the statement of the author in his preface, p. 4, where he speaks in his own person, with the definition of *Onore* given by Raffaella, pp. 50 and 51 of the Dialogue: 'L' onore non è riposto in altro, se non nella stimazione appresso agli uomini . . . l' onor della donna non consiste, come t' ho detto, nel fare o non fare, chè questo importa poco, ma nel credersi o non credersi.'

[3] This invective might be paralleled from one of Masuccio's Novelle (ed. Napoli, pp. 389, 390), in which he almost cynically exposes the inconvenience of self-respect and delicacy. The situation of two friends,

and Spain had communicated to aristocratic society in Italy an exotic sense of honour, yet a court poet dared to condemn it as unworthy of the *Bell' età dell' oro*, because it interfered with pleasure and introduced disagreeable duties into life. Such a tirade would not have been endured in the London of Elizabeth or in the Paris of Louis XIV. Tasso himself, it may be said in passing, was almost feverishly punctilious in matters that touched his reputation.

An important consideration, affecting the whole question of Italian immorality, is this. Whereas the northern races had hitherto remained in a state of comparative poverty and barbarism, distributed through villages and country districts, the people of Italy had enjoyed centuries of wealth and civilisation in great cities. Their towns were the centres of luxurious life. The superfluous income of the rich was spent in pleasure, nor had modern decorum taught them to conceal the vices of advanced culture beneath the cloak of propriety. They were at the same time both indifferent to opinion and self-conscious in a high degree. The very worst of them was seen at a glance and recorded with minute particularity. The depravity of less cultivated races remained unnoticed because no one took the trouble to describe mere barbarism.[1] Vices of the same sort, but less widely dispersed, perhaps, throughout the people, were notorious in Italy, because they were combined with so much that was beautiful and splendid. In a word, the faults of the Italians were such as belong to a highly intellectualised society, as yet but imperfectly penetrated with culture, raised above the brutishness of barbarians, but not advanced to the self-control of civilisation, hampered by the corruption of a Church that trafficked in crime, tainted by uncritical contact with pagan art and literature, and

who agree that honour is a nuisance and share their wives in common, is a favourite of the Novelists.

[1] Read, however, the Saxon Chronicles or the annals of Ireland in Froude.

emasculated by political despotism. Their vices, bad as they were in reality, seemed still worse because they attacked the imagination instead of merely exercising the senses. As a correlative to their depravity, we find a sobriety of appetite, a courtesy of behaviour, a mildness and cheerfulness of disposition, a widely diffused refinement of sentiment and manners, a liberal spirit of toleration, which can nowhere else be paralleled in Europe at that period. It was no small mark of superiority to be less ignorant and gross than England, less brutal and stolid than Germany, less rapacious than Switzerland, less cruel than Spain, less vain and inconsequent than France.

Italy again was the land of emancipated individuality. What Mill in his Essay on Liberty desired, what seems every day more unattainable in modern life, was enjoyed by the Italians. There was no check to the growth of personality, no grinding of men down to match the average. If great vices emerged more openly than they did elsewhere in Europe, great qualities also had the opportunity of free development in heroes like Ferrucci, in saints like Savonarola, in artists like Michael Angelo. While the social atmosphere of the Papal and despotic courts was unfavourable to the highest type of character, we find at least no external engine of repression, no omnipotent inquisition, no overpowering aristocracy.[1] False political systems and a corrupt Church created a malaria, which poisoned the noble spirits of Machiavelli, Ariosto, Guicciardini, Giuliano della Rovere. It does not, however, follow therefore that the humanities of the race at large, in spite of superstition and bad government, were vitiated.

We have positive proofs to the contrary in the art of the Italians. The April freshness of Giotto, the piety of Fra

---

[1] I am of course speaking of the Renaissance as distinguished from that new phase of Italian history which followed the Council of Trent and the Spanish despotism.

Angelico, the virginal purity of the young Raphael, the sweet
gravity of John Bellini, the philosophic depth of Da Vinci,
the sublime elevation of Michael Angelo, the suavity of Fra
Bartolommeo, the delicacy of the Della Robbia, the restrained
fervour of Rosellini, the rapture of the Sienese and the reverence of the Umbrian masters, Francia's pathos, Mantegna's
dignity, and Luini's divine simplicity, were qualities which
belonged not only to these artists but also to the people of
Italy from whom they sprang. If men not few of whom were
born in cottages and educated in workshops could feel and
think and fashion as they did, we cannot doubt that their
mothers and their friends were pure and pious, and that the
race which gave them to the world was not depraved.
Painting in Italy, it must be remembered, was nearer to the
people than literature : it was less a matter of education than
instinct, a product of temperament rather than of culture.

   Italian art alone suffices to prove to my mind that the
immorality of the age descended from the upper stratum of
society downwards. Selfish Despots and luxurious priests
were the ruin of Italy ; and the bad qualities of the princes,
secular and ecclesiastical, found expression in the literature
of poets and humanists, their parasites. But in what other
nation of the fifteenth century can we show the same amount
of social urbanity and intellectual light diffused throughout all
classes from the highest to the lowest? It is true that the sixteenth century cast a blight upon their lustre. But it was not
until Italian taste had been impaired by the vices of Papal
Rome and by contact with the Spaniards that the arts became
either coarse or sensual. Giulio Romano (1492–1546) and
Benvenuto Cellini (1500–70) mark the beginning of the
change. In Ribera, a Spaniard, in Caravaggio, and in the
whole school of Bologna, it was accomplished. Yet never at
any period did the native Italian masters learn to love ugliness
with the devotion that reveals innate grossness. It remained

for Dürer, Rembrandt, and Hogarth to elevate the grotesque into the region of high art, for Rubens to achieve the apotheosis of pure animalism, for Teniers to devote distinguished genius to the service of the commonplace.

In any review of Italian religion and morality, however fragmentary it may be, as this indeed is, one feature which distinguishes the acute sensibility of the race ought not to be omitted. Deficient in profound intellectual convictions, incapable of a fixed and radical determination towards national holiness, devoid of those passionate and imaginative intuitions into the mysteries of the world which generate religions and philosophies, the Italians were at the same time keenly susceptible to the beauty of the Christian faith revealed to them by inspired orators. What we call Revivalism was an institution in Italy, which the Church was too wise to discountenance or to suppress, although the preachers of repentance were often insubordinate and sometimes even hostile to the Papal system. The names of Arnold of Brescia, San Bernardino of Siena, John of Vicenza, Jacopo Bussolari, Alberto da Lecce, Giovanni Capistrano, Jacopo della Marca, Girolamo Savonarola, bring before the memory of those who are acquainted with Italian history innumerable pictures of multitudes commoved to tears, of tyrannies destroyed and constitutions founded by tumultuous assemblies, of hostile parties and vindictive nobles locked in fraternal embraces, of cities clothed in sackcloth for their sins, of exhortations to peace echoing by the banks of rivers swollen with blood, of squares and hillsides resonant with sobs, of Lenten nights illuminated with bonfires of Vanity.[1] In the midst of these melodramatic scenes towers the single form of a Dominican or Franciscan friar: while one voice thundering woe or pleading peace dominates the crowd. Of the temporary effects

---

[1] I have thrown into an appendix some of the principal passages from the chronicles about revivals in mediæval Italy.

produced by these preachers there can be no question. The changes which they wrought in states and cities prove that the enthusiasm they aroused was more than merely hysterical. Savonarola, the greatest of the class, founded not only a transient commonwealth in Florence, but also a political party of importance, and left his lasting impress on the greatest soul of the sixteenth century in Italy—Michael Angelo Buonarroti. There was a real religious vigour in the people corresponding to the preacher's zeal. But the action of this earnest mood was intermittent and spasmodic. It coexisted with too much superstition and with passions too vehemently restless to form a settled tone of character. In this respect the Italian nation stands not extravagantly pictured in the life of Cellini, whose violence, self-indulgence, keen sense of pleasure, and pagan delight in physical beauty were interrupted at intervals by inexplicable interludes of repentance, Bible-reading, psalm-singing, and visions. To delineate Cellini will be the business of a distant chapter. The form of the greatest of Italian preachers must occupy the foreground of the next.

Before closing the imperfect and scattered notices collected in this chapter, it will be well to attempt some recapitulation of the points already suggested. Without committing ourselves to the dogmatism of a theory, we are led to certain general conclusions on the subject of Italian society in the sixteenth century. The fierce party quarrels which closed the Middle Ages had accustomed the population to violence, and this violence survived in the too frequent occurrence of brutal crimes. The artificial sovereignty of the Despots being grounded upon perfidy, it followed that guile and fraud came to be recognised in private no less than public life. With the emergence of the bourgeois classes a self-satisfied positivism, vividly portrayed in the person of Cosimo de' Medici, superseded the passions and enthusiasms of a previous age. Thus force, craft, and practical materialism formed the basis of Italian immorality. Vehement contention in the sphere of politics, restless speculation, together with the loosening of every tie that bound society together in the Middle Ages, emancipated personality and substituted the freedom of self-centred vigour and virility (*Virtù*) for the prescriptions of civil or religious order. In the nation that had shaken off both Papal and Imperial authority no conception of law remained to control caprice. Instead of law, men obeyed the instincts of their several characters, swayed by artistic taste or tyrannous appetite, or by the splendid heroism of extinct antiquity. The Church had alienated the people from true piety. Yet no new form of religious belief arose; and partly through respect for the past, partly through the convenience of clinging to existing institutions, Catholicism was indulgently tolerated. At the same time the humanists introduced an ideal antagonistic to Christianity of the monastic type. Without abruptly severing themselves from the communion of the Church, and while in form at least observing all its ordinances, they thought, wrote, spoke, felt, and acted like Pagans. To the hypocrisies of obsolete asceticism were added the affectations of anachronistic license. Meanwhile, the national genius for art attained its fullest development, simultaneously with the decay of faith, the extinction of political liberty, and the anarchy of ethics. So strong was the æsthetic impulse that it seemed for a while capable of drawing all the forces of the nation to itself. A society that rested upon force and fraud, corroded with cynicism, cankered with hypocrisy, recognising no standard apart from success in action and beauty in form, so conscious of its own corruption that it produced no satirist among the many who laughed lightly at its vices, wore the external aspect of exquisite refinement, and was delicately sensitive to every discord. Those who understood the contradictions of the age most deeply were the least capable of rising above them. Consequently we obtain in Machiavelli's works the ideal picture of personal character, moving to calculated ends by scientifically selected means, none of which are sanctioned by the unwritten code of law that governs human progress. Cosimo's positivism is reduced to theory. Fraud becomes a rule of conduct. Force is advocated, when the dagger or the poisoned draught or the extermination of a city may lead the individual straight forward to his object. Religion is shown to be a political engine. Hypocrisy is a mask that must be worn. The sanctities of ancient use and custom controlling appetite have no place assigned them in the system. Action is analysed as a branch of the fine arts; and the spirit of the age, of which the philosopher makes himself the hierophant, compels him to portray it as a sinister and evil art.

In the civilisation of Italy, carried prematurely beyond the conditions of the Middle Ages, before the institutions of mediævalism had been destroyed or its prejudices had been overcome, we everywhere discern the want of a co-ordinating principle. The old religion has died; but there is no new faith. The Communes have been proved inadequate; but there is no nationality. Practical positivism has obliterated the virtues of a chivalrous and feudal past; but science has not yet been born. Scholarship floods the world with the learning of antiquity; but this knowledge is still undigested. Art triumphs; but the æsthetic instinct has invaded the regions of politics and ethics, owing to defective analysis in theory, and in practice to over-confident reliance on personal ability. The individual has attained to freedom; but he has not learned the necessity of submitting his volition to law. At all points the development of the Italians strikes us as precocious, with the weakness of precocity scarcely distinguishable from the decay of old age. A transition from the point attained in the Renaissance to some firmer and more

solid ground was imperatively demanded. But the fatality of
events precluded the Italians from making it. Their evolution,
checked in mid career by the brilliant ambition of France
and the cautious reactionary despotism of Spain, remained
suspended. Students are left, face to face with the sixteenth
century, to decipher an inscription that lacks its leading
verb, to puzzle over a riddle whereof the solution is hidden
from us by the ruin of a people. It must ever be an
undecided question whether the Italians, undisturbed by
foreign interference, could have passed beyond the artificial
and exceptional stage of the Renaissance to a sounder and
more substantial phase of national vitality ; or whether, as
their inner conscience seems to have assured them, their
disengagement from moral obligation and their mental
ferment foreboded an inevitable catastrophe.

CHAPTER IX

SAVONAROLA

The Attitude of Savonarola toward the Renaissance—His Parentage, Birth, and Childhood at Ferrara—His Poem on the Ruin of the World—Joins the Dominicans at Bologna—Letter to his Father—Poem on the Ruin of the Church—Begins to preach in 1482—First Visit to Florence—San Gemignano—His Prophecy—Brescia in 1486—Personal Appearance and Style of Oratory—Effect on his Audience—The three Conclusions—His Visions—Savonarola's Shortcomings as a patriotic Statesman—His sincere Belief in his Prophetic Calling—Friendship with Pico della Mirandola—Settles in Florence, 1490—Convent of San Marco—Savonarola's Relation to Lorenzo de' Medici—The Death of Lorenzo—Sermons of 1493 and 1494—The Constitution of 1495—Theocracy in Florence—Piagnoni, Bigi, and Arrabbiati—War between Savonarola and Alexander VI.—The Signory suspends him from preaching in the Duomo in 1498—Attempts to call a Council—The Ordeal by Fire—San Marco stormed by the Mob—Trial and Execution of Savonarola.

NOTHING is more characteristic of the sharp contrasts of the Italian Renaissance than the emergence not only from the same society, but also from the bosom of the same Church, of two men so diverse as the Pope Alexander VI. and the Prophet Girolamo Savonarola. Savonarola has been claimed as a precursor of the Lutheran Reformers, and as an inspired exponent of the spirit of the fifteenth century. In reality he neither shared the revolutionary genius of Luther, which gave a new vitality to the faiths of Christendom, nor did he sympathise with that free movement of the modern mind which found its first expression in the arts and humanistic studies of Renaissance Italy. Both toward Renaissance and Reform he preserved the attitude of a monk, showing on the one hand an austere mistrust of pagan culture, and on the other no desire to alter either the creeds or the traditions of the Romish Church. Yet the history of Savonarola is not to be dissociated from that of the Italian Renaissance. He more clearly than any other man discerned the moral and political situation of his country. When all the states of Italy seemed sunk in peace and cradled in prosperity, he predicted war, and felt the imminence of overwhelming calamity. The purification of customs which he preached was demanded by the flagrant vices of the Popes and by the wickedness of the tyrants. The scourge which he prophesied did in fact descend upon Italy. In addition to this clairvoyance, by right of which we call him prophet, the hold he took on Florence at a critical moment of Italian history is alone enough to entitle him to more than merely passing notice.

Girolamo Savonarola was born at Ferrara in 1452.[1] His grandfather Michele, a Paduan of noble family, had removed to the capital of the Este princes at the beginning of the fifteenth century. There he held the office of court physician ; and Girolamo was intended for the same profession. But early in his boyhood the future prophet showed signs of disinclination for a worldly life, and an invincible dislike of the court. Under the House of Este, Ferrara was famous throughout Italy for its gaiety and splendour. No city enjoyed more brilliant and more frequent public shows. Nowhere did the aristocracy maintain so much of feudal magnificence and chivalrous enjoyment. The square castle of red brick, which still stands in the middle of the town, was thronged with poets, players, fools who enjoyed an almost European reputation, court flatterers, knights, pages, scholars, and fair ladies. But beneath its cube of solid masonry, on a

[1] In this chapter on Savonarola I have made use of Villari's *Life* (translated by Leonard Horner, Longmans, 1863, 2 vols.), Michelet's *Histoire de France*, vol. vii., Milman's article on Savonarola (John Murray, 1870), Nardi's *Istoria Fiorentina*, book ii., and the *Memoirs* of De Comines.

level with the moat, shut out from daylight by a sevenfold series of iron bars, lay dungeons in which the objects of the Duke's displeasure clanked chains and sighed their lives away.[1] Within the precincts of this palace the young Savonarola learned to hate alike the worldly vices and the despotic cruelty against which in after-life he prophesied and fought unto the death.

Of his boyhood we know but little. His biographers only tell us that he was grave and solitary, frequenting churches, praying with passionate persistence, obstinately refusing, though otherwise docile, to join his father in his visits to the court. Aristotle and S. Thomas Aquinas seem to have been the favourite masters of his study. In fact he refused the new lights of the humanists, and adhered to the ecclesiastical training of the schoolmen. Already at the age of twenty we find him composing a poem in Italian on the Ruin of the World, in which he cries : 'The whole world is in confusion ; all virtue is extinguished, and all good manners ; I find no living light abroad, nor one who blushes for his vices.' His point of departure had been taken, and the keynote of his life had been struck. The sense of intolerable sin that came upon him in Ferrara haunted him through manhood, set his hand against the Popes and Despots of Italy, and gave peculiar tone to his prophetic utterances.

The attractions of the cloister, as a refuge from the storms of the world, and as a rest from the torments of the sins of others, now began to sway his mind.[2] But he communicated his desire to no one. It would have grieved his father and his mother to find that their son, who was, they hoped, to be a shining light at the court of Ferrara, had

[1] See p. 332.

[2] Often in later life Savonarola cried that he had sought the cloister to find rest, but that God had chosen, instead of bringing him into calm waters, to cast him on a tempest-swollen sea. See the Sermon quoted by Villari, vol. i. p. 298.

determined to assume the cowl. At length, however, came
the time at which he felt that leave the world he must. 'It was
on the 23rd of April, 1475,' says Villari; 'he was sitting with
his lute and playing a sad melody; his mother, as if moved
by a spirit of divination, turned suddenly round to him, and
exclaimed mournfully, My son, that is a sign we are soon to
part. He roused himself, and continued, but with a trembling
hand, to touch the strings of the lute, without raising his
eyes from the ground.' This would make a picture; spring
twilight in the quaint Italian room, with perhaps a branch of
fig-tree or of bay across the open window; the mother looking
up with anxious face from her needlework; the youth,
dressed almost for the last time in secular attire, with those
terrible eyes and tense lips and dilated nostrils of the future
prophet, not yet worn by years of care, but strongly marked
and unmistakable, bending over the melancholy chords of
the lute.

On the very next day Girolamo left Ferrara in secret and
journeyed to Bologna. There he entered the order of S.
Dominic, the order of the Preachers, the order of his master
S. Thomas, the order too, let us remember, of inquisitorial
crusades. The letter written to his father after taking this
step is memorable. In it he says: 'The motives by which I
have been led to enter into a religious life are these: the great
misery of the world; the iniquities of men, their rapes,
adulteries, robberies, their pride, idolatry, and fearful blas-
phemies: so that things have come to such a pass that no
one can be found acting righteously. Many times a day
have I repeated with tears the verse:

Heu, fuge crudeles terras, fuge littus avarum!

I could not endure the enormous wickedness of the blinded
people of Italy; and the more so because I saw everywhere
virtue despised and vice honoured.' We see clearly that

Savonarola's vocation took its origin in a deep sense of the wickedness of the world. It was the same spirit as that which drove the early Christians of Alexandria into the Thebaid. Austere and haggard, consumed with the zeal of the Lord, he had moved long enough among the Ferrarese holiday-makers. Those elegant young men in tight hose and particoloured jackets, with oaths upon their lips and deeds of violence and lust within their hearts, were no associates for him. It is touching, however, to note that no text of Ezekiel or Jeremiah, but Virgil's musical hexameter, sounded through his soul the warning to depart.

In this year Savonarola composed another poem: this time on the Ruin of the Church. In his boyhood he had witnessed the pompous shows which greeted Æneas Sylvius, more like a Roman general than a new-made Pope, on his entrance into Ferrara. Since then he had seen the monster Sixtus mount the Papal throne. No wonder if he, who had fled from the world to the Church for purity and peace, should need to vent his passion in a song. 'Where,' he cries, 'are the doctors of old times, the saints, the learning, charity, chastity of the past?' The Church answers by displaying her rent raiment and wounded body, and by pointing to the cavern in which she has to make her home. 'Who,' exclaims the poet, 'has wrought this wrong?' *Una fallace, superba meretrice*—Rome! Then indeed the passion of the novice breaks in fire:—

> Deh! per Dio, donna,
> Se romper si potria quelle grandi ale!

The Church replies:—

> Tu piangi e taci: e questo meglio parmi.

No other answer could be given to Savonarola's impatient yearnings even by his own hot heart, while he yet remained a young and unknown monk in Bologna. Nor, strive as he might strive through all his life, was it granted to him to break those outspread wings of arrogant Rome.

The career of Savonarola as a preacher began in 1482, when he was sent first to Ferrara and then to Florence on missions by his superiors. But at neither place did he find acceptance. A prophet has no honour in his own country; and for pagan-hearted Florence, though destined to be the theatre of his life-drama, Savonarola had as yet no thundrous burden of invective to utter. Besides, his voice was sharp and thin; his face and person were not prepossessing. The style of his discourse was adapted to cloistral disputations, and overloaded with scholastic distinctions. The great orator had not yet arisen in him. The friar, with all his dryness and severity, was but too apparent. With what strange feelings must the youth have trodden the streets of Florence! In after-days he used to say he foreknew those streets and squares were destined to be the scene of his labours. But then, voiceless, powerless, without control of his own genius, without the consciousness of his prophetic mission, he brooded alone and out of harmony with the beautiful and mundane city. The charm of the hills and gardens of Valdarno, the loveliness of Giotto's tower, the amplitude of Brunelleschi's dome—these may have sunk deep into his soul. And the subtle temper of the Florentine intellect must have attracted his own keen spirit by a secret sympathy. For Florence ere long became the city of his love, the first-born of his yearnings.

In the cloisters of San Marco, enriched with splendid libraries by the liberality of the Medicean princes, he was at peace. The walls of that convent had recently been decorated with frescoes by Fra Angelico, even as a man might crowd the leaves of a missal with illuminations. Among these Savonarola meditated and was happy. But in the pulpit and in contact with the holiday folk of Florence he was ill at ease. Lorenzo de' Medici overshadowed the whole city.

Lorenzo, in whom the pagan spirit of the Renaissance, the spirit of free culture, found a proper incarnation, was the very opposite of Savonarola, who had already judged the classical revival by its fruits, and had conceived a spiritual resurrection for his country. At Florence a passionate love of art and learning—the enthusiasm which prompted men to spend their fortunes upon MSS. and statues, the sensibility to beauty which produced the masterworks of Donatello and Ghiberti, the thirst for knowledge which burned in Pico and Poliziano and Ficino—existed side by side with impudent immorality, religious deadness, cold contempt for truth, and cynical admiration of successful villany. Both the good and the evil which flourished on this fertile soil so luxuriantly were combined in the versatile genius of the merchant prince, whose policy it was to stifle freedom by caressing the follies, vices, and intellectual tastes of his people.

The young Savonarola was as yet no match for Lorenzo. And whither could he look for help? The reform of morals he so ardently desired was not to be expected from the Church. Florence well knew that Sixtus had plotted to murder the Medici before the altar at the moment of the elevation of the Host. Excommunicated for a deed of justice after the failure of this Popish plot, the city had long been at war with the pontiff. If anywhere it was in the cells of the philosophers, in that retreat where Ficino burned his lamp to Plato, in that hall where the Academy crowned their master's bust with laurels, that the more sober-minded citizens found ghostly comfort and advice. But from this philosophy the fervent soul of Savonarola turned with no less loathing, and with more contempt, than from the Canti Carnascialeschi and Aristophanic pageants of Lorenzo, which made Florence at Carnival time affect the fashions of Athens during the Dionysia. It is true that Italy owed much to the elevated theism developed by Platonic students. While the humanists were exalting pagan license, and while the Church was teaching the worst kinds of immorality, the philosophers kept alive in cultivated minds a sense of God.

But the monk, nourished on the Bible and S. Thomas, valued this confusion of spirits and creeds in a chaos of indiscriminate erudition at a small price. He had the courage in the fifteenth century at Florence to proclaim that the philosophers were in hell, and that an old woman knew more of saving faith than Plato. Savonarola and Lorenzo were opposed as champions of two hostile principles alike emergent from the very life of the Renaissance: paganism reborn in the one, the spirit of the gospel in the other. Both were essentially modern; for it was the function of the Renaissance to restore to the soul of man its double heritage of the classic past and Christian liberty, freeing it from the fetters which the Middle Ages had forged. Not yet, however, were Lorenzo and Savonarola destined to clash. The obscure friar at this time was preaching to an audience of some thirty persons in San Lorenzo, while Poliziano and all the fashion of the town crowded to the sermons of Fra Mariano da Genezzano in Santo Spirito. This man flattered the taste of the moment by composing orations on the model of Ficino's addresses to the Academy, and by complimenting Christianity upon its similarity to Platonism. Who could then have guessed that beneath the cowl of the harsh-voiced Dominican, his rival, burned thoughts that in a few years would inflame Florence with a conflagration powerful enough to destroy the fabric of the Medicean despotism?

From Florence, where he had met with no success, Savonarola was sent to San Gemignano, a little town on the top of a high hill between Florence and Siena. We now visit San Gemignano in order to study some fading frescoes of Gozzoli and Ghirlandajo, or else for the sake of its strange feudal towers, tall pillars of brown stone, crowded together within the narrow circle of the town walls. Very beautiful is the prospect from these ramparts on a spring morning, when the song of nightingales and the scent of acacia flowers ascend together from the groves upon the slopes beneath. The grey Tuscan landscape for scores and scores of miles all round melts into blueness, like the blueness of the sky, flecked here and there with wandering cloud-shadows. Let those who pace the grass-grown streets of the hushed city remember that here the first flash of authentic genius kindled in Savonarola's soul. Here for the first time he prophesied: 'The church will be scourged, then regenerated, and this quickly.' These are the celebrated three conclusions, the three points to which Savonarola in all his prophetic utterances adhered.

But not yet had he fully entered on his vocation. His voice was weak; his style uncertain; his soul, we may believe, still wavering between strange dread and awful joy, as he beheld, through many a backward rolling mist of doubt, the mantle of the prophets descend upon him. Already he had abandoned the schoolmen for the Bible. Already he had learned by heart each verse of the Old and New Testaments. Pondering on their texts, he had discovered four separate interpretations for every suggestion of Sacred Writ. For some of the pregnant utterances of the prophets he found hundreds, pouring forth metaphor and illustration in wild and dazzling profusion of audacious, uncouth imagery. The flame which began to smoulder in him at San Gemignano burst forth into a blaze at Brescia, in 1486. Savonarola was now aged thirty-four. 'Midway upon the path of life' he opened the Book of Revelation: he figured to the people of Brescia the four-and-twenty elders rising to denounce the sins of Italy, and to declare the calamities that must ensue. He pictured to them their city flowing with blood. His voice, which now became the interpreter of his soul, in its resonance

and earnestness and piercing shrillness, thrilled his hearers
with strange terror. Already they believed his prophecy;
and twenty-six years later, when the soldiers of Gaston de
Foix slaughtered six thousand souls in the streets of Brescia,
her citizens recalled the Apocalyptic warnings of the Dominican monk.

As Savonarola is now launched upon his vocation of prophecy, this is the right moment to describe his personal
appearance and his style of preaching. We have abundant
material for judging what his features were, and how they
flashed beneath the storm of inspiration.[1] Fra Bartolommeo,
one of his followers, painted a profile of him in the character
of S. Peter Martyr. This shows all the benignity and grace
of expression which his stern lineaments could assume. It is
a picture of the sweet and gentle nature latent within the
fiery arraigner of his nation at the bar of God. In contemporary medals the face appears hard, keen, uncompro-
mising, beneath its heavy cowl. But the noblest portrait is
an intaglio engraved by Giovanni della Corniole, now to
be seen in the Uffizzi at Florence. Of this work Michael
Angelo, himself a disciple of Savonarola, said that art could
go no further. We are therefore justified in assuming that
the engraver has not only represented faithfully the outline
of Savonarola's face, but has also indicated his peculiar expression. A thick hood covers the whole head and shoulders.
Beneath it can be traced the curve of a long and somewhat
flat skull, rounded into extraordinary fulness at the base and
side. From a deeply sunken eye-socket emerges, scarcely
seen, but powerfully felt, the eye that blazed with lightning.
The nose is strong, prominent, and aquiline, with wide
nostrils, capable of terrible dilation under the stress of

[1] Engravings of the several portraits may be seen in Harford's
Life of Michael Angelo Buonarroti (Longmans, 1857, vol. i.), and
also in Villari.

vehement emotion. The mouth has full, compressed, projecting lips. It is large, as if made for a torrent of eloquence : it is supplied with massive muscles, as if to move with energy and calculated force and utterance. The jawbone is hard and heavy ; the cheek-bone emergent : between the two the flesh is hollowed, not so much with the emaciation of monastic vigils as with the athletic exercise of wrestlings in the throes of prophecy. The face, on the whole, is ugly, but not repellent ; and, in spite of its great strength, it shows signs of feminine sensibility. Like the faces of Cicero and Demosthenes, it seems the fit machine for oratory. But the furnaces hidden away behind that skull, beneath that cowl, have made it haggard with a fire not to be found in the serener features of the classic orators. Savonarola was a visionary and a monk. The discipline of the cloister left its trace upon him. The wings of dreams have winnowed and withered that cheek as they passed over it. The spirit of prayer quivers upon those eager lips. The colour of Savonarola's flesh was brown : his nerves were exquisitely sensitive yet strong ; like a network of wrought steel, elastic, easily overstrained, they recovered their tone and temper less by repose than by the evolution of fresh electricity. With Savonarola fasts were succeeded by trances, and trances by tempests of vehement improvisation. From the midst of such profound debility that he could scarcely crawl up the pulpit steps, he would pass suddenly into the plenitude of power, filling the Dome of Florence with denunciations, sustaining his discourse by no mere trick of rhetoric that flows to waste upon the lips of shallow preachers, but marshalling the phalanx of embattled arguments and pointed illustrations, pouring his thought forth in columns of continuous flame, mingling figures of sublimest imagery with reasonings of severest accuracy, at one time melting his audience to tears, at another freezing them with terror, again quickening their souls with prayers and pleadings and

blessings that had in them the sweetness of the very spirit
of Christ.   His sermons began with scholastic exposition ; as
they advanced, the ecstasy of inspiration fell upon the
preacher, till the sympathies of the whole people of Florence
gathered round him,[1] met, and attained, as it were, to single
consciousness in him.   He then no longer restrained the impulse of his oratory, but became the mouthpiece of God, the
interpreter to themselves of all that host. In a fiery crescendo,
never flagging, never losing firmness of grasp or lucidity of
vision, he ascended the altar steps of prophecy, and, standing
like Moses on the mount between the thunders of God and
the tabernacles of the plain, fulminated period after period of
impassioned eloquence.   The walls of the church re-echoed
with sobs and wailings dominated by one ringing voice.   The
scribe to whom we owe the fragments of these sermons, at
times breaks off with these words : ' Here I was so overcome
with weeping that I could not go on.'   Pico della Mirandola
tells us that the mere sound of Savonarola's voice, startling
the stillness of the Duomo, thronged through all its space
with people, was like a clap of doom : a cold shiver ran
through the marrow of his bones, the hairs of his head stood
on end, as he listened.   Another witness reports : ' These
sermons caused such terror, alarm, sobbing, and tears that
everyone passed through the streets without speaking, more
dead than alive.'

Such was the preacher : and such was the effect of his
oratory. The theme on which he loved to dwell was this.

[1] Nardi, in his *Istorie di Firenze* (lib. ii. cap. 16), describes the
crowd assembled in the Duomo to hear Savonarola preach : ' Per la
moltitudine degli uditori non essendo quasi bastante la chiesa cattedrale
di santa Maria del Fiore, ancora che molto grande e capace sia, fu
necessario edificar dentro lungo i pareti di quella, dirimpetto al pergamo,
certi gradi di legname rilevati con ordine di sederi, a guisa di teatro, e
così dalla parte di sopra all' entrata del coro e dalla parte di sotto in
verso le porte della detta chiesa.'

Repent! A judgment of God is at hand. A sword is suspended over you. Italy is doomed for her iniquity—for the sins of the Church, whose adulteries have filled the world—for the sins of the tyrants, who encourage crime and trample upon souls—for the sins of you people, you fathers and mothers, you young men, you maidens, you children that lisp blasphemy! Nor did Savonarola deal in generalities. He described in plain language every vice; he laid bare every abuse; so that a mirror was held up to the souls of his hearers, in which they saw their most secret faults appallingly portrayed and ringed around with fire. He entered with particularity into the details of the coming woes. One by one he enumerated the bloodshed, the ruin of cities, the trampling down of provinces, the passage of armies, the desolating wars that were about to fall on Italy.[1] You may read pages of his sermons which seem like vivid narratives of what afterwards took place in the sack of Prato, in the storming of Brescia, in the battle of the Ronco, in the cavern-massacre of Vicenza. No wonder that he stirred his audience to their centre. The hell within them was revealed. The coming doom above them was made manifest. Ezekiel and Jeremiah were not more prophetic. John crying to a generation of vipers,

[1] Savonarola's whole view of the situation and of the perils of Italy was that of a prophet. He saw more clearly than other people what was inevitable. But his disciples and the vulgar believed implicitly in his prophetic gift in the narrower sense, that is, in his power to predict events, such as the deaths of Lorenzo and the King of Naples, the punishment of Charles VIII. in the loss of the dauphin, &c. Pico says: 'Savonarola could read the future as clearly as one sees the whole is greater than the part.' And there is no doubt that, as time went on, Savonarola himself came to believe that he possessed this faculty. After his trial and execution a very uncomfortable sense of doubt remained upon the minds of those who had been witnesses of his life-drama. Upon this topic Guicciardini, *Stor. Fior.*, *Op. Ined.* vol. iii. p. 179; Nardi, *Stor. Fior.* lib. ii. caps. 16 and 36, may be read with advantage.

'Repent ye, for the kingdom of heaven is at hand!' was not more weighty with the mission of authentic inspiration.

'I began'—Savonarola himself writes with reference to a course of sermons delivered in 1491—'I began publicly to expound the Revelation in our Church of S. Mark. During the course of the year I continued to develop to the Florentines these three propositions: That the Church would be renewed in our time; that before that renovation God would strike all Italy with a fearful chastisement; that these things would happen shortly.' It is by right of the foresight of a new age contained in these three famous so-called conclusions that Savonarola deserves to be named the Prophet of the Renaissance. He was no apostle of reform: it did not occur to him to reconstruct the creed, to dispute the discipline, or to criticise the authority of the Church. He was no founder of a new order: unlike his predecessors, Dominic and Francis, he never attempted to organise a society of saints or preachers; unlike his successors, Caraffa the Theatine and Loyola the Jesuit, he enrolled no militia for the defence of the faith, constructed no machinery for education. Starting with simple horror at the wickedness of the world, he had recourse to the old prophets. He steeped himself in Bible studies. He caught the language of Malachi and Jeremiah. He became convinced that for the wickedness of Italy a judgment was imminent. From that conclusion he rose upon the wings of faith to the belief that a new age would dawn. The originality of his intuition consisted in this, that while Italy was asleep, and no man trembled for the future, he alone felt that the stillness of the air was fraught with thunder, that its tranquillity was like that which precedes a tempest blown from the very nostrils of the God of Hosts.

To the astonishment of his hearers, and perhaps also of himself, his prophecies began to fulfil themselves. Within three years after his first sermon in S. Mark's, Charles VIII.

had entered Italy, Lorenzo de' Medici was dead, and politicians no less than mystics felt that a new chapter had been opened in the book of the world's history.   The Reform of the Church was also destined to follow.   What Savonarola had foreseen, here too happened ; but not in the way he would have wished, nor by the means he would have used.   It is one thing to be a prophet in the sense of discerning the catastrophe to which circumstances must inevitably lead, another thing to trace beforehand the path which will be taken by the hurricanes that change the face of the world.   Remaining in his soul a monk, attached by education and by natural sympathy to the past rather than the future, he felt in spite of himself the spirit of the coming age.   Had he lived but one century earlier, we should not have called him prophet.   It was the Renaissance which set the seal of truth upon his utterances.   Yet in his vision of the world to be, he was like Balaam prophesying blindly of a star.

Sixtus IV. had died and been succeeded by Innocent VIII. Innocent had given place to Alexander.   The very nadir of the abyss had been reached.   Then Savonarola saw a vision and heard a voice : *Ecce gladius Domini super terram cito et velociter.*   The sword turned earthward ; the air was darkened with fiery sleet and arrows ; thunders rolled ; the world was filled with pestilences, wars, famines.   At another time he dreamed and looked toward Rome.   From the Eternal City there rose a black cross, reaching to heaven, and on it was inscribed *Crux iræ Dei.*   Then too the skies were troubled ; clouds rushed through the air discharging darts and fire and swords, and multitudes below were dying.   These visions he published in sermons and in print.   Pictures were made from them.   They and the three conclusions went abroad through Italy.   Again, Charles was preparing for his expedition. Savonarola took the Ark of Noah for his theme.   The deluge was at hand ; he bade his hearers enter the ship of refuge

before the terrible and mighty nation came : ' O Italy ! O
Rome ! I give you over to the hands of a people who will wipe
you out from among the nations ! I see them descending like
lions. Pestilence comes marching hand in hand with war.
The deaths will be so many that the buriers shall go through
the streets crying out : Who hath dead, who hath dead ? and
one will bring his father, and another his son. O Rome ! I
cry again to you to repent ! Repent, Venice ! Milan, repent !'
' The prophets a hundred years ago proclaimed to you the
flagellation of the Church. For five years I have been announcing it : and now again I cry to you. The Lord is full
of wrath. The angels on their knees cry to Him : Strike,
strike ! The good sob and groan : We can no more. The
orphans, the widows say : We are devoured, we cannot go on
living. All the Church triumphant hath cried to Christ :
Thou diedst in vain. It is heaven which is in combat. The
saints of Italy, the angels, are leagued with the barbarians.
Those who called them in have put the saddles to the horses.
Italy is in confusion, saith the Lord ; this time she shall be
yours. And the Lord cometh above his saints, above the
blessed ones who march in battle-array, who are drawn up in
squadrons. Whither are they bound ? S. Peter is for Rome,
crying : To Rome, to Rome ! and S. Paul and S. Gregory
march, crying : To Rome ! And behind them go the sword,
the pestilence, the famine. S. John cries : Up, up, to
Florence ! And the plague follows him. S. Anthony cries :
Ho for Lombardy ! S. Mark cries : Haste we to the city that
is throned upon the waters ! And all the angels of heaven,
sword in hand, and all the celestial consistory, march on unto
this war.'

Then he speaks of his own fate : ' What shall be the end
of our war, you ask ? If this be a general question, I shall
answer Victory ! If you ask it of myself in particular, I
answer, Death, or to be hewn in pieces. This is our faith,

this is our guerdon, this is our reward! We ask for no more than this. But when you see me dead, be not then troubled. All those who have prophesied have suffered and been slain. To make my word prevail, there is needed the blood of many.'

These are the prophecies with which Savonarola anticipated the coming of a foreign conqueror. It is interesting to trace in his apostrophes the double feeling of the prophet. Desire for the advent of Charles as a Messiah, liberator, and purifier of the Church, contends with an instinctive horror of the barbarian. Savonarola, like Dante, like all Italian patriots, except only Machiavelli, who too late had been lessoned by bitter experience to put no trust in foreign princes, could not refrain from hoping even against hope that good might come from beyond the Alps. Yet when the foreigners appeared, he trembled at the violence they wrought upon the ancient liberties of Italy. Savonarola's chief shortcoming as a patriot consisted in this, that he strengthened the old folly of the Florentines in leaning upon strangers.[1] Had he taught the Italians to work out their self-regeneration from within, instead of preparing them to accept an alien's yoke, he would have won a far more lasting meed of fame. As it was, together with the passion for liberty which became a religion with his followers, he strove to revive the obsolete tactics of an earlier age, and bequeathed to Florence the weak policy of waiting upon France. This legacy bore bitter fruits in the next century. If it was the memory of the Friar which nerved the citizens of Florence to sustain the siege of 1528, the same memory bound them to seek aid from inconsequent Francis, and to hope that at the last moment a cohort of seraphim would defend their walls.[2]

[1] Segni, *Ist. Fior.* lib. i. p. 23, records a saying of Savonarola's, *Gigli con gigli dover fiorire*, as one of the causes of the obstinate French partiality of the Florentines in 1529.

[2] See Varchi, Segni, and Nardi, who agree on these points.

That Savonarola believed in his own prophecies there is no doubt. They were in fact, as I have already tried to show, a view of the political and moral situation of Italy, expressed with the force of profound religious conviction and based upon a theory of the divine government of the world. But how far he allowed himself to be guided by visions and by words uttered to his soul in trance, is a somewhat different question. It is just at this point that a man possessed of acute insight and trusting to the truth of his instincts may be tempted under strong devotional excitement to pass the border land which separates healthy intuition from hallucination. If Savonarola's studies of the Hebrew prophets inclined him to believe in dreams and revelations, yet on the other hand the strong logic of his intellect, trained in scholastic distinctions, taught him to mistrust the promptings of a power that spoke to him when he was somewhat more or less than his prosaic self. How could he be sure that the spirit came from God? We know for certain that he struggled against the impulse of divination and refused at times to obey it. But it overcame him. Like the Cassandra of Æschylus, he panted in the grasp of one mightier than himself. 'An inward fire,' he cried, ' consumes my bones and forces me to speak out.' And again : 'I have, O Lord, burnt my wings of contemplation, and I have launched into a tempestuous sea, where I have found contrary winds in every quarter. I wished to reach a harbour, but could not find the way thither ; I wished to lay me down, but could meet with no resting-place. I longed to be silent and to utter not a word. But the word of the Lord is in my heart; and if it does not come forth, it must consume the marrow of my bones. Thus, O Lord, if it be Thy will that I should navigate in deep waters, Thy will be done.'

At another time he says: 'I remember well that upon one occasion, in the year 1491, when I was preaching in the

Duomo, having composed my sermon entirely upon these visions, I determined to abstain from all allusion to them, and in future to adhere to this resolution. God is my witness that the whole of Saturday and the whole of the succeeding night I lay awake, and could see no other course, no other doctrine. At daybreak, worn out and depressed by the many hours I had lain awake, while I was praying I heard a voice that said to me : " Fool that thou art, dost thou not see that it is God's will that thou shouldst keep to the same path ? " The consequence of which was that on the same day I preached a tremendous sermon.'

These passages leave upon the mind no doubt of Savonarola's sincerity. If he deceived others, he was himself the first to be deceived, and that too not before he had subjected himself to the most searching examination, seeking in vain to escape from the force which compelled him to play the part of prophet. Terrible, indeed, must have been the wrestlings and the questionings of this strong-fibred intellect, alone and diffident, within the toils of ecstasy.

Returning to the details of Savonarola's biography, we find him still in Lombardy in 1486. After leaving Brescia he moved to Reggio, where he made the friendship of the famous Giovanni Pico della Mirandola. They continued intimate till the death of the latter in 1494 ; it was his nephew, Giovanni Francesco Pico della Mirandola, who afterwards wrote the Life of Savonarola. From Reggio the friar went to Genoa ; and by this time his fame as a prophet in the north of Lombardy was well established. Now came the turning point in his life. Fourteen hundred and ninety is the date which determined his public action as a man of power in Italy. Lorenzo de' Medici, strangely enough, was the instrument of his recall in this year to Florence. Lorenzo, who, if he could have foreseen the future of his own family in Florence, would rather have stifled this monk's voice in his cowl, took pains

to send for him and bring him to S. Mark's, the convent
upon which his father had lavished so much wealth. He
hoped to add lustre to his capital by the preaching of the most
eloquent friar in Italy. Clear-sighted as he was, he could not
discern the flame of liberty which burned in Savonarola's
soul. Savonarola, the democratic party leader, was a force in
politics as incalculable beforehand as Ferrucci the hero. On
August 1, 1490, the monk ascended the pulpit of S. Mark's,
and delivered a tremendous sermon on a passage from the
Apocalypse. On the eve of this commencement he is reported
to have said : ' To-morrow I shall begin to preach, and I shall
preach for eight years.' The Florentines were greatly moved.
Savonarola had to remove from the Church of S. Mark to
the Duómo ; and thus began the spiritual dictatorship which
he exercised thenceforth without intermission till his death.

Lorenzo soon began to resent the influence of this un-
compromising monk, who, not content with moral exhortations, confidently predicted the coming of a foreign conqueror,
the fall of the Magnificent, the peril of the Pope, and the
ruin of the King of Naples. Yet it was no longer easy to
suppress the preacher. Very early in his Florentine career
Savonarola had proved himself to be fully as great an
administrator as an orator. The Convent of San Marco,
dominated by his personal authority, had made him Prior in
1491, and he was already engaged in a thorough reform of all
the Dominican monasteries of Tuscany. It was usual for the
Priors elect of S. Mark to pay a complimentary visit to the
Medici, their patrons. Savonarola, thinking this a worldly
and unseemly custom, omitted to observe it. Lorenzo,
noticing the discourtesy, is reported to have said, with a
smile : ' See now ! here is a stranger who has come into *my
house*, and will not deign to visit me.' He forgot that
Savonarola looked upon his convent as a house of God. At
the same time the prince made overtures of good-will to the

Prior, frequently attended his services, and dropped gold into the alms-box of S. Mark's. Savonarola took no notice of him, and handed his florins over to the poor of the city. Then Lorenzo stirred up Fra Mariano da Genezzano, Savonarola's old rival, against him; but the clever rhetorician was no longer a match for the full-grown athlete of inspired eloquence. Da Genezzano was forced to leave Florence in angry discomfiture. With such unbending haughtiness did Savonarola already dare to brave the powers that be. He had recognised the oppressor of liberty, the corrupter of morality, the opponent of true religion, in Lorenzo. He hated him as a tyrant. He would not give him the right hand of friendship or the salute of civility. In the same spirit he afterwards denounced Alexander, scorned his excommunication, and plotted with the kings of Christendom for the convening of a Council. Lorenzo, however, was a man of supreme insight into character, and knew how to value his antagonist. Therefore, when the hour for dying came, and when, true child of the Renaissance that he was, he felt the need of sacraments and absolution, he sent for Savonarola, saying that he was the only honest friar he knew. The magnanimity of the Medici was only equalled by the firmness of the monk. Standing by the bedside of the dying man, who had confessed his sins, Savonarola said: 'Three things are required of you: to have a full and lively faith in God's mercy; to restore what you have unjustly gained; to give back liberty to Florence.' Lorenzo assented readily to the first and second requisitions. At the third he turned his face in silence to the wall. He must indeed have felt that to demand and promise this was easier than to carry it into effect. Savonarola left him without absolution. Lorenzo died.[1]

[1] It is just to observe that great doubt has been thrown on the facts above related concerning Lorenzo's death. Poliziano, who was with Lorenzo during his last illness, does not mention them in his letter to

The third point insisted upon by the friar, Restore liberty to Florence, not only broke the peace of the dying prince, but it also afterwards for ever ruled the conduct of Savonarola. From this time his life is that of a statesman no less than of a preacher. What Lorenzo refused, or was indeed upon his deathbed quite unable to perform, the monk determined to achieve. Henceforth he became the champion of popular liberty in the pulpit. Feeling that in the people alone lay any hope of regeneration for Italy, he made it the work of his whole life to give the strength and sanction of religion to republican freedom. This work he sealed with martyrdom. The spirit of the creed which he bequeathed to his partisans in Florence was political no less than pious. Whether Savonarola was right to embark upon the perilous sea of statecraft cannot now be questioned. What prophet of Israel from Samuel to Isaiah was not the maker and destroyer of kings and constitutions? When we call him by their title, we mean to say that he, like them, controlled by spiritual force the fortunes of his people. Whether he sought it or not, this rôle of politician was thrust upon him by the course of events: nor was the history of Italian cities defi-

Jacobus Antiquarius (xv. Kal. Jun. 1492). But Burlamacchi, Pico, Barsanti, Razzi, and others of the Frate's party, agree in the story. What Poliziano wrote was that Savonarola confessed Lorenzo and retired without volunteering the blessing. Razzi says the interview between Savonarola and Lorenzo took place without witnesses; Pico and Burlamacchi relate the event as they heard of it from the lips of Savonarola. We have therefore to judge between the testimony of Poliziano, who held no communication with the friar, and the veracity of several narrators, biassed indeed by hostility toward the Medici, but in direct intercourse with the only man who could tell the exact truth of what passed—the confessor, Savonarola, who had been alone with Lorenzo. Villari, after sifting the evidence, arrives at the conclusion that we may believe Burlamacchi. The Baron Reumont, in his recent *Life of Lorenzo*, vol. ii. p. 590, gives some solid reasons for accepting this conclusion with caution, and Gino Capponi expresses a distinct disbelief in Burlamacchi's narration.

cient in precedents of similar functions assumed by preaching friars.[1]

To Lorenzo succeeded the incompetent Piero de' Medici, who surrendered the fortresses of Tuscany to the French army. While Savonarola was prophesying a sword, a scourge, a deluge, Charles VIII. rode at the head of his knighthood into Florence. The city was leaderless, unused to liberty. Who but the monk who had predicted the invasion should now attempt to control it? Who but he whose voice alone should have power to assemble and to sway the Florentines should now direct them? His administrative faculty in a narrow sphere had been proved by his reform of the Dominican Convents. His divine mission was authenticated by the arrival of the French. The Lord had raised him up to act as well as to utter. He felt this: the people felt it. He was not the man to refuse responsibility.

During the years of 1493 and 1494, when Florence together with Italy was in imminent peril, the voice of Savonarola never ceased to ring. His sermons on the psalm 'Quam bonus' and on the Ark of Noah are among the most stupendous triumphs of his eloquence. From his pulpit beneath the sombre dome of Brunelleschi he kept pouring forth words of power to resuscitate the free spirit of his Florentines. In 1495, when the Medici had been expelled and the French army had gone upon its way to Naples, Savonarola was called upon to reconstitute the state. He bade the people abandon their old system of Parlamenti and Balia, and establish a Grand Council after the Venetian type.[2] This

[1] It is enough to allude to Arnold of Brescia in Rome, to Fra Bussolari in Pavia, and to John of Vicenza. See Appendix iv.

[2] This change was certainly wrought out by the influence of the friar and approved by him. Segni, lib. i. p. 15, speaks clearly on the point, and says that the friar for this service to the city 'debbe esser messo tra buoni datori di leggi, e debbe essere amato e onorato da' Fiorentini non altrimenti che Numa dai Romani e Solone dagli Ateniesi

institution, which seemed to the Florentines the best they
had ever adopted, may be regarded by the historian as only
one among their many experiments in constitution-making,
if Savonarola had not stamped it with his peculiar genius by
announcing that Christ was to be considered the Head of the
State.[1]   This step at once gave a theocratic bias to the
government, which determined all the acts of the monk's
administration.   Not content with political organisation, too
impatient to await the growth of good manners from sound
institutions, he set about a moral and religious reformation.   Pomps, vanities, and vices were to be abandoned.
Immediately the women and the young men threw aside their
silks and fine attire.   The Carnival songs ceased.   Hymns
and processions took the place of obscene choruses and pagan
triumphs.   The laws were remodelled in the same severe and
abrupt spirit.   Usury was abolished.   Whatever Savonarola

e Licurgo da' Lacedemoni.'   The evil of the old system was that the
Parlamento, which consisted of the citizens assembled in the Piazza,
was exposed to intimidation, and had no proper initiative, while the
Balia, or select body, to whom they then entrusted plenipotentiary
authority, was always the faction for the moment uppermost.   For the
mode of working the Parlamento and Balia see Segni, p. 199 ; Nardi,
lib. vi. cap. 4 ; Varchi, vol. ii. p. 372.   Savonarola inscribed this octave
stanza on the wall of the Consiglio Grande :

> ' Se questo popolar consiglio e certo
> Governo, popol, de la tua cittate
> Conservi, che da Dio t' è stato offerto,
> In pace starai sempre e libertate :
> Tien dunque l' occhio della mente aperto,
> Chè molte insidie ognor ti fien parate ;
> E sappi che chi vuol far parlamento
> Vuol tôrti dalle mani il reggimento.'

[1] See Varchi, vol. i. p. 169.   Niccolo Capponi, in 1527, returning to
the policy of Savonarola, caused the Florentines to elect Christ for their
king, and inscribed upon the door of the Palazzo Pubblico :—

I. H. S. CHRISTUS REX FLORENTINI
POPULI S. P. DECRETO ELECTUS.

ordained, Florence executed.   By the magic of his influence
the city for a moment assumed a new aspect.   It seemed as
though the old austerity which Dante and Villani praised
were about to return without the factious hate and pride that
ruined mediæval Tuscany.   In everything done by Savonarola
at this epoch there was a strange combination of political
sagacity with monastic zeal.   Neither Guicciardini nor
Machiavelli, writing years afterwards, when Savonarola had
fallen and Florence was again enslaved, could propose anything wiser than his Consiglio Grande.   Yet the fierce revivalism advocated by the friar—the bonfire of Lorenzo di
Credi's and Fra Bartolommeo's pictures, of MSS. of Boccaccio
and classic poets, and of all those fineries which a Venetian Jew
is said to have valued in one heap at 22,000 florins—the
recitation of such Bacchanalian songs as this—

> Never was there so sweet a gladness,
> Joy of so pure and strong a fashion,
> As with zeal and love and passion
> Thus to embrace Christ's holy madness!
> Cry with me, cry as I now cry,
> Madness, madness, holy madness!

—the procession of boys and girls through the streets, shaming
their elders into hypocritical piety, and breeding in their own
hearts the intolerable priggishness of premature pietism—
could not bring forth excellent and solid fruits.   The change
was far too violent.   The temper of the race was not prepared
for it.   It clashed too rudely with Renaissance culture.   It
outraged the sense of propriety in the more moderate citizens,
and roused to vindictive fury the worst passions of the self-
indulgent and the worldly.   A reaction was inevitable.[1]

[1] The position of the Puritan leaders in England was somewhat
similar to Savonarola's.   But they had, at the end of a long war, the
majority of the nation with them.   Besides, the English temperament
was more adapted to Puritanism than the Italian, nor were the manifestations of piety prescribed by Parliament so extravagant.   And yet
even in England a reaction took place under the Restoration.

Meanwhile the strong wine of prophecy intoxicated Savonarola. His fiery temperament, strained to the utmost by the dead weight of Florentine affairs that pressed upon him, became more irritable day by day. Vision succeeded vision ; trance followed upon trance ; agonies of dejection were suddenly transformed into outbursts of magnificent and soul-sustaining enthusiasm. It was no wonder if, passing as he had done from the discipline of the cloister to the dictatorship of a republic, he should make extravagant mistakes. The tension of this abnormal situation in the city grew to be excessive, and cool thinkers predicted that Savonarola's position would become untenable. Parties began to form and gather to a head. The followers of the monk, by far the largest section of the people, received the name of Piagnoni or Frateschi. The friends of the Medici, few at first and cautious, were called Bigi. The opponents of Savonarola and of the Medici, who hated his theocracy, but desired to see an oligarchy and not a tyranny in Florence, were known as the Arrabbiati.

The discontent which germinated in Florence displayed itself in Rome. Alexander found it intolerable to be assailed as Antichrist by a monk who had made himself master of the chief Italian republic. At first he used his arts of blandishment and honeyed words in order to lure Savonarola to Rome. The friar refused to quit Florence. Then Alexander suspended him from preaching. Savonarola obeyed, but wrote at the same time to Charles VIII., denouncing his indolence and calling upon him to reform the Church. At the request of the Florentine Republic, though still suffering from the Pope's interdict, he then resumed his preaching. Alexander sought next to corrupt the man he could not intimidate. To the suggestion that a Cardinal's hat might be offered him, Savonarola replied that he preferred the red crown of martyrdom. Ascending the pulpit of the Duomo in 1496, he preached the most fiery of all his Lenten courses. Of this series of orations Milman writes: 'His triumphal career began with the Advent of 1494 on Haggai and the Psalms. But it is in the Carême of 1496 on Amos and Zechariah that the preacher girds himself to his full strength, when he had attained his full authority, and could not but be conscious that there was a deep and dangerous rebellion brooding in the hearts of the hostile factions at Florence, and when already ominous rumours began to be heard from Rome. He that would know the power, the daring, the oratory of Savonarola, must study this volume.' [1]

Very terrific indeed are the denunciations contained in these discourses—denunciations fulminated without disguise against the Pope and priests of Rome, against the Medici, against the Florentines themselves, in whom the traces of rebellion were beginning to appear. Mingled with these vehement invectives, couched in Savonarola's most impassioned style and heightened by his most impressive imagery, are political harangues and polemical arguments against the Pope. The position assumed by the friar in his war with Rome was not a strong one, and the reasoning by which he supported it was marked by curious self-deception mingled with apparent efforts to deceive his audience. He had not the audacious originality of Luther. He never went to the length of braving Alexander by burning his bulls and by denying the authority of popes in general. Not daring to break all connection with the Holy See, he was driven to quibble about the distinction between the office and the man, assuming a hazardous attitude of obedience to the Church, whose head and chief he daily outraged. At the same time he took no pains to enlist the sympathies of the Italian princes, many of whom might presumably have been hostile to the Pope, on his side of the

[1] These sermons were printed from the notes taken by Lorenzo Violi in one volume at Venice, 1534.

quarrel. All the tyrants came in for a share of his prophetic
indignation. Lodovico Sforza, the lord of Mirandola, and
Piero de' Medici felt themselves specially aggrieved, and kept
urging Alexander to extinguish this source of scandal to
established governments. Against so great and powerful a
host one man could not stand alone. Savonarola's position
became daily more dangerous in Florence. The merchants,
excommunicated by the Pope, and thus exposed to pillage in
foreign markets, grumbled at the friar who spoiled their trade.
The ban of interdiction lay upon the city, where the sacraments
could no longer be administered or the dead be buried with
the rites of Christians. Meanwhile, a band of high-spirited
and profligate young men, called Compagnacci, used every
occasion to insult and interrupt him. At last in March 1498
his staunch friends, the Signory, or supreme executive of
Florence, suspended him from preaching in the Duomo.
Even the populace were weary of the protracted quarrel with
the Holy See; nor could any but his own fanatical adherents
anticipate the wars which threatened the State, with
equanimity.

Savonarola himself felt that the supreme hour was come.
One more resource was left; to that he would now betake
himself; he could afterwards but die. This last step was the
convening of a general council.[1] Accordingly he addressed
letters to all the European potentates. One of these, inscribed
to Charles VIII., was despatched, intercepted, and conveyed
to Alexander. He wrote also to the Pope and warned him of
his purpose. The termination of that epistle is noteworthy:
'I can thus have no longer any hope in your Holiness, but

---

[1] This scheme was by no means utterly unpractical. The Borgia
had only just escaped deposition in 1495 by the gift of a Cardinal's hat
to the Bishop of S. Malo. He was hated no less than feared through
the length and breadth of Italy. But Savonarola had allowed the
favourable moment to pass by.

must turn to Christ alone, who chooses the weak of this world to confound the strong lions among the perverse generations. He will assist me to prove and sustain, in the face of the world, the holiness of the work for the sake of which I so greatly suffer : and He will inflict a just punishment on those who persecute me and would impede its progress. As for myself, I seek no earthly glory, but long eagerly for death. May your Holiness no longer delay, but look to your salvation.'

But while girding on his armour for this single-handed combat with the Primate of Christendom and the Princes of Italy, the martyrdom to which Savonarola now looked forward fell upon him. Growing yearly more confident in his visions and more willing to admit his supernatural powers, he had imperceptibly prepared the pit which finally engulfed him. Often had he professed his readiness to prove his vocation by fire. Now came the moment when this defiance to an ordeal was answered.[1] A Franciscan of Apulia offered to meet him in the flames and see whether he were of God or not. Fra Domenico, Savonarola's devoted friend, took up the gauntlet and proposed himself as champion. The furnace was prepared : both monks stood ready to enter it : all Florence was assembled in the Piazza to witness what should happen. Various obstacles, however, arose ; and after waiting a whole day for the Friar's triumph, the people had to retire to their homes under a pelting shower of rain, unsatisfied, and with a dreary sense that after all their prophet was but a mere man. The Compagnacci got the upper hand. S. Mark's convent was besieged. Savonarola was led to prison, never to issue till the day of his execution by the rope and faggot. We may

---

[1] There seems to be no doubt that this Ordeal by Fire was finally got up by the Compagnacci with the sanction of the Signory, who were anxious to relieve themselves by any means of Savonarola. The Franciscan chosen to enter the flames together with Fra Domenico was a certain Giuliano Rondinelli. Nardi calls him Andrea Rondinelli.

draw a veil over those last weeks. Little indeed is known
about them, except that in his cell the Friar composed his
meditations on the 31st and 51st Psalms, the latter of which
was published in Germany with a preface by Luther in 1573.
Of the rest we hear only of prolonged torture before stupid
and malignant judges, of falsified evidence, and of contradictory confessions. What he really said and chose to stand
by, what he retracted, what he shrieked out in the delirium
of the rack, and what was falsely imputed to him, no one
now can settle.[1] Though the spirit was strong, the flesh was
weak ; he had the will but not the nerve to be a martyr. At
ten o'clock on the 23rd of May, 1498, he was led forth together
with brother Salvestro, the confidant of his visions, and
brother Domenico, his champion in the affair of the ordeal,
to a stage prepared in the Piazza.[2] These two men were

---

[1] Nardi, lib. ii. vol. i. p. 128, treats the whole matter of Savonarola's
confessions under torture with good sense. He says : 'Avendo doman-
dato il frate quello che diceva e affermava delle sue esamine fatte infino
a quel dì, rispose, che ciò ch' egli aveva ne' tempi passati detto e predetto
era la pura verità, e che quello di che s' era ridetto e aveva ritratto, era
tutto falso e era seguito per il dolor grande e per la paura che egli aveva
de' tormenti, e che di nuovo si ridirebbe e ritratterebbe tante volte,
quante ei fusse di nuovo tormentato, perciò che si conosceva molto
debole e inconstante nel sopportare i supplicii.' Burchard, in his Diary,
reports the childish, foul, malignant gossip current in Rome. This may
be read in the 'Preuves et Observations' appended to the Memoirs of
De Comines, vol. v. p. 512. See the Marchese Gino Capponi's Storia
della Firenze (tom. ii. pp. 248-51) for a critical analysis of the deposi-
tions falsely ascribed to Savonarola.

[2] There is a curious old picture in the Pinacoteca of Perugia which
represents the burning of the three friars. The whole Piazza della
Signoria is shown, with the houses of the fifteenth century, and without
the statues which afterwards adorned it. The spectator fronts the
Palazzo, and has to his extreme right the Loggia de' Lanzi. The centre
of the square is occupied by a great circular pile of billets and faggots,
to which a wooden bridge of scaffolding leads from the left angle of the
Palazzo. From the middle of the pile rises a pole, to which the bodies
of the friars in their white clothes are suspended. Sta. Maria del Fiore,
the Badia tower, and the distant hills above Fiesole complete a scene
which is no doubt accurate in detail.

hanged first. Savonarola was left till the last. As the hangman tied the rope round his neck, a voice from the crowd
shouted: 'Prophet, now is the time to perform a miracle!'
The Bishop of Vasona, who conducted the execution, stripped
his friar's frock from him, and said, 'I separate thee from
the Church militant and triumphant.' Savonarola, firm
and combative even at the point of death, replied, 'Militant, yes: triumphant, no: *that* is not yours.' The last
words he uttered were, 'The Lord has suffered as much
for me.' Then the noose was tightened round his neck.
The fire beneath was lighted. The flames did not reach his
body while life was in it; but those who gazed intently
thought they saw the right hand give the sign of benediction.
A little child afterwards saw his heart still whole among the
ashes cast into the Arno; and almost to this day flowers have
been placed every morning of the 23rd of May upon the slab
of the Piazza where his body fell.

Thus died Savonarola: and immediately he became a saint.
His sermons and other works were universally distributed.
Medals in his honour were struck. Raphael painted him
among the Doctors of the Church in the Camera della
Segnatura of the Vatican. The Church, with strange incon-
sistency, proposed to canonise the man whom she had burned
as a contumacious heretic and a corrupter of the people.
This canonisation never took place; but many Dominican
churches used a special office with his name and in his
honour.[1] A legend similar to that of S. Francis in its wealth
of mythical details embalmed the memory of even the smallest
incidents of his life. But, above all, he lived in the hearts of
the Florentines. For many years to come his name was the
watchword of their freedom; his prophecies sustained their

---

[1] *Officio del Savonarola*, with preface by Cesare Guasti. Firenze,
1863.

spirit during the siege of 1528;[1] and it was only by returning
to his policy that Niccolo Capponi and Francesco Carducci
ruled the people through those troublous times.   The political
action of Savonarola forms but a short episode in the history
of Florence.   His moral revival belongs to the history of
popular enthusiasm.   His philosophical and theological
writings are chiefly interesting to the student of post-mediæval
scholasticism.   His attitude as a monastic leader of the
populace, attempting to play the old game whereby the
factious warfare of a previous age had been suspended by
appeals to piety, and politicians had looked for aid outside
the nation, was anachronistic.   But his prophecy, his insight
into the coming of a new era for the Church and for Italy, is
a main fact in the psychology of the Renaissance.

[1] Guicciardini, in his *Ricordi*, No. i., refers the incredible obstinacy
of the Florentines at this period in hoping against all hope and reason
to Savonarola: 'Questa ostinazione ha causata in gran parte la fede
di non potere perire, secondo le predicazioni di Fra Jeronimo da
Ferrara.'

CHAPTER X

CHARLES VIII

The Italian States confront the Great Nations of Europe—Policy of Louis XI. of France—Character of Charles VIII.—Preparations for the Invasion of Italy—Position of Lodovico Sforza—Diplomatic Difficulties in Italy after the Death of Lorenzo de' Medici—Weakness of the Republics—Il Moro—The year 1494—Alfonso of Naples—Inefficiency of the Allies to cope with France—Charles at Lyons is stirred up to the Invasion of Italy by Giuliano della Rovere—Charles at Asti and Pavia—Murder of Gian Galeazzo Sforza—Mistrust in the French Army—Rapallo and Fivizzano—The Entrance into Tuscany—Part played by Piero de' Medici—Charles at Pisa - His Entrance into Florence—Piero Capponi—The March on Rome—Entry into Rome—Panic of Alexander VI.—The March on Naples—The Spanish Dynasty: Alfonso and Ferdinand—Alfonso II. escapes to Sicily—Ferdinand II. takes Refuge in Ischia—Charles at Naples—The League against the French—De Comines at Venice—Charles makes his Retreat by Rome, Siena, Pisa, and Pontremoli—The Battle of Fornovo—Charles reaches Asti and returns to France—Italy becomes the Prize to be fought for by France, Spain, and Germany—Importance of the Expedition of Charles VIII.

ONE of the chief features of the Renaissance was the appearance for the first time on the stage of history of full-formed and colossal nations. France, Spain, Austria, and England are now to measure their strength. Venice, Florence, Milan, Naples, even Rome, are destined in the period that is opening for Europe to play but secondary parts. Italy, incapable of coping with these great Powers, will become the mere arena of their contests, the object of their spoliations. Yet the Italians themselves were far from being conscious of this change. Accustomed through three centuries to a system of diplomacy and intrigue among their own small states, they still thought more of the balance of power within the peninsula than of the means to be adopted for repelling foreign force. Their petty jealousies kept them disunited at an epoch when the best chance of national freedom lay in a federation. Firmly linked together in one league, or subject to a single prince, the Italians might not only have met their foes on equal ground, but even have taken a foremost place among the modern nations.[1] Instead of that, their princes were foolish enough to think that they could set France, Germany, or Spain in motion for the attainment of selfish objects within the narrow sphere of Italian politics, forgetting the disproportion between these huge monarchies and a single city like Florence, a mere province like the Milanese. It was just possible for Lorenzo de' Medici to secure the tranquillity of Italy by combining the Houses of Sforza and of Aragon with the Papal See in the chains of the same interested policy with the Commonwealth of Florence. It was ridiculous of Lodovico Sforza to fancy that he could bring the French into the game of peninsular intrigue without irrevocably ruining its artificial equilibrium. The first sign of the alteration about to take place in European history was the invasion of Italy by Charles VIII. This holiday excursion of a hare-brained youth was as transient as a border-foray on a large scale. The so-called conquest was only less sudden than the subsequent loss of Italy by the French. Yet the tornado which swept the peninsula from north to south, and returned upon its path from south to north within the space of a few months, left ineffaceable traces on the country which it

[1] Read, however, Sismondi's able argument against the view that Italy, united as a single nation under a sovereign, would have been better off, vol. vii. p. 298 et seq. He is of opinion that her only chance lay in a Confederation. See chapter ii. above, for a discussion of this chance.

traversed, and changed the whole complexion of the politics of Europe.

The invasion of Italy had been long prepared in the counsels of Louis XI. After spending his lifetime in the consolidation of the French monarchy, he constructed an inheritance of further empire for his successors by dictating to the old King René of Anjou (1474) and to the Count of Maine (1481) the two wills by which the pretensions of the House of Anjou to the Crown of Naples were transmitted to the royal family of France.[1] On the death of Louis, Charles VIII. became king in 1483. He was then aged only thirteen, and was still governed by his elder sister, Anne de Beaujeu.[2] It was not until 1492 that he actually took the reins of the kingdom into his own hands. This year, we may remark, is one of the most memorable dates in history. In 1492 Columbus discovered America : in 1492 Roderigo Borgia was made Pope : in 1492 Spain became a nation by the conquest of Granada. Each of these events was no less fruitful of consequences to Italy than was the accession of Charles VIII. The discovery of America, followed in another six years by Vasco de Gama's exploration of the Indian seas, diverted the commerce of the world into new channels ; Alexander VI. made the Reformation and the Northern Schism certainties ; the consolidation of Spain prepared a way for the autocracy of Charles V. Thus the commercial, the spiritual, and the political sceptre fell in this one year from the grasp of the Italians.

Both Philip de Comines and Guicciardini have described

---

[1] Sismondi, vol. vi. p. 285. The Appendix of Pièces Justificatives to Philip de Comines' *Memoirs* contains the will of René, King of Sicily, Count of Provence, dated July 22, 1474, by which he constitutes his nephew, Charles of Anjou, Duke of Calabria, Count of Maine, his heir in-chief ; as well as the will of Charles of Anjou, King of Sicily, Count of Provence, dated December 10, 1481, by which he makes Louis XI. his heir, naming Charles the Dauphin next in succession.

[2] Her husband was a cadet of the House of Bourbon.

the appearance and the character of the prince who was
destined to play a part so prominent, so pregnant of results,
and yet so trivial in the affairs of Europe. Providence,
it would seem, deigns frequently to use for the most
momentous purposes some pantaloon or puppet, environing
with special protection and with the prayers and aspirations
of whole peoples a mere mannikin. Such a puppet was
Charles. 'From infancy he had been weak in constitution
and subject to illnesses. His stature was short, and his face
very ugly, if you except the dignity and vigour of his glance.
His limbs were so disproportioned that he had less the
appearance of a man than of a monster. Not only was he
ignorant of liberal arts, but he hardly knew his letters.
Though eager to rule, he was in truth made for anything
but that ; for while surrounded by dependents, he exercised
no authority over them and preserved no kind of majesty.
Hating business and fatigue, he displayed in such matters as
he took in hand a want of prudence and of judgment. His
desire for glory sprang rather from impulse than from reason.
His liberality was inconsiderate, immoderate, promiscuous.
When he displayed inflexibility of purpose, it was more often
an ill-founded obstinacy than firmness, and that which
many people called his goodness of nature rather deserved
the name of coldness and feebleness of spirit.' This is
Guicciardini's portrait. De Comines is more brief: 'The
King was young, a fledgling from the nest ; provided neither
with money nor with good sense ; weak, wilful, and surrounded
by foolish counsellors.'

These foolish counsellors, or, as Guicciardini calls them,
'men of low estate, body-servants for the most part of the
king,' were headed by Stephen de Vesc, who had been raised
from the post of the king's valet de chambre to be the
Seneschal de Beaucaire, and by William Briçonnet, formerly
a merchant, now Bishop of S. Malo. These men had every-

thing to gain by an undertaking which would flatter the vanity of their master, and draw him into still closer relations with themselves. Consequently, when the Count of Belgioioso arrived at the French Court from Milan, urging the king to press his claims on Naples, and promising him a free entrance into Italy through the province of Lombardy and the port of Genoa, he found ready listeners. Anne de Beaujeu in vain opposed the scheme. The splendour and novelty of the proposal to conquer such a realm as Italy inflamed the imagination of Charles, the cupidity of his courtiers, the ambition of de Vesc and Briçonnet. In order to assure his situation at home, Charles concluded treaties with the neighbouring great Powers. He bought peace with Henry VII. of England by the payment of large sums of money. The Emperor Maximilian, whose resentment he had aroused by sending back his daughter Margaret after breaking his promise to marry her, and by taking to wife Anne of Brittany, who was already engaged to the Austrian, had to be appeased by the cession of provinces. Ferdinand of Spain received as the price of his neutrality the strong places of the Pyrenees which formed the key to France upon that side. Having thus secured tranquillity at home by ruinous concessions, Charles was free to turn his attention to Italy. He began by concentrating stores and ships on the southern ports of Marseilles and Genoa; then he moved downward with his army, to Lyons, in 1494.

At this point we are called to consider the affairs of Italy, which led the Sforza to invite his dangerous ally. Lorenzo de Medici during his lifetime had maintained a balance of power between the several states by his treaties with the Courts of Milan, Naples, and Ferrara. When he died, Piero at once showed signs of departure from his father's policy. The son and husband of Orsini,[1] he embraced the feudal pride

---

[1] His mother Clarice and his wife Alfonsina were both of them Orsini.

and traditional partialities of the great Roman House who had
always been devoted to the cause of Naples. The suspicions
of Lodovico Sforza were not unreasonably aroused by noticing
that the tyrant of Florence inclined to the alliance of King
Ferdinand rather than to his own friendship. At this same
time Alfonso, the Duke of Calabria, heir to the throne of
Naples, was pressing the rights of his son-in-law, Gian
Galeazzo Sforza, on the attention of Italy, complaining loudly
that his uncle Lodovico ought no longer to withhold from
him the reins of government.[1] Gian Galeazzo was in fact
the legitimate successor of Galeazzo Maria Sforza, who had
been murdered in Santo Stefano in 1476. After this assassination Madonna Bona of Savoy and Cecco Simonetta, who had
administered the Duchy as grand vizier during three reigns
extending over a period of half a century, governed Milan as
regents for the young duke. But Lodovico, feeling himself
powerful enough to assume the tyranny, beheaded Simonetta
at Pavia in 1480, and caused Madonna Bona, the duke's
mother, on the pretext of her immorality, to quit the regency.
Thus he took the affairs of Milan into his own hands, confined
his nephew in an honourable prison, and acted in a way to
make it clear that he intended thenceforth to be duke in
fact.[2] It was the bad conscience inseparable from this usurpation which made him mistrust the princes of the house of
Aragon, whose rights in Isabella, wife of the young duke,

Guicciardini, in his 'Dialogo del Reggimento di Firenze' (*Op. Ined.* vol. ii.
p. 46), says of him : ' Sendo nato di madre forestiera, era imbastardito in
lui il sangue Fiorentino, e degenerato in costumi esterni, e troppo insolenti
e altieri al nostro vivere.' Piero, nevertheless, refused to accept estates
from King Alfonso which would have made him a baron and feudatory
of Naples. See *Arch. Stor.* vol. i. p. 347.

[1] The young duke was aged twenty-four in 1493.

[2] Lodovico had taken measures for cloaking his usurpation with the
show of legitimate right. He betrothed his niece Bianca Maria, in 1494,
to the Emperor Maximilian, with a dower of 400,000 ducats, receiving in
return an investiture of the Duchy, which, however, he kept secret.

were set at nought by him. The same uneasy sense of wrong inclined him to look with dread upon the friendship of the Medici for the ruling family of Naples.

While affairs were in this state, and as yet no open disturbance in Lorenzo's balance of power had taken place, Alexander VI. was elected to the Papacy. It was usual for the princes and cities of Italy to compliment the Pope with embassies on his assumption of the tiara; and Lodovico suggested that the representatives of Milan, Florence, Ferrara, and Naples should enter Rome together in a body. The foolish vanity of Piero, who wanted to display the splendour of his own equipage without rivals, induced him to refuse this proposal, and led to a similar refusal on the part of Ferdinand. This trivial circumstance confirmed the suspicions of Lodovico, who, naturally subtle and intriguing, thought that he discerned a deep political design in what was really little more than the personal conceit of a broad-shouldered simpleton.[1] He already foresaw that the old system of alliances established by Lorenzo must be abandoned.

Another slight incident contributed to throw the affairs of Italy into confusion by causing a rupture between Rome and Naples. Lorenzo, by the marriage of his daughter to Franceschetto Cibo, had contrived to engage Innocent VIII. in the scheme of policy which he framed for Florence, Naples, Milan, and Ferrara. But on the accession of Alexander, Franceschetto Cibo determined to get rid of Anguillara, Cervetri, and other fiefs, which he had taken with his father's connivance from the Church. He found a purchaser in Virginio Orsini. Alexander complained that the sale was an infringement of his rights. Ferdinand supported the title of

---

[1] Piero de' Medici was what the French call a *bel homme*, and little more. He was tall, muscular, and well-made, the best player at *pallone* in Italy, a good horseman, fluent and agreeable in conversation, and excessively vain of these advantages.

the Orsini to his new acquisitions. This alienated the Pope from the King of Naples, and made him willing to join with Milan and Venice in a new league formed in 1493.

Thus the old equilibrium was destroyed, and fresh combinations between the disunited powers of Italy took place. Lodovico, however, dared not trust his new friends. Venice had too long hankered after Milan to be depended upon for real support; and Alexander was known to be in treaty for a matrimonial alliance between his son Geoffrey and Donna Sancia of Aragon. Lodovico was therefore alone, without a firm ally in Italy, and with a manifestly fraudulent title to maintain. At this juncture he turned his eyes towards France; while his father-in-law, the Duke of Ferrara, who secretly hated him, and who selfishly hoped to secure his own advantage in the general confusion which he anticipated, urged him to this fatal course. Alexander at the same time, wishing to frighten the princes of Naples into a conclusion of the projected marriage, followed the lead of Lodovico, and showed himself at this moment not averse to a French invasion.

It was in this way that the private cupidities and spites of princes brought woe on Italy: Lodovico's determination to secure himself in the usurped Duchy of Milan, Ercole d' Este's concealed hatred, and Alexander's unholy eagerness to aggrandise his bastards, were the vile and trivial causes of an event which, however inevitable, ought to have been as long as possible deferred by all true patriots in Italy. But in Italy there was no zeal for freedom left, no honour among princes, no virtue in the Church. Italy, which in the thirteenth century numbered 1,800,000 citizens—that is, members of free cities, exercising the franchise in the government of their own states—could show in the fifteenth only about 18,000 such burghers:[1] and these in Venice were subject to the tyranny of

[1] This is Sismondi's calculation (vol. vii. p. 305). It must be taken

the Council of Ten, in Florence had been enervated by the Medici, in Siena were reduced by party feuds and vulgar despotism to political imbecility. Amid all the splendours of revived literature and art, of gorgeous courts and refined societies, this indeed was the right moment for the Dominican visionary to publish his prophecies, and for the hunchback puppet of destiny to fulfil them. Guicciardini deplores, not without reason, the bitter sarcasm of fate which imposed upon his country the insult of such a conqueror as Charles. He might with equal justice have pointed out in Lodovico Sforza the actor of a tragi-comic part upon the stage of Italy. Lodovico, called Il Moro, not, as the great historian asserts, because he was of dark complexion, but because he had adopted the mulberry tree for his device,[1] was in himself an epitome of all the qualities which for the last two centuries had contributed to the degradation of Italy in the persons of the despots. Gifted originally with good abilities, he had so accustomed himself to petty intrigues that he was now incapable of taking a straightforward step in any direction. While he boasted himself the Son of Fortune and listened with complacency to a foolish rhyme that ran : *God only and the Moor foreknow the future safe and sure,* he never acted without blundering, and lived to end his days in the intolerable tedium of imprisonment at Loches. He was a thoughtful and

as a rough one. Still students who have weighed the facts presented in Ferrari's *Rivoluzioni d' Italia* will not think the estimate exaggerated. In the municipal and civil wars, free burghs were extinguished by the score.

[1] See Varchi, vol. i. p. 49. Also the *Elogia* of Paulus Jovius, who remarks that the complexion of Lodovico was fair. His surname, however, provoked puns. He had, for example, a picture painted, in which Italy, dressed like a queen, is having her robe brushed by a Moorish page. A motto ran beneath, *Per Italia nettar d' ogni bruttura.* He adopted the mulberry because Pliny called it the most prudent of all trees, inasmuch as it waits till winter is well over to put forth its leaves, and Lodovico piqued himself on his sagacity in choosing the right moment for action.

painstaking ruler; yet he so far failed to win the affection of his subjects that they tossed up their caps for joy at the first chance of getting rid of him.   He disliked bloodshed; but the judicial murder of Simonetta, and the arts by which he forced his nephew into an early grave, have left an ineffaceable stain upon his memory.   His court was adorned by the presence of Lionardo da Vinci; but at the same time it was so corrupt that, as Corio tells us,[1] fathers sold their daughters, brothers their sisters, and husbands their wives there.   In a word Lodovico, in spite of his boasted prudence, wrought the ruin of Italy and himself by his tortuous policy, and contributed by his private crimes and dissolute style of living no little to the general depravity of his country.[2]

Amid this general perturbation of the old political order the year 1494, marked in its first month by the death of King Ferdinand, began ‘a year,’ to quote from Guicciardini, ‘the most unfortunate for Italy, the very first in truth of our disastrous years, since it opened the door to numberless and horrible calamities, in which it may be said that a great portion of the world has subsequently shared.’   The expectation and uneasiness of the whole nation were proportioned to the magnitude of the coming change.   On every side the invasion of the French was regarded with that sort of fascination which a very new and exciting event is wont to inspire.   In one mood the Italians were inclined to hail Charles as a general pacificator and restorer of old liberties.[3]   Savonarola had

[1] *L' Historia di Milano*, Vinegia, 1554, p. 448: ‘A quella (scola di Venere) per ogni canto vi si convenivan bellissimi giovani.   I padri vi concedevano le figliuole, i mariti le mogliere, i fratelli le sorelle; e per sifatto modo senz’ alcun riguardo molti concorreano all’ amoroso ballo, che cosa stupendissima era riputata per qualunque l’ intendeva.’

[2] Guicciardini, *Storia d’ Italia*, lib. iii. p. 35, sums up the character of Lodovico with masterly completeness.

[3] This was the strictly popular as opposed to the aristocratic feeling. The common folk, eager for novelty and smarting under the bad rule of monsters like the Aragonese princes, expected in Charles VIII. a

preached of him as the *flagellum Dei*, the minister appointed to regenerate the Church and purify the fount of spiritual life in the peninsula. In another frame of mind they shuddered to think what the advent of the barbarians—so the French were called—might bring upon them. It was universally agreed that Lodovico by his invitation had done no more than bring down, as it were, by a breath the avalanche which had been long impending. 'Not only the preparations made by land and sea, but also the consent of the heavens and of men, announced the woes in store for Italy. Those who pretend either by art or divine inspiration to the knowledge of the future, proclaimed unanimously that greater and more frequent changes, occurrences more strange and awful than had for many centuries been seen in any part of the world, were at hand.' After enumerating divers signs and portents, such as the passing day after day in the region round Arezzo of innumerable armed men mounted on gigantic horses with a hideous din of drums and trumpets, the great historian resumes : 'These things filled the people with incredible fear; for, long before, they had been terrified by the reputation of the power of the French and of their fierceness, seeing that histories are full of their deeds—how they had already overrun the whole of Italy, sacked the city of Rome with fire and sword, subdued many provinces of Asia, and at one time or another smitten with their arms all quarters of the world.'

Among all the potentates of Italy, Alfonso of Naples had the most to dread : for against him the invasion was specially directed. No time was to be lost. He assembled his allies at Vicovaro near Tivoli in July and explained to them his theory of resistance. The allies were Florence, Rome, Bologna, and all the minor powers of Romagna.[1] For once the

Messiah, and cried 'Benedictus qui venit in nomine Domini.' See passages quoted in a note below.

[1] Venice remained neutral. She had refused to side with Charles, on the pretext that the fear of the Turk kept her engaged. She declined to

southern and the middle states of Italy were united against a
common foe. After Alfonso, Alexander felt himself in greatest peril, for he dreaded the assembly of a Council which
might depose him from the throne he had bought by simony.
So strong was his terror that he had already sent ambassadors
to the Sultan imploring him for aid against the Most Christian King, and had entreated Ferdinand the Catholic, instead
of undertaking a crusade against the Turk, to employ his arms
in opposition to the French. But Bajazet was too far off to
be of use; and Ferdinand was prudent. It remained for the
allies to repel the invader by their unassisted force. This
might have been done if Alfonso's plan had been adhered to.
He designed sending a fleet, under his brother Don Federigo,
to Genoa, and holding with his own troops the passes of the
Apennines to the North, while Piero de' Medici undertook
to guard the entrances to Tuscany on the side of Lunigiana.
The Duke of Calabria meanwhile was to raise Gian Galeazzo's
standard in Lombardy. But that absolute agreement which
is necessary in the execution of a scheme so bold and comprehensive was impossible in Italy. The Pope insisted that
attention should first be paid to the Colonnesi—Prospero and
Fabrizio being secret friends of France, and their castles
offering a desirable booty. Alfonso, therefore, determined to
occupy the confines of the Roman territory on the side of the
Abruzzi, while he sent his son, with the generals Giovan
Jacopo da Trivulzi and the Count of Pitigliano, into Lombardy.
They never advanced beyond Cesena, where the troops of the
Sforza, in conjunction with the French, held them at bay.
The fleet under Don Federigo sailed too late to effect the

join the league of Alfonso by saying it was mad to save others at the
risk of drawing the war into your own territory. Nothing is more
striking than the want of patriotic sentiment or generous concurrence
to a common end in Italy at this time. Florence, by temper and
tradition favourable to France, had been drawn into the league by
Piero de' Medici, whose sympathies were firm for the Aragonese princes.

desired rising in Genoa. The French, forewarned, had thrown 2,000 Swiss under the Baily of Dijon and the Duke of Orleans into the city, and the Neapolitan admiral fell back upon Leghorn. The forces of the league were further enfeebled and divided by the necessity of leaving Virginio Orsini to check the Colonnesi in the neighbourhood of Rome. How utterly Piero de' Medici by his folly and defection ruined what remained of the plan will be seen in the sequel. This sluggishness in action and dismemberment of forces—this total inability to strike a sudden blow—sealed beforehand the success of Charles. Alfonso, a tyrant afraid of his own subjects, Alexander, a Pope who had bought the tiara to the disgust of Christendom, Piero, conscious that his policy was disapproved by the Florentines, together with a parcel of egotistical petty despots, were not the men to save a nation. Italy was conquered, not by the French King, but by the vices of her own leaders. The whole history of Charles's expedition is one narrative of headlong rashness triumphing over difficulties and dangers which only the discord of tyrants and the disorganisation of peoples rendered harmless. The Atè of the gods had descended upon Italy, as though to justify the common belief that the expedition of Charles was divinely sustained and guided.[1]

While Alfonso and Alexander were providing for their safety in the South, Charles remained at Lyons, still uncertain whether he should enter Italy by sea or land, or indeed whether he should enter it at all. Having advanced so far as the Rhone valley, he felt satisfied with his achievement and indulged himself in a long bout of tournaments and pastimes. Besides, the want of money, which was to be his chief em-

[1] This, of course, was Savonarola's prophecy. But both Guicciardini and De Comines use invariably the same language. The phrase *Dieu monstroit conduire l'entreprise* frequently recurs in the *Memoirs* of De Comines.

barrassment throughout the expedition, had already made itself felt.[1] It was an Italian who at length roused him to make good his purpose against Italy—Giuliano de la Rovere,[2] the haughty nephew of Sixtus, the implacable foe of Alexander, whom he was destined to succeed in course of time upon the Papal throne. Burning to punish the Marrano, or apostate Moor, as he called Alexander, Giuliano stirred the king with taunts and menaces until Charles felt he could delay his march no longer. When once the French army got under weigh, it moved rapidly. Leaving Vienne on August 23, 1494, 3,600 men-at-arms, the flower of the French chivalry, 6,000 Breton archers, 6,000 crossbowmen, 8,000 Gascon infantry, 8,000 Swiss and German lances, crossed the Mont Genevre, debouched on Susa, passed through Turin, and entered Asti on September 19.[3] Neither Piedmont nor Montferrat stirred to resist them. Yet at almost any point upon the route they might have been at least delayed by hardy mountaineers until the commissariat of so large a force had proved an insurmountable difficulty. But before this hunch-back conqueror with the big head and little legs, the valleys had been exalted and the rough places had been made plain. The princes whose interest it might have been to throw obstacles in the way of Charles were but children. The Duke of Savoy

[1] 'La despense de ces navires estoit fort grande, et suis d'advis qu'elle cousta trois cens mille francs, et si ne servit de rien, et y alla tout l'argent contant que le Roy peut finer de ses finances : car comme j'ay dit, il n'estoit point pourveu ne de sens, ne d'argent, ny d'autre chose nécessaire à telle entreprise, et si en vint bien à bout, moyennant la grâce de Dieu, qui clairement le donna ainsi à cognoistre.' De Comines, lib. vii.

[2] Guicciardini calls him on this occasion 'fatale instrumento e allora e prima e poi de' mali d' Italia.' Lib. i. cap. 3.

[3] I have followed the calculation of Sismondi (vol. vii. p. 383), to which should be added perhaps another 10,000 in all attached to the artillery, and 2,000 for sappers, miners, carpenters, &c. See Dennistoun, *Dukes of Urbino*, vol. i. p. 433, for a detailed list of Charles's armaments by land and sea.

was only twelve years old, the Marquis of Montferrat fourteen; their mothers and guardians made terms with the French king, and opened their territories to his armies.

At Asti Charles was met by Lodovico Sforza and his father-in-law, Ercole d'Este. The whole of that Milanese Court which Corio describes [1] followed in their train. It was the policy of the Italian princes to entrap their conqueror with courtesies, and to entangle in silken meshes the barbarian they dreaded. What had happened already at Lyons, what was going to repeat itself at Naples, took place at Asti. The French King lost his heart to ladies, and confused his policy by promises made to Dalilahs in the ball-room. At Asti he fell ill of the small-pox, but after a short time he recovered his health and proceeded to Pavia. Here a serious entanglement of interests arose. Charles was bound by treaties and engagements to Lodovico and his proud wife Beatrice d'Este; the very object of his expedition was to dethrone Alfonso and to assume the crown of Naples; yet at Pavia he had to endure the pathetic spectacle of his forlorn cousin [2] the young Giovanni Galeazzo Sforza in prison, and to hear the piteous pleadings of the beautiful Isabella of Aragon. Nursed in chivalrous traditions, incapable of resisting a woman's tears, what was Charles to do, when this princess in distress the wife of his first cousin, the victim of his friend Lodovico, the sister of his foe Alfonso, fell at his feet and besought him to have mercy on her husband, on her brother, on herself? The situation was indeed enough to move a stouter heart than that of the feeble young king. For the moment Charles returned evasive answers to his petitioners; but the trouble of his soul was manifest, and no sooner had he set forth on his way to Piacenza than the Moor resolved to remove the cause of

[1] See above, p. 430.
[2] The mothers of Charles VIII. and Gian Galeazzo were sisters, princesses of Savoy.

further vacillation. Sending to Pavia, Lodovico had his nephew poisoned.[1] When the news of Gian Galeazzo's death reached the French camp, it spread terror and embittered the mistrust which was already springing up between the frank cavaliers and the plausible Italians with whom they had to deal.

What was this beautiful land in the midst of which they found themselves, a land whose marble palaces were thronged with cut-throats in disguise, whose princes poisoned while they smiled, whose luxuriant meadows concealed fever, whose ladies carried disease upon their lips ? To the captains and the soldiery of France, Italy already appeared a splendid and fascinating Circe, arrayed with charms, surrounded with illusions, hiding behind perfumed thickets her victims changed to brutes, and building the couch of her seduction on the bones of murdered men. Yet she was so beautiful that, halt as they might for a moment and gaze back with yearning on the Alps that they had crossed, they found themselves unable to resist her smile. Forward they must march through the garden of enchantment, henceforth taking the precaution to walk with drawn sword, and, like Orlando in Morgana's park, to stuff their casques with roses that they might not hear the siren's voice too clearly. It was thus that Italy began the part she played through the Renaissance for the people of the

---

[1] Sismondi does not discuss the fact minutely, but he inclines to believe that Gian Galeazzo was murdered. Michelet raises a doubt about it, though the evidence is such as he would have accepted without question in the case of a Borgia. Guicciardini, who recounts the whole matter at length, says that all Italy believed the duke had been murdered, and quotes Teodoro da Pavia, one of the royal physicians, who attested to having seen clear signs of a slow poison in the young man. Pontano, *de Prudentiá*, lib. 4, repeats the accusation. Guicciardini only doubts Lodovico's motives. He inclines to think the murder had been planned long before, and that Charles was invited into Italy in order that Lodovico might have a good opportunity for effecting it, while at the same time he had taken care to get the investiture of the Duchy from the Emperor ready against the event.

North. 'The White Devil of Italy' is the title of one of
Webster's best tragedies. A white Devil, a radiant daughter
of sin and death, holding in her hands the fruit of the knowledge of good and evil, and tempting the nations to eat : this
is how Italy struck the fancy of the men of the sixteenth
century. She was feminine, and they were virile ; but she
could teach and they must learn. She gave them pleasure ;
they brought force. The fruit of her embraces with the
nations was the spirit of modern culture, the genius of the
age in which we live.

Two terrible calamities warned the Italians with what new
enemies they had to deal. Twice at the commencement of
the invasion did the French use the sword which they had
drawn to intimidate the sorceress. These terror-striking
examples were the massacres of the inhabitants of Rapallo on
the Genoese Riviera, and of Fivizzano in Lunigiana. Soldiers
and burghers, even prisoners and wounded men in the hospitals,
were butchered, first by the Swiss and German guards, and
afterwards by the French, who would not be outdone by them
in energy. It was thus that the Italians, after a century
of bloodless battles and parade campaigning, learned a new
art of war, and witnessed the first act of those Apocalyptic
tragedies which were destined to drown the peninsula with
French, Spanish, German, Swiss, and native blood.

Meanwhile the French host had reached Parma, traversing,
all through the golden autumn weather, those plains where
mulberry and elm are married by festoons of vines above a billowy
expanse of maize and corn.   From Parma, placed beneath the
northern spurs of the Apennines, to Sarzana, on the western
coast of Italy, where the marbles of Carrara build their
barrier against the Tyrrhene Sea, there leads a winding barren
mountain pass.   Charles took this route with his army, and
arrived in the beginning of November before the walls of
Sarzana.   Meanwhile we may well ask what Piero de' Medici

had been doing, and how he had fulfilled his engagement with Alfonso. He had undertaken, it will be remembered, to hold the passes of the Apennines upon this side. To have embarrassed the French troops among those limestone mountains, thinly forested with pine and chestnut trees, and guarded here and there with ancient fortresses, would have been a matter of no difficulty. With like advantages 2,000 Swiss troops during their wars of independence would have laughed to scorn the whole forces of Burgundy and Austria. But Piero, a feeble and false tyrant, preoccupied with Florentine factions, afraid of Lucca, and disinclined to push forward into the territory of the Sforza, had as yet done nothing when the news arrived that Sarzana was on the point of capitulation. In this moment of peril he rode as fast as horses could carry him to the French camp, besought an interview with Charles, and then and there delivered up to him the keys of Sarzana and its citadel, together with those of Pietra Santa, Librafratta, Pisa, and Leghorn. Any one who has followed the sea-coast between Pisa and Sarzana can appreciate the enormous value of these concessions to the invader. They relieved him of the difficulty of forcing his way along a narrow belt of land, which is hemmed in on one side by the sea and on the other by the highest and most abrupt mountain range in Italy. To have done this in the teeth of a resisting army and beneath the walls of hostile castles would have been all but impossible. As it was, Piero cut the Gordian knot by his incredible cowardice, and for himself gained only ruin and dishonour. Charles, the foe against whom he had plotted with Alfonso and Alexander, laughed in his face, and marched at once into Pisa. The Florentines, whom he had hitherto engaged in an unpopular policy, now rose in fury, expelled him from the city, sacked his palace, and erased from their memory the name of Medici except for execration. The unsuccessful tyrant, who had proved a traitor to his allies, to his country, and to himself, saved his life by flying first to Bologna and thence to Venice, where he remained in a sort of polite captivity—safe, but a slave, until the Doge and his council saw which way affairs would tend.

On the 9th of November Florence after a tyranny of fifty years, and Pisa after the servitude of a century, recovered their liberties and were able to reconstitute republican governments. But the situation of the two states was very different. The Florentines had never lost the name of liberty, which in Italy at that period meant less the freedom of the inhabitants to exercise self-government than the independence of the city in relation to its neighbours. The Pisans on the other hand had been reduced to subjection by Florence; their civic life had been stifled, their pride wounded in the tenderest point of honour, their population decimated by proscription and exile. The great sin of Florence was the enslavement of Pisa: and Pisa in this moment of anarchy burned to obliterate her shame with bloodshed. The French, understanding none of the niceties of Italian politics, and ignorant that in giving freedom to Pisa they were robbing Florence of her rights, looked on with wonder at the citizens who tossed the lion of the tyrant town into the Arno and took up arms against its officers. It is sad to witness this last spasm of the long-suppressed passion for liberty in the Pisans, while we know how soon they were reduced again to slavery by the selfish sister state, herself too thoroughly corrupt for liberty. The part of Charles, who espoused the cause of the Pisans with blundering carelessness, pretended to protect the new republic, and then abandoned it a few months later to its fate, provokes nothing but the languid contempt which all his acts inspire.

After the flight of Piero and the proclamation of Pisan liberty the King of France was hailed as saviour of the free Italian towns. Charles received a magnificent address from

Savonarola, who proceeded to Pisa, and harangued him as the chosen vessel of the Lord and the deliverer of the Church from anarchy. At the same time the Friar conveyed to the French King a courteous invitation from the Florentine republic to enter their city and enjoy their hospitality. Charles, after upsetting Piero de' Medici with the nonchalance of a horseman in the tilting yard, and restoring the freedom of Pisa for a caprice, remained as devoid of policy and as indifferent to the part assigned him by the prophet as he was before. He rode, armed at all points, into Florence on November 17, and took up his residence in the palace of the Medici. Then he informed the elders of the city that he had come as conqueror and not as guest, and that he intended to reserve to himself the disposition of the state.

It was a dramatic moment. Florence, with the Arno flowing through her midst, and the hills around her grey with olive-trees, was then even more lovely than we see her now. The whole circuit of her walls remained, nor had their crown of towers been levelled yet to make resistance of invading force more easy. Brunelleschi's dome and Giotto's tower and Arnolfo's Palazzo and the Loggie of Orcagna gave distinction to her streets and squares. Her churches were splendid with frescoes in their bloom, and with painted glass, over which as yet the injury of but a few brief years had passed. Her palaces, that are as strong as castles, overflowed with a population cultivated, polished, elegant, refined, and haughty. This Florence, the city of scholars, artists, intellectual sybarites, and citizens in whom the blood of the old factions beat, found herself suddenly possessed as a prey of war by flaunting Gauls in their outlandish finery, plumed Germans, kilted Kelts, and particoloured Swiss. On the other hand these barbarians awoke in a terrestrial paradise of natural and æsthetic beauty. Which of us who has enjoyed the late gleams of autumn in Valdarno, but can picture to himself the revelation of the inner meaning of the world, incomprehensible yet soul subduing, which then first dawned upon the Breton bowmen and the bulls of Uri? Their impulse no doubt was to pillage and possess the wealth before them, as a child pulls to pieces the wonderful flower that has surprised it on some mountain meadow. But in the very rudeness of desire they paid a homage to the new-found loveliness of which they had not dreamed before.

Charles here as elsewhere showed his imbecility. He had entered and laid hands on hospitable Florence like a foe. What would he now do with her—reform the republic—legislate—impose a levy on the citizens, and lead them forth to battle? No. He asked for a huge sum of money, and began to bargain. The Florentine secretaries refused his terms. He insisted. Then Piero Capponi snatched the paper on which they were written, and tore it in pieces before his eyes. Charles cried: 'I shall sound my trumpets.' Capponi answered: 'We will ring our bells.' Beautiful as a dream is Florence; but her sombre streets, overshadowed by gigantic belfries and masked by grim brown palace-fronts, contained a menace that the French King could not face. Let Capponi sound the tocsin, and each house would become a fortress, the streets would be barricaded with iron chains, every quarter would pour forth men by hundreds well versed in the arts of civic warfare. Charles gave way, covering with a bad joke the discomfiture he felt: *Ah, Ciappon, Ciappon, voi siete un mal Ciappon!* The secretaries beat down his terms. All he cared for was to get money.[1] He agreed to content himself with

[1] The want of money determined all Charles's operations in this expedition. Borrowing from Lodovico, laying requisitions on Piero and the Florentines, pawning the jewels of the Savoy princesses, he passed from place to place, bargaining and contracting debts instead of dictating laws and founding constitutions. *La carestia dei danari* is a phrase continually recurring in Guicciardini. Speaking of the jewels lent to Charles by the royal families of Savoy and Montferrat at Turin,

120,000 florins. A treaty was signed, and in two days he quitted Florence.

Hitherto Charles had met with no serious obstacle. His invasion had fallen like the rain from heaven, and like rain, as far as he was concerned, it ran away to waste. Lombardy and Tuscany, the two first scenes in the pageant displayed by Italy before the French army, had been left behind. Rome now lay before them, magnificent in desolation; not the Rome which the Farnesi and Chigi and Barberini have built up from the quarried ruins of amphitheatres and baths, but the Rome of the Middle Ages, the city crowned with relics of a pagan past, herself still pagan, and holding in her midst the modern Antichrist. The progress of the French was a continued triumph. They reached Siena on the second of December. The Duke of Urbino and the lords of Pesaro and Bologna laid down their arms at their approach. The Orsini opened their castles : Virginio, the captain-general of the Aragonese army and grand constable of the kingdom of Naples, hastened to win for himself favourable terms from the French sovereign. The Baglioni betook themseves to their own rancours in Perugia. The Duke of Calabria retreated. Italy seemed bent on proving that cowardice and selfishness and incapacity had conquered her. Viterbo was gained : the Ciminian heights were traversed : the Campagna, bounded by the Alban and the Sabine hills, with Rome, a bluish cloud upon the lowlands of the Tiber, spread its solemn breadth of beauty at the invader's feet. Not a blow had been struck, when he reached the Porta del Popolo upon the 31st of December, 1494. At three o'clock in the afternoon began the entry of the French army. It was nine at night before the last soldiers, under the flaring light of torches and flambeaux, defiled through the gates, and took their quarters in the

de Comines exclaims : 'Et pouvez voir quel commencement de guerre c'estoit, si Dieu n'eut guidé l'œuvre.'

streets of the Eternal City. The gigantic barbarians of the
cantons, flaunting with plumes and emblazoned surcoats,
the chivalry of France, splendid with silk mantles and gilded
corslets, the Scotch guard in their wild costume of kilt and
philibeg, the scythe-like halberds of the German lanzknechts,
the tangled elf-locks of stern-featured Bretons, stamped an
ineffaceable impression on the people of the South. On this
memorable occasion, as in a show upon some holiday, marched
past before them specimens and vanguards of all those
legioned races which were soon to be too well at home in
every fair Italian dwelling-place. Nothing was wanting to
complete the symbol of the coming doom but a representative
of the grim, black, wiry infantry of Spain.

The Borgia meanwhile crouched within the Castle of
S. Angelo. How would the Conqueror, now styled Flagellum
Dei, deal with the abomination of desolation seated in the
holy place of Christendom? At the side of Charles were the
Cardinals Ascanio Sforza and Giuliano della Rovere, urging
him to summon a council and depose the Pope. But still
closer to his ear was Briçonnet, the *ci-devant* tradesman, who
thought it would become his dignity to wear a Cardinal's hat.
On this trifle turned the destinies of Rome, the doom of
Alexander, the fate of the Church. Charles determined to
compromise matters. He demanded a few fortresses, a red
hat for Briçonnet, Cesare Borgia as a hostage for four months,
and Djem, the brother of the Sultan.[1] After these agreements had been made and ratified, Alexander ventured to
leave his castle and receive the homage of the faithful.

Charles stayed a month in Rome, and then set out for

---

[1] See above, p. 325, for the history of this unfortunate prince.
When Alexander ceded Djem, whom he held as a captive for the Sultan
at a yearly revenue of 40,000 ducats, he was under engagements with
Bajazet to murder him. Accordingly Djem died of slow poison soon
after he became the guest of Charles. The Borgia preferred to keep
faith with the Turk.

Naples. The fourth and last scene in the Italian pageant was now to be displayed. After the rich plain and proud cities of Lombardy, beneath their rampart of perpetual snow; after the olive gardens and fair towns of Tuscany; after the great name of Rome; Naples, at length, between Vesuvius and the sea, that first station of the Greeks in Italy, world-famed for its legends of the Sibyl and the sirens and the sorcerer Virgil, received her king. The very names of Par-thenope, Posilippo, Inarime, Sorrento, Capri, have their fascination. There too the orange and lemon groves are more luxuriant; the grapes yield sweeter and more intoxicat-ing wine; the villagers are more classically graceful; the volcanic soil is more fertile; the waves are bluer and the sun is brighter than elsewhere in the land. None of the conquerors of Italy have had the force to resist the allurements of the bay of Naples. The Greeks lost their native energy upon these shores, and realised in the history of their colonies the myth of Ulysses' comrades in the gardens of Circe. Hannibal was tamed by Capua. The Romans in their turn dreamed away their vigour at Baiæ, at Pompeii, at Capreæ, until the whole region became a byword for voluptuous living. Here the Saracens were subdued to mildness, and became phy-sicians instead of pirates. Lombards and Normans alike were softened down, and lost their barbarous fierceness amid the enchantments of the southern sorceress.

Naples was now destined to ruin for Charles whatever nerve yet remained to his festival army. The witch too, while brewing for the French her most attractive potions, mixed with them a deadly poison—the virus of a fell disease, memorable in the annals of the modern world, which was destined to infect the nations of Europe from this centre, and to prove more formidable to our cities than even the leprosy of the Middle Ages.[1]

[1] Those who are curious to trace the history of the origin of syphilis

The kingdom of Naples, through the frequent uncertainty which attended the succession to the throne, as well as the suzerainty assumed and misused by the Popes, had been for centuries a standing cause of discord in Italy. The dynasty which Charles now hoped to dispossess was Spanish. After the death of Joanna II. in 1435, Alfonso, King of Aragon and Sicily, who had no claim to the crown beyond what he derived through a bastard branch of the old Norman dynasty, conquered Naples, expelled Count René of Anjou, and established himself in this new kingdom, which he preferred to those he had inherited by right. Alfonso, surnamed the Magnanimous, was one of the most brilliant and romantic personages of the fifteenth century. Historians are never weary of relating his victories over Caldora and Francesco Sforza, the coup-de-main by which he expelled his rival René, and the fascination which he exercised in Milan, while a captive, over the jealous spirit of Filippo Maria Visconti.[1]

should study the article upon the subject in Von Hirsch, *Historisch-geo-graphische Pathologie* (Erlangen, 1860), and in Rosenbaum, *Geschichte der Lustseuche im Alterthum* (Halle, 1845). Some curious contemporary observations concerning the rapid diffusion of the disease in Italy, its symptoms, and its cure, are contained in Matarazzo's *Cronaca di Perugia* (*Arch. Stor. It.* vol. xvi. part ii. pp. 32–36), and in Porto-venere (*Arch. St.* vol. vi. pt. ii. p. 338). The celebrated poem of Fracastorius deserves to be read both for its fine Latinity and for its information. One of the earliest works issued from the Aldine press in 1497 was the *Libellus de Epidemiâ quam vulgo morbum Gallicum vocant*. It was written by Nicolao Leoniceno, and dedicated to the Count Francesco de la Mirandola.

[1] Mach. *Ist. Fior.* lib. v. cap. 5. Corio, pp. 332, 333, may be consulted upon the difficulties which Alfonso overcame at the commencement of his conquest. Defeated by the Genoese near the Isle of Ponza, and carried a prisoner to Milan, he succeeded in proving to Filippo Visconti that it was more to his interest to have him king of Naples than to keep the French there. Upon this the Duke of Milan restored him with honour to his throne, and confirmed him in the conquest which before he had successfully opposed. It is a singular instance of the extent to which Italian princes were controlled by policy and reason.

Scholars are no less profuse in their praises of his virtues, the justice, humanity, religion, generosity, and culture which rendered him pre-eminent among the princes of that splendid period.[1] His love of learning was a passion. Whether at home in the retirement of his palace, or in his tent during war, he was always attended by students, who read aloud and commented on Livy, Seneca, or the Bible. No prince was more profuse in his presents to learned men. Bartolommeo Fazio received 500 ducats a year for the composition of his histories, and when, at their conclusion, the scholar asked for a further gift of 200 or 300 florins, the prince bestowed upon him 1,500. The year he died, Alfonso distributed 20,000 ducats to men of letters alone. This immoderate liberality is the only vice of which he is accused. It bore its usual fruits in the disorganisation of finance.

The generous humanity of Alfonso endeared him greatly to the Neapolitans. During the half-century in which so many Italian princes succumbed to the dagger of their subjects, he, in Naples, where, according to Pontano, 'nothing was cheaper than the life of a man,' walked up and down unarmed and unattended. 'Why should a father fear among his children?' he was wont to say in answer to suggestions of the danger of this want of caution. The many splendid qualities by which he was distinguished were enhanced rather than obscured by the romance of his private life. Married to Margaret of Castile, he had no legitimate children; Ferdinand, with whom he shared the government of Naples in 1443, and whom he designated as his successor in 1458, was supposed to be his son by Margaret de Hijar. It was even whispered that this Ferdinand was the child of

---

[1] Vespasiano's *Life of Alfonso* (*Vite di Uomini Illustri*, pp. 48–72) is a model of agreeable composition and vivid delineation. It is written of course from the scholar's more than the politician's point of view. Compare with it Giovio, *Elogia*, and Pontanus, *de Liberalitate*.

Catherine, the wife of Alfonso's brother Henry, whom Margaret, to save the honour of the king, acknowledged as her own. Whatever may have been the truth of this dark history, it was known for certain that the queen had murdered her rival, the unhappy Margaret de Hijar, and that Alfonso never forgave her or would look upon her from that day. Pontano, who was Ferdinand's secretary, told a different tale. He affirmed that the real father of the Duke of Calabria was a Marrano of Valentia. This last story is rendered probable by the brusque contrast between the character of Alfonso and that of Ferdinand.

It would be terrible to think that such a father could have been the parent of such a son. In Ferdinand the instinct of liberal culture degenerated into vulgar magnificence; courtesy and confidence gave place to cold suspicion and brutal cruelty. His ferocity bordered upon madness. He used to keep the victims of his hatred in cages, where their misery afforded him the same delight as some men derived from watching the antics of monkeys.[1] In his hunting establishment were repeated the worst atrocities of Bernabo Visconti: wretches mutilated for neglect of his hounds extended their handless stumps for charity to the travellers through his villages.[2] Instead of the generosity for which Alfonso had been famous, Ferdinand developed all the arts of avarice. Like Sixtus IV. he made the sale of corn and oil a royal monopoly,

[1] See Pontanus, *de Immanitate*, Aldus, 1518, vol. i. p. 318: 'Ferdinandus Rex Neapolitanorum præclaros etiam viros conclusos carcere etiam bene atque abunde pascebat, eandem ex iis voluptatem capiens quam pueri e conclusis in caveâ aviculis: quâ de re sæpenumero sibi ipsi inter intimos suos diu multumque gratulatus subblanditusque in risum tandem ac cachinnos profundebatur.'

[2] *Ibid.* vol. i. p. 320: 'Ferd. R. N. qui cervum aprumve occidissent furtimve palamve, alios remo addixit, alios manibus mutilavit, alios suspendio affecit: agros quoque serendos interdixit dominis, legendasque aut glandes aut poma, quæ servari quidem volebat in escam feris ad venationis suæ usum.'

trafficking in the hunger of his subjects.[1]   Like Alexander **VI.**
he fattened his viziers and secretaries upon the profits of
extortion which he shared with them, and when they were
fully gorged he cut their throats and proclaimed himself the
heir through their attainder.[2]   Alfonso had been famous for
his candour and sincerity.   Ferdinand was a demon of dissimulation and treachery.   His murder of his guest Jacopo
Piccinino at the end of a festival, which extended over
twenty-seven days of varied entertainments, won him the
applause of Machiavellian spirits throughout Italy.   It
realised the ideal of treason conceived as a fine art.   Not less
perfect as a specimen of diabolical cunning was the vengeance
which Ferdinand, counselled by his son Alfonso, inflicted on
the barons who conspired against him.[3]   Alfonso was a son
worthy of this terrible father.   The only difference between
them was that Ferdinand dissembled, while Alfonso, whose
bravery at Otranto against the Turks had surrounded him
with military glory, abandoned himself with cynicism to his
passions.   Sketching characters of both in the same paragraph, de Comines writes : ' Never was man more cruel than
Alfonso, nor more vicious, nor more wicked, nor more
poisonous, nor more gluttonous.   His father was more
dangerous, because he could conceal his mind and even his
anger from sight ; in the midst of festivity he would take and

---

[1] Caracciolo, *de Varietate Fortunæ*, Muratori, vol. xxii. p. 87, exposes
this system in a passage which should be compared with Infessura on
the practices of Sixtus.   De Comines, lib. vii. cap. 11, may be read with
profit on the same subject.

[2] See Caracciolo, loc. cit. pp. 88, 89, concerning the judicial murder
of Francesco Coppola and Antonello Perucci, both of whom had been
raised to eminence by Ferdinand, used through their lives as the
instruments of his extortion, and murdered by him in their rich old age.

[3] See De Comines, lib. vii. cap. 11 ; Sismondi, vol. vii. p. 229.   Read
also the short account of the massacre of the Barons given in the
Chronicon Venetum, Muratori, xxiv. p. 15, where the intense loathing
felt throughout Italy for Ferdinand and his son Alfonso is powerfully
expressed.

slaughter his victims by treachery. Grace or mercy was never found in him, nor yet compassion for his poor people. Both of them laid forcible hands on women. In matters of the Church they observed nor reverence nor obedience. They sold bishoprics, like that of Tarento, which Ferdinand disposed of for 13,000 ducats to a Jew in favour of his son whom he called a Christian.'

This kind of tyranny carried in itself its own deathwarrant. It needed not the voice of Savonarola to proclaim that God would revenge the crimes of Ferdinand by placing a new sovereign on his throne. It was commonly believed that the old king died in 1494 of remorse and apprehension, when he knew that the French expedition could no longer be delayed. Alfonso, for his part, bold general in the field and able man of affairs as he might be, found no courage to resist the conqueror. It is no fiction of a poet or a moralist, but plain fact of history, that this King of Naples, grandson of the great Alfonso and father of the Ferdinand to be, quailed before the myriads of accusing dead that rose to haunt his tortured fancy in the supreme hour of peril. The chambers of his palace in Naples were thronged with ghosts by battalions, pale spectres of the thousands he had reduced to starvation, bloody phantoms of the barons he had murdered after nameless tortures, thin wraiths of those who had wasted away in dungeons under his remorseless rule. The people around his gates muttered in rebellion. He abdicated in favour of his son, took ship for Sicily, and died there conscience-stricken in a convent ere the year was out.

Ferdinand, a brave youth, beloved by the nation in spite of his father's and grandfather's tyranny, reigned in his stead. Yet even for him the situation was untenable. Everywhere he was beset by traitors—by his whole army at San Germano, by Trivulzi at Capua, by the German guide at Naples. Without soldiers, without allies, with nothing to rely upon but the untried goodwill of subjects who had just reason to execrate his race, and with the conquerors of Italy advancing daily through his states, retreat alone was left to him. After abandoning his castles to pillage, burning the ships in the harbour of Naples, and setting Don Federigo together with the Queen dowager and the Princess Joanna upon a quick-sailing galley, Ferdinand bade farewell to his kingdom. Historians relate that as the shore receded from his view he kept intoning in a loud voice this verse of the 127th Psalm: 'Except the Lord keep the city, the watchman waketh but in vain.' Between the beach of Naples and the rocky shore of Ischia, for which the exiles were bound, there is only the distance of some seventeen miles. It was in February, a month of mild and melancholy sunshine in those southern regions, when the whole bay of Naples with its belt of distant hills is wont to take one tint of modulated azure, that the royal fugitives performed this voyage. Over the sleeping sea they glided ; while from the galley's stern the king, with a voice as sad as Boabdil's when he sat down to weep for Granada, cried : 'Except the Lord keep the city, the watch-man waketh but in vain.'

There was no want of courage in the youth. By his simple presence he had intimidated a mob of rebels in Naples. By the firmness of his carriage he subdued the insolent governor of Ischia, and made himself master of the island. There he waited till the storm was overpast. Ten times more a man than Charles, he watched the French King depart from Naples leaving scarcely a rack behind—some troops decimated by disease and unnerved by debauchery, and a general or two without energy or vigour. Then he returned and entered on a career of greater popularity than could have been enjoyed by him if the French had never made the fickle race of Naples feel how far more odious is a foreign than a familiar yoke.[1]

[1] The misfortunes and the bravery of this young prince inspire a

Charles entered Naples as a conqueror or liberator on February 22, 1495. He was welcomed and fêted by the Neapolitans, than whom no people are more childishly delighted with a change of masters. He enjoyed his usual sports, and indulged in his usual love affairs. With suicidal insolence and want of policy he alienated the sympathies of the noble families by dividing the titles, offices, and fiefs of the kingdom among his retinue.[1] Without receiving so much as a provisional investiture from the Pope, he satisfied his vanity by parading on May 12 as sovereign, with a ball in one hand and a sceptre in the other, through the city. Then he was forced to return upon his path and to seek France with the precipitancy he had shown in gaining Naples. Alexander, who was witty, said the French had conquered Italy with lumps of chalk and wooden spurs, because they rode unarmed in slippers and sent couriers before them to select their quarters. It remained to be seen that the achievements of this conquest could be effaced as easily as a chalk mark is rubbed out, or a pair of wooden spurs are broken.

While Charles was amusing himself at Naples, a storm was gathering in his rear. A league against him had been formed in April by the great Powers of Europe. Venice, alarmed for the independence of Italy, and urged by the Sultan, who had reason to dread Charles VIII.,[2] headed the league.

deep feeling of interest. It is sad to read that after recovering his kingdom in 1496, he died in his twenty-eighth year, worn out with fatigue and with the pleasures of his marriage to his aunt Joanna, whom he loved too passionately. His uncle Frederick, the brother of Alfonso II., succeeded to the throne. Thus in three years Naples had five sovereigns.

[1] 'Tous estats et offices furent donnez aux Francois, à deux ou trois,' says De Comines.

[2] Charles, by an act dated A.D. 1494, September 6, had bought the title of Emperor of Constantinople and Trebizond from Andrew Palæologus (see Gibbon, vol. viii. p. 183, ed. Milman). When he took Djem from Alexander in Rome, his object was to make use of him in a

Lodovico, now that he had attained his selfish object in the quiet possession of Milan, was anxious for his safety. The Pope still feared a general council. Maximilian, who could not forget the slight put upon him in the matter of his daughter and his bride, was willing to co-operate against his rival. Ferdinand and Isabella, having secured themselves in Roussillon, thought it behoved them to re-establish Spaniards of their kith and kin in Naples. Each of the contracting parties had his rôle assigned to him. Spain undertook to aid Ferdinand of Aragon in Calabria. Venice was to attack the seaports of the kingdom; Lodovico Sforza, to occupy Asti; the King of the Romans, to make a diversion in the North. Florence alone, though deeply injured by Charles in the matter of Pisa, kept faith with the French.

The danger was imminent. Already Ferdinand the Catholic had disembarked troops on the shore of Sicily, and was ready to throw an army into the ports of Reggio and Tropea. Alexander had refused to carry out his treaty by the surrender of Spoleto. Cesare Borgia had escaped from the French camp. The Lombards were menacing Asti, which the Duke of Orleans held, and without the possession of which there was no safe return to France. Asti indeed at this juncture would have fallen, and Charles would have been caught in a trap, if the Venetians had only been quick or wary enough to engage German mercenaries.[1] The danger of the situation may best be judged by reading the Memoirs of De Comines, who was then ambassador at Venice. 'The league was concluded very late one evening. The next morning the Signory sent for me earlier than usual. They were assembled in great numbers, perhaps a hundred or more, and held their heads high, made a good cheer, and had not

war against Bajazet; and the Pope was always impressing on the Turk the peril of a Frankish crusade.

[1] See De Comines, lib. vii. cap. 15, pp. 78, 79.

the same countenance as on the day when they told me of the capture of the citadel of Naples.[1]   My heart was heavy, and I had grave doubts about the person of the king and about all his company ; and I thought their scheme more ripe than it really was, and feared they might have Germans ready : and if it had been so, never could the king have got safe out of Italy.'   Nevertheless De Comines put a brave face on the matter, and told the council that he had already received information of the league and had sent despatches to his master on the subject.[2]   'After dinner,' continues De Comines, 'all the ambassadors of the league met for an excursion on the water, which is the chief recreation at Venice, where everyone goes according to the retinue he keeps, or at the expense of the Signory.   There may have been as many as forty gondolas, all bearing displayed the arms of their masters upon banners.   I saw the whole of this company pass before my windows, and there were many minstrels on board.   Those of Milan, one at least of them who had often kept my company, put on a brave face not to know me ; and for three days I remained without going forth into the town, nor my people, nor was there all that time a single courteous word said to me or to any of my suite.'

Returning northward by the same route, Charles passed Rome and reached Siena on June 13.   The Pope had taken refuge, first at Orvieto, and afterwards at Perugia, on his

[1] De Comines' account of the alarm felt at Venice on that occasion is very graphic : ' They sent for me one morning, and I found them to the number of fifty or sixty in the Doge's bedchamber, for he was ill of colic ; and there he told me the news with a good countenance.   But none of the company knew so well how to feign as he.   Some were seated on a wooden bench, leaning their heads on their hands, and others otherwise ; and all showed great heaviness at heart.   I think that when the news reached Rome of the battle of Cannæ, the senators were not more confounded or frightened.'

[2] Bembo, in his *Venetian History* (lib. ii. p. 32), tells a different tale. He represents De Comines quite unnerved by the news.

approach; but he made no concessions. Charles could not obtain from him an investiture of the kingdom he pretended to have conquered, while he had himself to surrender the fortresses of Civita Vecchia and Terracina. Ostia alone remained in the clutch of Alexander's implacable enemy, the Cardinal de la Rovere. In Tuscany the Pisan question was again opened. The French army desired to see the liberties of Pisa established on a solid basis before they quitted Italy. On their way to Naples the misfortunes of that ancient city had touched them: now on their return they were clamorous that Charles should guarantee its freedom. But to secure this object was an affair of difficulty. The forces of the league had already taken the field, and the Duke of Orleans was being besieged in Novara. The Florentines, jealous of the favour shown, in manifest infringement of their rights, to citizens whom they regarded as rebellious bondsmen, assumed an attitude of menace. Charles could only reply with vague promises to the solicitations of the Pisans, strengthen the French garrisons in their fortresses, and march forward as quickly as possible into the Apennines. The key of the pass by which he sought to regain Lombardy is the town of Pontremoli. Leaving that in ashes on June 29, the French army, distressed for provisions and in peril among those melancholy hills, pushed onward with all speed. They knew that the allied forces, commanded by the Marquis of Mantua, were waiting for them at the other side upon the Taro, near the village of Fornovo. Here, if anywhere, the French ought to have been crushed. They numbered about 9,000 men in all, while the allies were close upon 40,000. The French were weary with long marches, insufficient food, and bad lodgings. The Italians were fresh and well cared for. Yet in spite of all this, in spite of blind generalship and total blundering, Charles continued to play his part of fortune's favourite to the end. A bloody battle, which lasted for an hour, took place upon the banks of the Taro.[1] The Italians suffered so severely that, though they still far outnumbered the French, no persuasions could make them rally and renew the fight. Charles in his own person ran great peril during this battle; and when it was over, he had still to effect his retreat upon Asti in the teeth of a formidable army. The good luck of the French and the dilatory cowardice of their opponents saved them now again for the last time. On July 15, Charles at the head of his little force marched into Asti and was practically safe. Here the young king continued to give signal proofs of his weakness. Though he knew that the Duke of Orleans was hard pressed in Novara, he made no effort to relieve him; nor did he attempt to use the 20,000 Switzers who descended from their Alps to aid him in the struggle with the league. From Asti he removed to Turin, where he spent his time in flirting with Anna Soléri, the daughter of his host. This girl had been sent to harangue him with a set oration, and had fulfilled her task, in the words of an old witness, 'without wavering, coughing, spitting, or giving way at all.' Her charms delayed the king in Italy until October 19, when he signed a treaty at Vercelli with the Duke of Milan. At this moment Charles might have held Italy in his grasp. His forces, strengthened by the unexpected arrival of so many Switzers, and by a junction with the

[1] The action at Fornovo lasted a quarter of an hour, according to De Comines. The pursuit of the Italians occupied about three-quarters of an hour more. Unaccustomed to the quick tactics of the French, the Italians, when once broken, persisted in retreating upon Reggio and Parma. The Gonzaghi alone distinguished themselves for obstinate courage, and lost four or five members of their princely house. The Stradiots, whose scimitars ought to have dealt rudely with the heavy French men-at-arms, employed their time in pillaging the Royal pavilion, very wisely abandoned to their avarice by the French captains. To such an extent were military affairs misconstrued in Italy, that, on the strength of this brigandage, the Venetians claimed Fornovo for a victory. See my essay 'Fornovo,' in *Sketches and Studies in Italy*, for a description of the ground on which the battle was fought.

Duke of Orleans, would have been sufficient to overwhelm the army of the league, and to intimidate the faction of Ferdinand in Naples. Yet so light-minded was Charles, and so impatient were his courtiers, that he now only cared for a quick return to France. Reserving to himself the nominal right of using Genoa as a naval station, he resigned that town to Lodovico Sforza, and confirmed him in the tranquil possession of his Duchy. On October 22 he left Turin, and entered his own dominions through the Alps of Dauphiné. Already his famous conquest of Italy was reckoned among the wonders of the past, and his sovereignty over Naples had become the shadow of a name. He had obtained for himself nothing but momentary glory, while he imposed on France a perilous foreign policy, and on Italy the burden of bloody warfare in the future.

A little more than a year had elapsed between the first entry of Charles into Lombardy and his return to France. Like many other brilliant episodes of history, this conquest, so showy and so ephemeral, was more important as a sign than as an actual event. 'His passage,' says Guicciardini, 'was the cause not only of change in states, downfalls of kingdoms, desolations of whole districts, destructions of cities, barbarous butcheries ; but also of new customs, new modes of conduct, new and bloody habits of war, diseases hitherto unknown. The organisation upon which the peace and harmony of Italy depended was so upset that, since that time, other foreign nations and barbarous armies have been able to trample her under foot and to ravage her at pleasure.' The only error of Guicciardini is the assumption that the holiday excursion of Charles VIII. was in any deep sense the cause of these calamities.[1] In truth the French invasion

[1] Guicciardini's *Dialogo del Reggimento di Firenze* (*Op. Ined.* vol. ii. p 94) sets forth the state of internal anarchy and external violence which followed the departure of Charles VIII., with wonderful acuteness. 'Se per sorte l' uno Oltramontano caccerà l' altro, Italia resterà

opened a new era for the Italians, but only in the same sense as a pageant may form the prelude to a tragedy. Every monarch of Europe, dazzled by the splendid display of Charles and forgetful of its insignificant results, began to look with greedy eyes upon the wealth of the peninsula. The Swiss found in those rich provinces an inexhaustible field for depredation. The Germans, under the pretence of religious zeal, gave a loose rein to their animal appetites in the metropolis of Christendom. France and Spain engaged in a duel to the death for the possession of so fair a prey. The French, maddened by mere cupidity, threw away those chances which the goodwill of the race at large afforded them.[1] Louis XII. lost himself in petty intrigues, by which he finally weakened his own cause to the profit of the Borgias and Austria. Francis I. foamed his force away like a spent wave at Marignano and Pavia. The real conqueror of Italy was Charles V. Italy in the sixteenth century was destined to

in estrema servitù,' is an exact prophecy of what happened before the end of the sixteenth century, when Spain had beaten France in the duel for Italy.

[1] Matarazzo, in his *Cronaca della Città di Perugia* (*Arch. St.*, vol. xvi. part 2, p. 23), gives a lively picture of the eagerness with which the French were greeted in 1495, and of the wanton brutality by which they soon alienated the people. In this he agrees almost textually with De Comines, who writes: 'Le peuple nous advouoit comme Saincts, estimans en nous toute foy et bonté; mais ce propos ne leur dura gueres, tant pour nostre desordre et pillerie, et qu'aussi les ennemis oppreschoient le peuple en tous quartiers,' &c., lib. vii. cap. 6. In the first paragraph of the *Chronicon Venetum* (Muratori, vol. xxiv. p. 5), we read concerning the advent of Charles: 'I popoli tutti dicevano *Benedictus qui venit in nomine Domini*. Nè v' era alcuno che li potesse contrastare, nè resistere, tanto era da tutti i popoli Italiani chiamato.' The Florentines, as burghers of a Guelf city, were always loyal to the French. Besides, their commerce with France (*e.g.* the wealth of Filippo Strozzi) made it to their interest to favour the cause of the French. See Guicc. i. 2, p. 62. This loyalty rose to enthusiasm under the influence of Savonarola, survived the stupidities of Charles VIII. and Louis XII., and committed the Florentines in 1528 to the perilous policy of expecting aid from Francis I.

receive the impress of the Spanish spirit, and to bear the yoke of Austrian dukes. Hand in hand with political despotism marched religious tyranny. The Counter-Reformation over which the Inquisition presided was part and parcel of the Spanish policy for the enslavement of the nation no less than for the restoration of the Church. Meanwhile the weakness, discord, egotism, and corruption which prevented the Italians from resisting the French invasion in 1494, continued to increase. Instead of being lessoned by experience, Popes, Princes, and Republics vied with each other in calling in the strangers, pitting Spaniard against Frenchman, and paying the Germans to expel the Swiss, oblivious that each new army of foreigners they summoned was in reality a new swarm of devouring locusts. In the midst of this anarchy it is laughable to hear the shrill voice of priests, like Julius and Leo, proclaiming before God their vows to rid Italy of the barbarians. The confusion was tenfold confounded when the old factions of Guelf and Ghibelline put on a new garb of French and Spanish partisanship. Town fought with town and family with family, in the cause of strangers whom they ought to have resisted with one will and steady hatred. The fascination of fear and the love of novelty alike swayed the fickle population of Italian cities. The foreign soldiers who inflicted on the nation such cruel injuries made a grand show in their streets, and there will always be a mob so childish as to covet pageants at the expense of freedom and even of safety.

In spite of its transitory character the invasion of Charles VIII., therefore, was a great fact in the history of the Renaissance. It was, to use the pregnant phrase of Michelet, no less than the revelation of Italy to the nations of the North. Like a gale sweeping across a forest of trees in blossom, and bearing their fertilising pollen, after it has broken and deflowered their branches, to far-distant trees that hitherto have bloomed in barrenness, the storm of Charles's army carried far and wide through Europe thought-dust imperceptible, but potent to enrich the nations. The French alone, says Michelet, understood Italy. How terrible would have been a conquest by Turks with their barbarism, of Spaniards with their Inquisition, of Germans with their brutality! But France, impressible, sympathetic, ardent for pleasure, generous, amiable and vain, was capable of comprehending the Italian spirit. From the Italians the French communicated to the rest of Europe what we call the movement of the Renaissance. There is some truth in this panegyric of Michelet's. The passage of the army of Charles VIII. marks a turning-point in modern history, and from this epoch dates the diffusion of a spirit of culture over Europe. But Michelet forgets to notice that the French never rightly understood their vocation with regard to Italy, They had it in their power to foster that free spirit which might have made her a nation capable, in concert with France, of resisting Charles V. Instead of doing so, they pursued the pettiest policy of avarice and egotism. Nor did they prevent that Spanish conquest the horrors of which their historian has so eloquently described. Again, we must remember that it was the Spaniards and not the French who saved Italy from being barbarised by the Turk.

For the historian of Italy it is sad and humiliating to have to acknowledge that her fate depended wholly on the action of more powerful nations, that she lay inert and helpless at the discretion of the conqueror in the duels between Spain and France and Spain and Islam. Yet this is the truth. It would seem that those peoples to whom we chiefly owe advance in art and knowledge, are often thus the captives of their intellectual inferiors. Their spiritual ascendency is purchased at the expense of political solidity and national prosperity. This was the case with Greece, with Judah, and with Italy. The civilisation of the Italians, far in advance of that of other

European nations, unnerved them in the conflict with robust barbarian races. Letters and the arts and the civilities of life were their glory. 'Indolent princes and most despicable arms' were their ruin. Whether the Renaissance of the modern world would not have been yet more brilliant if Italy had remained free, who shall say? The very conditions which produced her culture seem to have rendered that impossible.

APPENDICES

APPENDIX I

Blood-madness.   See Chapter iii. p. 84.

ONE of the most striking instances afforded by history of Hæmatomania in a tyrant is Ibrahim ibn Ahmed, prince of Africa and
Sicily (A.D. 875).   This man, besides displaying peculiar ferocity in
his treatment of enemies and prisoners of war, delighted in the
execution of horrible butcheries within the walls of his own palace.
His astrologers having once predicted that he should die by the
hands of a 'small assassin,' he killed off the whole retinue of his
pages, and filled up their places with a suite of negroes whom he
proceeded to treat after the same fashion.   On another occasion,
when one of his three hundred eunuchs had by chance been
witness of the tyrant's drunkenness, Ibrahim slaughtered the whole
band.   Again, he is said to have put an end to sixty youths,
originally selected for his pleasures, burning them by gangs of five
or six in the furnace, or suffocating them in the hot chambers of
his baths.   Eight of his brothers were murdered in his presence ;
and when one, who was so diseased that he could scarcely stir,
implored to be allowed to end his days in peace, Ibrahim answered :
' I make no exceptions.'   His own son Abu l-Aghlab was beheaded
by his orders before his eyes ; and the execution of chamberlains,
secretaries, ministers, and courtiers was of common occurrence.
But his fiercest fury was directed against women.   He seems to
have been darkly jealous of the perpetuation of the human race.
Wives and concubines were strangled, sawn asunder, and buried
alive, if they showed signs of pregnancy.   His female children were
murdered as soon as they saw the light ; sixteen of them, whom
his mother managed to conceal and rear at her own peril, were

massacred upon the spot when Ibrahim discovered whom they claimed as father. Contemporary Arab chroniclers, pondering upon the fierce and gloomy passions of this man, arrived at the conclusion that he was the subject of a strange disease, a portentous secretion of black bile producing the melancholy which impelled him to atrocious crimes. Nor does the principle on which this diagnosis of his case was founded appear unreasonable. Ibrahim was a great general, an able ruler, a man of firm and steady purpose; not a weak and ineffectual libertine whom lust for blood and lechery had placed below the level of brute beasts. When the time for his abdication arrived, he threw aside his mantle of state and donned the mean garb of an Arab devotee, preached a crusade, and led an army into Italy, where he died of dysentery before the city of Cosenza. The only way of explaining his eccentric thirst for slaughter is to suppose that it was a dark monomania, a form of psychopathy analogous to that which we find in the Maréchal de Retz and the Marquise de Brinvilliers. One of the most marked symptoms of this disease was the curiosity which led him to explore the entrails of his victims, and to feast his eyes upon their quivering hearts. After causing his first minister Ibn-Semsâma to be beaten to death, he cut his body open, and with his own knife sliced the brave man's heart. On another occasion he had 500 prisoners brought before him. Seizing a sharp lance he first explored the region of the ribs, and then plunged the spear-point into the heart of each victim in succession. A garland of these hearts was made and hung up on the gate of Tunis. The Arabs regarded the heart as the seat of thought in man, the throne of the will, the centre of intellectual existence. In this preoccupation with the hearts of his victims we may therefore trace the jealousy of human life which Ibrahim displayed in his murder of pregnant women, as well as a tyrant's fury against the organ which had sustained his foes in their resistance. We can only comprehend the combination of sanguinary lust with Ibrahim's vigorous conduct of civil and military affairs, on the hypothesis that this man-tiger, as Amari, to whom I owe these details, calls him, was possessed with a specific madness.

APPENDIX II

Nardi, Istorie di Firenze, lib. i. cap. 4. See Chap. **iv. p. 153.**

AFTER the freedom regained by the expulsion of the Duke of Athens and the humbling of the nobles, regularity for the future in the government might have been expected, since a very great equality among the burghers had been established in consequence of those troubles. The city too had been divided into quarters, and the supreme magistracy of the republic assigned to the eight priors, called *Signori Priori di libertà*, together with the Gonfalonier of Justice. The eight priors were chosen, two for each quarter; the Gonfalonier, their chief, differed in no respect from his colleagues save in precedence of dignity; and as the fourth part of the honours pertained to the members of the lesser arts, their turn kept coming round to that quarter to which the Gonfalonier belonged. This magistracy remained for two whole months, always living and sleeping in the Palace; in order that, according to the notion of our ancestors, they might be able to attend with greater diligence to the affairs of the commonwealth, in concert with their colleagues, who were the sixteen gonfaloniers of the companies of the people, and the twelve *buoni uomini*, or special advisers of the Signory. These magistrates collectively in one body were called the College, or else the Signory and the Colleagues. After this magistracy came the Senate, the number of which varied, and the name of which was altered several times up to the year 1494, according to circumstances. The larger councils, whose business it was to discuss and make the laws and all provisions both general and particular, were until that date two; the one called the Council of the people, formed only by the *cittadini popolani*, and the other the Council of the Commune, because it embraced both nobles and plebeians from the date of the formation of these councils.[1] The appointment of the magistrates, which of old times and under the best and most equitable govern-

---

[1] Lorenzo de' Medici superseded these two councils by the Council of the Seventy, without, however, suppressing them.

ments was made on the occasion of each election, in this more modern period was consigned to a special council called *Squittino*.[1] The mode and act of the election was termed *Squittinare*, which is equivalent to *Scrutinium* in the Latin tongue, because minute investigation was made into the qualities of the eligible burghers. This method, however, tended greatly to corrupt the good manners of the city, inasmuch as, the said scrutiny being made every three or five years, and not on each occasion, as would have been right, considering the present quality of the burghers and the badness of the times, those who had once obtained their nomination and been put into the purses thereto appointed, being certain to arrive some time at the honours and offices for which they were designed, became careless and negligent of good customs in their lives. The proper function of the Gonfaloniers was, in concert with their Gonfalons and companies, to defend with arms the city from perils foreign and civil, when occasion rose, and to control the fire-guards specially deputed by that magistracy in four convenient stations. All the laws and provisions, as well private as public, proposed by the Signory, had to be approved and carried by that College, then by the Senate, and lastly by the Councils named above. Notwithstanding this rule, everything of high importance pertaining to the State was discussed and carried into execution during the whole time that the Medici administered the city by the Council vulgarly called *Balia*, composed of men devoted to that government. While the Medici held sway, the magistracy of the *Dieci della Guerra* or of Liberty and Peace were superseded by the *Otto della Pratica* in the conduct of all that concerned wars, truces, and treaties of peace, in obedience to the will of the chief agents of that government. The *Otto di guardia e balia* were then as now delegated to criminal business, but they were appointed by the forenamed Council of Balia, or rather such authority and commission was assigned them by the Signory, and this usage was afterwards continued on their entry into office. Let this suffice upon these matters. Now the burghers who have the right of discussing and determining the affairs of the republic were and still are called privileged *benefiziati* or *statuali*, of that quality and condition to which, according to the laws of our city, the government belongs; in other words they are eligible for office, as distinguished from those who have not this privilege. Consequently the *benefiziati*

---

[1] A corruption of Scrutinio.

and *statuali* of Florence correspond to the *gentiluomini* of Venice. Of these burghers there were about 400 families or houses, but at different times the number was larger, and before the plague of 1527 they made up a total of about 4,000 citizens eligible for the Consiglio Grande. During the period of freedom between 1494 and 1512 the other or non-privileged citizens could be elevated to this rank of enfranchisement according as they were judged worthy by the Council; at the present time they gain the same distinction by such merits as may be pleasing to the ruler of the city for the time being : our commonwealth from the year 1433 having been governed according to the will of its own citizens, though one faction has from time to time prevailed over another, and though before that date the republic was distressed and shaken by the divisions which affected the whole of Italy, and by many others which are rather to be reckoned as sedition peculiar and natural to free cities. Seeing that men by good and evil arts in combina- tion are always striving to attain the summit of human affairs, together also with the favour of fortune, who ever insists on having her part in our actions.

Varchi : Storia Fiorentina, lib. iii. caps. 20, 21, 22.

THE whole city of Florence is divided into four quarters, the first of which takes in the whole of that part which is now called Beyond the Arno, and the chief church of the district gives it the name of Santo Spirito. The other three, which embrace all that is called This side the Arno, also take their names from their chief churches, and are the Quarters of Sta. Croce, Sta. Maria Novella, and San Giovanni. Each of these four quarters is divided into four gonfa- lons, named after the different animals or other things they carry painted on their ensigns. The quarter of Santo Spirito includes the gonfalons of the Ladder, the Shell, the Whip, and the Dragon ; that of Santa Croce, the Car, the Ox, the Golden Lion, and the Wheels ; that of Santa Maria Novella, the Viper, the Unicorn, the Red Lion, and the White Lion ; that of San Giovanni, the Black Lion, the Dragon, the Keys, and the Vair. Now all the households and families of Florence are included and classified under these four quarters and sixteen gonfalons, so that there is no burgher of Florence who does not rank in one of the four quarters and one of the sixteen gonfalons. Each gonfalon had its standard-bearer who carried the standard like captains of bands; and their chief office was to run with arms whenever they were called by the Gonfalonier of Justice, and to defend, each under his own ensign, the palace of the Signory, and to fight for the people's liberty; wherefore they were called Gonfaloniers of the companies of the people, or more briefly, from their number, the Sixteen. Now since they never assembled by themselves alone, seeing that they could not propose or carry any measure without the Signory, they were also called the Colleagues, that is, the companions of the Signory, and their title was venerable. This, after the Signory, was the first and most honourable magistracy of Florence; and after them came the Twelve Buonuomini, also called, for the like reason, Colleagues. So the Signory with the Gonfalonier of Justice, the Sixteen, and the Twelve were called the Three Greater. No man was said to have the franchise (*aver lo stato*), and in consequence to frequent the council, or to exercise any office, whose grandfather or father had not occupied or been passed for (*seduto o veduto*) one of these three magistracies. To be passed (*veduto*) Gonfalonier or Colleague meant this: when a man's name was drawn from the purse of the Gonfaloniers or of the College to exercise the office of Gonfalonier or Colleague, but by reason of being below the legal age, or for some other cause, he never sat himself upon the Board or was in fact Gonfalonier or Colleague, he was then said to have been passed; and this held good of all the other magistracies of the city.

It should also be known that all the Florentine burghers were obliged to rank in one of the twenty-one arts: that is, no one could be a burgher of Florence unless he or his ancestors had been approved and matriculated in one of these arts, whether they practised it or no. Without the proof of such matriculation he could not be drawn for any office, or exercise any magistracy, or even have his name put into the bags. The arts were these: i. Judges and Notaries (for the doctors of the law were styled of old in Florence Judges); Merchants, or the Arts of; ii. Calimala,[1] iii. Exchange, iv. Wool; Porta Santa Maria, or the Arts of v. Silk; vi. Physicians and Apothecaries; vii. Furriers. The others were viii. Butchers, ix. Shoemakers, x. Blacksmiths, xi. Linen-drapers and Clothesmen, xii. Masters, or Masons, and Stonecutters, xiii.

---

[1] The name Calimala was given to a trade in cloth carried on at Florence by merchants who bought rough goods in France, Flanders, and England, and manufactured them into more delicate materials.

Vintners, xiv. Innkeepers, xv. Oilsellers, Pork-butchers, and Rope-makers, xvi. Hosiers, xvii. Armourers, xviii. Locksmiths, xix. Saddlers, xx. Carpenters, xxi. Bakers. The last fourteen were called Lesser Arts; whoever was enrolled or matriculated into one of these was said to rank with the lesser (*andare per la minore*); and though there were in Florence many other trades than these, yet having no guild of their own they were associated with one or other of those that I have named. Each art had, as may still be seen, a house or mansion, large and noble, where they assembled, appointed officers, and gave account of debit and credit to all the members of the guild.[1] In processions and other public assemblies the heads (for so the chiefs of the several arts were called) had their place and precedence in order. Moreover, these arts at first had each an ensign for the defence, on occasion, of liberty with arms. Their origin was when the people in 1282 overcame the nobles (*Grandi*), and passed the Ordinances of Justice against them, whereby no nobleman could exercise any magistracy; so that such of the patricians as desired to be able to hold office had to enter the ranks of the people, as did many great houses of quality, and matriculate into one of the arts. Which thing, while it partly allayed the civil strife of Florence, almost wholly extinguished all noble feeling in the souls of the Florentines; and the power and haughtiness of the city were no less abated than the insolence and pride of the nobles, who since then have never lifted up their heads again. These arts, the greater as well as the lesser, have varied in numbers at different times; and often have not only been rivals, but even foes, among themselves; so much so that the lesser arts once got it passed that the Gonfalonier should be appointed only from their body. Yet after long dispute it was finally settled that the Gonfalonier could not be chosen from the lesser, but that he should always rank with the greater, and that in all other offices and magistracies the lesser should always have a fourth and no more. Consequently of the eight Priors, two were always of the lesser; of the Twelve, three; of the Sixteen, four; and so on through all the magistracies.

As a consequence from what has been said, it is easy to perceive that all the inhabitants of Florence (by inhabitants I mean those only who are really settled there, for of strangers, who are

---

[1] Marco Foscari, quoted lower down, estimates the property of the Arts at 200,000 ducats.

passing or sojourning a while, we need not here take any account)
are of two sorts. The one class are liable to taxation in Florence,
that is, they pay tithes of their goods, and are inscribed upon the
books of the Commune, and these are called contributors. The
others are not taxed nor inscribed upon the registers of the Commune, inasmuch as they do not pay the tithes or other ordinary
imposts; and these are called non-contributors: who, seeing that
they live by their hands, and carry on mechanical arts and the
vilest trades, should be called plebeians; and though they have
ruled Florence more than once, ought not even to entertain a
thought about public affairs in a well-governed state. The contributors are of two sorts: for some, while they pay the taxes, do
not enjoy the citizenship (*i.e.* cannot attend the council or take any
office); either because none of their ancestors, and in particular
their father or their grandfather, has sat or been passed for any of
the three greater magistracies; or else because they have not had
themselves submitted to the scrutiny,[1] or, if they have advanced so
far, have not been approved and nominated for office. These are
indeed entitled citizens: but he who knows what a citizen is really,
knows also that, being unable to share either the honours or the
advantages of the city, they are not truly citizens; therefore let us
call them burghers, without franchise. Those again who pay taxes
and enjoy the citizenship (whom we will therefore call enfranchised
burghers) are in like manner of two kinds. The one class, inscribed
and matriculated into one of the seven first arts, are said to rank
with the greater; whence we may call them Burghers of the
Greater: the others, inscribed and matriculated into the fourteen
lesser arts, are said to rank with the lesser; whence we may call
them Burghers of the Lesser. This distinction had the Romans,
but not for the same reason.

Varchi: Storia Fiorentina, lib. ix. caps. 48, 49, 46.

As for natural abilities, I for my part cannot believe that any one
either could or ought to doubt that the Florentines, even if they do
not excel all other nations, are at least inferior to none in those
things to which they give their minds. In trade, whereon of a
truth their city is founded, and wherein their industry is chiefly

[1] For an explanation of *Squittino* and *Squittinare*, see Nardi, p. 464
above.

exercised, they ever have been and still are reckoned not less trusty and true than great and prudent : but besides trade, it is clear that the three most noble arts of painting, sculpture, and architecture have reached that degree of supreme excellence in which we find them now, chiefly by the toil and by the skill of the Florentines, who have beautified and adorned not only their own city but also very many others, with great glory and no small profit to themselves and to their country. And, seeing that the fear of being held a flatterer should not prevent me from testifying to the truth, though this will turn to the highest fame and honour of my lords and patrons, I say that all Italy, nay the whole world, owes it solely to the judgment and the generosity of the Medici that Greek letters were not extinguished to the great injury of the human race, and that Latin literature was restored to the incalculable profit of all men.

I am wholly of opinion opposed to that of some, who, because the Florentines are merchants, hold them for neither noble nor high-spirited, but for tame and low.[1] On the contrary, I have often wondered with myself how it could be that men who have been used from their childhood upwards for a paltry profit to carry bales of wool and baskets of silk like porters, and to stand like slaves all day and great part of the night at the loom, could summon, when and where was need, such greatness of soul, such high and haughty thoughts, that they have wit and heart to say and do those many noble things we know of them. Pondering on the causes of which, I find none truer than this, that the Florentine climate, between the fine air of Arezzo and the thick air of Pisa,

---

[1] Compare, however, Varchi, quoted above, p. 191. The report of Marco Foscari, *Relazioni Venete*, serie ii. vol. i. p. 9 et seq., contains a remarkable estimate of the Florentine character. He attributes the timidity and weakness which he observes in the Florentines to their mercantile habits, and notices, precisely what Varchi here observes with admiration : ' li primi che governano lo stato vanno alle loro botteghe di seta, e gittati li lembi del mantello sopra le spalle, pongonsi alla caviglia e lavorano pubblicamente che ognuno li vede; ed i figliuoli loro stanno in bottega con li grembiuli dinanzi, e portano il sacco e le sporte alle maestre con la seta e fanno gli altri esercizi di bottega.' A strong aristocratic prejudice transpires in every line. This report was written early in 1527. The events of the Siege must have surprised Marco Foscari. He notices among other things, as a source of weakness, the country villas which were all within a few months destroyed by their armies for the public good.

infuses into their breasts the temperament of which I spoke. And whoso shall well consider the nature and the ways of the Florentines, will find them born more apt to rule than to obey. Nor would it be easily believed how much was gained for the youth of Florence by the institution of the militia; for whereas many of the young men, heedless of the commonwealth and careless of themselves, used to spend all the day in idleness, hanging about places of public resort, girding at one another, or talking scandal of the passers-by, they immediately, like beasts by some benevolent Circe transformed again to men, gave all their heart and soul, regardless of peril or loss, to gaining fame and honour for themselves, and liberty and safety for their country. I do not by what I have been saying mean to deny that among the Florentines may be found men proud, ambitious, and greedy of gain; for vices will exist as long as human nature lasts: nay, rather, the ungrateful, the envious, the malicious, and the evil-minded among them are so in the highest degree, just as the virtuous are supremely virtuous. It is indeed a common proverb that Florentine brains have no mean either way; the fools are exceeding simple, and the wise exceeding prudent.

Their mode of life is simple and frugal, but wonderfully and incredibly clean and neat; and it may be said with truth that the artisans and handicraftsmen live at Florence even better than the citizens themselves: for whereas the former change from tavern to tavern, according as they find good wine, and only think of joyous living; the latter in their homes, with the frugality of merchants, who for the most part make but do not spend money, or with the moderation of orderly burghers, never exceed mediocrity. Nevertheless there are not wanting families, who keep a splendid table and live like nobles, such as the Antinori, the Bartolini, the Tornabuoni, the Pazzi, the Borgherini, the Gaddi, the Rucellai, and among the Salviati, Piero d' Alamanno and Alamanno d' Jacopo, and some others. At Florence every one is called by his proper name or his surname: and the common usage, unless there be some marked distinction of rank or age, is to say *thou* and not *you*; only to knights, doctors, and prebendaries is the title of *messere* allowed: to doctors that of *maestro*, to monks *don* and to friars *padre*. True, however, is it that since there was a Court at Florence, first that of Giulio, the Cardinal de' Medici, then that of the Cardinal of Cortona, which enjoyed more license than the former, the manners of the city have become more re-fined—or shall I say more corrupt?

APPENDIX III

The Character of Alexander VI., from Guicciardini's Storia Fiorentina, cap. 27.   See Chap. vii. p. 323 above.

So died Pope Alexander, at the height of glory and prosperity; about whom it must be known that he was a man of the utmost power and of great judgment and spirit, as his actions and behaviour showed.   But as his first accession to the Papacy was foul and shameful, seeing he had bought with gold so high a station, in like manner his government disagreed not with this base foundation.   There were in him, and in full measure, all vices both of flesh and spirit; nor could there be imagined in the ordering of the Church a rule so bad but that he put it into work-ing.   He was most sensual toward both sexes, keeping publicly women and boys, but more especially toward women; and so far did he exceed all measure that public opinion judged he knew Madonna Lucrezia, his own daughter, toward whom he bore a most tender and boundless love.   He was exceedingly avaricious, not in keeping what he had acquired, but in getting new wealth: and where he saw a way toward drawing money, he had no respect whatever; in his days were sold as at auction all benefices, dis-pensations, pardons, bishoprics, cardinalships, and all court dignities: unto which matters he had appointed two or three men privy to his thought, exceeding prudent, who let them out to the highest bidder.   He caused the death by poison of many cardinals and prelates, even among his intimates, those namely whom he noted to be rich in benefices and understood to have hoarded much, with the view of seizing on their wealth.   His cruelty was great, seeing that by his direction many were put to violent death: nor was the ingratitude less with which he caused the ruin of the Sforzeschi and Colonnesi, by whose favour he acquired the Papacy. There was in him no religion, no keeping of his troth: he promised all things liberally, but stood to nought but what was useful to himself: no care for justice, since in his days Rome was like a den of thieves and murderers: his ambition was boundless, and such that it grew in the same measure as his state increased: never-

theless, his sins meeting with no due punishment in this world, he
was to the last of his days most prosperous. While young and
still almost a boy, having Calixtus for his uncle, he was made
Cardinal and then Vice-Chancellor: in which high place he continued till his papacy, with great revenue, good fame, and peace
Having become Pope, he made Cesare, his bastard son and bishop
of Pampeluna, a Cardinal, against the ordinances and decrees of
the Church, which forbid the making of a bastard Cardinal even
with the Pope's dispensation, wherefore he brought proof by false
witnesses that he was born in wedlock. Afterwards he made him
a layman and took away the Cardinal's dignity from him, and
turned his mind to making a realm; wherein he fared far better
than he purposed, and beginning with Rome, after undoing the
Orsini, Colonnesi, Savelli, and those barons who were wont to be
held in fear by former Popes, he was more full master of Rome
than ever had been any pope before. With greatest ease he got
the lordships of Romagna, the March, and the Duchy; and having
made a most fair and powerful state, the Florentines held him in
much fear, the Venetians in jealousy, and the King of France in
esteem. Then having got together a fine army, he showed how
great was the might of a Pontiff when he hath a valiant general
and one in whom he can place faith. At last he grew to that
point that he was counted the balance in the war of France and
Spain. In one word he was more evil and more lucky than ever
for many ages peradventure had been any pope before.

APPENDIX IV

Religious Revivals in Mediæval Italy.   See Chap. viii.
p. 384 above.

It would be unscientific to confound events of such European importance as the foundation of the orders of S. Francis and S. Dominic with the phenomena in question. Still it may be remarked, that the sudden rise and the extraordinary ascendency of the mendicants and preachers were due in a great measure to the sensitive and lively imagination of the Italians. The Popes of the first half of the Thirteenth century were shrewd enough to discern the political and ecclesiastical importance of movements which seemed at first to owe their force to mere fanatical revivalism. They calculated on the intensely excitable temperament of the Italian nation, and employed the Franciscans and Dominicans as their militia in the crusade against the Empire and the heretics. Again, it is necessary to distinguish what was essentially national from what was common to all Europeans in the Middle Ages. Every country had its wandering hordes of flagellants and penitents, its crusaders and its pilgrims. The vast unsettled populations of mediæval Europe, haunted with the recurrent instinct of migration, and nightmare-ridden by imperious religious yearnings, poured flood after flood of fanatics upon the shores of Palestine. Half-naked savages roamed, dancing and groaning and scourging their flesh, from city to city, under the stress of semi-bestial impulses. Then came the period of organised pilgrimages. The celebrated shrines of Europe—Rome, Compostella, Monte Gargano, Canterbury —acted like lightning-conductors to the tempestuous devotion of the mediæval races, like setons to their over-charged imagination. In all these universal movements the Italians had their share ; though being more advanced in civilisation than the Northern peoples, they turned the crusades to commercial account, and maintained some moderation in the *fakir* fury of their piety. It is not, therefore, with the general history of religious enthusiasm in the Middle Ages that we have to do, but rather with those intermittent manifestations of revivalism which were peculiar to the

Italians   The chief points to be noticed are the political influence
acquired by monks in some of the Italian cities, the preaching of
peace and moral reformation, the panics of superstitious terror
which seized upon wide districts, and the personal ascendency of
hermits unaccredited by the Church, but believed by the people to
be divinely inspired.

One of the most picturesque figures of the first half of the
Thirteenth century is the Dominican monk, John of Vicenza.   His
order, which had recently been founded, was already engaged in
the work of persecution.   France was reeking with the slaughter of
the Albigenses, and the stakes were smoking in the town of Milan,
when this friar undertook the noble task of pacifying Lombardy.
Every town in the north of Italy was at that period torn by the
factions of the Guelfs and Ghibellines; private feuds crossed and
intermingled with political discords; and the savage tyranny of
Ezzelino had shaken the fabric of society to its foundations.   It
seemed utterly impossible to bring this people for a moment to
agreement.   Yet what popes and princes had failed to achieve, the
voice of a single friar accomplished.   John of Vicenza began his
preaching in Bologna during the year 1233.   The citizens and the
country folk of the surrounding districts flocked to hear him.   It
was noticed with especial wonder that soldiers of all descriptions
yielded to the magic of his eloquence.   The themes of his discourse
were invariably reconciliation and forgiveness of injuries.   The heads
of rival houses, who had prosecuted hereditary feuds for generations, met before his pulpit, and swore to live thenceforth in amity.
Even the magistrates entreated him to examine the statutes of
their city, and to point out any alterations by which the peace of
the commonwealth might be assured.   Having done his best for
Bologna, John journeyed to Padua, where the fame of his sanctity
had been already spread abroad.   The *carroccio* of the city, on
which the standard of Padua floated, and which had led the
burghers to many a bloody battle, was sent out to meet him at
Monselice, and he entered the gates in triumph.   In Padua the
same exhortations to peace produced the same results.   Old
enmities were abandoned and hands were clasped which
had often been raised in fierce fraternal conflict.   Treviso, Feltre,
Belluno, Conegliano, and Romano, the very nests of the grim
brood of Ezzelino, yielded to the charm.   Verona, where the
Scalas were about to reign, Vicenza, Mantua, and Brescia,

all placed themselves at the disposition of the monk, and prayed him to reform their constitution. But it was not enough to restore peace to each separate community, to reconcile household with household, and to efface the miseries of civil discord. John of Vicenza aimed at consolidating the Lombard cities in one common bond. For this purpose he bade the burghers of all the towns where he had preached to meet him on the plain of Paquara, in the country of Verona. The 28th of August was the day fixed for this great national assembly. More than four hundred thousand persons, according to the computation of Parisio di Cereta, appeared upon the scene. This multitude included the populations of Verona, Mantua, Brescia, Padua and Vicenza, marshalled under their several standards, together with contingents furnished by Ferrara, Modena, Reggio, Parma, and Bologna. Nor was the assembly confined to the common folk. The bishops of these flourishing cities, the haughty Marquis of Este, the fierce lord of Romano, and the Patriarch of Aquileia, obeyed the invitation of the friar. There, on the banks of the Adige, and within sight of the Alps, John of Vicenza ascended a pulpit that had been prepared for him, and preached a sermon on the text, *Pacem meam do vobis, pacem relinquo vobis.* The horrors of war, and the Christian duty of reconciliation, formed the subject of his sermon, at the end of which he constrained the Lombards to ratify a solemn league of amity, vowing to eternal perdition all who should venture to break the same, and imprecating curses on their crops, their vines, their cattle, and everything they had. Furthermore, he induced the Marquis of Este to take in marriage a daughter of Alberico da Romano. Up to this moment John of Vicenza had made a noble use of the strange power which he possessed. But his success seems to have turned his head. Instead of confining himself to the work of pacification so well begun, he now demanded to be made lord of Vicenza, with the titles of Duke and Count, and to receive the supreme authority in Verona. The people, believing him to be a saint, readily acceded to his wishes; but one of the first things he did, after altering the statutes of these burghs, was to burn sixty citizens of Verona, whom he had himself condemned as heretics. The Paduans revolted against his tyranny. Obliged to have recourse to arms, he was beaten and put in prison; and when he was released, at the intercession of the Pope, he found his wonderful prestige annihilated.[1]

[1] The most interesting accounts of Fra Giovanni da Vicenza are to

The position of Fra Jacopo del Bussolaro in Pavia differed from that of Fra Giovanni da Vicenza in Verona. Yet the commencement of his political authority was very nearly the same. The son of a poor boxmaker of Pavia, he early took the habit of the Augustines, and acquired a reputation for sanctity by leading the austere life of a hermit. It happened in the year 1356 that he was commissioned by the superiors of his order to preach the Lenten sermons to the people of Pavia. 'Then,' to quote Matteo Villani, 'it pleased God that this monk should make his sermons so agreeable to every species of people, that the fame of them and the devotion they inspired increased marvellously. And he, seeing the concourse of the people, and the faith they bare him, began to denounce vice, and specially usury, revenge, and ill-behaviour of women ; and thereupon he began to speak against the disorderly lordship of the tyrants ; and in a short time he brought the women to modest manners, and the men to renunciation of usury and feuds.' The only citizens of Pavia who resisted his eloquence were the Beccaria family, who at that time ruled Pavia like despots. His most animated denunciations were directed against their extortions and excesses. Therefore they sought to slay him. But the people gave him a bodyguard, and at last he wrought so powerfully with the burghers that they expelled the house of Beccaria and established a republican government. At this time the Visconti were laying siege to Pavia ; the passes of the Ticino and the Po were occupied by Milanese troops, and the city was reduced to a state of blockade. Fra Jacopo assembled the able-bodied burghers, animated them by his eloquence, and led them to the attack of their besiegers. They broke through the lines of the beleaguering camp, and re-established the freedom of Pavia. What remained, however, of the Beccaria party passed over to the enemy, and threw the whole weight of their influence into the scale of the Visconti ; so that at the end of a three years' manful conflict, Pavia was delivered to Galeazzo Visconti in 1359. Fra Jacopo made the best terms that he could for the city, and took no pains to secure his own safety. He was consigned by the conquerors to the superiors of his order, and died in the dungeons of a convent at Vercelli. In his case, the sanctity of an austere life, and the eloquence of an authoritative

be found in Muratori, vol. viii., in the Annals of Rolandini and Gerardus Maurisius.

preacher of repentance, had been strictly subordinated to political aims in the interest of republican liberty. Fra Jacopo deserves to rank with Savonarola; like Savonarola, he fell a victim to the selfish and immoral oppressors of his country. As in the case of Savonarola, we can trace the connection which subsisted in Italy between a high standard of morality and patriotic heroism.[1]

San Bernardino da Massa heads a long list of preachers, who, without taking a prominent part in contemporary politics, devoted all their energies to the moral regeneration of the people. His Life, written by Vespasiano da Bisticci, is one of the most valuable documents which we possess for the religious history of Italy in the first half of the fifteenth century. His parents, who were people of good condition, sent him at an early age to study the Canon law at Siena. They designed him for a lucrative and important office in the Church. But, while yet a youth, he was seized with a profound conviction of the degradation of his countrymen. The sense of sin so weighed upon him that he sold all his substance, entered the order of S. Francis, and began to preach against the vices which were flagrant in the great Italian cities. After travelling through the length and breadth of the peninsula, and winning all men by the magic of his eloquence, he came to Florence. 'There,' says Vespasiano, 'the Florentines being by nature very well disposed indeed to truth, he so dealt that he changed the whole State and gave it, one may say, a second birth. And in order to abolish the false hair which the women wore, and games of chance, and other vanities, he caused a sort of large stall to be raised in the Piazza di Santa Croce, and bade every one who possessed any of these vanities to place them there; and so they did; and he set fire thereto and burned the whole.' S. Bernardino preached unremittingly for forty-two years in every quarter of Italy, and died at last worn out with fatigue and sickness. 'Of many enmities and deaths of men he wrought peace and removed deadly hatreds; and numberless princes, who harboured feuds to the death, he reconciled, and restored tranquillity to many cities and peoples.' A vivid picture of the method adopted by S. Bernardino in his dealings with these cities is presented to us by Graziani, the chronicler of Perugia: 'On September 23, 1425,

[1] The best authorities for the life and actions of Fra Jacopo are Matteo Villani, bks. 8 and 9, and Peter Azarius, in his Chronicle (Grævius, vol. ix.)

a Sunday, there were, as far as we could reckon, upwards of 3,000 persons in the Cathedral. His sermon was from the Sacred Scripture, reproving men of every vice and sin, and teaching Christian living. Ther. he began to rebuke the women for their paints and cosmetics, and false hair, and such like wanton customs; and in like manner the men for their cards and dice-boards and masks and amulets and charms: insomuch that within a fortnight the women sent all their false hair and gewgaws to the Convent of S. Francis, and the men their dice, cards, and such gear, to the amount of many loads. And on October 29 Fra Bernardino collected all these devilish things on the piazza, where he erected a kind of wooden castle between the fountain and the Bishop's palace; and in this he put all the said articles, and set fire to them; and the fire was so great that none durst go near; and in the fire were burned things of the greatest value, and so great was the haste of men and women to escape that fire that many would have perished but for the quick aid of the burghers.' Together with this onslaught upon vanities, Fra Bernardino connected the preaching of peace and amity. It is noticeable that while his sermon lasted and the great bell of S. Lorenzo went on tolling, no man could be taken or imprisoned in the city of Perugia.[1]

The same city was the scene of many similar displays. During the fifteenth century it remained in a state of the most miserable internal discord, owing to the feuds of its noble families. Graziani gives an account of the preaching there of Fra Jacopo della Marca in 1445: on this occasion a temporary truce was patched up between old enemies, a witch was burned for the edification of the burghers, the people were reproved for their extravagance in dress, and two peacemakers (*pacieri*) were appointed for each gate. On March 22, after undergoing this discipline, the whole of Perugia seemed to have repented of its sins; but the first entry for April 15 is the murder of one of the Ranieri family by another of the same house. So transitory were the effects of such revivals.[2] Another entry in Graziani's ' Chronicle' deserves to be noticed. He describes how, in 1448, Fra Roberto da Lecce (like S. Bernardino and Fra Jacopo della Marca, a Franciscan of the Order of Observance) came to preach in January. He was only twenty-two years of age; but

---

[1] See Vespasiano, *Vite di Uomini Illustri*, pp. 185–92. Graziani, *Archivio Storico*, vol. xvi. part i. pp. 313, 314.

[2] See Graziani, pp. 565–68.

his fame was so great that he drew about 15,000 persons into the piazza to listen to him. The stone pulpit, we may say in passing, is still shown, from which these sermons were delivered. It is built into the wall of the Cathedral, and commands the whole square. Roberto da Lecce began by exhibiting a crucifix, which moved the audience to tears; 'and the weeping and crying, *Jesu misericordia!* lasted about half an hour. Then he made four citizens be chosen for each gate as peacemakers.' What follows in Graziani is an account of a theatrical show, exhibited upon the steps of the Cathedral. On Good Friday the friar assembled all the citizens, and preached; and when the moment came for the elevation of the crucifix, 'there issued forth from San Lorenzo Eliseo di Christoforo, a barber of the quarter of Sant Angelo, like a naked Christ with the cross on his shoulder, and the crown of thorns upon his head, and his flesh seemed to be bruised as when Christ was scourged.' The people were immensely moved by this sight. They groaned and cried out, '*Misericordia!*' and many monks were made upon the spot. At last on April 7, Fra Roberto took his leave of the Perugians, crying as he went, '*La pace sia con voi!*' [1] We have a glimpse of the same Fra Roberto da Lecce at Rome, in the year 1482. The feuds of the noble families della Croce and della Valle were then raging in the streets of Rome. On the night of April 3 they fought a pitched battle in the neighbourhood of the Pantheon, the factions of Orsini and Colonna joining in the fray. Many of the combatants were left dead before the palaces of the Vallensi; the numbers of the wounded were variously estimated; and all Rome seemed to be upon the verge of civil war. Roberto da Lecce, who was drawing large congregations, not only of the common folk, but also of the Roman prelates, to his sermons at Santa Maria sopra Minerva, interrupted his discourse upon the following Friday, and held before the people the image of their crucified Saviour, entreating them to make peace. As he pleaded with them, he wept; and they too fell to weeping—fierce satellites of the rival factions and worldly prelates lifting up their voice in concert with the friar who had touched their hearts.[2] Another member of the Franciscan Order of Observance should be mentioned after Fra Roberto. This was Giovanni da Capistrano, of whose preaching at Brescia in 1451 we

---

[1] Graziani, pp. 597–601.

[2] See Jacobus Volaterrauus. Muratori, xxiii. pp. 126, 166, 167.

have received a minute account. He brought with him a great reputation for sanctity and eloquence, and for the miraculous cures which he had wrought. The Rectors of the city, together with 300 of the most distinguished burghers upon horseback, and a crowd of well-born ladies on foot, went out to meet him on February 9. Arrrangements were made for the entertainment of himself and 100 followers, at public cost. Next morning, three hours before dawn, there were already assembled upwards of 10,000 people on the piazza, waiting for the preacher. 'Think, therefore,' says the 'Chronicle,' 'how many there must have been in the day time ! and mark this, that they came less to hear his sermon than to see him.' As he made his way through the throng, his frock was almost torn to pieces on his back, everybody struggling to get a fragment.[1]

It did not always need the interposition of a friar to arouse a strong religious panic in Italian cities. After an unusually fierce bout of discord the burghers themselves would often attempt to give the sanction of solemn rites and vows before the altar to their temporary truces. Siena, which was always more disturbed by civil strife than any of her neighbours, offered a notable example of this custom in the year 1494. The factions of the Monti de' Nove and del Popolo had been raging ; the city was full of feud and suspicion, and all Italy was agitated by the French invasion. It seemed good, therefore, to the heads of the chief parties that an oath of peace should be taken by the whole body of the burghers. Allegretti's account of the ceremony, which took place at dead of night in the beautiful Cathedral of Siena, is worthy to be translated. 'The conditions of the peace were then read, which took up eight pages, together with an oath of the most horrible sort, full of maledictions, imprecations, excommunications, invocations of evil, renunciation of benefits temporal and spiritual, confiscation of goods, vows, and so many other woes that to hear it was a terror *et etiam* that *in articulo mortis* no sacrament should accrue to the salvation, but rather to the damnation, of those who might break the said conditions; insomuch that I, Allegretto di Nanni Allegretti, being present, believe that never was made or heard a more awful and horrible oath. Then the notaries of the Nove and the Popolo, on either side of the altar, wrote down the names of all the citizens, who swore upon the crucifix, for on each side there was one, and every couple of the one and the other faction kissed:

[1] See *Istoria Bresciana*. Muratori, xxi. 865.

and the bells clashed, and "Te Deum laudamus" was sung with the organs and the choir while the oath was being taken. All this happened between one and two hours of the night, with many torches lighted. Now may God will that this be peace indeed, and tranquillity for all citizens, whereof I doubt.'[1] The doubt of Allegretti was but too reasonable. Siena profited little by these dreadful oaths and terrifying functions. Two years later on, the same chronicler tells how it was believed that blood had rained outside the Porta a Laterino, and that various visions of saints and spectres had appeared to holy persons, proclaiming changes in the state, and commanding a public demonstration of repentance. Each parish organised a procession, and all in turn marched, some by day and some by night, singing Litanies, and beating and scourging themselves, to the Cathedral, where they dedicated candles; and 'one ransomed prisoners, for an offering, and another dowered a girl in marriage.'

In Bologna in 1457 a similar revival took place on the occasion of an outbreak of the plague. 'Flagellants went round the city, and when they came to a cross, they all cried with a loud voice: "Misericordia! misericordia!" For eight days there was a strict fast; the butchers shut their shops.' What follows in the 'Chronicle' is comic: 'Meretrices ad concubita nullum admittebant. Ex eis quâdam quæ cupiditate lucri adolescentem admiserat, deprehensâ, aliæ meretrices ita illius nates nudas corrigiis percusserunt, ut sanguinem emitteret.'[2] Ferrara exhibited a like devotion in 1496, on even a larger scale. About this time the entire Italian nation was panic-stricken by the passage of Charles VIII., and by the changes in states and kingdoms which Savonarola had predicted. The Ferrarese, to quote the language of their chronicler, expected that 'in this year, throughout Italy, would be the greatest famine, war, and want that had ever been since the world began.' Therefore they fasted, and 'the Duke of Ferrara fasted together with the whole of his court.' At the same time a proclamation was made against swearing, games of hazard, and unlawful trades: and it was enacted that the Jews should resume their obnoxious yellow gaberdine with the O upon their breasts. In 1500 these edicts were repeated. The condition of Italy had grown worse and worse: it was necessary to besiege the saints with still more energetic

---

[1] See Muratori, vol. xxiii. p. 839.
[2] *Annales Bononienses.* Mur. xxiii. 890.

demonstrations. Therefore 'the Duke Ercole d'Este, for good reasons to him known, *and because it is always well to be on good terms with God*, ordained that processions should be made every third day in Ferrara, with the whole clergy, and about 4,000 children or more from twelve years of age upwards, dressed in white, and each holding a banner with a painted Jesus. His lordship, and his sons and brothers, followed this procession, namely the Duke on horseback because he could not then walk, and all the rest on foot, behind the Bishop.'[1] A certain amount of irony transpires in this quotation, which would make one fancy that the chronicler suspected the Duke of ulterior, and perhaps political, motives.

It sometimes happened that the contagion of such devotion spread from city to city; on one occasion, in 1399, it travelled from Piedmont through the whole of Italy. The epidemic of flagellants, of which Giovanni Villani speaks in 1310 (lib. viii. cap. 121), began also in Piedmont, and spread along the Genoese Riviera. The Florentine authorities refused entrance to these fanatics into their territory. In 1334, Villani mentions another outburst of the same devotion (lib. xi. cap. 23), which was excited by the preaching of Fra Venturino da Bergamo. The penitents on this occasion wore for badge a dove with the olive-branch. They stayed fifteen days in Florence, scourging themselves before the altars of the Dominican churches, and feasting, five hundred at a time, in the Piazza di S. M. Novella. Corio, in the 'Storia di Milano' (p. 281), gives an interesting account of these 'white penitents,' as they were called, in the year 1399: 'Multitudes of men, women, girls, boys, small and great, townspeople and countryfolk, nobles and burghers, laity and clergy, with bare feet and dressed in white sheets from head to foot,' visited the towns and villages of every district in succession. 'On their journey, when they came to a cross-road or to crosses, they threw themselves on the ground, crying "Misericordia" three times; then they recited the Lord's Prayer and the Ave Mary. On their entrance into a city, they walked singing "Stabat Mater dolorosa" and other litanies and prayers. The population of the places to which they came were divided: for some went forth and told those who stayed that they should assume the same habit, so that at one time there were as many as 10,000, and at another as many as 15,000 of them.' After admitting that the fruit of this

[1] *Diario Ferrarese.* Mur. xxiv. pp. 17–386.

devotion was in many cases penitence, amity, and almsgiving, Corio
goes on to observe: 'However, men returned to a worse life than
ever after it was over.' It is noticeable that Italy was devastated
in 1400 by a horrible plague; and it is impossible not to believe
that the crowding of so many penitents together on the highways
and in the cities led to this result.

During the anarchy of Italy between 1494—the date of the
invasion of Charles VIII.—and 1527—the date of the sack of Rome
—the voice of preaching friars and hermits was often raised, and
the effect was always to drive the people to a frenzy of revivalistic
piety. Milan was the centre of the military operations of the
French, the Swiss, the Spaniards, and the Germans. No city
suffered more cruelly, and in none were fanatical prophets received
with greater superstition. In 1516 there appeared in Milan 'a
layman, large of stature, gaunt, and beyond measure wild, without
shoes, without shirt, bareheaded, with bristly hair and beard, and
so thin that he seemed another Julian the hermit.' He lived on
water and millet-seed, slept on the bare earth, refused alms of all
sorts, and preached with wonderful authority. In spite of the opposition of the Archbishop and Chapter, he chose the Duomo for
his theatre; and there he denounced the vices of the priests and
monks to vast congregations of eager listeners. In a word, he
engaged in open warfare with the clergy on their own ground.
But they of course proved too strong for him, and he was driven
out of the city. He was a native of Siena, aged thirty.[1] We may
compare with this picturesque apparition of Jeronimo in Milan
what Varchi says about the prophets who haunted Rome like birds
of evil omen in the first years of the pontificate of Clement VII.
'Not only friars from the pulpit, but hermits on the piazza, went
about preaching and predicting the ruin of Italy and the end of
the world with wild cries and threats.'[2] In 1523 Milan beheld the
spectacle of a parody of the old preachers. There appeared a
certain Frate di S. Marco, whom the people held for a saint and
who 'encouraged the Milanese against the French, saying it was a
merit with Jesus Christ to slay those Frenchmen, and that they

[1] See Prato and Burigozzo, *Arch. Stor.* vol. iii. pp. 357, 431. It is
here worth noticing that Siena, the city of civil discord, was also the
city of frenetic piety. The names of S. Caterina, S. Bernardino, and
Bernardo Tolomei occur to the mind.

[2] *Storia Fiorentina*, vol. i. p. 87.

were pigs.' He seems to have been a feeble and ignorant fellow,
whose head had been turned by the examples of Bussolaro and
Savonarola.[1] Again, in 1529, we find a certain monk, Tommaso,
of the order of S. Dominic, stirring up a great commotion of piety
in Milan. The city had been brought to the very lowest state of
misery by the Spanish occupation ; and, strange to say, this friar
was himself a Spaniard. In order to propitiate offended deities, he
organised a procession on a great scale. 700 women, 500 men,
and 2,500 children assembled in the Cathedral. The children were
dressed in white, the men and women in sackcloth, and all were
barefooted. They promenaded the streets of Milan, incessantly
shouting ' Misericordia ! ' and besieged the Duomo with the same
dismal cry, the Bishop and the Municipal authorities of Milan
taking part in the devotion.[2] These gusts of penitential piety were
matters of real national importance. Writers imbued with the
classic spirit of the Renaissance thought them worthy of a place in
their philosophical histories. Thus we find Pitti, in the ' Storia
Fiorentina ' (' Arch. Stor.' vol. i. p. 112), describing what happened
at Florence in 1514 : ' There appeared in Santa Croce a Frate
Francesco da Montepulciano, very young, who rebuked vice with
severity, and affirmed that God had willed to scourge Italy, especially
Florence and Rome, in sermons so terrible that the audience kept
crying with floods of tears, " Misericordia ! " ' The whole people was
struck dumb with horror, for those who could not hear the friar by
reason of the crowd, listened with no less fear to the reports of
others. At last he preached a sermon so awful that the congre-
gation stood like men who had lost their senses ; for he promised
to reveal upon the third day how and from what source he had
received this prophecy. However, when he left the pulpit, worn
out and exhausted, he was seized with an illness of the lungs, which
soon put an end to his life.' Pitti goes on to relate the frenzy of
revivalism excited by this monk's preaching, which had roused all
the old memories of Savonarola in Florence. It became necessary
for the Bishop to put down the devotion by special edicts, while the
Medici endeavoured to distract the minds of the people by tournaments and public shows.

Enough has now been quoted from various original sources to
illustrate the feverish recurrences of superstitious panics in Italy
during the Middle Ages and the Renaissance. It will be observed,

---

[1] *Arch. Stor.* vol iii. p. 443.   [2] Burigozzo, pp. 485–89.

from what has been said about John of Vicenza, Jacopo del Bussolaro, S. Bernardino, Roberto da Lecce, Giovanni della Marca, and Fra Capistrano, that Savonarola was by no means an extraordinary phenomenon in Italian history. Combining the methods and the aims of all these men, and remaining within the sphere of their conceptions, he impressed a rôle, which had been often played in the chief Italian towns, with the stamp of his peculiar genius. It was a source of weakness to him in his combat with Alexander VI. that he could not rise above the monastic ideal of the prophet which prevailed in Italy, or grasp one of those regenerative conceptions which formed the motive force of the Reformation. The inherent defects of all Italian revivals, spasmodic in their paroxysms, vehement while they lasted, but transient in their effects, are exhibited upon a tragic scale by Savonarola. What strikes us, after studying the records of these movements in Italy, is chiefly their want of true mental energy. The momentary effect produced in great cities like Florence, Milan, Verona, Pavia, Bologna, and Perugia is quite out of proportion to the slight intellectual power exerted by the prophet in each case. He has nothing really new or life-giving to communicate. He preaches indeed the duty of repentance and charity, institutes a reform of glaring moral abuses, and works as forcibly as he can upon the imagination of his audience. But he sets no current of fresh thought in motion. Therefore, when his personal influence was once forgotten, he left no mark upon the nation he so deeply agitated. We can only wonder that, in many cases, he obtained so complete an ascendency in the political world. All this is as true of Savonarola as it is of S. Bernardino. It is this which removes him so immeasurably from Huss, from Wesley, and from Luther.

APPENDIX V

The Sommario della Storia d' Italia dal 1511 al 1527,' by Francesco Vettori[1]

I HAVE reserved for special notice in this Appendix the short history written of the period between 1511 and 1527 by Francesco Vettori; not because I might not have made use of it in several of the previous chapters, but because it seemed to me that it was better to concentrate in one place the illustrations of Machiavelli and Guicciardini which it supplies. Francesco Vettori was born at Florence in 1474 of a family which had distinguished itself by giving many able public servants to the Commonwealth. He adopted the politics of the Medicean party, remaining loyal to his aristocratic creed all through the troublous times which followed the French invasion of 1494, the sack of Prato in 1512, the sack of Rome in 1527, and the murder of Duke Alessandro in 1536. Even when he seemed to favour a republican policy, he continued in secret stanch to the family by whom he hoped to obtain honours and privileges in the state. Like all the Ottimati, so furiously abused by Pitti, Francesco Vettori found himself at last deceived in his expectations. To the Medici they sold the freedom of their native city, and in return for this unpatriotic loyalty they were condemned to exile, death, imprisonment, or frosty toleration by the prudent Cosimo. Two years after Cosimo had been made Duke, Vettori died, aged upwards of sixty, without having shared in the prosperity of the princes to whose service he had consecrated his life and for whose sake he had helped to enslave Florence. To respect this species of fidelity, or to feel any pity for the men who were so cruelly disappointed of their selfish expectations, is impossible.

Francesco Vettori held offices of importance on various occasions in the Commonwealth of Florence. In 1520, for example, he entered the Signory; and in 1521 he was Gonfalonier of Justice. Many years of his life were spent on foreign missions, as ambas-

---

[1] Printed in *Arch. Stor. It.* Appendice No. 22, vol. vi.

sador to the Emperor Maximilian, resident ambassador at the
Courts of Julius and Leo, ambassador together with Filippo Strozzi
to the Court of Francis I., and orator at Rome on the election of
Clement. He had therefore, like Machiavelli and Guicciardini, the
best opportunities of forming a correct judgment of the men whose
characters he weighed in his 'Sommario,' and of obtaining a
faithful account of the events which he related. He deserves a
place upon the muster-roll of literary statesmen mentioned by me
in Chapter v.; nor should I have omitted him from the company of
Segni and Varchi, had not his history been exclusively devoted to
an earlier period than theirs. At the same time he was an intimate
friend both of Guicciardini and Machiavelli. Some of the most
precious compositions of the latter are letters addressed from
Florence or San Casciano to Francesco Vettori, at the time
when the ex-war-secretary was attempting to gain the favour of the
Medici. The clairvoyance and acuteness, the cynical philosophy
of life, the definite judgment of men, the clear comprehension of
events, which we trace in Machiavelli, are to be found in Vettori.
Vettori, however, had none of Machiavelli's genius. What he writes
is, therefore, valuable as proving that the Machiavellian philosophy
was not peculiar to that great man, but was shared by many
inferior thinkers. Florentine culture at the end of the fifteenth
century culminated in these statists of hard brain and stony hearts,
who only saw the bad in human nature, but who were not led by
cynicism or scepticism to lose their interest in the game of politics.

In the dedication of the 'Sommario della Storia d' Italia' to
Francesco Scarfi, Vettori says that he composed it at his villa,
whither he retired in 1527. I do not purpose to extract portions of
the historical narrative contained in this sketch; to do so indeed
would be to transcribe the whole, so closely and succinctly is it
written; but rather to quote the passages which throw a light upon
the opinions of Machiavelli and Guicciardini, or confirm the views
of men and morals adopted in my previous chapters.

After touching on the sack of Prato and the consternation which
ensued in Florence, Vettori describes the return of the Medici in
1512. Giuliano, the son of Lorenzo, was the first to appear: after
him came the Cardinal Giovanni, and Giuliano's son Giulio.[1] The
elder among their partisans persuaded them to call a Parlamento
and assume the government in earnest. On September 16,

[1] Giovanni and Giulio were afterwards Leo X. and Clement VII.

accordingly, the Cardinal took possession of the palace—*fece pigliare il Palazzo*; the Signory summoned the people into the piazza—a mere matter of form; a Balia of forty men was appointed; the Gonfalonier Ridolfi resigned; and the city was reduced to the will and pleasure of the Cardinal de' Medici. Then reasons Vettori:[1] 'This was what is called an absolute tyranny; yet, speaking of the things of this world without prejudice and according to the truth, I say that if it were possible to institute republics like that imagined by Plato, or feigned to exist in Utopia by Thomas More, we might affirm they were not tyrannical governments: but all the commonwealths or kingdoms I have seen or read of, have, it seems to me, a savour of tyranny. Nor is it a matter for astonishment that parties and factions have often prevailed in Florence, and that one man has arisen to make himself the chief, when we reflect that the city is very populous, that many of the burghers desire to share in its advantages, and that there are few prizes to distribute: wherefore one party always must have the upper hand and enjoy the honours and benefits of the state, while the other stands by to watch the game.' He then proceeds to criticise France, where the nobles alone bear arms and pay no taxes, and where the administration of justice is slow and expensive; and Venice, where three thousand gentlemen keep more than 100,000 of the inhabitants below their feet, unhonoured, powerless, unprivileged, oppressed. Having demonstrated the elements of tyranny and injustice both in a kingdom and a common-wealth reputed prosperous and free, he shows that, according to his own philosophy, no blame attaches to a burgher who succeeds in usurping the sole mastery of a free state, provided he rule wisely; for all kingdoms were originally founded either by force or by craft. 'We ought not therefore to call that private citizen a tyrant who has usurped the government of his state, if he be a good man: nor again to call a man the real lord of a city who, though he has the investiture of the Emperor, is bad and malevolent.' This critique of constitutions from the pen of a doctrinaire, who was also a man of experience, is interesting, partly for its positive frankness, and partly as showing what elementary notions still prevailed about the purposes of government. Vettori's ultimate criterion is the personal quality of the ambitious ruler.

Passing to what he says about Leo X.,[2] it is worth while to note that he attributes his election chiefly to the impression produced upon the Cardinals by Alexander and Julius. 'During the reign of two fierce and powerful Pontiffs, Cardinals had been put to death, imprisoned, deprived of their property, exiled, and kept in continual alarm; and so great was the dread among them now of electing another such Pope, that they unanimously chose Giovanni de' Medici. Up to that time he had always shown himself liberal and easy, or, rather, prodigal in squandering the little that he owned; he had moreover managed so to dissemble as to acquire a reputation for most excellent habits of life.' Vettori adds that his power in Florence helped him, and that he owed much to the ability displayed by Bernardo da Bibbiena in winning votes. The joy of the Florentines at his election is attributed to mean motives: 'being all of them given over to commerce and gain, they thought they ought to get some profit from this Papacy.'[1]

The government which Lorenzo, afterwards Duke of Urbino, now established in Florence is very favourably described by Vettori.[2] 'Lorenzo, though still a young man, applied himself with great attention to the business of the city, providing that equal justice should be administered to all, that the public moneys should be levied and spent with frugality, and that disputes should be settled to the satisfaction of all parties. His rule was tolerated, because, while the revenues were large and the expenses small, the citizens were not troubled with taxes; and this is the chief way to please a people, seeing their affection for a prince is measured by the good they get from him.' Taking this opinion of Lorenzo, it is possible for Vettori in another place to say of him that ' he governed Florence like a citizen;'[3] and on the occasion of his death in 1520, he passes what amounts to a panegyric on his character. 'His death was a misfortune for Florence, which it would be difficult to describe. Though young he had the qualities of virtuous maturity. He bore a real affection toward the citizens, was parsimonious of the moneys of the Commune, prodigal of his own; while a foe to vice, he was not too severe on those who erred. Though he began his military life at twenty-three, he always bore the cuirass of a man-at-arms upon his shoulders day and night on active service. He slept very little, was sober in his diet, temperate in love. The Florentines did not love him, because it is

---

[1] P. 300.   [2] Ibid.   [3] P. 306.

not possible for men used to freedom to love a ruler; but he, for his part, had not sought the office which was thrust upon him by the will of others. Madonna Alfonsina, his mother, brought unpopularity upon him; for she was avaricious, and the Florentines, who notice every detail, thought her grasping: and though he wanted to restrain her, he found himself unable to do so through the high esteem in which he held her. Maddalena, his wife, died six days before him, after giving birth to a daughter Catherine.' This is the, no doubt, highly favourable portrait of the man to whom Machiavelli dedicated his ' Principe.' The somewhat negative good qualities of Lorenzo, his prudence and parsimony, his freedom from despotic ambition, and dislike of dangerous service, combined with his deference to the powerful members of his own family, are very unlike Machiavelli's ideal of the founder of a state. Cesare Borgia was almost the exact opposite. The impression produced by Vettori's panegyric is further confirmed by what he says about Lorenzo's disinclination to undertake the Duchy of Urbino.[1]

But to return to the early days of Leo's pontificate. Vettori marks his interference in the affairs of Lucca as the first great mistake he made.[2] His advisers in Florence had not reflected 'what infamy it would bring upon the Pope in the opinion of all men, or what suspicion it would rouse among the princes, if in the first months of his power he were led to sanction an attack by the Florentines upon the Lucchese, their neighbours and allies. How too could the burghers of Florence, who had urged him to this step, remind the pontiff that he ought to moderate his desire of gaining dominion for the Church, and for his kin, by the example of former Popes, all of whom, in the interest of their dependants, had acquired to their own dishonour with peril and expense what in a few days upon their death returned to the old and rightful owners?' The conduct of Leo with regard to Lucca, his policy in Florence, and the splendour maintained by his brother at Rome, did in fact rouse the jealousy of the Italian powers both great and small.[3] ' King Ferdinand remarked; if Giuliano has left Florence, he must be aiming at something better, which can be nothing but the realm of Naples. The Dukes of Milan, Ferrara, and Urbino said the same. The Sienese thought; if the Pope allows the Florentines to attack Lucca, which is so strong, well furnished, and harmonious, far more will he consent to their encroaching upon us, who are weak, ill-provided, and at odds among ourselves. The Duke of Ferrara had further reasons for discontent in respect to Modena and Reggio.' Altogether, Leo began to lose credit. Secret alliances were formed against him by the della Rovere, the Baglioni, and the Petrucci; and though he took care to attend public services and to fast more than etiquette required, nobody believed in him. Vettori's comment reads like an echo of Machiavelli and Guicciardini.[1] 'Assuredly it is most difficult to combine temporal lordship with a reputation for religion: for they are two things which will not harmonise. He who well considers the law of the Gospel will observe that the pontiffs, though called Christ's vicars, have originated a new religion unlike that of Christ except in name. His enjoins poverty; they desire riches. He preached humility; they follow after pride. He commanded obedience; they aim at universal sovereignty. I could enlarge upon their other vices; but it is enough to allude to these, without entering into inconvenient discourses.' While treating of the affairs of Urbino,[2] however, Vettori remarks that Leo could not have done otherwise than punish Francesco Maria della Rovere, if he wished to maintain the Papacy at the height of reputation to which it had been raised by his predecessors.

In his general estimate of Leo, Vettori confirms all that we know about this Pope from other sources. He insists more perhaps than other historians upon the able diplomacy by which Lodovico Canossa, Bishop of Tricarico, made terms with Francis after Marignano,[3] and traces Leo's fatal alliance with Charles V. in 1520 to the influence of Jeronimo Adorno.[4] The secret springs of Leo's conduct, when he was vainly endeavouring to steer to his own profit between the great rivals for power in Europe, are exposed with admirable precision at both of these points. Of the prodigality which helped to ruin this Pope, and which made his two successors impotent, he speaks with sneering sarcasm. 'It was as easy for him to keep 1,000 ducats together as for a stone to fly into the air by its own weight.'[5] When the news of the capture of Milan reached him on November 27, 1520, Leo was at the Villa Magliana in the neighbourhood of Rome.[6] Whether he took cold at a window, or whether his anxiety and jealousy disturbed his

---

[1] P. 304. [2] P. 319. [3] P. 313. [4] P. 334.
[5] P. 322. [6] P. 338.

constitution, Vettori remains uncertain. At any rate, he was attacked with fever, returned to Rome, and died. 'It was said that his death was caused by poison; but these stories are always circulated about men of high estate, especially when they succumb to acute disease. Those, however, who knew the constitution and physical conformation of Leo, and his habits of life, will rather wonder that he lived so long.' After summing up the vicissitudes of his career and passing a critique upon his vacillating policy, Vettori resumes:[1] 'while on the one hand he would fain have never had one care to trouble him; on the other he was desirous of fame and sought to aggrandise his kindred. Fortune, to rid him of this ambition, removed his brother and his nephew in his lifetime, Lastly, when he had engaged in a war against the King of France, in which, if he won, he lost, and was going to meet obvious ruin, fortune removed him from the world so that he might not see his own mischance. In his pontificate at Rome there was no plague, no poverty, no war. Letters and the arts flourished, and the vices were also at their height. Alexander and Julius had been wont to seize the inheritance not only of the prelates but of every little priest or clerk who died in Rome. Leo abstained entirely from such practices. Therefore people came in crowds; and it may be said for certain that in the eight years of his papacy, the population of Rome increased by one third.' Vettori prudently refuses to sum up the good and bad of Leo's character in one decisive sentence. He notes, however, that he was blamed for not keeping to his word: 'it was a favourite expression with him, that princes ought to give such answers as would send petitioners away satisfied; accordingly he made so many promises, and fed people with such great expectations, that it became impossible to please them.'

The election of Adrian is attributed by Vettori to the mutual hatred and jealousy of the Cardinals.[2] He ascribes the loss of Rhodes to the Pope's want of interest in great affairs, adds his testimony to his private excellence and public incapacity, and dismisses him without further notice.[3]

What he tells us about Clement is more interesting. In the dedication to the 'Sommario' he apologised in express terms for the high opinion recorded of this Pope. Yet the impression which he leaves upon our mind by what he writes is so unfavourable as to make it clear what Clement's foes habitually said against him. He remarks, as one excuse for his ill-success in office, that he succeeded to a Papacy ruined by the prodigality in war and peace of Leo.[1] As knight of Rhodes, as governor of Florence, and as Cardinal, Clement had shown himself an able man. Fortune heaped her favours on him then. As soon as he was made Pope, she veered round, 'From a puissant and respected Cardinal, he became a feeble and discredited Pope.' His first care was to provide for the government of Florence. In order to arrive at a decision, he asked counsel of the Florentine orators and four other noble burghers then in Rome, as to whether he could advantageously entrust the city to the Cardinal of Cortona in guardianship over Ippolito and Alessandro, the young bastards of the Medici.[2] 'All men nearly,' says Vettori, 'are flatterers, and say what they believe will please great folk, although they think the contrary. Of the thirteen whom the Pope consulted, ten advised him to send Ippolito to Florence under the guardianship of the Cardinal of Cortona.' The remaining three, who were Ruberto Acciajuoli, Lorenzo Strozzi, and Francesco Vettori, pointed out the impropriety of administering a free city through a priest who held his title from a subject town. They recommended the appointment of a Gonfalonier for one year, and so on, till a member of the Medicean family could take the lead. Clement, however, decided on the other course; and to this cause may be traced half the troubles of his reign.

The greater part of what remains of the 'Sommario' is occupied with the wars and intrigues of Francis, Charles, and Clement. Vettori, it may be said in passing, records a very unfavourable opinion of the Marquis of Pescara, who was, he hints, guilty of first turning a favourable ear to Moroni's plot and then of discovering the whole to his master.[3] A few days after his breach of faith with the Milanese, he fell ill and died. 'He was a man whose military excellence cannot be denied; but proud beyond all measure, envious, ungrateful, avaricious, venomous, cruel, without religion or humanity, he was born to be the ruin of Italy; and it may be truly said that of the evil she has suffered and still suffers a large part was caused by him.'

Of the breach of faith of Francis, after he had left his Spanish prison, Vettori speaks in terms of the very highest commendation.[4]

[1] P. 348.   [2] P. 349. They were 14 and 13 years of age respectively.
     [3] Pp. 358, 359.   [4] P. 362.

His refusal to cede Burgundy to Charles was just and patriotic.
That he broke his faith was no crime; for, though a man ought
rather to die than forswear himself, yet his first duty is to God, his
second to his country. Francis was clearly acting for the benefit
of his kingdom; and had he not left his two sons as hostages in
Spain? The whole defence is a good piece of special pleading,
and might be used to illustrate the chapter on the Faith of Princes
in the 'Principe.'

By far the most striking passage in Vettori's 'Sommario' is the
description of the march of Frundsberg's and De Bourbon's army
upon Rome.[1] He makes it clear to what extent the calamity of
the sack was due to the selfishness and cowardice of the Italian
princes. First of all the Venetians refused to offer any obstacles
before the passage of the Po, feeling that by doing so they might
draw trouble on their own provinces. Then the Duke of Ferrara
supplied the Lutherans with artillery, of which they hitherto had
stood in need. The first use they made of their fire-arms was to
shoot the best captain in Italy, Giovanni de' Medici of the Black
Bands. The Duke of Urbino, the Marquis of Saluzzo, and Guido
Rangoni watched them cross the river and proceed by easy stages
through the district of Piacenza, 'following them like lacqueys
waiting on their lords.' The same thing happened at Parma and
Modena, while the Duke of Ferrara kept supplying the foreigners
with food and money. Clement meanwhile was penniless in
Rome. Rich as the city was, he had so utterly lost credit that he
dared not ask for loans, and was so feeble that he could not rob.
The Colonnesi, moreover, who had recently plundered the Vatican,
kept him in a state of terror. As the invaders, now commanded by
the Constable de Bourbon, approached Tuscany, the youth of
Florence demanded to be armed in defence of their hearths and
homes. The Cardinal of Cortona, fearing a popular rising, refused
to grant their request. A riot broke out, and the Medici were
threatened with expulsion: but by the aid of influential citizens a
revolution was averted. The Constable, avoiding Florence and
Siena, marched straight on Rome, still watched but unmolested by
the armies of the League. He left his artillery on the road, and
as is well known, carried the walls of Rome by assault on the
morning of May 3, dying himself at the moment of victory. From
what has just been rapidly narrated, it will be seen how utterly
abject was the whole of Italy at this moment, when a band of

---

[1] Pp. 372-82.